Communicating Effectively For Dummies®

Cheat Sheet

Ten Ways to Listen Well

The following are ten ways to utilize the active-listening tools found in Part II of this book:

- ✔ Concentrate on what the speaker has to say.
- ✔ Listen for content and emotion to understand the entire message.
- ✔ Maintain steady eye contact so speakers know your attention is with them.
- ✔ Reflect back with verbal feedback to confirm your understanding of the message.
- ✔ Stay patient when people talk to you.
- ✔ Keep your tone sincere and nonjudgmental when you listen.

- ✔ When you give feedback to check understanding, do so in one sentence.
- ✔ Tune into *how* the message is being said, not just what the words are.
- ✔ Acknowledge feelings that are important to the message you're hearing.
- ✔ Make your goal in conversations to show understanding of what the speaker truly means.

Ten Tips for Delivering Positive and Confident Messages

When you speak — no matter what your forum — you want to sound positive and confident (see Part III for details). Here's a summary of how you can achieve this:

- ✔ Speak up so others can easily hear you, especially in group situations.
- ✔ Make your message as concise as possible; wordiness is not needed or wanted.
- ✔ Use language in the best way possible to make your points.
- ✔ Talk with your hands and use them to emphasize your key points.
- ✔ Be direct and honest with people as a consistent practice.
- ✔ Provide steady eye contact with your listeners to engage their attention when you talk.

- ✔ Maintain an alert body posture when you speak to put life behind your message.
- ✔ Pause to gather your thoughts so you avoid extraneous sounds, such as "um" that clutter your message.
- ✔ Focus on getting solutions when you talk about problems.
- ✔ Be sincere: People respond best to those who are genuine and respectful in their delivery.

Copyright © 2001 Wiley Publishing, Inc. All rights reserved.

Cheat Sheet $2.95 value. Item 5319-4.

For more information about Wiley Publishing, call 1-800-762-2974.

For Dummies®: Bestselling Book Series for Beginners

Communicating Effectively For Dummies®

Cheat Sheet

Ten Communication Efforts that Build Strong Working Relationships

To build strong working relationships with clients and customers, team members, managers, and internal customers, do the following:

- Respond to requests by emphasizing what you can do to help meet them.
- Follow through and do what you say you'll do.
- Listen without passing judgment and don't rush in to give advice.
- When you have concerns, work them out with the source, not with others.
- Communicate with respect in every interaction regardless of whether you like the person.

- When others give you assistance or support, express appreciation for it.
- Focus on issues, not personalities, when you discuss work matters and problems.
- When differences in views or ideas occur, work first to understand them from the other person's perspective.
- Be direct and sincere as normal practices.
- Use humor in good taste.

Ten Pitfalls to Avoid in Workplace Communications

Avoid the following pitfalls to effective communication:

- **Using e-mail to express concerns.** Instead, go to the source to work out problems in person.
- **Talking too much in sales situations.** Instead, learn to understand the customer's needs and then speak to indicate how you can help meet those needs.
- **Responding to requests by immediately saying it can't be done.** Instead, emphasize what you *can* do and *when* you can meet the request.
- **Providing your employees, if you are a manager, with opinionated criticism when their performance needs improvement.** Instead, provide employees with specific performance-focused feedback based on your observations.
- **Saying yes when you really don't mean it.** Instead, express your concerns constructively and offer alternatives as to what you think will work better in the situation.
- **Sitting by quietly and passively when people discuss issues with you.** Instead, interact with the message you're hearing and provide verbal feedback to check your understanding of the message.

- **Dwelling on what's wrong or who's at fault when dealing with problem situations.** Instead, put your focus on working out solutions with others and on how to make the situation better.
- **Focusing on yourself — what you like and don't like — as you receive others' messages.** Instead, shift your focus from yourself to concentrating on your speaker's message and work to understand what that message means without passing judgment on it.
- **Attempting to soften a point when addressing tough or sensitive issues.** Instead, be direct, constructive, and straightforward so that your message and its importance come across clearly and respectfully.
- **Pushing forward with your idea and disregarding concerns that people have with it.** Instead, listen to and acknowledge the concerns and address them. Sometimes the best way to gain support for an idea about which others have reservations is to show that you hear those concerns.

For Dummies®: Bestselling Book Series for Beginners

Praise for Communicating Effectively For Dummies

"The information Marty has in this book has made a dramatic positive impact on my ability to communicate on the job. The managers in my department also have implemented Marty's assertive speaking and active listening techniques with great benefit to themselves, their productivity, and to our company as a whole. I highly recommend this book to everyone who wants to improve their personal communication skills and effectiveness."

> — Robert Faulhaber, Senior Vice President, Customer Services and Support, Fujistu PC

"*Communicating Effectively For Dummies* helps hone the skills of even the most experienced communicator. Clever tips and workable techniques all come to life with realistic examples on everything from listening to co-workers to voice-mailing strangers. The conflict-resolution section is a vital guide to anyone who works with people under pressure. Business life would be so much better if only everyone would read this book."

> — Ed Niehaus, President and CEO, Niehaus Ryan Wong, Inc.

"What a dynamic resource and excellent coaching tool to use in all types of business communications! The real-life examples are easy to relate to, as they often hit very close to home; and the light-hearted writing style is an added pleasure for the reader."

> — Deb Eppert, Senior Director of Human Resources, Innunity, Inc.

"*Communicating Effectively* is more than a book; it is a way of life. Practicing and believing this philosophy will change the way you relate to your customers, employees, family, friends and even your competitors! Believe in it, internalize it, and it will have a positive impact on everything you say and hear."

> — Louis F. Rickley, Vice President and Chief Operating Officer, TRS Staffing Solutions

Communicating Effectively

FOR DUMMIES®

Communicating Effectively

FOR

DUMMIES®

by Marty Brounstein

Wiley Publishing, Inc.

Communicating Effectively For Dummies®

Published by
Wiley Publishing, Inc.
909 Third Avenue
New York, NY 10022
www.wiley.com

Copyright © 2001 by Wiley Publishing, Inc., Indianapolis, Indiana

Published by Wiley Publishing, Inc., Indianapolis, Indiana

Published simultaneously in Canada

For general information on our other products and services or to obtain technical support, please contact our Customer Care Department within the U.S. at 800-762-2974, outside the U.S. at 317-572-3993, or fax 317-572-4002.

Wiley also publishes its books in a variety of electronic formats. Some content that appears in print may not be available in electronic books.

Library of Congress Cataloging-in-Publication Data:

Library of Congress Control Number: 00-111140

ISBN: 0-7645-5319-4

Manufactured in the United States of America

10 9 8 7 6

About the Author

 **Marty Brounstein** is the Principal of The Practical Solutions Group, a training and consulting firm based in the San Francisco Bay area that specializes in management and organizational effectiveness. Marty's consulting work includes one-on-one coaching with managers and executives, assistance to groups working to become productive teams, and guidance and direction for organizations establishing practices for high performance and employee retention. His training programs target management as well as employee-development issues including leadership, team development, customer service, and effective communications.

As a consultant, speaker, and trainer since 1991, Marty has served a wide variety of organizations from high tech to government, for profit to not-for-profit. He has a bachelor's degree in education and history and a master's degree in industrial relations. Prior to beginning his consulting career, he spent a couple of years as a human resources executive.

This is Marty's fourth book and second for Hungry Minds, Inc. He is the coauthor of *Effective Recruiting Strategies: A Marketing Approach* and author of *Handling the Difficult Employee: Solving Performance Problems.* In 2000, he wrote *Coaching and Mentoring For Dummies.*

To contact Marty regarding consulting, speaking, or training services, call 650-341-8001 or e-mail him at mabruns@earthlink.net.

Dedication

To the best father I've got. He used to tell me this when I was a kid, and I always reminded him that the competition was rather thin. But as I finish this book, he has just turned 80 years young and is still going strong — for which I am very grateful. So thank you, Cyril Brounstein, for still being the best father I've got as I dedicate this book to you.

Acknowledgments

While writing a book is a difficult task in the midst of running a business, to be able to write a book for a major publisher is a wonderful opportunity. I want to thank Kathy Welton and Holly McGuire of Hungry Minds for giving me another opportunity to write a book for you. You've been a pleasure to work with on this project. Thanks also goes out to Tere Drenth, whose upfront edits and project assistance made my job as an author so much easier, and thanks to Suzanne Snyder who handled the internal project workings at Hungry Minds. Thanks also to Neil Johnson and Pam Mourouzis for their copy editing skills. My appreciation also goes out to friend and colleague, Carl Welte, for serving as my technical support person on the book.

Publisher's Acknowledgments

We're proud of this book; please send us your comments through our Online Registration Form located at www.dummies.com/register.

Some of the people who helped bring this book to market include the following:

Acquisitions, Editorial, and Media Development

Project Editor: Suzanne Snyder

Acquisitions Editor: Holly McGuire

Copy Editor: Neil Johnson

Acquisitions Coordinator: Lauren Cundiff

Technical Editor: Carl Welte

Editorial Manager: Pam Mourouzis

Editorial Assistant: Carol Strickland

Cover Photos: © VCP-FPG

Production

Project Coordinator: Bill Ramsey

Layout and Graphics: Amy Adrian, Barry Offringa, Jill Piscitelli, Jeremey Unger

Proofreaders: Jennifer Mahern, Angel Perez, York Production Services, Inc.

Indexer: York Production Services, Inc.

Publishing and Editorial for Consumer Dummies

Diane Graves Steele, Vice President and Publisher, Consumer Dummies

Joyce Pepple, Acquisitions Director, Consumer Dummies

Kristin A. Cocks, Product Development Director, Consumer Dummies

Michael Spring, Vice President and Publisher, Travel

Brice Gosnell, Publishing Director, Travel

Suzanne Jannetta, Editorial Director, Travel

Publishing for Technology Dummies

Andy Cummings, Acquisitions Director

Composition Services

Gerry Fahey, Vice President, Production Services

Debbie Stailey, Director of Composition Services

Contents at a Glance

Introduction 1

Part I: Communicating Successfully 5
Chapter 1: Working at Communicating and Communicating at Work 7
Chapter 2: Understanding How People Express Themselves to Others 15
Chapter 3: Are You Really Listening? 27

Part II: Tuning In to the Power of Active Listening 41
Chapter 4: Fixing Your Radar on the Speaker 43
Chapter 5: Putting Active Listening Tools to Work 57
Chapter 6: Giving a Dose of Empathy a la Mode 77

Part III: Speaking Assertively 95
Chapter 7: It Isn't Just What You Say, but How You Say It 97
Chapter 8: Speaking in the Positive 113
Chapter 9: Keeping Your Listener Engaged 133

Part IV: Win-Win Conflict Resolution 153
Chapter 10: Approaching Conflicts Constructively 155
Chapter 11: Communicating to Keep Conflicts Cool 175
Chapter 12: Bringing the Conflict to Resolution 197

Part V: Tackling Communication Challenges 225
Chapter 13: You've Got Mail: Managing E-Mail Communications 227
Chapter 14: Oh, No! I Have to Do a Presentation! 235
Chapter 15: Hurdling Customer Challenges 259
Chapter 16: Interviewing from Both Sides of the Table 281
Chapter 17: Conquering the Challenges of Management 307

Part VI: The Part of Tens 321
Chapter 18: Ten Ideas for Effectively Handling Telephone Interactions 323
Chapter 19: Ten Tips to Enhance Teamwork 329
Chapter 20: Ten Actions that Lend Credibility to Your Communications 335

Index 341

Cartoons at a Glance

By Rich Tennant

page 321

page 5

page 153

page 41

page 95

page 225

Cartoon Information:
Fax: 978-546-7747
E-Mail: richtennant@the5thwave.com
World Wide Web: www.the5thwave.com

Table of Contents

Introduction *1*

   About This Book 1
   Conventions Used in This Book 2
   How This Book Is Organized 2
      Part I: Communicating Successfully 2
      Part II: Tuning In to the Power of Active Listening 2
      Part III: Speaking Assertively 3
      Part IV: Win-Win Conflict Resolution 3
      Part V: Tackling Communication Challenges 3
      Part VI: The Part of Tens 4
   Icons Used in This Book 4
   Where to Go from Here 4

Part 1: Communicating Successfully *5*

   Chapter 1: Working at Communicating
   and Communicating at Work *7*
      Sharing the Rope Versus Tugging on It 8
         Understanding where the tug-of-war comes from 8
         Achieving the goal in communicating: Mutual understanding 9
      Hold the Pickles, Lettuce, and Assumptions 10
         Understanding assumptions and how they can help 11
         Avoiding the downside of assumptions 11
         Becoming aware of your own assumptions 13

   Chapter 2: Understanding How People Express
   Themselves to Others *15*
      Understanding the Four Approaches to Speaking 15
         My way or the highway: The aggressive approach 16
         The appeasing way: The nonassertive approach 17
         Subtle but aggravating: The passive-aggressive approach 18
         Straight and positive: The assertive approach 20
      Contrasting the Four Approaches to Speaking 22
      Becoming an Assertive Speaker 24

   Chapter 3: Are You Really Listening? *27*
      Recognizing the Impact of Listening 28
         Accentuate the positives 28
         Minimize the negatives 29

Following the Three Stages of the Listening Process 29
Avoiding Ineffective Patterns for Listening 30
Seeing How People Listen 33
    Is anybody really home? The passive approach 34
    Getting what you want, not what you need:
        The selective approach 35
    Grabbing the facts: The attentive approach 36
    Capturing and confirming the message: The active approach 37
Batteries Required: Making Active Listening Work 38

Part II: Tuning In to the Power of Active Listening 41

Chapter 4: Fixing Your Radar on the Speaker 43
Capturing the Whole Message 44
    Understanding the impact of the unspoken message 44
    The feelings behind the facts 45
Attending or Pretending to Listen? 47
    Giving yourself to the speaker 47
    Adding concentration to the attending mix 49
Avoiding Barriers to Listening 51
    Poor eye contact 51
    Unfavorable facial expressions 52
    Unwelcoming posture 52
    Too much movement 53
    Ineffective placement 54
    Uninviting tone of voice 54

Chapter 5: Putting Active Listening Tools to Work 57
Drawing Out the Speaker's Message 58
    Letting the speaker in: Door openers 58
    Verbal door openers 59
    Say again: Echoing 60
    Digging deeper: Probing 61
    Making sure you're following along: Checking the subject 63
Verifying Your Understanding of the Message 65
    Capturing the emotions: Reflecting feelings 67
    Capturing the content: Paraphrasing 68
    Utilizing the combo version: Reflective paraphrasing 69
    Relating when it counts: Sharing a relevant example 70
Watching Active Listening in Action 72
    Bringing listening alive 72
    Contrasting listener talk with speaker talk 75

Chapter 6: Giving a Dose of Empathy a la Mode **77**

Showing Empathy, Not Sympathy 78
Defining empathy and sympathy in listening 78
Contrasting empathetic and sympathetic listening 79
Avoiding Verbal Barriers: Nonempathetic Modes of Listening 81
The critic mode 81
The identifier mode 82
The defensive mode 82
The denying mode 83
The being-right mode 84
The interrogator mode 84
The sparring mode 85
The diagnostic mode 86
The advice mode 87
Seeing Empathy in Action 88
Working with a complaining client 88
Helping an overworked employee 89
Responding to an upset employee 90
Discovering Seven Listening Tips 91

Part III: Speaking Assertively *95*

Chapter 7: It Isn't Just What You Say, but How You Say It **97**

The Eyes Have It: Communicating with Eye Contact 98
Using eye contact to effectively get your message across 98
Avoiding eye-contact pitfalls 99
Your Body Is Talking; Make Sure It's Supporting Your Message 100
Using body language to effectively get your message across 101
Avoiding body-language pitfalls 103
Putting the Oomph in Your Voice 104
Using your voice to effectively get your message across 105
Avoiding vocal pitfalls 106
Managing Your Pace 108
Using pace to effectively get your message across 108
Avoiding pace pitfalls 110

Chapter 8: Speaking in the Positive **113**

Being Powerfully Positive: The Can-Do and Will-Do
Uses of Language 114
Speaking in the positive 114
Avoiding sugarcoating or putting
a positive spin on your words 115
Emphasizing what you can do instead of what you can't 117
Emphasizing what you will do 120

Say What? Communicating Your Messages with Clarity 122
    Making your message short and sweet 122
    Speaking in terms your audience understands 123
Employing the Language of Solutions 124
    Avoiding language that dwells on problems 124
    Using language that focuses on solutions 125
Staying Away from Speaking in the Negative 127
    Avoiding language that hinders your message 127
    Responding in the positive 130

Chapter 9: Keeping Your Listener Engaged **133**
Making Your Conversations Open-and-Shut Cases 134
    Staging the grand opening 134
    Putting on the finishing touches 138
Helping Your Listener Stay Involved 140
    Adding meaning to your message 141
    Adding good sense to your humor 143
    Getting your listener to respond 144
Developing a Plan for Sensitive Issues 147
    Knowing when to map out your plan 147
    Mapping out your plan 148
    Tasting a sample plan 150

Part IV: Win-Win Conflict Resolution **153**

Chapter 10: Approaching Conflicts Constructively **155**
Taking the High Road or the Low Road? 155
    The low road: What not to do in conflict situations 156
    The keys for driving on the high road 158
Get Mad? Get Even? Get Over It? Oh, So Many Choices 161
    The four approaches for handling conflict 161
    Scenario #1: A bad idea 165
    Scenario #2: The disagreement on who's to do what ...166
Using the Assertive — and Best — Approach 167
    Now or later? When to deal with the problem 168
    Should I talk about this now? Assessing your own readiness 168
Becoming Assertive: A Guide for Those Who Aren't 169
    Paving the road to productive working relationships 170
    Keys to being consistently respectful 171
    The benefits of being consistently respectful 172

Chapter 11: Communicating to Keep Conflicts Cool **175**
Getting Started on the Right Foot 176
    Letting your positive intentions be known 176
    Setting an agenda 179

Be First in Showing Understanding 181
 Making the shift and showing understanding 181
 Shifting into gear with the tool 182
 Taking the tool for a spin 184
Give Me a Description of the Suspect 186
 Describing describing 186
 Reviewing the guidelines for the describing tool 188
 Describing tool scenario 190
I've Got a Thought and a Feeling to Share 191
 Stating thoughts 192
 Feelings, nothing more than feelings 193

Chapter 12: Bringing the Conflict to Resolution **197**
Preparing for Solutions and Success 198
 Crafting the plan 198
 Thinking with a solutions focus 199
Using the Resolving-Concerns Conflict-Resolution Model 202
 Going through the model step by step 202
 Case study: The case of the overzealous boss 208
Understanding the Needs-Based Conflict-Resolution Model ...212
 Going through the model step by step 213
 Case study: The case of the staffing dilemma 217
Dealing with the Challenging Reactions 220
 Handling the defensive blows 221
 Dealing with the reluctant solution-maker 222

Part V: Tackling Communication Challenges 225

**Chapter 13: You've Got Mail: Managing
E-Mail Communications** **227**
To E-Mail or Not to E-Mail, That Is the Question 227
 Knowing when to use e-mail 228
 Recognizing when not to use e-mail 229
Staying on the Right Track When Writing E-Mail 232

Chapter 14: Oh, No! I Have to Do a Presentation! **235**
Hitting the Essentials of Effective Presentations 236
 What breaks a presentation 236
 What makes a presentation 238
 On your mark, get set 240
Becoming Content with Your Content 241
 In the beginning: The introduction 242
 Shaping up: The body of a presentation 244
 That's all, folks: The conclusion 246

Special Delivery: It's a Presentation Given with Impact 247
    Here's looking at you, kid: Making eye contact 248
    Getting your hands up: Using gestures 248
    Atten-hut: Paying attention to your posture
        and body position 249
    I can't hear you: Using your voice 249
    Whoa, Nellie: Pacing yourself 251
For Best Supporting Actor, Your Supporting Materials 252
    Avoiding the pitfalls 252
    Preparing useful visual aids 253
Live on Stage in Front of an Audience 254
    Responding to audience questions 254
    Overcoming stage fright 256

Chapter 15: Hurdling Customer Challenges **259**
You're Selling, but Are They Buying? 260
    Identifying needs and selling to meet them 260
    Negotiating to seal the deal 264
Quality Customer Service Is Not an Oxymoron 267
    Following the Golden Rule 267
    Communicating with impact to deliver quality service 269
Say, Mate, Your Customer Is Irate 272
    Problem solving with difficult customers 272
    The great eight for dealing with customers who are irate 274
Remember the Alamo and Your Internal Customers 276

Chapter 16: Interviewing from Both Sides of the Table **281**
Knowing What You're Looking For 282
    Can-do factors 283
    Will-do factors 284
Asking Your Questions 286
    Ways of asking questions 287
    Types of questions to ask 288
    Avoiding common interviewing pitfalls 289
All Aboard: Conducting an Effective Interview 291
    Stay organized; don't wing it 291
    Promoting goodwill 294
The Other Side of the Table: Preparing Yourself to Win the Job 295
    Say it and prove it 296
    Handling your dark-cloud issues 298
Scoring a Big Hit in the Interview 301
    Winners and losers 301
    You're on: Succeeding in the interview 303

Chapter 17: Conquering the Challenges of Management 307

Coaching Your Staff 308
   State performance expectations and emphasize results
     over methods 308
   Ask more than you tell 309
   Give ongoing feedback on performance 310
   Listen first and give advice — framed as suggestions —
     when asked 310
   Invite feedback and input in return 311
   Address issues directly with a focus on solutions 311
Managing Upward 312
   You have a problem — so what? 312
   Don't worry, be happy boss 314
Managing Outward 317

Part VI: The Part of Tens 321

Chapter 18: Ten Ideas for Effectively
Handling Telephone Interactions 323

Start with a Smile in Your Voice 323
Give a Professional Greeting 324
Direct People to the Right Resources 324
Put the Caller on Hold Smoothly 325
Sound Alive, Not Scripted 325
Converse with Patience 326
Tune In to Your Speaker's Tone 326
If Your Time Is Short, Say So 326
Close the Call before You End It 327
Leave Messages Worth Returning 327

Chapter 19: Ten Tips to Enhance Teamwork 329

Make Newcomers Feel Welcome 329
Keep Information Flowing 330
Teach So that Others Can Learn 330
Offer Assistance 331
Ask for Help 331
Speak Up in Meetings 331
Talk in Terms of Outcomes 332
Give Feedback Supportively 332
Take Problems to the Right Source 332
Maintain a Sense of Humor 333

**Chapter 20: Ten Actions that Lend Credibility
to Your Communications** **335**

    Following Through 335

    Returning Phone Calls 336

    Being Passionate 336

    Demonstrating Expertise 336

    Disagreeing without Being Disagreeable 337

    Staying Calm under Pressure 337

    Taking Positive Approaches to Problems 337

    Listening First, Acting Second 338

    Showing Sincerity 338

    Being Straightforward 339

Index *341*

Introduction

*I*f you're like most people I meet, you find applying your knowledge and skills to the tasks of your job is pretty easy. The harder part of your job is interacting with people. Aside from working in a lighthouse, few jobs exist in which working with and getting along well with others is unimportant.

As you probably know, success in your work comes from more than just having expertise in your field or discipline. It also comes from being able to express that expertise so that others can understand it, from hearing what others need so you apply that expertise to serve them, and from working with others in ways that build, not damage, relationships — especially when you're in a leadership role.

For many people, the biggest challenges they face in their jobs deal with communicating with others. From coworkers and direct reports to your boss and other members of management, from customers to vendors, you have to communicate with people to get your job done.

About This Book

I wrote this book to help you — someone who takes your job seriously, who wants to perform to your best, and who realizes that the greatest challenges at work usually come from dealing with others. The words in this book apply to you whether you're an individual contributor or a top executive.

This book provides you with tips and tools to handle these communication challenges and achieve results such as the following:

- Be heard in the way you want to be heard.
- Solve problems and conflicts.
- Understand what others really mean regardless of their communication styles.
- Serve customers in ways that meet their needs.
- Influence and build cooperation with others to get work done.
- Present ideas that capture the attention of others.
- Hire well and get hired.
- Use e-mail effectively.

The book helps you discover the best ways to maximize your interactions with others — listening actively and expressing your messages to others assertively — even when resolving conflicts, dealing with customers, giving presentations, and so on.

Conventions Used in This Book

Throughout this book, you'll see references to active listening and assertive speaking. People listen in a variety of ways, but active listening is the most effective. When you listen actively, you achieve an understanding of the speaker's message as that person meant it. People also speak (express themselves to others) in many ways. Assertive speaking is the most effective way: You express your messages in a direct, positive, and confident way that maintains respect for those who hear them.

This book gives you tools to become an active listener and an assertive speaker. *Tools* is a term that participants in my seminars often use; it refers to techniques and skills that you can apply on the job right away.

How This Book Is Organized

This book first lays a conceptual framework to get you thinking about how you communicate. The rest of the book shows you how to communicate effectively at work in your person-to-person interactions. Here's an overview of what you'll find in each part of the book.

Part I: Communicating Successfully

In this part, you explore the four ways in which people express themselves and the four ways in which people commonly listen to others. You see the behaviors in each way of expressing yourself and listening, many of which come from old habits and are spurred by feelings of stress. I also introduce you to the most effective forms of each side of the interaction, assertive speaking and active listening.

Part II: Tuning In to the Power of Active Listening

In Part II, you find out all about active listening — how to do it and what it takes to make it work. You discover what to listen for when others speak to you and find out how to draw out their messages and understand them. In addition, I tell you about verbal and nonverbal behaviors to avoid when listening because they turn off the speaker and interfere with your effort to truly capture what the speaker means. Most important, you find out that active listening works best with empathy: the sincerity and understanding that make you genuine — someone worth talking to.

Part III: Speaking Assertively

In this part, you discover how to express your messages assertively and learn that *how* you say things often carries more weight than *what* you say. You find out all about the nonverbal tools of assertive speaking, gain tips and tools on improving the content of your messages, and discover how to use language in its most powerful and positive form to convey your messages. You also find new ways to organize your messages so that your listener understands them clearly and receives them positively.

Part IV: Win-Win Conflict Resolution

Conflicts — differences — are a part of every workplace, but handling them constructively is no small feat. This part gives you tools and problem-solving models that can help you deal effectively with any kind of conflict situation. You also uncover an assertive approach to working relationships, being consistently respectful, that builds relationships long before conflicts happen.

Part V: Tackling Communication Challenges

This part takes you through some of the most common challenges people face in their jobs and uses the tools of active listening and assertive speaking to deal effectively with them. It starts by exploring the technology of e-mail and its use in person-to-person communications — how best to use it and the pitfalls to avoid. You also find out how to organize and deliver formal presentations effectively, manage sales situations and service challenges, and deal with difficult customer situations. This part also shows you how to interview effectively, whether you're interviewing prospective employees or trying to land a job yourself. Finally, I let you in on some communication tips that help you coach employees, run meetings, and manage upward and across your organization.

Part VI: The Part of Tens

This part gives you quick tips and ideas for specific communication situations. You find out how to handle telephone interactions effectively and how to enhance teamwork. You also get a summary of ten actions that make you more credible in your business communication.

Icons Used in This Book

Throughout this book you may notice small graphics in the margins, called *icons*, which are meant to grab your attention and support what you're reading. Here are the icons you'll see in this book:

This icon points to practical ideas and tips that enhance your interpersonal communications.

This symbol serves as a reminder about an idea or point that you'll want to keep in mind.

The icon alerts you to behaviors you want to avoid — ones that will hinder your effectiveness in communicating with others on the job.

Where you see this icon, I provide either a more-detailed explanation of a communication skill or an anecdote that gives you a clearer picture of that skill and how to put it into practice.

This icon symbolizes a how-to skill that you'll want to apply in your communication practices on the job.

Where to Go from Here

I wrote this book so that each chapter stands on its own, so if you want to skip around when you read, you can do so and not feel out of place. Sometimes, I refer to key skills or tools covered in other chapters, but you can easily turn to that chapter to find what you need. You may, however, want to start with Chapters 1, 2, and 3 because they give the conceptual foundation that the rest of the book builds upon.

Part I

Communicating Successfully

The 5th Wave   By Rich Tennant

SCREW-U

Screws 'n Screwdrivers
CUSTOMER SERVICE

Screw-U! How can
I... Hello? Dang!

Another, hang
up Dave? Just
a tip—next time try
answering with a smile
on your
face.

In this part . . .

People express themselves and listen to others in a variety of ways. In this part, you find out what these common ways are and what makes assertive speaking and active listening the most effective ways to communicate at work.

Chapter 1

Working at Communicating and Communicating at Work

In This Chapter

▶ Recognizing the goal — and challenge — of effective communication

▶ Exploring the impact of assumptions in interpersonal communications

*W*ho needs to communicate effectively with others to be successful at work? In today's often fast-paced and ever-changing world of work, the far more enlightened answer to this simple question is: "Who doesn't?" Most must interact in the workplace with bosses and low-level employees, superiors and underlings, managers and the managed — co-workers in some way, shape, or form — to be successful at their jobs. That challenge begins here.

Fewer and fewer jobs today require employees to do tasks by themselves. Instead, many organizations, in the public as well as private sectors, stress that all have customers that they must serve. The two basic types are

✔ **External customers:** These are people outside your organization who need the products and services that your business provides. In the broadest sense, external customers are people outside the workplace with whom you need to build good working relationships for success on the job. That includes a variety of folks ranging from suppliers to investors.

✔ **Internal customers:** These are your fellow employees, inside and outside the department where you work, to whom you provide services or assistance.

In addition, the workplace is often structured so that employees do their jobs in cooperative, team-like situations for part or most of their workdays. And if you work in management, most of the demands placed on your job require being able to effectively interact with others — staff, peers, and bosses.

In fact, you'd be hard-pressed to find any job function or field of employment where communicating effectively with people isn't vital. Regardless of your job title or the type of organization or industry you work for, if you're like most people, the greatest challenges you face lean less toward the technical side of your job (your area of expertise) than they do toward interacting with other people.

Sharing the Rope Versus Tugging on It

Ever play tug-of-war? The two teams on opposing ends of a rope try to pull each other across a dividing center line — sometimes across and into a hole filled with water and mud. It's a really dirty competition.

Interactions between people at work often are like tugs-of-war. The rope serves as a metaphor for the bond or connection between two people as they interact. The more it gets tugged between the two parties, the higher the tension, and the less productive the conversations. Alternatively, when neither party makes an effort to hold onto the rope, the bond is broken. In either case, you have varying degrees of a tug-of-war — the stresses and strains that block effective communications.

The goal of successful communications is sharing the rope so that it is strongly held but no one gets dirty — a big challenge but key to the success of communicating on the job.

Understanding where the tug-of-war comes from

As a human being, you communicate with other human beings through four means:

- Listening
- Speaking
- Reading
- Writing

While the advent of the computer and the Internet increased the use of the reading and writing as channels of communication, human beings generally spend more time in the live person-to-person forms of communication: listening and speaking. And remember, speaking includes both the verbal and nonverbal ways people express their messages to one another.

Although you're taught the traditional Three Rs (Reading, wRiting, and aRithmetic) from elementary school through high school, if you can read and write, you're considered literate. On the other hand, you probably didn't receive any formal instruction about how to listen effectively and express yourself constructively while interacting with others. Seldom are these interpersonal channels of communication a part of the curriculum in basic education. Yet listening and speaking are more critical for people to understand each other, work together, and solve problems with one another.

While you probably weren't exactly schooled in how to listen, you've been told certain things about listening, such as, "Listen up," "Be quiet," or the ever-popular "Shut up (and listen)." Imagine if you were taught to read that way — "Here's the book, read it!" You'd be illiterate.

Add elements like stress, tension, and challenge to your picture of the workplace — from encountering differences of opinion to facing demanding customers — and you see how easy it is to get caught up in that tug-of-war feeling. Because the skills needed to effectively handle stressful situations seldom are taught, you may have trouble sharing the rope. Instead, communication is more adversarial, ranging from waging verbal war against the other person to appeasing that person just to get past a difficult situation to using a subtle but negative *get-even* approach. Adversarial ways of communicating, represented by the tug-of-war, block people from working out their differences and interacting respectfully.

Achieving the goal in communicating: Mutual understanding

Interpersonal communications involves senders and receivers. A *sender* is the speaker, expressing his or her message to other parties. A *receiver,* on the other hand, is a person who listens to one or more speakers. In a good conversation, participants take turns being senders and receivers. When participants in a conversation try to be senders at the same time, the tug-of-war rope stretches taut. Or if one participant is a receiver but tunes out the sender, shows little interest in the conversation, or passes judgment on nearly every point that the sender makes, the tension mounts as the tug-of-war goes on.

The goal of the communication process is mutual understanding — sharing the rope together and maintaining its strength. When this goal is achieved, participants hear each other out and understand where everyone is coming from. They don't battle as adversaries or competitors. Instead, they communicate in a collaborative fashion — a conversation characterized by respect and sincerity. They may have their differences, but differences aren't an excuse to have a tug-of-war; rather, differences are issues to work through to reach the desired outcome.

Achieving mutual understanding is no small feat because most people aren't taught how to communicate as senders and receivers. As a result, when they express messages (that is, when they speak), they use four common approaches that are primarily based on old habits (discussed in further detail in Chapter 2). Those four approaches include

- Aggressive speaking
- Nonassertive speaking
- Passive-aggressive speaking
- Assertive speaking

People commonly engage in four similar ways of receiving (that is, listening) messages (see Chapter 3 for further details), including the following:

- Passive listening
- Selective listening
- Attentive listening
- Active listening

Of these common approaches to speaking and listening, the more effective forms of communication — the ways that help you achieve the goal of mutual understanding — are:

- **Assertive speaking,** or the act of expressing yourself directly, positively, and with confidence, so that your point comes across clearly and so that you maintain respect toward others.
- **Active listening,** or the act of providing nonverbal and verbal feedback to a speaker that allows his or her message to be expressed and shows understanding of that message.

To communicate successfully, you must be able to combine active listening and assertive speaking.

Keep in mind that active listening and assertive speaking don't provide you with special formulas to get people to do what you want. If that is your only intent, you'll come across as a manipulator.

Hold the Pickles, Lettuce, and Assumptions

To listen actively and speak assertively, you must first become aware of and perhaps even change the pattern of your *assumptions* when interacting with others. That is no easy feat.

Understanding assumptions and how they can help

An *assumption* is a belief that something is true without proof or demonstration, or that a person is going to behave a certain way before that person has a chance to act. Assumptions are part of the human condition. You've probably been making them (and have had them made about you, too) all your life. But not all assumptions are negative:

✔ **Processing stimuli:** Assumptions help you gather the information and stimuli to make sense of the world around you. When you're driving, for example, assumptions help keep you alert and aware of what other drivers may do so that you stay safe.

✔ **Anticipating problem situations:** Assumptions can help you prepare for problems and plan how to respond appropriately if difficult challenges arise.

✔ **Trying new things:** Assumptions can help you make educated guesses about new people or situations. They can aid you in drawing upon past experiences and determining how to apply them in future situations — in essence, allowing you to take risks and do something new and different.

Avoiding the downside of assumptions

You've no doubt heard that old saying that goes something like this:

"When you assume, you make an A S S out of U and ME."

Reporting the downside of assumptions

A reporter for a local newspaper wrote a story about an accident. A priest from the local parish was struck by a car and suffered a head injury while riding his bicycle. The reporter writing the story assumed that the good father was not wearing a helmet when the accident occurred.

The next day, the priest called the reporter to inform him of a major error in the story: The priest had, in fact, been wearing a helmet at the time of the accident and the assumption made him look irresponsible. By acting on his assumption without knowing all the facts first, the reporter was the biggest donkey of all.

When you assume, you make a donkey out of yourself, but you also affect others and make them look or feel pretty silly, too. Worst of all, by acting on your assumption, you've probably hurt someone else. In other words, using assumptions a lot, especially when dealing with other people, is a mistake.

The problem with assumptions is that they can lead to mistakes, misunderstandings, and strained relationships when they're acted upon as absolute facts. The following is a list of common assumptions that people make:

- **Jumping to conclusions:** In this scenario, you *know* what someone is going to say or whether something can work before you get the whole story. This assumption usually manifests itself in several annoying ways, including

    - Finishing people's sentences for them

    - Interrupting before a message has been fully stated

    - Tuning out as soon as a person whom you find unfavorable starts talking

    - Dismissing a new idea before hearing the rationale for it

    Although jumping to conclusions can be useful if you're playing *Name That Tune,* it tends to have little benefit in work situations.

- **Focusing on intentions:** People have intentions and they have actions, and you can only see the actions. Yet people often make assumptions on what they perceive are someone else's intentions — and quite often assume the worst about those intentions. Focusing on intentions instead of actions sometimes causes you to interpret inconsequential actions (the little things) as destructive or of ill will. When you focus on someone's intentions, you often approach people with undue suspicion.

- **Thinking you know best:** When you think you know best, you're already taking actions or making decisions for someone else without first checking with the person who is affected directly by what you do. These actions range from making commitments to initiating changes. Quite often, the person most affected doesn't find out about these changes until after they're made. Save such surprises for birthdays.

- **Stereotyping:** The term *stereotyping* means assuming that anyone who is from a different group than you — whether in race, ethnicity, gender, religion, sexual orientation, occupation, or other grouping — behaves and thinks in the same way as the group. Engineers all do one thing, men are all like that, all women do that, and so on. Stereotypical remarks often offend others and do nothing more than show your ignorance and biases.

Becoming aware of your own assumptions

Although assumptions are a normal part of the human thought process, you need to become aware of your own assumptions to have effective interactions. Here are a few tips to help:

- **Deal with each person as an individual.** One person doesn't represent millions. Get to know each person you work with or each customer you serve as an individual. The more you understand others, the better you can communicate with them.

- **Listen first.** Hear people out. Ask questions and check your understanding after you've heard the message so that you know what someone really means. When something sounds contrary to your thoughts, avoid reacting quickly with a negative comment or disagreement. Instead, ask the person the rationale or benefits of the idea or proposal at hand. Get the facts first.

- **Avoid generalizations.** Generalizations about people often come off as stereotypical remarks. By taking a few experiences with a limited number of people and attempting to make those experiences sound like absolute facts, you ignore profound individual differences. Rather than talking in generalizations, tie the comments you make to your own experiences and do so only when it is relevant.

- **Communicate first; act second.** Because so much of work requires cooperating and coordinating efforts with others, check with the people involved first, making sure that everyone is on the same page before you take action. No matter how well intentioned you are or how brilliant an idea you have, when you don't consult important people first, they're often upset, and as a result, may even reject a legitimate action or idea.

- **Make the safest assumption of them all.** The safest assumption to make when working with others is to assume that the other person means well. Put all conspiracy theories aside. (What a relief!) This assumption allows you to see and deal with the actions and ideas of others at face value.

Chapter 2

Understanding How People Express Themselves to Others

In This Chapter

▶ Outlining the four ways in which people express themselves to others

▶ Understanding how to begin speaking assertively

The strain (or tug-of-war) that stems from the stressful and challenging situations you encounter often mars your interactions. What those stressful and challenging situations are, how often they occur, and with whom they occur vary greatly from individual to individual. One person's stressful encounter can be a no-big-deal situation to someone else. For some people, the workday is filled with constant stress, while for others, the day is peaceful and friendly. Your approach to interacting with others greatly influences how stressful and challenging your work situations have been and will become.

People express themselves to others through four approaches. This chapter outlines each of the four approaches and helps you understand what makes assertiveness the most effective approach.

Understanding the Four Approaches to Speaking

People express themselves in four ways: aggressively, nonassertively, passive-aggressively, and assertively. This section discusses each of the four patterns of communication in detail so that you can recognize each pattern and begin to move your own way of speaking toward assertiveness.

If you're like most people, you've used all four speaking approaches at various times. But you may find that when you deal with certain people or encounter certain situations — especially challenging and stressful ones — you often fall into one of the less-productive patterns of expressing yourself

(aggressive, nonassertive, or passive-aggressive). If you do, join the club known as the human race. You become a successful communicator by dealing with these situations assertively, the most positive and respectful way of resolving issues with others.

My way or the highway: The aggressive approach

Aggressive speaking is a hard-charging approach that's often hostile and comes across as controlling or dominating. Here are some common messages you may hear when someone speaks aggressively:

- ✔ "You must. . . ."
- ✔ "Because I said so."
- ✔ "You idiot!"
- ✔ "You always/never. . . ."
- ✔ "Who screwed this up?"

There's nothing subtle to the aggressive approach. The following are common behaviors that an aggressive speaker displays:

- ✔ **Blaming, accusing:** In problem situations, an aggressive speaker is quick to find fault and focus on the wrongs that the other person supposedly committed.

- ✔ **Intimidating body language:** An aggressive speaker sometimes uses threatening or intimidating body language, such as demonstrative finger pointing, moving closer to you, getting in your face to argue a point, or pounding on a table with his or her fist.

- ✔ **Demanding, ordering:** The aggressive approach to getting something from another person is to demand it or give orders. An aggressive speaker tells you what you must do.

- ✔ **Raised voice:** As you may have guessed, when someone is making a point aggressively, his or her voice gets louder and the tone becomes sharper.

- ✔ **Harsh, personal language:** An aggressive speaker focuses more on the person than on the issue. The language is often filled with a lot of *you* insults and, at times, with profanity. Tact or diplomacy is tossed aside.

- ✔ **Verbal browbeating:** When you have a difference of opinion with an aggressive speaker who feels strongly about a point, or when something isn't going the way that person desires, the conversation quickly turns into a competition — a battle to be won. The way to *win* is not to listen, to interrupt, to talk louder, to argue, and to verbally attack the other person.

Getting a point across the aggressive way

Derek's approach as a supervisor was to make requests of his staff nicely. But if they didn't follow through on those requests, no more Mr. Nice Guy.

For example, because Ken, an employee, was often out and about in the plant doing maintenance work, Derek asked Ken to carry a beeper and to keep it on at all times. Derek wanted to be able to reach Ken when he needed him for an assignment. The first couple of days wearing the beeper, Ken often forgot to turn it on. Derek got frustrated because he couldn't get timely responses from Ken. Instead of asking Ken what was happening, Derek got into Ken's face, shook his index finger at him, and yelled at him never to have his beeper off again. For the next two days, Ken's beeper was on at all times. On the third day, Ken gave Derek the beeper and his resignation.

The appeasing way: The nonassertive approach

Nonassertive speaking comes off as the softest of the four approaches. A nonassertive speaker is passive and allows others to dominate the conversation. Here are some common messages you hear when someone speaks in a nonassertive manner:

- ✔ "Uh . . . if that's the way you want to do it . . . um, that's fine with me."
- ✔ "I don't know if I could do that."
- ✔ "I'll talk to him soon about that problem; I've just been really busy."
- ✔ "I'm sorry to ask you."
- ✔ "I hate to bother you."
- ✔ "Maybe that's a good idea."

There's nothing strong or certain about the nonassertive approach. Instead, nonassertive speakers often display the following behaviors:

- ✔ **Soft voice:** In nonassertive speaking, the volume in the speaker's voice is often low and sometimes hard to hear, especially in group settings. The tone also may come across as meek.

- ✔ **Overly agreeable, no point of view expressed:** A nonassertive speaker agrees with you in order to go along and keep everything nice. A nonassertive speaker also seldom expresses his or her point of view and certainly doesn't express an opinion that's contrary to yours.

✔ **Avoidance:** The nonassertive way to deal with a concern is to avoid dealing with it: Avoid talking to the person, let the problem linger, and try to put off dealing with the situation for as long as possible. The more uncomfortable the matter is, the more effort a nonassertive person puts into avoiding it.

✔ **Withdrawn body language:** A nonassertive speaker doesn't make direct eye contact with other people, stays at a distance, and may slump or cower. Nothing confident comes across in the speaker's physical effort to communicate the message.

✔ **Sounding unsure:** When someone speaks nonassertively, he or she hesitates and sounds unsure. A nonassertive speaker may use qualifier language such as *perhaps, maybe,* or *hopefully,* or may start sentences with comments like, "I don't know if this idea will help."

✔ **Beating around the bush:** Nonassertive speakers express critical or sensitive points by talking around the issue and rambling, leaving the point — at best — implied. The speaker never states the point clearly and directly.

✔ **Sounding hopeless or helpless:** Another common nonassertive speaking characteristic is language of despair or inaction. A typically resigned or hopeless message, such as, "I tried that once, but it didn't work, so what can you do?" is common. You may hear a lot of *I can'ts* and *I don't knows* such that no plan of action or possible solution is introduced.

Subtle but aggravating: The passive-aggressive approach

Passive-aggressive speaking is an approach in which a person comes off as subtle and indirect, but whose underlying tone may hurt or manipulate others. Take a look at some messages you hear when someone speaks in a passive-aggressive manner:

✔ "I knew that wouldn't work."

✔ "If that's the way you want it. . . ."

✔ "How could you even think that?"

✔ "When was the last time you helped me?"

✔ "The problem with Joe is. . . ."

The subtleties of the passive-aggressive approach are not pleasant. Someone speaking passive-aggressively often displays the following behaviors:

Dealing with problems the nonassertive way

For quite a while, Jim had put off addressing some performance issues with Greg, one of his team members. The pressure to do so was growing from both his boss and his team members because Greg's performance was negatively impacting the team.

Finally, Jim got up the nerve and sat down with Greg to have a heart-to-heart talk about the problems. During the meeting, Jim talked about how a good team needs members who are supportive and follow through on their assignments. Greg agreed that those are good qualities for a team member to have. This 15-minute meeting ended with Jim feeling that Greg understood the problem and with Greg feeling that this was a strange conversation — and nothing he needed to be concerned about.

✔ **Appears to agree but really does not agree:** One of the common behaviors of passive-aggressiveness is that the speaker sounds as though he or she is going along with or agreeing to something, but his or her actions that follow don't show support or commitment. Instead, the passive-aggressive speaker claims that any agreement was actually a misunderstanding, or the speaker carries out actions that are contrary to the supposed commitment.

✔ **Tells others but not the source of the concern:** A passive-aggressive person does not deal directly with concerns about others. Complaining about that person to other people — behind that person's back — is a common way to handle concerns. Generally, such behavior stirs up gossip and divisiveness.

✔ **Makes subtle digs and sarcastic remarks:** Heard the old line that many a truth is said in jest? This line summarizes one behavior of passive-aggressive speakers: Put-downs are concealed with sarcasm. When the speaker uses no sarcasm, his or her tone may be condescending and hurtful to the person hearing it. Sometimes a passive-aggressive speaker expresses displeasure not through words but through nonverbal means, such as rolling the eyes, shaking the head, or making sighs of disgust.

✔ **Keeps score, sets conditions:** In the passive-aggressive approach, cooperation comes with limitations or conditions. Ask a passive-aggressive speaker for support and you'll likely meet reluctance. Memories are long and forgiveness is short. Sometimes a passive-aggressive speaker comes off sounding like a martyr: "For all the work I've done for you, this is the appreciation I get!"

A passive-aggressive speaker also may try to settle the score by giving you the silent treatment, not showing up when help is needed, sabotaging your efforts behind the scenes, and sending harsh messages via e-mail and copying others on them (see Chapter 13 for more on communicating via e-mail).

✔ **Nonverbal message contradicts the verbal message:** In passive-aggressive behavior, stated words sound positive, but body language or tone of voice gives the words the opposite meaning. *Everything is fine* means that something *is* wrong, *Nothing is bothering me* means that something *is* bothering me. *That's a good idea* means that it *isn't,* and so on.

✔ **Holds back expressing concerns or providing assistance:** A passive-aggressive speaker may withhold information or other forms of support when others can use it to get a job done. In addition, he or she holds emotions in, although you may get a sense of them in the speaker's body language or from implied negative messages. But nothing is said directly, and when asked about a concern or issue, the passive-aggressive speaker often responds to the inquiry by saying "Never mind" or "No big deal."

✔ **Criticizes after the fact:** This behavior is sometimes referred to as *second-guessing* or *armchair quarterbacking.* After an event or action has taken place, a passive-aggressive communicator responds with what you should've done or what you did wrong — sometimes even when you requested input beforehand and he or she gave none. A passive-aggressive speaker is quick to pass judgment.

Straight and positive: The assertive approach

The last of the four common speaking approaches that people use to express messages to others is assertiveness. *Assertive speaking* involves expressing yourself in a positive and confident way and allowing and encouraging others to do the same. This pattern of speaking requires the most skill and effort, for unlike the other three approaches, it requires you to think before you speak. Here are some common messages you hear from assertive speakers:

✔ "Yes, that was my mistake."

✔ "As I understand your point . . ."

✔ "Let me explain why I disagree with that point."

✔ "Let's define the issue and then explore some options to help resolve it."

✔ "Please hear me out and then work with me to resolve my concern."

The following are some of the behaviors that someone who speaks in an assertive fashion displays:

✔ **Takes responsibility:** The assertive approach says that each individual is responsible for his or her own actions — no excuses, no woe-is-me language, no blaming others for problems. The speaker accepts what has happened and focuses on what needs to be done next.

Reeling in the company critic

Tom led a special cross-functional task team. Its purpose was to come up with policies and programs to help build a stronger workplace that would retain good employees. Mary was an influential middle manager who was asked to be on the task force but declined.

The task team members showed much enthusiasm and worked hard to come up with ideas they thought would strengthen the organization. When they presented recommendations to management, Mary attended and was quick to point out everything she thought was wrong with the task team's work — which delayed

acceptance of the recommendations. After going through this experience twice, Tom invited Mary to one of the team's meetings and explained to her the team's latest proposal. He then asked her to tell the team everything she believed was wrong with this proposal. After Mary left, the team incorporated the parts of her criticism they thought were most useful and then went forward to present at the next management meeting. At that meeting, Mary smiled and said little, and the recommendations were approved on the spot.

✔ **Takes initiative:** An assertive speaker doesn't play games. If something needs to happen, he or she takes the initiative to get the process rolling — no waiting for others to say what to do and when to act. The assertive approach is action oriented.

✔ **Listens actively:** Assertiveness allows for two-way conversation. Assertive speakers show a willingness to hear the other person out and understand his or her point of view.

✔ **Speaks up, is direct and constructive:** If a point needs to be made or a thought needs to be expressed, an assertive communicator speaks up. He or she states the point directly without beating around the bush. Assertive speakers use language *constructively;* that is, they communicate the message in the best way possible and make the point clearly. The language focuses on the issue at hand.

✔ **Shows sincerity:** When you express yourself sincerely, you say what you mean and mean what you say — and do so with respect for others.

✔ **Is solutions focused:** In problem situations, an assertive speaker takes a problem-solving approach. He or she examines the problem, not to blame or find fault with anyone but to understand the issue and move toward developing a solution. Creating the solution becomes the main focus in working with others.

✔ **Assumes a confident voice and body language:** The voice of an assertive speaker sounds strong, certain, and firm when needed. The speaker's posture, gestures, and facial expressions support his or her message. He or she sounds and looks alive when speaking, coming across nonverbally as positive and enthusiastic to an appropriate degree.

Assertively rallying the team

Lynn was growing frustrated with her team of employees. After all her hard work to coach and build them into a productive unit, performance among the group had begun to slip in recent months. Production was down, follow-through with customers was inconsistent, and error rates were increasing. This overall lax performance had Lynn frustrated and ready to come down hard on everyone on the team — the aggressive approach.

Instead, Lynn called a team meeting. At the beginning of the meeting, she outlined her agenda, which was to be in a problem-solving format. Then, in a serious and firm tone, she outlined directly and specifically her concerns regarding the team's recent performance. She

had everyone's attention. She then reiterated what she said in her introduction so that people could comment on what they saw happening, but her emphasis was on problem solving, not on problem dwelling. After a few comments from team members, all in support of Lynn's observations, Lynn brainstormed with the group for ideas on improving performance. Everyone got involved as Lynn facilitated. The team set goals and generated an action plan. Team members walked away with high, positive energy, and many commented that this was one of their best team meetings ever.

The team followed up on the plans, and performance picked up again. Lynn had faced the problem head-on without being aggressive.

✔ **Addresses concerns directly to the source:** An assertive speaker addresses issues directly to the source as opposed to telling others about the problems. At the same time, the speaker states the problem constructively and places the emphasis on collaborating with the other person to work out a resolution. No browbeating or blaming occurs.

✔ **Requests needs:** Whereas an aggressive speaker demands or orders to get what's needed, an assertive speakers *asks for* or *requests* what's needed. The message makes the sense of importance clear so that the request and any rationale for it are understood.

Contrasting the Four Approaches to Speaking

One of the fun activities in my communication seminars involves taking a situation and demonstrating each of the four common speaking approaches for that situation. Here's one such scenario:

Say you just received an important assignment with a tight deadline. You know that you need assistance from Sue, a co-worker, to get it done. Using each approach, how would you communicate this need? Take your thoughts and compare them to the following samples.

- **Aggressive approach:** "Sue, look, I'm in a jam right now. You need to help me get this critical project done right away! I don't have time to hear that you're busy with something else. That excuse just won't fly. So come on, sit down and let me show you what I need you to do."

- **Nonassertive approach:** "Hi, Sue. I hate to bother you. I know you're probably busy with a lot of other issues right now. I have one of those tough assignments. If you have a chance, maybe you could lend me a hand for a little bit. But, uh, it's okay if you don't want to."

- **Passive-aggressive approach:** "Sue, I know you're the type who doesn't want to put yourself out too much. Hey, I'm just kidding. But look, when you were in a pinch last week, who helped you out? That's right — me. So look, I'm in the same boat now. Don't worry, I won't have you do most of the work anyway."

- **Assertive approach:** "Sue, I was just assigned a critical project that needs to be done in a week. I would appreciate it if you could lend some assistance. The project involves an area in which your experience will really come in handy. What I'd like to do is take a few minutes with you now or this afternoon to determine what time and support you can lend and to fill you in on the needs of the project. Does that work for you, and if so, what time can we meet?"

Don't confuse aggressive with assertive

People sometimes confuse the words *aggressive* and *assertive.* What they share in common is that the speaker is willing to share his or her viewpoint and is willing to take action to deal with issues. But after that, the two approaches are quite different:

Aggressive	Assertive
Blunt	Direct
In conflict situations, harsh in tone	In conflict situations, firm in tone
In conflict situations, blame and browbeat the other person	In conflict situations, collaborate on solutions
Push your own way	Speak up, yet hear what the other person has to say
One-way conversation flow	Two-way conversation flow

As you see in this example, the same message can be communicated in four different ways. Only an assertive speaker is able to directly and positively request Sue's help and communicate the importance of the situation. The aggressive message comes on as a strong demand, the nonassertive approach leaves you wondering whether anything is being asked at all, and the passive-aggressive message tinges with sarcasm and you-owe-me conditions — all of which are turnoffs to most fellow team members.

Becoming an Assertive Speaker

As you read through the descriptions of the four ways people commonly express themselves (see the preceding section), you probably noticed that the assertive approach is the most effective for achieving success on the job. If you're like many people I encounter in my seminars, you can see yourself in each of the other approaches — and probably see people you've encountered in both your professional and personal lives in each approach, too.

Speaking assertively is the toughest approach — not in terms of difficulty but in terms of effort. It requires more effort than the aggressive, nonassertive, and passive-aggressive approaches because you have to be aware of your own behavior and be considerate of the other person.

You may have noticed that you have to listen effectively to speak assertively. The better you understand where the other person is coming from — you do so through active listening — the better you can tailor your message so that the other person understands it well (which is a great definition for assertive speaking). See Chapter 3 for more on active listening.

To change your pattern of behavior so that you become an assertive speaker, apply the following principles:

- **Collaboration:** Conversations work best when they're two-way — that is, where both parties contribute and work to understand each other.

- **Flexibility:** Not everyone you interact with is the same; however, being direct, positive, confident, and willing to listen is a good place to start with everyone. From there, you can adjust to the individual after you get to know the person. For example, with some people, the less you say, the better. With others, you have to be firm to be taken seriously. And with still others, you have to be patient in order to work effectively with them.

- **Self-control:** The toughest person to manage in any interaction is yourself. Assertive speakers are in control of their emotions. Aggressive, nonassertive, and passive-aggressive speakers allow their emotions to control them.

✔ **Continuous respect:** Assertive speakers take a long-term view to working relationships. People you deal with today will remember you tomorrow. If you treat everyone with unconditional respect, you build more partners and allies for the future. (You may not like everyone you encounter in doing your job, but you don't have to take them home with you, either.) Disrespectful actions received are not met with disrespectful actions in return; otherwise, you go down the aggressive or passive-aggressive tracks for tug-of-war relationships. You can take actions to deal with situations you don't like (covered in Part IV), but you always do so with respect for the other person.

✔ **Fix problems, not blame:** Problems are inevitable in any work situation, and many involve other people. When speaking assertively, your focus is on problem solving versus problem dwelling — on creating solutions together versus blaming one another.

Chapter 3

Are You Really Listening?

In This Chapter

▶ Looking at the positive impact of effective listening

▶ Exploring the three stages of the listening process

▶ Examining the four common ways that people engage in listening

▶ Outlining what's needed to make active listening really work

*I*f you're like most people, you interact with people every day in your job, so you do some talking and some listening. But are you *really* listening? This chapter can help you figure that out.

In conversations about the need to listen, people sometimes like to joke and ask, "What did you say?" That's not listening; that's hearing. In fact, as Chapter 1 points out, you spend much of your communication time speaking and listening, yet seldom throughout your basic education are you given formal instruction in how to improve these types of communication. Not surprisingly, then, many people don't know the difference between hearing and listening and don't know what effective listening really means.

Listening, as used throughout this book, is defined as the process of receiving a message from a speaker, processing that message to make sense of it, and then responding to it in ways that show understanding of what the speaker means. This chapter walks you through this process, shows you the ways that people commonly engage in listening, and helps you understand the most effective way to listen (called *active listening* and sometimes referred to as *reflective listening* or *responsive listening*). *Hearing* is simply the physical effort of taking in the speaker's message, but doesn't necessarily mean that the message was received, processed, or responded to.

Ever see a movie or television show where the heroes or heroines were applauded for their great listening? I can't think of one. You may not, therefore, have a lot of role models, in public forums or private ones, who demonstrate effective listening skills. So there's no need to feel bad if you aren't sure what effective listening is. What's important is to recognize that applying tools for listening effectively is crucial to success in your job.

Recognizing the Impact of Listening

You can gain a lot when you listen effectively; you can lose a lot when you don't. You've probably experienced both the benefits of good listening and the costs of poor listening. The key is to recognize both the benefits and the costs so that you can maximize the benefits of your own listening.

Accentuate the positives

How do you feel when someone really listens to you? When I ask this question in my seminars, these are the responses that people give the most:

- ✔ Respected
- ✔ Cared for
- ✔ That you've gained rapport
- ✔ Rewarded
- ✔ Satisfied
- ✔ Sense of achievement

What do these feelings have in common? They're all very positive. When someone listens well to you, the experience is definitely positive.

Here's the follow-up question I ask seminar participants: What would the impact on your job be if the people you interact with — from co-workers to customers — walked away from interactions with you with these kinds of positive feelings? Here are the responses that this question usually evokes:

- ✔ Increased productivity
- ✔ Stronger working relationships
- ✔ Better quality of work
- ✔ Greater customer satisfaction
- ✔ Repeat business
- ✔ Easier and better problem solving
- ✔ Greater cooperation and teamwork
- ✔ Less stress

Listening is a powerful means of communication that can increase your effectiveness on the job. People often overlook or take for granted the power (*power*, in this case, meaning "positive influence") of this tool. When you become aware of the power that active listening gives you, you're ready to develop and use listening tools (see Part II) and begin to have a positive impact on others.

Minimize the negatives

People have no problem telling stories about examples of poor listening. One story I recall being told went something like this: "I needed a package shipped overnight to a customer in Portland, Maine. It never got there, and we lost the customer's business as a result. A few days later, the package was discovered to have been sent to Portland, Oregon."

Stories of woes like this, from big to small, usually roll out when people are asked to tell about situations in which they were listened to poorly. Quite often, these experiences are more common than the ones in which effective listening occurs. When I ask about the impact that poor listening has, I get the following answers:

- ✔ Strained working relationships
- ✔ Messed-up customer orders
- ✔ Loss of current or potential business
- ✔ Dissatisfied customers
- ✔ Little problems escalating into big ones
- ✔ Increased errors and the need for rework
- ✔ Greater inefficiency

In simple terms, poor listening can be quite costly. You can't afford it. The key is to recognize the impact of effective listening and work hard to gain the benefits that come from it. Remember, too, that this stuff about listening makes your job easier, not harder.

Following the Three Stages of the Listening Process

Listening occurs in three stages:

- ✔ **Stage 1 — receiving:** In this first stage, you take in the speaker's message through your senses, most notably through hearing and seeing. In fact, you listen as much with your sense of sight as you do with your sense of hearing. (The exception is when you're talking to someone over the telephone.) Your eyes help you read the nonverbal cues that play a part in how the speaker expresses his or her message.

This is why, if you have an issue to work out with someone, you should get together face to face if possible. Seeing the person live helps you gain a better understanding of what that person is thinking and feeling.

✔ **Stage 2 — processing:** After you take in the speaker's message with your senses, the internal processing begins. This activity takes place in your mind and involves analyzing, evaluating, and synthesizing. It's done to make sense out of the speaker's message; that is, to help you figure out the answer to the question, "What does the speaker mean?" Because all this processing is internal, the speaker doesn't yet see any visible reaction from you, the listener.

If problems occur in this stage of the listening process, they're most often caused by attention levels and stress levels. When you're distracted or not fully tuned into the speaker's message, you don't get the intended meaning. When your stress level is high emotionally, you may react to bits and pieces of the message instead of capturing the whole thing. Therefore, the processing stage requires a great deal of concentration (see Chapter 4) so that you get what the speaker is truly saying.

✔ **Stage 3 — responding:** This third stage in the listening process is the one in which the speaker sees and hears what the listener does. In this stage, the listener verbally and nonverbally acknowledges that he or she has received and understood the message.

When the speaker feels respected and understood by the listener, a strong connection is made — and productivity goes up. When the speaker encounters barriers from the listener — nonverbal (see Chapter 4) as well as verbal barriers (check out Chapter 6) — the communication process breaks down. Productivity goes down and stress increases.

Avoiding Ineffective Patterns for Listening

One of the common ineffective patterns that occurs in conversations is that a speaker speaks to a speaker instead of a listener. Little true listening takes place. Table 3-1 illustrates this pattern, which makes for less-than-productive conversations. Check out this sample conversation between two co-workers, related to a customer order.

Table 3-1	Heated Conversation with No Listening
Ann's Role and Message	**Sue's Role and Message**
Begins as speaker: "Sue, that new account you have, Alpha Inc.? I'm running into a problem trying to fill the order for it."	**Reacts as speaker:** "Oh, no! I worked so hard to finally get business from this new customer, turn it over to you to get the order fulfilled, and then the very next day you show up with a problem. Why can't I get support for the sales I bring in, Ann?"
Reacts as speaker: "If you knew how to qualify customer orders, we wouldn't run into any problems."	**Reacts as speaker:** "This is the support I get. Every problem is my fault. If you folks in customer fulfillment understood how we in sales keep you employed, you would be a lot more helpful."

As the conversation in Table 3-1 shows, Ann and Sue are talking *at* each other. Turn up the volume on what they have to say, and you have an argument. This is a conversation with two people talking and no one listening.

Table 3-2 shows another example of what people commonly do in this less-than-productive conversation pattern.

Table 3-2	Calm Conversation with No Listening
Joe's Role and Message	**Ramon's Role and Message**
Begins as speaker: "Ramon, we need to increase efficiency in our operation by creating some process improvements."	**Reacts as speaker:** "Joe, I think the answer lies in putting in some organized training for the staff."
Reacts as speaker: "I disagree. The inefficiencies that occur in our operation are all process related. If we find ways to streamline our processes, we can serve our customers better."	**Reacts as speaker:** "No, Joe. If you look at the kinds of errors that staff members make, most are because of not knowing how the processes work. We tend to throw people into their jobs as opposed to training them how to do the job right."

The example in Table 3-2 again illustrates the pattern people often have in conversations: two people talking at each other and no one really listening. While the conversation between Joe and Ramon is less heated than the one between Ann and Sue in Table 3-1 — and they're talking on a related subject about making efficiency improvements — Joe and Ramon are still busy expressing opinions back and forth to each other. Neither is making the effort to understand the other's thinking.

Table 3-3 illustrates the pattern of more productive conversations. Take a look at Ann and Sue's conversation under this different pattern.

Table 3-3	Respectful Conversation with Active Listening
Ann's Role and Message	**Sue's Role and Message**
Begins as speaker: "Sue, that new account you have, Alpha Inc.? I'm running into a problem trying to fill the order for it."	**Responds as listener:** "A problem? Tell me about it."
Continues as speaker: "A couple of items. First, some of the prices quoted on the order form don't match what we have on our guide sheet in customer fulfillment. Second, a few of the part numbers listed on the order form don't match our listings."	**Responds as listener again:** "So what you're telling me is that you're running into some confusion in trying to fulfill the order here. Is that right?"
Confirms as speaker and then becomes listener: "Exactly. What can you do to help us out?"	**Becomes speaker:** "Let me take a look at the items in question on the order form. I can check to see whether they are just my clerical mistakes or whether I need to get back to the customer to clarify his needs for the order. I'll also check our guide sheets so that we're all on the same page. I should be able to get back to you with some answers by tomorrow."
Responds as listener and laughs: "Sounds like you've got a plan."	
Closes as speaker: "Thanks for your help. We'll talk tomorrow and get Alpha Inc. off to a good start."	

In productive conversations like this one, both people take turns being speaker and listener. They hold off on making assumptions (read more about assumptions in Chapter 1) and make every effort to find out more about each other's viewpoints. They are collaborative as opposed to adversarial in working out the issue.

Table 3-4 gives you a look at how Joe and Ramon's conversation can use this more productive pattern.

Table 3-4	Respectful Conversation with Active Listening
Joe's Role and Message	*Ramon's Role and Message*
Begins as speaker: "Ramon, we need to increase efficiency in our operation by creating some process improvements."	**Responds as listener:** "Help me understand more of your thinking behind this suggestion."
Continues as speaker: "From my thinking, Ramon, our current processes for order fulfillment can be quite cumbersome. They create a lot of work and often much confusion, too. If we can find ways to streamline them, I think we can better serve our customers."	**Responds as listener again:** "So you're seeing the root of our operational problems as being centered around processes?"
Confirms as speaker and then becomes listener: "That's right. What do you see as the main factors for our operational problems, Ramon?"	**Becomes speaker:** "In my view, the area we need to tackle most is training. That's the quickest and best way to start to make the improvements we need."
Responds as listener: "Training, hmm? What's your reasoning?"	
(And the conversation continues from there.)	

Unlike in their previous conversation (refer to Table 3-2), Joe and Ramon are now talking *with* each other as opposed to speaking *at* each other. They are expressing opinions, but this time the opinions are explored and heard out. The conversation flows as a two-way interaction instead of two one-way interactions.

Seeing How People Listen

As Chapter 2 discusses, people express their messages to each other by using four common approaches. The same applies to how people listen. Because most people don't receive formal instruction in how to listen effectively and don't usually have standout role models for it, either, they engage in listening in the following ways:

- Passive listening
- Selective listening
- Attentive listening
- Active listening

Sometimes, people consider ignoring to be another form of listening. However, consciously (or even unconsciously) tuning out the speaker is not listening because no message is received. Doing so in a one-on-one conversation indicates that you don't care about the other person and that the message being spoken is unimportant.

Of the four common patterns in how people listen to others, passive listening and selective listening occur the most often. As many people engage in listening, they tend to function in one pattern as a regular practice — whether in stressful or nonstressful situations. You may see yourself, plus others in your life, in the patterns described in the following sections.

Is anybody really home? The passive approach

Passive listening is a common way that people listen to others. In this approach, the listener is present nonverbally but verbally provides little feedback to the speaker. Here are some common behaviors exhibited by someone who is listening passively:

- Eye contact with the speaker
- Fairly expressionless look on the face
- Occasional nods of the head
- Occasional verbal acknowledgments, such as, "Uh huh," especially on the telephone

As you can see in these behaviors, the listener is with the speaker but adds little to stimulate the flow of conversation. As the speaker, you're on your own. Talking to a passive listener is quite frustrating because you generally want more participation from the other person and begin to wonder whether that listener really cares or is understanding anything about the message you're expressing.

Where does this common habit of passive listening come from? Much of it has to do with how children are raised. From experiences at home to experiences at school, where 30 or more children in a classroom together listen to one teacher, children frequently receive messages about how they should listen:

- Be quiet.
- Listen up.
- Shut up.
- Children are better seen than heard.

These kinds of messages and experiences condition people to think that good listening means to show up and be quiet. In other words, you let the other person talk, and when he or she is done, you speak up if you have something to say. The result is one-way conversations with little effort to connect to the other person's message.

Getting what you want, not what you need: The selective approach

Selective listening is nearly as common as passive listening. Selective listening is most commonly defined as hearing what you want to hear. When you hear the message you want to hear, you may function as a more engaged and understanding listener. But when you don't want to hear about the particular message being delivered, you tend to tune out or become reactive to the speaker. In other words, you're consistently inconsistent in your listening efforts when you function as a selective listener.

Someone who is listening in a selective manner to a message that he or she doesn't want to hear displays these behaviors:

- Gives looks of disinterest
- Looks away at other things — a watch, papers, and so on
- Sits by quietly
- Reacts with high degrees of emotion, such as being defensive or debating every point
- Jumps in before the speaker has finished and takes over the conversation as a speaker
- Changes the subject
- Asks a question about a point of self-interest, sometimes in an interrogating manner, that doesn't fit in the speaker's current message

Judgmental actions by a listener, from tuning out to reacting harshly, create barriers in conversation. They put up hurdles that cause the listener not to get the full message and add strain and tension to the working relationship.

Falling into the trap of being a selective listener is easy to do. Humans have emotions and biases, and sometimes, something a speaker says triggers those emotions and biases.

In addition, people are selective not just based on what they hear — the subject matter — but also on who is speaking and how the message is presented. For example, your department vice president comes into your office to make a request of you. You're fully attentive and receive the message well. A few minutes later, a co-worker stops by, one who turns you off because of his verbose nature. What do you do when he starts talking? Tune him right out. That's selective listening.

Grabbing the facts: The attentive approach

Functioning as an *attentive listener* is more productive than functioning as either a passive or a selective listener. When you function as an attentive listener, you're more engaged and less judgmental, both nonverbally and verbally. Attentive listeners display these behaviors:

- Give steady eye contact to the speaker.

- Show interested looks and sincere facial expressions.

- Nod to indicate understanding.

- Provide simple verbal acknowledgments ("I see," "Okay," "Yes," and so on) to encourage the speaker to express his or her message.

- Raise questions to begin to draw out the message.

- Ask questions that seek greater detail out of the message.

A speaker's message contains two parts: the facts or content and the feelings or emotions. Together, they comprise the meaning of the speaker's message. This concept is fundamental to results-oriented communication.

> Facts + emotions = The meaning of the message

Attentive listening focuses on the facts being heard in the message. The facts are the more tangible part of the message. Emotions tend to be stated less in words than in nonverbal behavior — emotions are much less tangible. (More about that in Chapter 4.) So when you function as an attentive listener, you take the *Dragnet* approach to listening — you become the Sergeant Joe Friday of communication, looking for "Just the facts."

As an attentive listener, you seek the facts and information that the speaker wants to relay to you in your conversation. When the message is mostly factual, you do well. When the message involves much emotion, you tend not to deal with it or neglect to acknowledge it directly. In essence, you say, "I can tell you what you're talking about, I hear your words, but I may not be able to tell fully what you mean." This is where attentive listeners fall short. They don't capture the entire message to get the full meaning — both the facts *and* the feelings.

Avoiding the selective-listening syndrome

Mark learned a lesson early in his career about what listening — truly effective listening — means. One of his initial assignments was to conduct interviews with a number of employees in his plant so that he could write job descriptions and determine what issues of concern existed.

As his manager explained the project, she made a key point to Mark about his role in this assignment. The manager told Mark that he would encounter a few employees who were known as the squeaky wheels in the plant — the chronic complainers for whom everything was always wrong. The manager explained that 90 percent of what these squeaky-wheel types had to say would be garbage, just whining over not much at all. But 10 percent of what they had to say would be of much value. The problem in the plant was that no one listened for the 10 percent, which kept the chronic complainers forever complaining. Mark's most important effort in carrying out this assignment, his manager emphasized, was to capture that 10 percent.

In other words, although some people may be difficult to listen to, you shouldn't allow yourself to become a selective listener and miss what they really have to say.

Capturing and confirming the message: The active approach

Active listening, sometimes referred to as *responsive listening* or *reflective listening,* is the most powerful way in which people engage in the effort of listening. An active listener receives a speaker's message with care and respect and then works to verify his or her understanding of that message — as the speaker meant it to be.

When you function as an active listener, you capture the speaker's whole message — the facts *and* the feelings. The speaker is able to get his or her message out and then walk away knowing that the listener has understood it. (Chapter 5 provides you with the tools to listen actively.)

Among the behaviors displayed by active listeners are the positive ones listed in the "Grabbing the facts: The attentive approach" section, plus the following:

- Showing patience
- Giving verbal feedback to summarize understanding of the message
- Acknowledging the emotions being expressed with the message to fully understand where the speaker is coming from

✔ Exploring the reasons for the emotions being expressed when they are significant to the overall message

✔ Speaking up when something is unclear or confusing

Active listeners do talk. But what they talk about and where their attention goes is the speaker's message — not their own message or their commentary on the speaker's message.

Batteries Required: Making Active Listening Work

Like many an electronic device that requires batteries to make it work, active listening requires "batteries" as well. "Batteries" in this case means your own hard work and ongoing effort. The tools you gain in Part II don't just happen when you show up to the conversation. They require concentration — focused mental energy and attention.

Overcoming objections

Diane had worked hard to prepare her public relations plan for launching the company's new product. Her meeting today was to review the plan with Terry, the vice president of marketing, so that the PR campaign could begin shortly. Diane had also worked hard in recent months to learn how to be an active listener. Her hard work would come in handy in this critical meeting.

This meeting represented Diane's first major piece of work for Terry. She wanted to show him that she could do an outstanding job and felt confident that her work would demonstrate this to Terry. Once the meeting kicked off, Terry expressed a couple of concerns about Diane's plan. He stated that he thought some rework would have to be done, and that this plan did not quite meet what was needed for the product launch.

Diane caught herself as she was feeling agitated by Terry's comments. Instead of arguing with him, she shifted to being a listener. She first asked questions to get Terry to explain his concerns one at a time. After each explanation, she gave verbal feedback to make sure that she understood Terry's points. After a few minutes of active listening, Diane had gained confirmation from Terry that she understood his concerns. With this new understanding in mind, Diane proceeded to address each item.

When she spoke, she directed Terry's attention to aspects of the PR plan and explained how those areas addressed his concerns. When she finished, Terry smiled and said that the plan looked great and that it indeed would work well, and then he commended Diane for her quality work. Diane's was off and running on the road to success.

The best aspect of active listening, which makes it more effective than attentive listening, is that it removes doubt from your conversations. When you function as an attentive listener, you walk away from interactions thinking that you understood the other person. The speaker often shares that view, thinking that you have understood him or her. With active listening, the parties no longer think that understanding has been achieved; they *know* that it has. Verbal feedback to confirm understanding of a speaker's message, given without being judgmental, makes active listening the most effective form of listening.

To prepare you to get the best out of the powerful tools of active listening, here are a few tips. Consider them the kit that holds the tools together.

- ✔ **Hold off on the assumptions.** Avoid jumping to the conclusion that you know what someone is saying before he or she states the entire message. (Chapter 1 covers the problems with making assumptions.) Hold back and hear the message all the way through. You may be surprised! Then, as needed, ask questions and check your understanding so that you don't act under a false assumption. When in doubt, check it out.

- ✔ **Avoid being quick to offer advice.** The old adage that advice is best received when asked for is important to keep in mind when becoming an active listener. Sometimes what sounds like a problem is merely the other person sharing the day's trials and tribulations — no more, no less. Your desire to be helpful may have you giving advice out freely, without knowing whether it's really wanted.

  The first step in problem solving is to understand what the problem is. Quite often, when you're quick to provide advice, you skip this key first step. In addition, many people are simply looking for a sounding board so that they can resolve their own problems. Unwanted advice may make the recipient feel dictated to or imposed upon — major turnoffs for most people.

- ✔ **Exercise patience.** *Patience* as used in active listening means exercising control over your own emotions. Your emotions are affected all the time when you interact with others. People have different communication styles, some of which may please you and others of which may be difficult to deal with. For active listening to work, you need to take control of your emotions so that you can deal with the variety of people who come your way.

- ✔ **Eliminate distractions and physical barriers.** This tip is about managing your physical environment. When someone is talking to you, keep your cell phone off and turn down the volume on your pager. Don't be quick to answer the phone simply because you hear it ring. Instead of sitting across from someone at a distance because of a huge desk between you, arrange your chair so that you can sit across from each other without a physical barrier in between. Within the environment in which you're working, create the best possible conditions to allow for a comfortable conversation.

✔ **Be continuously respectful.** Passing judgment on what people say or who they are turns you into a selective listener. When your actions or reactions come across as judgmental, you add tension to the relationship. When you come across as respectful, you build confidence and trust. Regardless of your intentions, people see only your actions. Without consistent efforts to show respect, active listening won't work.

✔ **Shift attention.** Everyone has a lot on his or her mind. Thoughts pass in and out all the time. If, as you attempt to listen, your mind's attention is focused more on what's going on around you or on what your next word back to the speaker is going to be, you're not really listening. Active listening puts attention on the speaker and his or her message, not on you.

Are you really listening?

I use the following activity in my communication seminars after we cover the common ways in which people engage in the effort of listening: passive, selective, attentive, and active listening.

I pair up the participants and have each pair go through two rounds of conversation, one at a time. They take turns in each round being the primary listener and primary speaker. The primary listener is instructed to interact as an active listener. The conversations of a few minutes are often lively as participants work to really be engaged with their speaking partners.

At the end of each round of conversation, the person who played the role of listener is asked to write a one-sentence summary capturing the essence of the speaker's message, both facts and feelings. Although trying to capture the message in one sentence is challenging for many participants, most find that they were close to right-on in capturing the main idea of the message when they show their summaries to their speakers.

Now the main point of the activity comes in. After the rounds of conversation are over, I ask the participants this question: When you were the listener, did you verbalize something close to what you summarized in writing about your speaker's message *while* the conversation took place? The answer for many is no. Only the handful who say yes functioned as active listeners in their conversations. Active listeners give their speakers verbal feedback to ensure that they understand the main idea of the message. Although everyone was pushed into being an active listener after the conversation by writing a summary and checking it out with his or her partners, few were fully active listeners during the conversation.

The key to success is to give verbal feedback during the conversation. Because most people aren't taught how to listen when they go through school, they tend not to give feedback to show understanding.

Part II
Tuning In to the Power of Active Listening

The 5th Wave — By Rich Tennant

"GET READY, I THINK THEY'RE STARTING TO DRIFT."

In this part . . .

This part shows you how to make active listening work for you. Here, you discover what to listen for when someone speaks to you and discover tools that help you capture the speaker's message and understand it with care and respect. You also uncover what not to do when you listen — nonverbal and verbal behaviors that create barriers to your communication.

Chapter 4

Fixing Your Radar on the Speaker

. . . .

In This Chapter

▶ Listening for the entire message

▶ Giving the speaker your full attention

▶ Avoiding habits in your listening that create barriers in the conversation

. . . .

*I*f you're like most people, at some point in a conversation, you've been turned off by your listener. You know what I mean. You've wanted someone to listen to exactly what you were saying, but your listener was either inattentive, distracted, or reacting in ways that showed displeasure with what you had to say.

You've also probably been in the listener's shoes: How the speaker's message was said carried much more meaning than the mere words spoken, making it challenging to pick up on all those cues while trying to figure out what the speaker truly meant.

Both experiences emphasize the importance of communication that goes beyond words. As a listener, it's crucial for you either to invite a speaker to go forward with a message or do the opposite by blocking the expression of that message. Similarly, as a listener, you need to tune into and read the speaker to gain a full understanding of his or her meaning. In each case, your *radar* — your openness and attentiveness — has a powerful effect on the flow of the conversation. Are you open to listening, or are you coming off as judgmental; are you tuned in, or are you tuned out?

This chapter shows you how the most effective form of listening — active listening — really works. It emphasizes the cues you need to listen for and how to situate yourself to receive and process the speaker's message accurately. This chapter also covers what not to do when listening. Most people are well experienced in the habits-to-avoid area, but as with any important behavioral skills, sometimes you need to know what old habits to break so you can put the new ones into practice.

Capturing the Whole Message

If you only hear my words, you won't understand my message. Every message you listen to is expressed by verbal and nonverbal means (or a combination of the two), and quite often, the nonverbal aspects have more to do with the meaning of the message than the verbal aspects.

An important part of listening effectively is knowing what to listen for as the speaker talks. A speaker's message contains three components:

- ✔ **Words:** The verbal component of the message; that is, *what* the speaker is saying.

- ✔ **Tone of voice:** The flavor that comes from your voice that impacts how the words are being said. Different from volume, which is how loud or soft you speak, tone involves the inflection being heard and the level of sincerity coming out of your voice.

- ✔ **Body language:** A nonverbal component that further describes *how* the speaker's message is being conveyed. Body language includes all the things you do with your body to express your message. This includes the use of gestures, eye contact, facial expressions, and posture.

Understanding the impact of the unspoken message

People use a wide variety of communication styles when expressing their messages. Many rely mostly on language and vocabulary — the verbal part of the message. And many express themselves quite differently: Some are reserved or low-key while others are highly active. Of course, some people are somewhere in between these two opposite ends of the scale, while others make use of the full range, sometimes showing little expression and other times exhibiting a great deal of expression in their messages.

Like signatures, individual communication styles have similarities, but each person's style is unique. This diversity represents a major challenge that listeners must face: If people didn't express themselves in different ways, communication would sure be a lot easier. However, if people expressed themselves in the same way, life would be a lot more boring. Although an individual's style of communication is greatly influenced by what is said, *how* the message is said through body language and tone of voice often provides even more of an impact.

Body language and tone of voice have great influence over the meaning of a speaker's message. To recognize their impact on the meaning of a message, try this out:

1. **Say the following sentence with a smile on your face: "Today is a beautiful day."**

2. **Now repeat the same sentence with a frown on your face.**

   What happened to your message from the first time to the second time it was said? When your facial expression changed, your message's meaning changed from a positive outlook to a negative one.

3. **Say the following sentence in a calm and sincere tone: "Today is a beautiful day."**

4. **Now repeat the same sentence with a sarcastic tone in your voice.**

   What happened to your message from the first time to the second time it was said? When your tone of voice changed, your message's meaning changed from one of patient truthfulness to one of annoyed deceit.

As these examples point out, body language and tone of voice greatly impact the overall meaning of a speaker's message. In many cases, they carry the vast majority of the meaning. If you tune in to only to the words you don't fully know what the speaker truly means.

Listening on the telephone is often harder than when you're listening in person. On the phone, you don't see the body language cues that help you pick up on what the person is really saying. So, in a phone conversation, you have to tune in even more closely to the tone, or how the words are being said, to give them meaning. As a listener, this means slowing your pace a bit to let the speaker finish his or her message.

Don't let silence make you uncomfortable. It's better to listen to the message all the way through than to step on it before you've heard it in total. When you're face to face, you can easily pick up when the speaker finishes a point. Let patience guide you even more on the phone, and then check your understanding of what the speaker means from what you have heard in the words, and — more important — in the tone of his or her voice (get the lowdown in Chapter 5).

The feelings behind the facts

As you gain a sense of what to listen for in the verbal and nonverbal components of a message, remember this formula:

Facts/content + Emotion = The meaning of the message

Don't worry, this isn't new math. What this formula represents is the substance you want to listen for when receiving a speaker's message. The content side is filled with the facts, information, and thoughts the speaker relates through the words — the verbal components of the message. The emotion side reflects the message that most often is expressed through the nonverbal components — body language and tone of voice.

Rather than sometimes merely stating their emotions in words — for example, "I am happy today," or, "I am sad from yesterday" — people more often *show* their emotions through nonverbal communication. For example, how would you know if a speaker in an interaction were angry with you if he or she doesn't say the words? The following are some examples of what you may see or hear, or see and hear from the speaker:

✔ Developing a flushed face

✔ Using a harsh or sharp tone of voice; raising the volume

✔ Sounding sarcastic

✔ Pounding his or her fist on a table

✔ Getting close and in your face

✔ Placing hands on hips and hovering over you

✔ Stomping feet

✔ Waving arms boisterously

✔ Saying nothing and looking away

✔ Clenching his or her teeth

✔ Slamming the door and walking away

Simply saying, "I am angry with you," is much clearer. Yet quite often people show their emotions much more than they state them. As these examples indicate, people express their emotions in different ways: Some are highly expressive while others are subtle to reserved.

To truly understand what the speaker means, you need to tune in to the feelings being expressed behind the facts. And when emotion carries much of a message's overall meaning, double-check that you understand it. In listening terms, this means acknowledging the emotion or reflecting the feelings.

Suppose, for example, a co-worker is telling you about an experience in which his proposal for a new work procedure was shot down by management without much thoughtful discussion. As he tells you about it, you can certainly hear that emotion is a strong part of the message. So to acknowledge that the emotion you hear is a significant part of the meaning, you may say something like, "Sounds like a very frustrating experience for you. Is that right?" To be effective when you're listening, capture the tangibles as well as the intangibles expressed in the speaker's message — the facts and the feelings.

Chapter 5 gets into more detail about reflecting feelings, an important active-listening tool. The idea here is that when positive or negative emotions play an important role in the message — acknowledge the existence of the respective emotion. Not doing so means that you don't truly understand what the speaker means.

Attending or Pretending to Listen?

Here is a fun activity I like to do in my communication seminars that people get a big kick out of and that makes a strong point about listening. It deals with what is called *attending to the speaker*. (Now don't try this at home!)

Participants are paired up and one partner steps outside for a moment. The individuals who stay in the room are instructed to play the role of active listeners when their partners return to the room. They are to highly engage in conversation with their partners for about one minute; that is, really get them going so the speakers are having a great time relating their stories. Then when given a signal from me, the listeners disengage; they no longer give direct eye contact or engage verbally in any way with their speakers.

When the partners are brought back in and the exercise starts, the room usually fills with a high level of energy and volume. The topic the speakers are given to talk about is an enjoyable experience they recently had. After talking for a minute, the signal is given and the listeners then disengage. What do you think happens in the conversations?

As you may have guessed, in most cases, the conversations die off and the volume in the room drops. Sometimes the speakers start to laugh because they guess that they've been set up, but the point is made about the importance of attending to the speaker.

Giving yourself to the speaker

To make active listening work, you need to attend to the speaker. Most people, when they are speaking, can pick up quickly on whether their listener is attending, or even pretending to listen — as often evident in glazed looks or automatic *uh-huh* responses. Two reactions usually occur with speakers when they discover listeners aren't attending or are only pretending to listen:

- ✔ The conversation begins to trail off and the speaker's voice and manner start to sound hesitant. After that, the conversation stops, and the speaker walks away with feelings of disappointment and disgust.

- ✔ On some occasions, the opposite occurs. The speaker rambles and talks on and on and on. The conversation has a void in it and the speaker fills it by talking enough for both parties.

Giving up on the conversation is the more common of the two reactions by the speaker when the listener is not attending. In either case, however, the flow of the conversation has been disrupted; the two-way nature of good conversations has been lost because the listener is no longer participating. Speakers, in most cases, notice even though they don't say anything directly to the listener.

Attending to the speaker involves shifting your attention from yourself to the speaker and focusing on what the speaker has to say — not on what's going on inside your head. It's what you do nonverbally with your behavior to show receptiveness toward the speaker. When you're attending, you gain some valuable benefits that help you listen more effectively:

- **You capture the whole message.** You are better able to pick up on the nonverbal components of the message — not just the verbal components — and thus can begin to figure out the real meaning of the speaker's message. You'll hear more of the feelings behind the facts.

- **You can gauge the flow.** By attending, you have a stronger sense of what is happening in the conversation. You pick up on the nonverbal cues as the words are said and gauge whether to remain patient, ask a question, or take your turn and say something as a speaker. Like a driver who is alert while traveling down a winding road, you too can follow the ebbs and flows of a conversation with greater skill.

- **You demonstrate respect.** When you're attending to the speaker, your nonverbal demeanor demonstrates receptiveness. Your behavior lets the speaker know that you're interested in hearing the message and allowing it to flow all the way through — the basic level of respect every speaker desires.

In fact, here are key nonverbal behaviors to work on that effectively attend to the speaker. These behaviors answer the question: What nonverbal efforts do listeners put forth that speakers see as positive behaviors?

- **Steady eye contact:** As much as anything a listener does in a conversation, making steady eye contact with the speaker is powerful and positive attending behavior. Eye contact tells the speaker, "My attention is with you and I care about what you have to say." It is eye contact, even when the speaker's eyes are wandering as he's deep in thought, that's still there when the speaker comes around and looks toward his listener.

- **Sincere facial expressions:** Sincere facial expressions fit the flow of the speaker's message — a smile when the message is upbeat, a look of concern when the message sounds serious, or a patient look when the speaker is contemplating his or her thoughts.

- **Open, receptive body language:** The most receptive body language shows that you're alert yet relaxed in posture. This may include turning to face the speaker to better receive the message or leaning in slightly to better hear it. These nonverbal cues communicate that your attention is with the speaker and that you're ready to receive the message.

✔ **Encouraging, nonjudgmental tones:** Your tone of voice in receiving a message plays a big part in attending to the speaker. When your tone stays nonjudgmental or when its responses say, in effect, "I'm with you, tell me more," the conversation flows and the speaker knows that you're ready and willing to take in the message.

Adding concentration to the attending mix

Nonverbal tools that help you attend to the speaker are the ones you use when responding to the speaker (see Chapter 3). The speaker sees your behavior and is encouraged to continue to express his or her message. Yet what helps you effectively attend to the speaker is what you do before you respond, when you're still processing the information the speaker is giving. To process information well, you must concentrate.

Simply defined, *concentration* is focused mental energy. It is the discipline of giving your full attention to the matter at hand and of being truly present in the conversation. In conversations in which you're the listener, the matters at hand are the speaker and that person's message.

You, too, can attend to the speaker!

Theresa was a manager who was given the opportunity, along with other managers in her company, to attend an interpersonal communications seminar. She got a lot out of the seminar and saw its importance not only for herself as a manager but also for her staff, many of whom were involved in heavy interactions with customers and each other. So within a couple of months, she arranged for the seminar instructor to give the course to her staff.

During the first segment of this two-day seminar, the nonverbal habits to avoid while listening were covered. The staff responded well to it. Interesting enough, for the rest of the first day and the second day, various staff members approached the instructor on breaks and gave unsolicited feedback about their manager, Theresa. They said that they had observed a change in her listening behavior after she had attended the seminar a few months earlier. In their fast-paced work environment, it used to be that they found Theresa in a whirlwind whenever they approached her. Her attention was focused on many things at once, even though she attempted to engage with the person at hand. Now if you knock on Theresa's door and ask to speak with her, she says yes and really means it. She sits patiently with her full attention directed at the speaker. Conversations with her have become easier now that the whirlwind has slowed down, and respect for her has grown.

All too often in conversations, people are creating distractions for themselves and for their speakers. They're thinking ahead to their next meeting, worrying about their own problems, daydreaming, or reacting to the bits and pieces of the speaker's message that they don't like. Creating these distractions gives you less of an opportunity to make sense out of the message; your time with the speaker is being wasted. In addition, selective and passive listening (covered in Chapter 3) often frustrate your speaker.

Concentration is hard work, but because it's at the foundation of active listening, it has its rewards. When you concentrate for a period of time while working at something, how do you feel? Most likely, you're tired! The exertion of mental energy is often as exhausting as the exertion of physical energy. That aside, you probably accomplish a lot and feel a great deal of satisfaction when you've concentrated well.

Your level of concentration makes a huge difference in how productive your conversations are. The more tuned in you are, the more you pick up on the speaker's entire message; therefore, the more you understand what the speaker truly means.

Here are a few tips to help you get the best out of focused mental energy:

- ✔ **Eliminate distractions.** Turn off that cellular phone and beeper. Let the phone ring into voice mail. Turn down the radio. Put aside those papers you were reading. Whatever else may grab your attention, put it aside so you're ready to focus on the speaker's message. Avoid trying to do another task when engaged in conversation. Full attention to the speaker maximizes your concentration.

- ✔ **Take notes.** Sometimes the speaker is relaying important information to you. Relying on memory is the worst thing you can do in these situations. Writing a few notes on the key points or action items engages your mind and helps you concentrate on what the speaker is saying. Taking notes may also prompt you to check your understanding along the way and reassures the speaker that you're taking his or her message seriously. Keep in mind that the shortest pencil will outlast the longest memory.

   You're taking a few notes, not transcribing every word heard. Because you want to maintain eye contact with your speaker, glance down and write quickly, periodically checking your understanding with the speaker so that you're getting the key points.

- ✔ **Visualize the message.** This tip is especially handy when you're in conversations on the telephone. *Visualizing the message* means picturing in your mind what the speaker is saying. It helps you tune in to closely follow the message. When you can see what someone is talking about, you can more easily make sense of what is being said. Because you don't have this direct sight while conversing on the telephone, visualization helps you focus and provides a sight substitute.

✔ **Speak up when you're slipping.** Sometimes, for whatever reason, you begin to lose what the speaker is saying. When you recognize that you missed something, give yourself permission to speak up. Sometimes this is as easy as saying, "Say again, please," or "Could you repeat that?" Passively sitting by and letting the message continue when you're not connected do you and the speaker a disservice. Instead, capture what you're missing as soon as it happens, and you'll be tuned in.

✔ **Clarify the uncertain or unclear.** When something is unfamiliar or doesn't make sense, ask the question to have it clarified, such as, "To clarify . . . your point is we need to have less food for lunch?" You're inviting the speaker to give you an explanation or verification to help you capture the message correctly.

Throw away the old thinking that asking questions or checking for clarification means you're not very smart. Quite the opposite, asking questions helps you concentrate and reassures your speaker that you're working to understand his or her message.

Avoiding Barriers to Listening

Sometimes as a listener you may knowingly or unknowingly create barriers in your conversations. These barriers can be verbal (explored further in Chapter 6) or nonverbal. *Barrier* here means a behavior that hinders the flow of meaningful, nonjudgmental conversation.

Part of listening effectively involves being aware of what not to do in your listening behaviors. Sometimes you need to know which old habits to curb so that new ones can kick in and work for you.

What follows are six nonverbal behavior categories; each with its respective habits that you — as a listener — should avoid. These habits or pitfalls create barriers that turn off your speaker and prevent the speaker's message from being communicated. If you're like most people, many of the behaviors on this list will be familiar to you — from the standpoints of being a listener or a speaker.

Poor eye contact

Eye contact is one of the more influential behaviors that affect the flow of conversations. Steady eye contact with your speaker enhances the flow, while these behaviors hinder it:

✔ **Looking away:** The occasional glance away is not a barrier, but when eye contact often breaks away, the speaker feels that your attention is drifting elsewhere. And, as covered in the previous section, when your eyes are not attending, the speaker becomes disheartened and quits the conversation.

✔ **Locking in:** This is the glare or stare that creates a great deal of discomfort for the speaker — even more so when your eyes are looking below the speaker's face level. Steady eye contact is a relaxed look, not an intense stare down.

✔ **Rolling your eyes:** This is one of the most judgmental looks you can ever give a speaker while he or she is talking. It communicates sarcasm and displeasure with the message being heard and sometimes even stops a speaker right in his tracks — a conversation barrier at its worst.

Unfavorable facial expressions

Without a mirror, you can't see your face. But your speaker sees it and often reacts to the unfavorable messages it may be sending. Here are a few of these barrier makers:

✔ **Giving a frown or scowl:** A frown or a scowl is a look of disapproval and dismissal. These looks sometimes are accompanied by a shaking of the head from side to side and often communicate to the speaker, regardless of intention, that you don't like the person and/or the message being heard.

✔ **Flashing a smirk:** The smirk is that half-smile that often comes out when the speaker is talking about something serious. Again, regardless of intent, it has a mocking effect on the speaker, as if his serious message is a big joke to you — a major turnoff when someone is talking to you.

✔ **Raising one eyebrow:** Similar to the scowl, this behavior comes across as a stern, disapproving, or questioning facial expression. Unlike a curious look in which the forehead scrunches a bit and both eyebrows go up slightly, this is a look in which one eyebrow goes up the moment something unpleasant is said. It's often a conversation stopper.

✔ **Displaying a blank look:** This is a passive, expressionless look. It leaves the speaker wondering what, if anything, is getting through to you. Is anyone home? Does anyone care? In many cases, this behavior is the most unnerving to speakers — they get the feeling that they're talking to a wall.

Unwelcoming posture

Posture is how you sit or stand as you receive a speaker's message. Here are some postures that can create barriers:

✔ **Slouching:** Slouching is sitting back in your chair almost to the point at times where your feet are nearly as high as your head. You may like to relax in your chairs — especially the big cushy ones. But instead of sitting up alertly to take in the speaker's message, slouching communicates a disinterest and inattentiveness to the speaker.

✔ **Being closed:** In this case, the listener's arms are tightly folded such that the entire body looks stiff, too. This behavior is often accompanied with a scowl or stern look. It gives the message to the speaker that you're not open and that you're sitting in judgment of what you're hearing. That's a conversation stopper.

Keep in mind that folding your arms doesn't necessarily mean your posture is closed. Quite often, the opposite is true. Try this out. First sit up and fold your arms tightly — most likely you have a closed, uninviting posture. Now stay sitting up and fold your arms in a relaxed way. This second posture shows an openness and a sense of being comfortable while being attentive — behaviors to which speakers favorably respond.

Too much movement

Movement refers to what you do with your body, including your hands, when you receive the speaker's message. Generally speaking, the sender in a conversation uses hands more than the receiver, because the speaker is expressing the message.

The receiver or listener occasionally uses gestures to check his understanding of the speaker's message. Otherwise, the expectation is for the receiver to sit patiently and hear the message all the way through. Of course, sometimes that isn't what's happening with the listener.

✔ **Fidgeting:** With this behavior, the hands are in frequent motion, such as playing with paper clips, pens, pencils, or whatever else you can get your hands on. When your hands are on display while someone is talking to you, they create a sense that your attention is elsewhere or that you are too nervous to tune in and fully understand the message.

✔ **Squirming:** Squirming is the habit of shifting around a lot in your seat. It lends the appearance that you just can't sit still, like having ants in your pants. This restless body movement becomes an annoyance to someone who is trying to express a message to you.

✔ **Pulling on yourself:** This is a habit in which, as you attempt to listen, your hands are occupied with something on your body. You're twirling a necklace, playing with a ring, constantly pulling on a tie, making a curl out of your hair, or rubbing your beard. The list goes on and can get downright personal. People often are unaware of these habits, but they nevertheless create a great distraction — if not a turnoff — for the speaker.

Handling interruptions positively

Attempting to attend to a speaker when you aren't ready to do so doesn't work. Giving subtle hints such as looking at your watch or continuing to work at what you're doing doesn't always help the person understand that now is not a good time for you to listen.

The key to managing interruptions — so as not to miss important messages you need to hear and not to turn off your speaker — is to be direct and courteous. Here are three actions that fit the bill:

- **Give the wait-a-moment signal:** Sometimes this signal is nonverbal such as with a hand up and your index finger slightly raised. Sometimes this signal is verbal such as saying, "Hang on just a moment and I'll be right with you." Sometimes the verbal and nonverbal signals are used together. In any case, the actions let your speaker know that you're willing to engage in conversation in just a moment. People usually don't mind waiting for a few minutes when their presence has been acknowledged. Of course, when you finish your task, fully attend to the speaker.

- **Schedule for later:** This action is more useful when you really don't have the time at hand

to deal with the other person's issue. It involves giving a brief explanation of what is happening for you and asking if that person can talk with you later. Then it is important that you schedule an appointment for the conversation, making sure that you keep it and engage in the conversation so your request doesn't turn into a brushoff. When you follow through and meet later, you increase the likelihood that your requests will be honored and your time respected.

- **Stop and engage now:** Sometimes the best thing you can do for yourself and your speaker is to stop what you are doing, look up, and receive the other person. Whatever you're working on will still be there when the conversation is over. If your time is tight and the conversation is going to be an involved one (you can determine that with the speaker at the beginning), rescheduling for when you have more time is all right to do. But the more you can stop and handle the issue right away, the more you save time for you and that other person. People greatly appreciate that, when they have an important issue, they can get your attention, even if only for a few minutes. This communicates that you're approachable.

Ineffective placement

This nonverbal behavior — where and how you place yourself to receive a speaker's message — is subtle yet powerful in its effect on the speaker. When you place yourself at a comfortable yet fairly close distance, without major physical barriers and in a face-to-face manner, the influence on the conversation flow is positive. However, communications barriers go up when you're:

✔ **Remaining distant:** This habit commonly shows itself in a couple of ways: Standing a good distance across the room instead of coming up close to easily hear the speaker or sitting behind a large desk instead of coming from behind the desk to sit side by side. While no one wants you to get up in his or her face — a habit more common to speakers than listeners — nonetheless, when you're too distant, you have the effect of discouraging the message from being openly received.

✔ **Facing away:** With this habit, you're turned away from the speaker. Sometimes, your back is turned while the person is talking to you, or you're staying shoulder to shoulder while listening rather than turning and directly facing the speaker. These behaviors often are discomforting to the speaker, because they communicate that, as the listener, you aren't comfortable engaging in conversation.

✔ **Being preoccupied with something else:** Some people refer to this behavior as multitasking; that is, doing two things at once. Unfortunately, quite often, both tasks suffer in the effort, especially the task of listening to and understanding a speaker's message. Holding onto reading material, working away at your computer, and even engaging in a telephone call while someone is talking to you are common ways to display this barrier-creating behavior. Even in your fast-paced worklife, doing two things at once often slows you down and hinders your productivity because you're blocking the speaker and, as a result, not getting the entire message the first time.

Uninviting tone of voice

As a listener, you may speak or make sounds in response to the speaker's message — and that makes your tone of voice important. It's a strong part of your behavior that greatly impacts how open or judgmental you are to the speaker and the message being expressed. A slight change of your tone from sounding receptive to becoming irritated or displeased can change and disrupt the flow of a conversation. Here are some tone-of-voice habits that may create a communications barrier:

✔ **Using harsh, reactive tones:** You hear an explanation from the other person and you give a response of, "You did what!" Sharpness in tone of voice has the effect of putting the speaker on the defensive. Often before the speaker has even finished the message, this tone — usually fueled by emotions of anger or displeasure — comes out strongly and harshly in response to the message heard.

✔ **Biting with sarcasm:** This behavior is usually a reaction to what the speaker has said. In this case, it is tinged with subtle put-downs and just-kidding humor, neither of which are funny to the person getting it in return, such as "Yeah, great idea, Joe," or "Sounds like you're giving your best effort." These comments, while sounding positive in words, are negated by the sarcastic tones that communicate the opposite meaning and pass degrading judgment on the speaker and the message heard.

✔ **Being monotone:** This is the tone in response to a speaker that comes across as bored or disinterested. It's that dull and lifeless sounding, "Oh, that's nice," when the speaker has enthusiastically discussed, for example, an exciting experience. A monotone response can quickly deflate a speaker.

Chapter 5

Putting Active Listening Tools to Work

In This Chapter
▶ Developing skills for drawing out the speaker's message
▶ Developing skills for showing an understanding of the speaker's message
▶ Looking at the active listening tools in practice

Listening is more than just showing up and being present for a conversa-tion, yet many people are conditioned to think that *passive listening* (sit-ting quietly while someone is talking to you) is the only way they can listen.

Moreover, many folks are *selective listeners:* They hear what they want to hear, and as a result, miss much of the message. When you make an effort, you can tune in and be an attentive listener to certain parts of the message but still not get its full meaning; that is, the feelings that are behind the facts or content.

As defined in Chapter 3, active or responsive listening is about showing an understanding of the speaker's entire message, not agreeing with or having opinions about that message. Achieving understanding is the emphasis of active listening, but doing so in a nonjudgmental manner is critical to the lis-tening behavior necessary to make it all work.

Chapter 4 prepares you for active listening by showing how to recognize the nonverbal and verbal components of a speaker's message and what to do and not to do with your own nonverbal behavior to be more openly receptive of the speaker's message.

This chapter provides you with eight tools that help you listen actively and effectively. Four of them are devoted to drawing out the speaker's message, and four help you verify your understanding of the message. Quite simply, to get more of the speaker's message — anywhere throughout the beginning, middle, or conclusion of a conversation — you apply the listening tools in the following sections.

By *tools,* I mean skills. It is a term I've developed over the years from my seminar participants who use it to mean practical, how-to practices that can immediately be put into action.

Drawing Out the Speaker's Message

Active listeners rely on the four tools covered in this section to help draw out and focus a message. They aid and stimulate the speaker to express the message freely. By using these four tools, the listener is better equipped to help the speaker express the content of the message and, as needed, explain the basis of the feelings being heard in the message.

Letting the speaker in: Door openers

Door openers are signals listeners use to encourage speakers to express and elaborate upon their messages. Like red lights changing to green for motorists, door openers tell speakers to proceed without caution in presenting their messages.

Door openers can be nonverbal or verbal expressions by the listener; however, nonverbal door openers are especially helpful because they can be given while the speaker is talking without being interpreted as interruptions. The following list describes nonverbal door openers:

- ✔ Nodding your head to acknowledge that you're following the message
- ✔ Giving a sincere smile for an upbeat message
- ✔ Showing a look of interest
- ✔ Showing a look of concern for a serious message
- ✔ Turning and facing the speaker
- ✔ Leaning in slightly toward the speaker
- ✔ Offering steady eye contact
- ✔ Providing a patient look with silence

Providing a patient look with silence is one of the more powerful and sophisticated nonverbal door openers. Use it when someone is expressing what sounds like a serious message.

When a speaker has something serious to say, he or she often expresses the message in a manner that's more deliberate than normal. Unless the speaker is extremely eloquent, such messages usually come out a piece at a time with noticeable pauses along the way. You can tell by the look on the speaker's face and the tone in his or her voice — these are called *nonverbal* cues — that the message is important and serious. When poor listeners don't tune into these nonverbal cues, they become disinterested and jump in after the speaker's first pause. They become speakers themselves, never allowing the original speaker to complete his or her message. Active listeners who use the silent, patient-look door opener signal the speaker to take the time necessary to tell the entire story. Without interruptions, the depth of the speaker's message comes out.

Sincerity is key to the effectiveness of nonverbal door openers. Facial expressions showing insincerity often close rather than open the door. If you're smiling when your speaker is saying something serious, the behavior may come off as a smirk, a major turnoff to the speaker. In fact, the exact opposites of these nonverbal door openers are detractors or barriers to a good flowing conversation as covered in Chapter 4.

Nonverbal door openers communicate to the speaker that you're attending to him or her and that you're really tuned in and want to hear what the he or she has to say.

Verbal door openers

Nonverbal door openers are only half of the green lights that stimulate a good flow of conversation. The other half are verbal door openers: one or two spoken words that have the same effect as their nonverbal counterparts. The following verbal door openers communicate to your speaker that, "I'm following along — go ahead and tell me more."

Uh-huh

Um-hum

Right

I see

Yeah

Yes

Really

Neat

Oh

Okay

Wow

The tone of your verbal door openers is critical. The tone needs to be non-judgmental — in a range that allows for curious, interested, and patient sounds. When the tone comes across as judgmental, you're creating a barrier to the conversation and are likely blocking the speaker from communicating the full message. For example, if you say "right" in a sarcastic tone as someone is talking to you, that door opener that then becomes a door closer.

Don't be monotone either! Keep your tone as alive and interested as possible when listening to a speaker's message.

Say again: Echoing

Echoing is repeating a key word or phrase of the speaker's message as a way to draw out more of the message and gain a clearer picture of it. Echoing works like little sparks, hardly noticed by the speaker, that help you ignite the vague and unknown elements of a message into fiery specifics and well-defined details. It involves two steps:

1. **Repeat the key word (or two) from the speaker's message (use the speaker's words, not your own).**

   That's the echo. Your voice inflection punctuates what you say with a question-mark sound. Your *inflection* is the pitch of your voice. In echoing, you want the pitch to go higher at the end of your remark.

2. **After making your echo response, wait patiently.**

   Sometimes the speaker responds right away to the stimulus of the echoing and explains what the word or term means. The inquisitive sound of the tool invites a response to come from the speaker without the listener having to ask a direct question. It creates a smooth, comfortable environment.

   Other times, the response from the speaker doesn't come as readily, especially when strong emotion lurks behind the words. Waiting patiently and allowing for silence puts the responsibility for clarification on the speaker. The silence acts as a door opener to encourage the speaker to take his or her time. When you wait patiently (as opposed to anxiously) in a matter of seconds, the speaker starts to express what's going on.

To echo correctly, you need to know when to use the technique. Three such situations work best:

 ✔ **Vague, general statements:** Vague, general statements tell you little and may mean a variety of things. For example, the person says to you, "That was a really interesting meeting yesterday." Who knows what that means? It's unclear.

   You, as the listener, should echo, " Interesting meeting?"

✔ **Vague yet loaded statements:** Vague yet loaded statements give you little substance or clarity, but by the tone of voice or body language, you can tell emotionally that a strong message lies beneath the surface. For example, you ask a co-worker how a meeting went, and you get a response with a very sharp tone: "Fine. Just fine!" What happened is vague, but the emotion is strong — in essence, loaded.

You should echo, "Fine?"

✔ **Unfamiliar word or term:** In this case, you hear a word that isn't familiar to you or that is being used in a way that seems unusual or different to you. Often this happens when a speaker uses various forms of *technical jargon* (language that isn't familiar to people who aren't connected to the subject of conversation). Sometimes the unfamiliar terms are *acronyms* (letters that stand for words) that not everyone knows. Here's an example:

Speaker says an unfamiliar term: "We got a new MRP system that I'm not sure will help us."

Listener uses echoing: "MRP system?"

In all three cases, echoing encourages the speaker to open up to you and explain his or her point. Using an inquisitive tone encourages the speaker to tell you more information about the message without your having to work hard to get it.

Digging deeper: Probing

Questions are phrased as either *close-ended* or *open-ended*. Close-ended questions solicit short definitive answers that more often can be said in a word or two. Here are a couple of examples:

✔ "Did you get that report done?" Answer: "Yes."

✔ "When is the meeting?" Answer: "2:00."

Although asking them can still result in verbose responses, close-ended questions nevertheless aim for brief and definitive answers. Open-ended questions, on the other hand, ask for information, explanation, expressions of thoughts and feelings — things that can't be said in a mere word or two. Here are a couple of examples:

✔ What are your ideas for solving this problem?

✔ How would you go about implementing that new program?

Probing is asking questions to gain more information and more depth below the surface of the message. As you see by this description, probing relies on open-ended questions.

To probe effectively, consider the tips in the following three sections.

Asking open-ended questions

Ask open-ended questions. A few of the following key words, used at the start of the sentence can help you shape open-ended questions (or questioning statements).

- ✔ **What:** "What happened at the meeting yesterday?"
- ✔ **How:** "How do you perform that new procedure?"
- ✔ **Why:** "Why do think the client opposes that idea we offered?"
- ✔ **Explain:** "Explain to me your thinking on that issue."
- ✔ **Describe:** "Describe the features of that product."
- ✔ **Elaborate:** "Elaborate on the pros and cons of that strategy."
- ✔ **Give:** "Please give me an example of what you mean."
- ✔ **Tell:** "Tell me more about that."

Grammatically speaking, imperatives that start with verbs such as explain, describe, elaborate, give, and tell are forms of probing because they solicit explanation and expression of thoughts and details. Let these verbs, along with what, how, and why words, start your sentences, and then insert the issue you want the speaker to address. Don't overload the speaker; go with one question at a time.

Giving the speaker some space

Make sure your questions don't crowd the speaker. That means that you shouldn't expect or anticipate a set answer, thus providing the speaker with the freedom to express what is on his or her mind in response to the question.

Avoid what I refer to as *leading-the-witness questions,* which many close-ended questions can do. Here are a couple of examples:

- ✔ Do you really think that idea is going to help the team?
- ✔ Don't you think my idea is really the best?

As these examples illustrate, you can guess what the answer *should* be. The speaker is being influenced to answer a certain way as opposed to having the space to express his or her own thoughts. Instead, ask the following in a probing manner:

- ✔ Please explain how that can help the team.
- ✔ What do you think of my idea?

Using a nonjudgmental and inquisitive tone

The tone of your questions needs to be nonjudgmental and inquisitive. This means inviting the speaker to feel comfortable expressing thoughts, providing information, and exploring issues on a deeper level.

Exercise caution when asking *why* questions. Why? Although why is a good first word to shape open-ended questions, it often carries a more judgmental tone. Here are a couple of examples:

✔ Why did you do that?

✔ Why would we ever want to try that way?

Why questions can have an accusatory or critical tone that can put a speaker on the defensive rather than inviting that person to speak freely. Therefore, either manage your tone carefully so as to sound inquisitive or rephrase the question. For example, instead of asking why did you do that, you could say, "Please explain your thinking on the handling of this issue."

Making sure you're following along: Checking the subject

Checking the subject is clarifying a detail of the speaker's topic or subject. Checking the subject enables you to follow the flow of the speaker's message without becoming sidetracked or confused. You can use the checking-the-subject tool when the topic of your speaker's message starts to become unclear or fuzzy, implicit instead of explicit, or off the subject instead of on the intended subject.

Instead of sitting back passively when the topic becomes unclear, implement the following steps:

1. **As soon as the speaker takes a breath, jump in.**

   Don't let the speaker continue. Interject the moment that the subject becomes unclear.

2. **In an inquisitive tone, state the subject you think the speaker means.**

   Sometimes you can use starter phrases like the following:

   • "You're referring to . . . (then say what you think the subject is)?"

   • "You're talking about . . . ?"

   • "You mean . . . ?"

Checking the subject by this two-step process invites an immediate response before the speaker has a chance to proceed with more of the message. The response you get either verifies what you thought the topic was or clarifies what it means. Here is an example:

Speaker: John and Bill finally got together and met yesterday. He came up with quite a creative idea.

He is the subject but who is he? Is it John or Bill? The subject has gotten fuzzy.

Listener: (Using the checking-the-subject tool) "You're talking about Bill?"

Sometimes you can skip the starter phrase ("You're referring to Bill?") and just say, inquisitively, "Bill?"

Speaker: (In return) "Yes." Or, "No, I meant John."

Now the speaker can continue with the message, and you can clearly follow the flow of information. Knowing the speaker's subject, you can connect the information you're hearing to it. When you let this uncertainty about the speaker's topic continue without checking it, the message you hear often becomes disjointed.

Repositioning the speaker

Sometimes checking the subject can reposition the speaker back onto the main subject when he or she goes off on a tangent. Every speaker does this at some time. The speaker announces that he wants to tell you about a topic, but as he gets into the subject, he diverts himself and takes a different path. A passive listener may lose track of what the original message was supposed to be. Here is an example of how checking the subject to reposition the speaker works:

Speaker: "I want to go over the proposal for executing this project. Projects like these can be very involved. I've been on a few that got way too complicated, like one just a few months ago."

Listener: (Spotting an unrelated tangent starting to divert attention from the main subject) "Now you wanted to review that proposal with me, right?"

Speaker: (Responding — as so often happens) "Oh yeah. Let me get to it."

Repositioning allows the speaker to clarify whether the tangent is indeed important and thus continue, but more often, it brings the speaker immediately back to the main topic.

Benefits of checking the subject

A couple of ways that checking the subject can help are by:

- ✔ Reassuring the speaker that you're following along with the message. Speakers like to know they have receptive and attentive listeners.

- ✔ Focusing the speaker. Clarifying keeps the speaker on topic and thus increases the likelihood for him or her to express a more coherent message. This is especially important when you have a speaker who has a tendency to ramble. If you sit back passively, you'll be lost and that speaker may never get back on track.

Of course, to make checking the subject work, you often have to break those passive-listening tendencies that you have. If you don't interject when the topic of the message starts to become unclear, you face a much harder time of helping the speaker stay on track and making sense out of the message you're hearing. This means you need to know the difference between *interjecting* and *interrupting* in a conversation.

Figure 5-1 shows you the flow and contrast between interjecting when checking the subject and interrupting in a conversation. The commonality of the two is that you're jumping into the conversation before the speaker has finished his or her message. People generally don't like to be interrupted, for as Figure 5-1 shows, the conversation gets taken away. You take over and become the speaker. When you're talking before the other person feels heard, you've interrupted, and more often than not, you've turned off the other person.

When checking the subject, your interjection is brief and it focuses on the speaker's message, not away from it. As a result, many speakers don't even notice this little clarifying effort by you. Instead, they end up benefiting from it.

Verifying Your Understanding of the Message

The active listening tools covered in the previous section draw out the speaker's message and help focus it. They stimulate the flow of the message and allow that message to be expressed. The active listening tools covered in this section go further. They have you checking whether what you heard the speaker say, nonverbally and verbally, is what the speaker really means. Checking understanding and not assuming you know what is being said are key here.

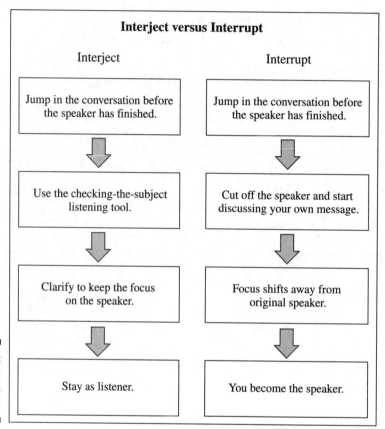

Using these tools as regular practice is what turns you into a full-fledged active listener. People often walk away from conversations *thinking* they understood what the other person meant. With these tools, you walk away *knowing* exactly what the other person meant and knowing that the person feels understood. That's how productivity increases and working relationships strengthen.

To use these tools you have to listen for the entire message. Keep the following formula in mind (as covered in Chapter 4) as you discover each of the tools in this second set:

Facts or content + Emotion = Meaning of the message

Capturing the emotions: Reflecting feelings

Reflecting feelings is checking your perception of the speaker's feelings in the message to understand the emotional meaning being expressed.

This tool is used when the feelings being expressed represent a great deal of the message's meaning. As discussed in Chapter 4, the speaker, through body language and tone of voice, often expresses this emotion. When that emotion carries a significant part of the message's meaning, reflecting feelings is a good tool to apply.

As the name of the tool says, you're acting like a mirror, reflecting the emotional meaning you're hearing from the speaker. Here are some tips:

✔ State the emotion you perceive is being expressed.

✔ Use the word "you" because the message is from the speaker not from you.

✔ Because you're checking, your voice inflection should pick up at the end of your statement to make it sound like a question. If you can't do that clearly with your voice, you can add a question to your reflecting statement, such as: "Is that right?"

The following are a few examples of reflecting feelings, based on what has been heard from the speaker:

✔ "Sounds like you're excited by that opportunity. Is that right?"

✔ "Seems like that was a frustrating experience for you?"

✔ "I sense you're irritated with Don. Is that correct?"

In each case, the emotion being expressed — excitement, frustration, irritation — is the main emphasis of the speaker's statement. It reflects the significance in the speaker's message.

On occasion I run into people who express discomfort with reflecting feelings. Who wants to deal with emotions, especially when they may be strong negative ones? Or is this some bunch of touchy-feely stuff? The key is to recognize that you're acknowledging what you're hearing. You're neither trying to play therapist nor judging the emotion being expressed as good or bad. Not acknowledging the emotion when it is a strong negative one may keep the speaker on edge and the tension in the interaction brewing. Not acknowledging the emotion when it is a positive one also serves to deflate the speaker. In both cases, not tuning in and reflecting the feeling that's so much a part of the speaker's meaning sends that person a message that is the opposite of your intentions: "I don't really care what's going on for you." Keep your tone sincere when you use the tool and your actions will match your intentions.

Here's an example of a brief conversation. A co-worker expresses the following remarks:

"This new customer I have has been quite difficult to deal with. He wants everything done a certain way. When I try to explain how things need to be done so the product works right for him, I'm lucky to get a word in. He doesn't seem to realize that I'm trying to help him and that I'm not his soldier taking orders."

You hear the emotion in this message and realize that it is a significant portion of the overall meaning. That's the time to reflect the speaker's feelings back to him. What would you say in response? How about something like: "Sounds like this is an aggravating situation for you. Is that right?"

Capturing the content: Paraphrasing

Paraphrasing is restating the main idea of the speaker's message in live conversation to show and check — verify or clarify — your understanding of the facts or content of that message. It's a restatement in your own words but not a reiteration of the speaker's exact words. The latter tends to be mimicking, which usually turns people off. Paraphrasing is similar to reflecting feelings except that its purpose is to establish understanding of the content side of the message.

In most cases, you can paraphrase in one sentence. You're looking to capture the essence of the speaker's message, not all the details. Quite often, you can set up the paraphrase with starter phrases that cue the speaker that you want to check your understanding. Here are some common starter phrases to use:

- ✔ What you're saying is. . . . (then comes the paraphrase)
- ✔ In other words. . . .
- ✔ What you mean is. . . .
- ✔ What you're telling me is. . . .
- ✔ If I understand your point correctly. . . .
- ✔ What I'm hearing you say is. . . .
- ✔ Sounds like you're saying. . . .

Like reflecting feelings, with paraphrasing you're checking your understanding, not assuming that you know what the speaker means. So you want to have that inquisitive inflection in your voice at the end of the paraphrase statement or add "Is that right?" so that you clearly sound like you're checking and asking for confirmation in return.

Here is an example of a paraphrase being used in a brief conversation with a co-worker:

"This special project is an opportunity for us to make some significant process improvements. We have a diverse group of participants with different perspectives that'll be involved in this project. I think we need to emphasize that people come ready to contribute, that they listen and be open, and that they take a cooperative approach to working together."

Your paraphrasing response may be: "So in other words, you see the key to success for this project is a strong sense of teamwork?"

Utilizing the combo version: Reflective paraphrasing

Sometimes, messages you hear have meanings that take in facts and feelings. In those cases, call upon the reflective paraphrasing tool. *Reflective paraphrasing* is a combination of reflecting feelings and paraphrasing, capturing the emotion and content being expressed to show and check understanding of the speaker's meaning. In most cases, you can check the meaning with just one sentence.

You identify the emotion in the meaning of the message and summarize in your own words the content that serves as the explanation for the emotion. Sometimes it's done by saying, "You're feeling (emotion you hear) because of (content you heard that explains the situation behind the emotion)." For example: "You're feeling frustrated because your proposal has gotten little response so far from management. Is that right?"

Here's an example of reflective paraphrasing put into action in a conversation you have with one of your staff members:

"I was excited when this project started a couple of months ago but that changed recently. We've lost a few resources who were helping us, and we've had changing directions hit us. I get the feeling now, it seems almost daily, that something is going to happen to make this project harder for us to do well and on time."

Your reflective paraphrasing response: "So you're feeling a loss of enthusiasm for this project because of these obstacles that keep getting in the way. Is that right?"

"I understand how you feel"

Avoid saying (even with good intentions), "I understand how you feel." This statement can rub people the wrong way and is sometimes met with an emphatic, "No you don't!" (Don't try this at home either.) Why is saying "I understand how you feel" a turn off? Sometimes it is perceived as patronizing, coming across as an assumption. As discussed in Chapter 1, assumptions annoy people and add tension to an interaction.

The following list shows how the "I understand how you feel" statement is inferior to the reflecting-feelings tool:

✔ **I-focused versus you-focused:** *I* is the subject of "I understand how you feel." It takes the focus away from the speaker and places it, instead, on the second party in the conversation. The reflecting-feelings tool, however, retains the focus — the *you*-focus — on the speaker.

✔ **A declaration versus a checking effort:** "I understand how you feel" checks nothing. It invites nothing in return from the speaker to verify whether you understand what that person means. By using the reflecting-feelings tool, on the other hand, an inquisitive, questioning sound invites the speaker to respond, verifying or clarifying the meaning of the message.

✔ **No emotion stated versus an emotion identified:** When someone says to me, "I understand how you feel," I wonder, feel what? No emotion is identified to indicate that you understand anything that's going on for the speaker. In reflecting feelings, though, you identify the emotion you perceive is being expressed without making any assumptions.

Relating when it counts: Sharing a relevant example

Sharing a relevant example is providing an example of a situation that relates to the point the speaker is making to show an understanding of where that person is coming from. Its use is more for special circumstances, and when done right, it can be powerful in a positive way.

You must meet a couple of prerequisites before you can use this tool:

✔ You've heard the whole story from the speaker.

✔ You have an example from your experience that you see as relevant and believe will help show the speaker that you understand his or her circumstance.

If those prerequisites have not been met, simply don't use the tool. You want to avoid giving your speaker a feeling of what's called *one-upmanship* — "If you think that's bad, you ought to hear what happened to me!" Your role is to keep the focus with the speaker, not take it away. That's why you want to use this tool only under special circumstances.

When the prerequisites have been met, you follow one of two processes in applying the tool. In either case, you may paraphrase or reflective paraphrase first to check if you do understand your speaker's situation. In one process, you give a brief, usually one-sentence, relevant example.

"So the struggles you've encountered with this client are much like what Joe went through last year when he was assigned this client, right?"

The second is a three-step process that is good to use when you have an example from your own experience that you want to share. Here are the three steps:

1. **Make a connecting statement from the speaker to you.**

   "Your situation sounds like something similar to what I went through."

2. **Tell your related story briefly, briefly, briefly.**

   Get to the point. Just because you heard a detailed story doesn't mean you offer one in return. Yours should be the concise highlights version that you're only sharing to show relevance to the speaker's situation.

   "I encountered this, that, and the other."

3. **Make a connecting statement back to the speaker.**

   "Much like you've experienced, right?"

Checking by asking, "Right?" at the end of the statement lets the speaker know he or she still is the focus of the conversation. You, on the other hand, merely shared something to add value to what you heard and to show that you understood where the speaker was coming from. Speakers greatly appreciate that.

You're having a conversation with a co-worker who has recently returned to work after being out for six months because of a serious injury. He explains his difficulty in adjusting back to work and shares his concern whether working at a job he did well before his injury is what's right for him now. Being off for awhile gave him time to reflect on what he wants to do and now he feels a dilemma in his life. You've heard the whole story and have a relevant experience to share that you think may help your co-worker, John, know you understand his situation. Here is an example of how to use this tool:

You: John, some years ago, I went through a quandary similar to the one you're going through now. I had taken a sabbatical leave and had a great time traveling around Europe. I knew it would end one day, and much to my displeasure, I'd have to go back to work. Although it took some adjustment and struggle, I knew I wanted to find a role where I felt that I was helping people. That led me to the job you and I do today. It sounds like you're trying to figure out that right path for you while struggling to adjust to working again. Is that right?

John: Exactly, that's a good way of putting it . . . where I am right now.

As you see in this example, the three-step process of using the tool was applied. The story shared was brief, and while it doesn't have to be exactly the same as your speaker's story, it was relevant to John's situation. The connection back to the speaker was made smoothly by letting John know he was the focus the whole time.

Watching Active Listening in Action

It's fun to put these tools into action as you find out how to use them in your own conversations and to watch what others do or don't do effectively in their conversations. In this section, you'll read about a conversation in which many of the active-listening tools come to life. As you see active listening in action, you'll also notice that active listeners do say things, but not the way speakers do.

Bringing listening alive

Before you watch the following conversation, keep in mind door openers, echoing, probing, checking the subject, reflecting feelings, paraphrasing, reflective paraphrasing, and sharing a relevant example, all the tools of active listening.

The conversation you're going to sit in on is between Bob and Sue. Sue is Bob's manager. For the purposes of this example, she's the primary listener. Bob is meeting with Sue today for a one-month checkin. He's been off on special assignment as part of a cross-functional team within their company, and he's letting Sue know how things have been going. After greeting each other, the dialogue begins.

Sue: So Bob, please tell me how the past month with this project has been going for you. (Probing)

Bob: To say the least, it's been quite a challenge.

Sue: A challenge? (Echoing)

Bob: Well yes. When you asked me to be a part of this process improvement team, I thought it would be an exciting assignment: A chance to do something different, help make a contribution, and get a broader exposure to the people and operations of this company. It turns out some of these people are not the easiest people in the world to deal with. This group is hard to get all focused together sometimes.

Sue: I sense you're frustrated. Is that right? (Reflecting feelings)

Bob: Definitely, that's been the case.

Sue: Uh huh. (Door opener)

Bob: Jim's been designated the task team leader.

Sue: You mean Jim Sanders, the finance manager? (Checking the subject)

Bob: Yes. Jim's facilitation skills are not the best. He sometimes pushes his agenda about how we should improve the customer-fulfillment order process. That led to some clashes with a couple of the people who work in sales and customer service. Some of the meetings ended up being arguments over solutions when we haven't yet done a thorough analysis of the process.

Sue: So you're frustrated because the team hasn't had focused leadership and isn't sticking to a systematic path of problem solving, right? (Reflective paraphrasing)

Bob: That sums it up pretty well. I'm also worried that this project could drag on and end up having nothing to show for our efforts.

Sue: So you feel like you're spinning your wheels, so to speak, and a part of a team that's going nowhere? (Reflective paraphrase)

Bob: Exactly.

Sue: Fill me in. As the team began losing its focus and the clashes occurred, what have you done? (Probing)

Bob: The tact I've been using with a little bit of success is to focus the team on working from a common agenda. So I've started meeting with Jim outside the team meetings to help shape the agendas.

Sue: Yes. (Door opener)

Bob: Then at the meetings I have been calling people's attention back to the agenda and suggesting that we agree upon some action items at the end of each meeting so that we're accomplishing some things.

Sue: Bob, it sounds like you're playing the facilitator role for the team. Is that right? (Paraphrasing)

Bob: Well in a way, I guess I'm starting to do that.

Sue: How's it been working? (Probing)

Bob: Outside of the meetings, Jim reacts positively to my planning with him what the agenda should be for the next meeting. In the meetings, he is still the designated facilitator, so my efforts to help focus the group are a little more difficult. Our last meeting yesterday was probably the first productive meeting we've had since we began as a team a month ago.

Sue: Oh? (Door opener)

Bob: For the first time, we started discussing some of the effects that cause our order fulfillment process not to work as efficiently as needed. We got some good input without any clashes. Everyone agreed to check back with their groups to gather more data about what's been happening in this area.

Sue: In other words, you have some movement in the right direction for this team? (Paraphrasing)

Bob: Yes. Team members responded well, but whether this momentum will continue, I don't know.

Sue: You don't know? (Echoing)

Bob: Jim's my concern. He doesn't really know how to facilitate. He'd do this team far better if he'd let me and Rhonda from customer service facilitate the team meetings. He could be our team leader, participate in the team meetings, and report our progress to management. But he doesn't know how to engage participation positively and keep people focused so we get something done.

Sue: So I hear an idea in the making about how to improve the functioning of this team. Am I picking that up right? (Paraphrasing)

Bob: Well, yes.

Sue: But I hear a worry, too? (Reflecting feelings)

Bob: I was thinking of suggesting this change to Jim, but I'm not sure how he'll take it. I could use your help.

Sue: What do you have in mind? (Probing)

Bob: I was thinking I could talk to Jim first and offer my suggestion for the change in roles. You know Jim well, and he knows you have a strong interest in wanting this task team to come up with some recommendations that are going to make a positive difference. So shortly after I speak to Jim, you follow up, talk to him, and basically close the deal. What do you say?

Sue: Your suggestion sounds like the story I've told you about where I got the president to quietly support me with a couple of vice presidents, which led to a significant change in our branding strategy. A sort of one-two punch. Kind of what you're looking for here, right? (Sharing a relevant example)

Bob: Exactly!

Sue: (Now as speaker) Bob, I'd be happy to help. That's why I assigned you to this team. I knew you'd help them focus. How about talking to Jim tomorrow and letting me know how it goes. Then I can check in with him the day after that.

Bob: That would be great. Thanks for meeting with me today.

Contrasting listener talk with speaker talk

The conversation between Bob and Sue (see the previous section) reveals Sue as an active participant in the conversation. She was talking throughout the conversation, but she was only a speaker in the end to wrap up the discussion. She was talking but not a speaker. Say what?

Speakers talk. Because people commonly don't understand what listening involves, they often don't realize that effective listening involves talking, too. Active or responsive listeners talk when they listen. But speaker talk differs from listener talk as follows:

- ✔ *You*-**focused versus** *me*-**focused:** Active listeners maintain the focus on the speaker and the speaker's message, not on themselves. With speaker talk, the focus is on the speaker saying what's on his or her mind.

- ✔ **Drawing out, reflecting back on the message versus telling, reporting:** Active listeners help the speaker to get his or her facts and feelings across and to reflect back the listener's understanding of that message. Speakers tell what's on their minds or report their information.

- ✔ **Receive and stay nonjudgmental versus expressing opinions, feelings, ideas, and information:** Active listeners receive; speakers give. Active listeners stay neutral and respectful; speakers, if they so desire, take a stand and give their opinions, ideas, or feelings.

✔ **Less said versus more said:** Active listeners talk, but they usually say much less than speakers in conversations. Using active listening tools is generally accomplished in a few words or a sentence or two. Speakers say that much and usually a whole lot more.

✔ **A difference in emphasis:** Active listeners work to gain an understanding of what speakers' messages mean. Speakers emphasize getting their messages across.

In truly productive conversations, people take turns being listeners and then being speakers — a nice ebb and flow takes place. When they're active listeners like Sue was with Bob in the previous section, they create an opportunity for issues to be heard and addressed and for speakers to walk away knowing that results were achieved and respect was maintained.

Chapter 6

Giving a Dose of Empathy a la Mode

. . . .

In This Chapter

▶ Listening with empathy as opposed to sympathy

▶ Avoiding verbal barriers that diminish empathy and results

▶ Putting active listening with empathy into practice

▶ Exploring some final tips to enhance listening effectiveness

. . . .

*E*ver have a conversation with someone in which the other person seemed to be hearing and receiving what you were saying, but you wondered whether he or she really cared? Ever have a conversation with someone in which the other individual reacted judgmentally toward what you were saying? These two types of conversations aren't unusual experiences. You've likely encountered them more than a few times in your working and personal lives.

By merely going through the motions without any hint of sincerity, many people fall short in their efforts to apply the active-listening skills they've discovered. Although they may allow the speaker to convey a message without taking over the conversation as a speaker themselves, other people show that they're not really listening by criticizing or debating the message or giving the speaker unsolicited advice. In each situation, *empathy* is the missing ingredient. Empathy is the care and feeding given by the listener to the speaker so that the speaker walks away from the conversation feeling respected and understood. When that happens, you make your job (as a listener) a whole lot easier.

Chapter 4 guides you through what you should listen for — the content and emotion of the message — and discusses how you can manage yourself better nonverbally to receive the speaker's message. Chapter 5 provides you with verbal tools that help you draw out, capture, and gain a full understanding of the speaker's message. This chapter combines those two concepts, topping them off with a heavy dose of empathy — kind of like the ice cream on the cake.

You need empathy to listen actively and to be able to offer sincere verbal or nonverbal input when you're listening. Keep in mind that empathy isn't the same as sympathy. In brief, it's gaining a truer understanding of the message by putting yourself in the speaker's position. That's a great expression we have in English — walking in another person's shoes. Aren't you glad you don't have to try on someone else's clothes to gain the other person's perspective?

This chapter helps you understand what listening with empathy is all about, and more important, it tweaks your awareness so that you avoid the nonempathetic modes of listening that people sometimes exhibit — the ones that create barriers in conversations.

Productive conversations are about opening two-way lines of communication in which each party shares the rope as a link or bond with others in the conversations as opposed to engaging in a tug-of-war, as discussed in Chapter 1. Listening with empathy helps make sharing the rope successful. So now it's time now for some empathy a la mode.

Showing Empathy, Not Sympathy

Active listening works best with empathy, as opposed to sympathy, yet people often get those two words mixed up, thinking of them as synonyms. They're not.

Moments of sympathy often are welcomed in interactions, but active listening, for the most part, is empathetic. Empathy goes further, working for all interactions. The following sections help you understand what empathy and sympathy mean and how they differ. The emphasis, however, is placed on using empathy in your active-listening efforts.

Defining empathy and sympathy in listening

Here's how empathy and sympathy relate to the effort of listening:

- **Active listening with empathy:** When listening with empathy, the receiver listens with care and respect and works to understand the message from the speaker's point of view. The listener doesn't pass judgment or do anything to take the focus away from the speaker's message.

  Listening with empathy is reflected to the speaker first by the manners you display toward the speaker (care and respect) and second by the emphasis you place on your listening efforts (understanding the message from the other person's perspective).

✔ **Listening with sympathy:** When listening with sympathy, the receiver tries to show compassion, pity, and even commiseration for the feelings expressed by the speaker.

Sympathetic listening makes the speaker aware that, in essence, you feel his or her pain or feelings. It lets the speaker know that you genuinely care and that you want to let him or her know you feel the same way.

Contrasting empathetic and sympathetic listening

As you look now at the differences between listening with empathy and listening with sympathy, remember the following formula about what you listen for as an active listener, and then keep the following tips in mind:

Facts or content + Emotion = The meaning of the message

✔ **Capturing the entire message as opposed to part of the message:** Listening with empathy deals with understanding the content and emotion of the speaker's message — the whole message. Sympathy focuses more toward the feelings side of the message, showing how you, too, are affected by the emotions the speaker expresses.

✔ **Understanding versus feeling:** Listening with empathy is about understanding the speaker's meaning and perspective. Sometimes emotion carries the weight of the meaning; sometimes content carries the message. Other times emotion and content share responsibility for carrying the meaning of a message. But by lending a sympathetic ear, you exhibit compassion for how and what the speaker feels. If that speaker feels bad, sympathy enables you to join in and participate in showing that you feel bad, too. On the other hand, empathy enables you to show an understanding . . . that you have had pain and know what it's all about, but unlike sympathy, you don't necessarily express sorrow for the speaker's pain.

✔ **Gaining recognition versus showing pity:** The old expression of "misery loves company" indicates that people don't mind, at times, receiving sympathy from others. But in many cases, when people express serious messages, they don't want someone feeling sorry in return. Such an effort from the listener does not exhibit recognition of what the speaker really means. Instead, it often comes across as being condescending or sappy, regardless of the intentions of the sympathetic soul.

As discussed in Chapter 5, avoid the well-intentioned yet sympathetic statement of "I understand how you feel." It's an assumption that strikes people as condescending. You're declaring that you understand what the other person is feeling even though you've made no effort to acknowledge and check the emotion the person has expressed (using the active listening tool of reflecting feelings). Identifying the feelings and facts you're hearing are the keys to moving from sympathy to empathy.

When listening with empathy, you recognize where the other person is coming from, but you don't have to outwardly express your feelings or experiences, as they relate to the feelings and experiences of the speaker, simply to show that you understand. The message you give to the speaker when you use active listening with empathy is: "I'll spare you my pity. Instead, I'll give you respect and understanding."

To contrast a little more, take a look at the empathetic and sympathetic responses in the following example: A co-worker, Larry, comes to you with the following concern:

"I know you're concerned that I have been coming late to our team meetings the last few weeks. Frankly, I don't see anything productive happening with this project as far as my involvement is concerned. As a result, I am having a hard time showing much interest in it. My input no longer seems needed, and you and the rest of the team seem to have everything under control. So I don't know if coming to the meetings any more is even necessary."

- ✔ **Empathetic response:** "So you're telling me you've lost your enthusiasm for this project because you don't see that your contributions are valued or needed any more. Is that right?"

- ✔ **Sympathetic response:** "Don't feel down, Larry. We truly want you on this project team. Really, don't feel sad about this."

The empathetic response addresses where the speaker is coming from — the heart of the message. The sympathetic response expresses a feeling of sorrow for the speaker but doesn't quite exhibit an understanding of his meaning. If you spend time feeling sorry for Larry, one possibility is that he may not mind the attention he's getting but then you don't get to the issue regarding his involvement in the team. The other possibility here is that the sympathetic response is likely to become a major turnoff to Larry.

Sometimes, people fear giving an empathetic response because it may come across as condescending just like a sympathetic response can. Can Larry respond with a retort like, "Of course, that's what I said. What are you, deaf?" Use the following tips to minimize these kinds of reactions and make sure that empathetic responses are well received:

- ✔ As you're identifying emotions that haven't been stated and using content to summarize the situation, use your own words not the speaker's words. You're more likely to get a negative reaction when you mimic someone.

- ✔ As you check your understanding (instead of declaring that you know something), do so with a tone of sincerity. Without sincerity, your words don't matter. People tend to respond well when others listen to understand the heart of their messages. Don't be afraid to do so.

A great aspect of active listening with empathy is that you don't have to agree with what you hear. Maybe in this example, you're thinking to yourself, "Larry, you big lump. What we need on this team is for you to get in there and make some contributions and not back away." Rather than verbalizing this judgmental response — and creating a huge barrier in the conversation as a result (more about the problem of creating barriers in the following section) — listening with empathy helps you first understand where Larry is coming from. When you gain that understanding, you're better able to reduce tension and come up with solutions.

Avoiding Verbal Barriers: Nonempathetic Modes of Listening

Chapter 4 discusses some nonverbal listening habits that create barriers to speakers. Listeners also sometimes react verbally to messages in ways that create barriers to the speaker. Although you may think you're actively listening, you may somehow be reacting in a judgmental or nonempathetic way, selectively listening to the speaker, or in other words, hearing only what you want to hear. In this section, I introduce you to nonempathetic modes or actions of listening that have you passing judgment and taking the focus of the conversation away from the speaker's message — the opposite of active listening with empathy. The effect of these modes is to block or prevent the speaker from getting the entire message across and being understood. These barriers can take a conversation down a nonproductive path.

As each barrier-creating mode is explained, it is applied to Larry's message in the previous section, thus giving you a chance to see how it contrasts with the empathetic example shown in the previous section.

The critic mode

As a listener in the *critic mode,* you criticize your speaker in response to the message that you hear. Often, your remarks are personal and make the speaker feel judged or put down.

The response of the critic mode listener may sound something like: "Larry, if you had something of value to add, you wouldn't feel this loss of interest, right?"

The critic mode response has a personal sting to it. It lets the speaker, Larry, know that you question his value — a nice little put-down. Instead of understanding where he's coming from, you pass judgment on his worth to the team.

The identifier mode

I often refer to the *identifier mode* as the me-too mode. When you listen in the identifier mode, the speaker says something to which you can relate, and before you know it, you launch into your own story, take over as speaker, and divert the conversation away from the speaker's message before you ever understand it.

Falling into the trap of the identifier mode is quite common. Your eagerness to show that you can relate ends up showing no understanding whatsoever. It's a far cry from the active listening tool known as *sharing a relevant example,* which is described in Chapter 5. With that tool, you use an example to illustrate your understanding while maintaining the focus on the speaker's message — far different than the identifier mode.

The identifier mode response to Larry may sound like: "You know, Larry, I've been on many a team where I questioned whether I should stay a part of the effort. But you know, I stuck it out and focused on what I could do to help this team to be successful. That's what we're paid for. And sure enough, my contributions mattered in the end."

As you can see with the identifier mode, the listener generally has the best of intentions, but nevertheless takes off with something the speaker has said and focuses it on himself. The fact that Larry's wondering whether he should stay with the project team has led the listener to talk about his own experiences regardless of whether Larry wanted to hear about them — in most cases, he doesn't. The experiences don't relate, and the speaker feels like he's sitting through a self-centered lecture without anyone understanding his message.

The defensive mode

What do you notice when you're trying to talk to someone who's getting defensive with you? Often you'll observe anxious and tense body language, a face scrunched or flushed, nervous or fidgety gestures, a sharper tone of voice, or louder volume. You'll be interrupted more and often face counterattack responses or he's-picking-on-me remarks. These are verbal as well as strong nonverbal reactions that often characterize how people listen when they're in the *defensive mode.* You get the feeling as a speaker that a wall is going up and that your message never will penetrate it. The defensive listener is liable to make you defensive in return and, at least, block your message from ever being understood the way it was intended.

A defensive mode response to Larry may be as follows: "Oh, thanks a lot Larry. I've been working so hard as team leader to pull everything together. We're over halfway into this project with high expectations and now you want to bail on me, right!"

You can hear the sharpness in the tone of the message striking back at Larry. The listener's response takes what Larry has said quite personally. All of these are common reactions when listeners fall into the defensive mode. It often is a common mode to fall into when people bring problems or negative feedback to you.

The key to avoiding these nonproductive modes, especially the defensive mode, is to shift the focus and your concentration from yourself onto what the speaker's message says and means. When you do, you're much more able to manage your stress level and deal with the issue at hand. The more you feel the need to defend yourself first before you understand what the other person means, the more you'll come across as defensive.

The denying mode

The *denying mode is* similar to the defensive mode. For example, in the defensive mode, you listen in a way that makes the speaker feel like he is being pushed away and that a wall is coming up between the two of you. The denying mode does essentially the same thing, but usually in a subtler, less anxious way.

In the denying mode, the responses are often dismissive in nature:

- ✔ "You're just too sensitive."
- ✔ "You wouldn't really understand."
- ✔ "Oh, not me."
- ✔ "You're making too big of a deal out of this."

These types of responses have the effect of greatly irritating your speaker. Like the defensive mode, the denying mode often shows itself in situations that involve problems or concerns.

A denying mode response to Larry may sound like the following: "Don't see anything productive happening, Larry? I see you just don't understand what this project is all about, right?"

Denying-mode responses like this one to Larry can make the speaker feel like he's received a subtle insult — like you're slapping him in the face. Sometimes you can see a combination of critic mode and defensive mode in them. In their own subtle way, they put the speaker down and push him away. Understanding first where the speaker is coming from? Forget about it.

The being-right mode

In the *being-right mode*, the listener is annoying, nitpicking what the speaker has said; that is, trying to correct little points that usually are unimportant details. In addition, the listener in the being-right mode comes across as rigid. Everything is right or wrong, one way or another — what is often referred to as *black and white thinking* with no gray in between. Of course, in this mode the listener insists on being right.

A being-right mode response to Larry may sound like this: "Actually Larry, you've been coming late to our team meetings for more than a month now, and it sounds like you think this is not a productive project. That's not the case."

As you can see from this response, the listener is showing Larry how he's wrong. An unimportant detail is pointed out first, and then Larry's view about the project is being corrected. Actually, Larry never expressed an opinion that the project was not productive; he stated he didn't see his involvement as being helpful and necessary for the team. As is often the case in the being-right mode, as well as the other modes, assumptions are made, and as a result, the whole message has neither been heard nor understood.

The interrogator mode

As you can guess by its name, the *interrogator mode* puts the speaker under the listener's microscope, grilling him or her with questions that sometimes come in rapid-fire fashion. Many closed-end, leading-the-witness questions like the following can be part of this interrogation:

- "Do you think implementing that idea is really going to help?"
- "Isn't it true that you really knew about the problem but just didn't want to say anything about it?"
- "How many times have you missed deadlines in the last quarter?"

In the interrogator mode, the listener usually knows or anticipates the answers to the questions he or she asks of the speaker. If any open-ended questions are used, they generally start with *why* to add to the speaker's feeling of being *on the spot* or accused — like being on the stand at your own trial with a hard-charging prosecuting attorney blasting away at your alibi.

An interrogator mode response to Larry may be like this: "So Larry, why haven't you been making something productive happen? When was the last time you gave the team much input that we could even use? And do you think coming late for the meetings helps the project team?"

I have to prove I'm right

When someone listens in the being-right mode, the efforts often focus on trying to show that he or she is right or *in the know* — a great distraction to most speakers. Through the years, seminar participants sometimes demonstrate these points without knowing they're doing it.

Once in a communications seminar, I asked the group if they knew what a particular term meant. To this day, I don't remember the question, just the response that ensued. The individual who first attempted to answer — I'll call him Bill — was not accurate, so the question was thrown out again to the group to see if anyone else knew. Two other people spoke up and correctly explained what the term meant.

We then moved ahead with this point in the lesson. About two minutes later Bill spoke up, again pushing hard that what he said earlier really tied in to this point. As the other participants chuckled, you could hear the message "I've got to prove I'm right," coming through in Bill's insistence that his earlier remarks did indeed fit.

As the example shows, more questions than one are asked in the interrogator mode, sometimes in rapid-fire succession, overwhelming and defeating the speaker before he or she has a chance to even think about it (let alone attempt to respond). Understanding where the speaker is coming from isn't part of the interrogation.

The sparring mode

The *sparring mode* means listening in much the same way as the interrogator mode and coming back with strong responses that usually put the speaker on the defensive. The difference here is that, instead of hard-charging questions, the conversation breaks up into a debate with point versus counterpoint, argument versus rebuttal flowing between speaker and listener. The listener often plays devil's advocate, challenging every point the speaker makes with the opposite point of view, even though the speaker has not been inclined to engage in such a great debate.

A sparring mode response to Larry may be as follows: "Larry, how can you say that! You've got assignments to do for this team. This project is important for the company. Sounds like you're making a bunch of excuses."

In the sparring mode, as is happening in the response to Larry, a rebuttal to much of what the speaker has said is followed by a challenge. If the conversation continues, a back-and-forth struggle may well ensue or, as happens with many speakers, Larry may just shut down and go away. People want to be understood first without having to defend themselves in verbal combat.

Whatever floats your boat

Some people enjoy engaging in heavy-duty sparring, interrogation, and other verbal banter in an attempt to outdo the other person in the conversation. In fact, for them, conversation is a place for competition, and no better modes in listening spur this competitive fire than the sparring and interrogator modes. In my seminars, these people are the ones who start smiling when the two modes are explained and, at first, have a hard time deciding what the issue is.

Certainly, for effective communications, you must know your audience. None of what is covered in this book is about right or wrong. The emphasis is on what's most effective for getting the results you need at work. When two people enjoy this verbal exchange of inquisition and debate and have an understanding between each other that no harm is intended, then let the fireworks happen. It can be fun to watch, too.

Recognizing that such hard-charging exchanges turn many people off is a key to good communication. Not everybody is the same. For some, such exchanges are intimidating and cause them to shut down. For others, such exchanges escalate tensions and cause them to engage in needless confrontations. Good listeners recognize these differences and seek understanding, not a chance to play with what you hear the speaker say. They push aside the rebuttal to see if they can feed back what the speaker means. Doing so moves you out of sparring or interrogator modes and into empathetic mode and saves the fireworks for those few who share such tastes for banter.

The diagnostic mode

Often fun to watch but never fun to experience are listeners who enter the *diagnostic mode,* analyzing and psychoanalyzing the speaker, making assumptions, and essentially telling the speaker what his motives are or why he is the way he is. Comments often are offensive to the speaker and usually go well beyond the scope of his or her message.

"You know what your problem is?" is one of the classic lines people say when they're in the diagnostic mode. The psychiatrist has arrived and already has figured you out, saying, "Here's your diagnosis!" long before gaining an understanding of what you truly had to say.

A diagnostic response to Larry may sound like the following: "So in other words Larry, you really resent that I was selected to be the team leader for this project, and you're basically giving up as a result, right?"

In this response to Larry, the listener leaps to a conclusion that provides Larry with the analysis for his concerns and makes several assumptions that are in no way connected to Larry's message. Aside from getting upset, Larry can do nothing more with this conversation — one of the effects all nonempathetic modes have in common.

The advice mode

In the *advice mode*, the listener often tries to be helpful but winds up dwelling on what he or she thinks the speaker should do. Quite often you hear what sounds like a problem and, BOOM! there you go announcing your solution to fix all the speaker's ills. Even when those ills are merely attempts by the speaker to share life's experiences or let off a little steam, the advice-mode listener jumps in to offer up a solution.

In the advice mode, the listener forgets a few basics about problem solving and advice. The first step in problem solving is understanding the problem, not running with a solution. Second, if a problem exists, the solution often rests with the person who's having the problem. That individual may need only for someone to be a sounding board to help him think through the issue. Last, advice is best received, of course, when someone asks for it. When you listen in the advice mode, you skip that request and let the advice fly free of charge, regardless of the outcome.

An advice-mode response to Larry may sound like the following: "Larry, you know what you need to do. You need to take a long weekend break, then come back and get refocused on what the team's goals are and what your part is in helping the team achieve those goals. Do that and your input will definitely be valued, don't you think?"

As this example shows, the listener has the answer or solution for Larry's situation. Although the problem is not yet understood, the solution nevertheless is ready to go. When people receive advice that they neither seek out nor desire, they're disappointed and often annoyed because their messages seldom are heard.

Falling into advice mode at work is easy because the nature of so many jobs involves problem solving. This is precisely where active listening can help you stay away from giving advice that isn't sought. First gain an understanding of what the speaker really means and feed that information back to the speaker to confirm your understanding. Determine from there whether the speaker is venting or sharing an experience or seeking help. If the former is the case, let it be. If it's the latter but a direct request for ideas or assistance has not been made, ask the speaker directly if help is desired. For example, "Would you like a suggestion about how to deal with that situation?" Keep the tone of your question light and friendly so that the speaker has permission to say no. If the answer is yes, go ahead and give your advice. If the answer is no, move forward with the conversation — the advice-mode trap has been avoided.

Seeing Empathy in Action

The preceding section gives you a preview of listening behaviors that create verbal barriers between the listener and speaker. Each of the nine nonempathetic listening modes mentioned in the preceding section makes the job of the speaker much more difficult. As the listener's uninformed reactions come across to the speaker as judgmental, the focus of the conversation is diverted from the speaker's true meaning, thereby creating a barrier between the two.

When you gain an accurate understanding of the speaker's message, you create a powerful connection that enables you to take positive actions to productively move a conversation forward. By showing empathy, for example, you can address the speaker's concerns as you understand them and perhaps persuade the speaker to consider other points of view. In so doing, the speaker can opt to dig deeper to find more perspective, or to do nothing at all and thus avoid saying something that may turn out to detract from the conversation — foot-in-mouth disease prevented.

In the following sections, you get a chance to see how empathy in action contrasts with the more detrimental nonempathetic responses that you may commonly give (even though the latter may sometimes be more fun). You see how the empathetic responses are the highest and most sincere form of listening because they're the only ones that go to the heart of the speaker's message without passing judgment.

Working with a complaining client

You're part of a group that works with the clients your company serves. A big part of the role is serving as liaison between the client and the technical teams that perform work for the client. In this scenario a fellow account manager, Alicia, shares her concern with you about a new client she has.

Alicia says to you, "I've recently taken on a new client who has become quite a challenge. Nearly every day he raises complaints about the project we're doing. He complains about the quality of the work, sometimes about cost issues, and sometimes about staff behavior. The problem is most of his complaints arrive through e-mail and voice mail. When I call him and leave a message, he doesn't return my phone calls. When I finally connect live with him on the phone, he usually can only talk for a minute or two because he's off to some other meeting. When I met with him in person a couple of weeks ago, all the concerns were addressed. Yet his complaining messages continue. If he wasn't located in another state, I'd be sitting at his doorstep until I could make some sense out of all his issues."

Possible responses to Alicia include the following:

- ✔ "Why don't you fly out and demand to see this client and not leave until he gives you some straight answers?"

- ✔ "Are you sure you've really been trying that hard to connect with this client?"

- ✔ "Sounds like what I call hit-and-run; that is, hit you with a complaint and run away before you can truly address it, which is quite frustrating. Is that the case here?"

Which response shows the most empathy with Alicia's situation, and in what modes are the less empathetic responses?

- ✔ The first response, in advice mode, is not empathetic. The idea offered in this response is possibly a good idea, but Alicia says she already has tried it once — the problem when advice is given even though it's not asked for.

- ✔ The second response is in critic mode. It questions Alicia's efforts, a sort of put-down to her. It overlooks the challenge Alicia is dealing with and takes a subtle but personal shot at her — critic mode at its best (or worst).

- ✔ The third response is the only response that first captures what is happening for Alicia, and then goes to the heart of the message, acknowledges the emotion she is experiencing, and recognizes the difficult client she has encountered. That's empathy.

Helping an overworked employee

You're a department manager who oversees three groups. Each group has its own supervisor, and Jim is one of the supervisors who reports to you. Jim's group is running lean in terms of staff resources right now and has just been given another critical project to handle. He has come to you, his manager, to talk about his thoughts for handling this situation.

Jim says to you, "I'm in a tight situation right now. My group has done its best to keep up with its workload while keeping costs down. Now this new project that was assigned to us a couple of weeks ago has us stretched way too thin. While I know I can hire a couple of new people, that's going to take some time. I thought that maybe a couple of the other groups might be able to share some of this new project in the meantime. Without this help, I'm afraid I'll lose some of the good staff I already have and then we'll really be in trouble."

Possible responses to Jim include the following:

- ✔ "Why are you coming to me now with this problem? Where were you about this issue when the project was assigned to your team? And what makes you think the other teams can just jump right in and help out on this project?"

- ✔ "So I hear a big worry for you right now, and the crux of it is that your group is overloaded and understaffed, which may cause people to walk. Is that right?"

- ✔ "So you're upset that I didn't let you go ahead and hire additional resources until now? And if staff quits, you think it's my fault. Is that right?"

Which response shows the most empathy to Jim's situation, and in what modes are the less empathetic responses?

- ✔ The first is in interrogator mode. Its sharp-toned, rapid-fire questions are grilling Jim for bringing forth a problem.

- ✔ The second response is the most empathetic. This comment is not likely to put him on the defensive, inhibit him from speaking, or prevent him from achieving any positive action. It works to capture what Jim's message is all about — the facts and feelings.

- ✔ The third response is in defensive mode. The response shows that the listener is taking the situation personally. You can hear an agitated tone in his response, which diverts the conversation away from understanding Jim's issue.

The second response is the only one that shows an understanding of Jim's situation and the difficulty he's facing. He's short-handed on resources and worried that the staff he has may quit because of the overload of work. Again, the other two responses make no direct effort to show understanding of where Jim is coming from — not unusual in such interactions.

Responding to an upset employee

You're a manager, and Julie is one of your staff members. She is a reliable employee who does quality work most of the time. Because of some issues you've had to deal with, you haven't been in the office much lately. Because you're back in the office today, you take the opportunity to provide Julie with some feedback on an assignment she left for you to review. It needs some correction.

Upon providing this feedback to Julie, she says to you, "What you pointed out that needs correction with the assignment, I recognize and will fix with no problem. Yet you barely take notice of all the other work I've done to keep the group running while you've been away. For the last few weeks, I've put in extra hours to help maintain the operations but haven't heard a peep from you about anything until today, and even then, that was only to point out a small mistake. If you think this is motivational management, then you're terribly mistaken. I've said enough here."

Possible responses to Julie include the following:

- ✔ "Julie, I hear an important point you're making here. In other words, you feel I've been taking you for granted and that's a big mistake on my part that needs to be corrected. Am I hearing that right?"

- ✔ "Julie, are you sure you're not just overreacting a bit here?"

- ✔ "Julie, you're just resentful because I asked you to postpone your vacation until my business trips slow down, right?"

Which response shows the most empathy to Julie's message, and in what modes are the less empathetic responses?

- ✔ The first response is the most empathetic one. It is the only one that goes beyond what may be coming across as venting. It picks up on where Julie is coming from and recognizes the lesson that the message conveys.

- ✔ The second is in denying mode. It dismisses what Julie has to say and avoids acknowledging her concern whatsoever. As denying mode does so well, it offers comments that are certain to irritate (if not greatly aggravate) and pushes attention away from the issue at hand.

- ✔ The third response is in diagnostic mode. It attempts to explain why Julie has a problem through a dose of psychoanalysis. As so often happens in this mode, conclusions are drawn from assumptions that go far beyond the message, casting a judgmental focus on the speaker and diverting attention away from what the message is saying.

Discovering Seven Listening Tips

You've no doubt heard about the Seven Wonders of the World. Or, maybe you've heard about how *lucky seven* is the number many people play in their gambling adventures. So, sticking with such an important theme, what follows are seven final tips to help you get the best out of your active listening efforts:

- ✔ **Listen for main ideas.** As you know and have experienced many times, speakers can talk a lot. They can ramble, or they can give you a ton of information. They can get all excited or anxious at the same time. It isn't difficult, therefore, as a listener, to get lost in all the detail and noise and miss what the message is truly telling you.

The emphasis of active listening first and foremost is grasping the main ideas. To fully understand what people are saying in terms of content and emotion, your attention and effort need to capture the essence of the message. Doing so steers you clear of confusion and the stifling effect of strong emotions and focuses you on understanding what's important from the speaker's point of view. That's how you start to build success in your working relationships and your job.

✔ **Use familiarity to your advantage, not your disadvantage.** As you spend time with your co-workers or with customers who you see time and again, you get to know them better. If you use this to your advantage, you can understand the context of their messages and know what's important to them.

Sometimes people do the opposite. Because I know you, for example, I start making assumptions about what you're going to say, or I form biases about you — all internal thoughts that block my ability to openly listen. These thoughts also are likely to turn into actions that create barriers in your conversations. They cause you to overlook that every day is a new day and that each day you need to let others be who they are. Like you, they may not want to be the same every day.

Used in a positive sense, familiarity serves as a basis for you to recognize when something may be different about someone else and allows you to check it out by listening rather than jumping to a hard-and-fast conclusion. It also helps you know how to receive speakers better and to go beyond their delivery styles to capture their messages.

✔ **Eliminate distractions and physical barriers.** Common sense and common courtesy, unfortunately, are not always common. Please turn off your pager and your cell phone when I'm talking to you. Don't automatically pick up your telephone when it rings while we are in the middle of a conversation. Please move that plant or box or stack of files and papers so we can see each other as we converse. Come out from behind your mammoth desk so we can comfortably be seated together to have a relaxed conversation. Invite me to sit down so I don't have to stand the whole time to explain my message to you. If your cube area is really noisy, and we really need to talk, then take me to a quieter place.

As you read the previous paragraph, you probably experienced flashes of your own various experiences. The tip here is quite simple: Take care of the logistics to make it easier for your speaker to talk to you. Then you can truly concentrate on that person's message and not cause a distraction for either of you.

✔ **Follow through on what you said you would do.** Sometimes the real test of whether you're listening comes from what you do after we talk. I remember a manager who viewed himself as a good listener with his staff. When he got some feedback from a survey done with his staff, their view was quite the opposite. Yes, he received people and let them say their messages. But all the actions he said he would take (from what people asked of him), he seldom took. Or when he asked for their ideas for improvements, he acted on none of them. So in their view, he didn't listen at all.

A big part of listening is receiving people's requests, ideas, and information, and then acting upon them. When you forget, do half of what was asked, or for one reason or another do nothing at all, you lack follow-through skills. You're ineffective as a worker and as a communicator. Certainly, taking notes so that you don't rely on memory can help, but follow-through goes one step further. It's acting upon what was heard and agreed upon without being reminded and doing so within the time frame that was expected. When you follow through, not only does your listening effectiveness greatly increase, so does your credibility and integrity.

✔ **Take an interest in what the speaker has to say.** This tip doesn't mean you have to find everything that you hear interesting or engage in heavy conversations when they have little value to you. Don't waste your time, but on the other hand, don't forget that this tip is all about maximizing your time *within* your conversations.

When you take an interest in what someone has to say, especially on the many work issues that you deal with, you communicate a sense of respect and importance to the other person. At the same time, the effort focuses your attention and pushes you to actively participate, figuring out what you need to understand from that speaker and thereby increasing your productivity. So save your daydreaming until after the conversation is over.

✔ **Remember that you have two ears, two eyes, and one mouth.** Sometimes people operate in conversations as if they have one ear, one eye, and two mouths. I'm sure you've done it more than a few times yourself. This tip reminds you that you listen with your eyes and ears, but trying to get in the first through the last words of a conversation keeps you in the role of speaker. The latter makes conversations more of a contest than the two-way dialogue that is characteristic of the most productive conversations described in Chapter 3.

✔ **Keep your supply of patience full.** For you to get the best out of applying the tools of active listening, patience is required. Lack of patience is a stumbling block that causes many people to function more as selective listeners than active listeners.

Patience in terms of listening means exercising control over your own emotions. Take a moment to think about that. When you have control, you can manage your stress level, you can handle any message regardless of how it's delivered, and you can focus in positive directions. Conversations break down and destructive conflicts arise when you don't have this control.

You don't control anyone else, but you can influence. The person you have the most control over is you. When you demonstrate patience as defined here, you're composed, ready to listen, and able to figure out what people truly mean. With your judgment much more clear as a result, you have far more potential to create positive outcomes when it's your turn to speak. After all, you're being paid to deliver results and that's what active listening with empathy and patience helps you do.

Part III
Speaking Assertively

The 5th Wave — By Rich Tennant

IT'S REALLY QUITE SIMPLE. WITH THE REVISED MAINFRAME PRICING POLICY, YOU'LL BE CHARGED ONE-QUARTER OF THE PREVIOUS PRICE PER CPU BASED ON A 3-TIERED SITE LICENSING AGREEMENT FOR UP TO 12 USERS, AFTER WHICH A 5-TIERED SYSTEM IS EMPLOYED FOR UP TO 64 USERS WITHIN THE ORIGINAL 4-TIERED SYSTEM FOR NEW CUSTOMERS USING OLD SOFTWARE OR OLD CUSTOMERS USING NEW SOFTWARE ON EACH OF THREE CPUs RUNNING A NEW OLD OPERATING SYSTEMS SITE LICENSED UNDER THE OLD NEW AGREEMENT BUT ONLY ON THURSDAYS WITH LESS THAN 10 PEOPLE IN THE ROOM, ...

In this part . . .

In this part, you find out how to express yourself in ways that command attention and respect. You discover how best to use nonverbal behaviors to come across as positive and confident, as well as how to use language to state your messages in the best way possible while making your points clear. I also give you tips and strategies for keeping your listeners tuned in to you and helping them understand your messages as you intend them.

Chapter 7

It Isn't Just What You Say, but How You Say It

In This Chapter

▶ Making eye contact to connect to your listener

▶ Using body language to deliver a confident message

▶ Engaging your listener: Getting the best out of your voice

▶ Managing your pace to have a positive effect

*P*eople listen in many different ways (see Chapter 3). Active, or responsive, listening is the most effective approach (covered in Chapters 4, 5, and 6). The same holds true for the speaking side of interpersonal communications. When expressing their messages, people speak in four different ways. Chapter 2 highlights assertive speaking, the most effective approach to speaking, and contrasts it with three other approaches: aggressive speaking, nonassertive speaking, and passive-aggressive speaking.

Assertive speaking is about delivering your message in a positive, direct, and confident manner while maintaining respect for the person or persons to whom you're expressing that message. When your audience feels respected as you use this form of expression, you'll be effective in your interactions at work, or anywhere for that matter. This chapter provides you some of the tools of assertive speaking.

It's interesting that the tools explained in this chapter are all nonverbal. That's right, they have nothing to do with *what* you say but rather *how* you say it! The nonverbal tools discussed throughout this chapter can greatly impact how your message is expressed and received by others. Your words alone — that verbal stuff — aren't the only component of speaking. In fact, the following is true:

✔ **What you say is important, but how you say it often carries more weight.** As discussed in Chapter 4, much of the emotion in a speaker's message is presented through nonverbal means of communication — body language and tone of voice. Emotion is what engages people's attention as they listen to you — or causes them to disengage and not listen. When the emotion is channeled in positive ways, people tune in and want to hear what you have to say.

✔ **Most people haven't been taught how to truly listen; therefore, you can't count on them to listen fully and effectively when you speak to them.** The nonverbal tools explored in this chapter help you engage your listeners and keep their attention focused on your message.

You don't have to use one particular speaking style to be effective at assertive speaking. What a relief! You can be anywhere from reserved to highly expressive, as long as you're assertive. The idea here is to get the most out of your style so that others receive your messages the way that you intend for them to be heard. When people receive your message the way that you intend, you're communicating assertively.

The Eyes Have It: Communicating with Eye Contact

Your eyes lend credibility to your spoken messages. They give the message much of its meaning and affect whether the listener believes and trusts your message. So open your eyes, and in the next two sections, look at how to use eye contact assertively and at a few no-nos to avoid.

Using eye contact to effectively get your message across

In conversation, who provides more direct eye contact to the other person, the listener or the speaker? More often than not, it's the listener (as long as that individual is making the effort to listen).

What is the speaker doing with his eyes? At times, the speaker looks at the person with whom he's conversing, but quite often, his eyes are wandering around gathering thoughts about what to say next. Some also are

✔ Looking skyward

✔ Looking at the floor

> ✔ Looking over your shoulder
>
> ✔ Almost looking within themselves

The eye-contact assertive-speaking tool works differently: You provide steady and sincere eye contact with the other person while expressing your message. Here's how you use this tool:

✔ **Make steady eye contact.** The idea is to look at people when you're talking to them. Steady eye contact is the key. Steady does not, however, mean constant. Blinking and occasional glances away are expected and normal. Add a touch of sincerity to your looks and you'll attract people's attention to you and your message. This subtle tool has a positive and powerful effect.

Try this out. Ask someone to receive your message and give it to them twice. Make it a short message of two to three sentences and start out by saying, "Something important to me is. . . ." First say your message while giving steady eye contact; and then repeat the exact same message while looking away most of the time. Ask your test subject to let you know which message evokes a more favorable response.

To which method did the other person respond more favorably? You'll find steady eye contact wins every time. People listen less when the speaker gives little eye contact. Their attention wanders. But when the steady eye contact is maintained, the effect is magnetic. It attracts people's attention toward you and helps them tune in to your message.

✔ **Maintain eye contact.** People often ask how long you should continue eye contact. Certainly, no set time exists for maintaining eye contact and then momentarily glancing away. Life and interactions don't exist by formulas. Instead, the more familiar and comfortable a relationship you have with someone, the longer the eye contact can be maintained without discomfort for either party. In general, eye contact can range comfortably from 6 to 20 seconds in one-on-one interactions, while in group situations, the time is less per individual — three to six seconds — because you want to address everybody in the group.

✔ **Look in the right places.** Look directly at your listener's face, near the eyes. Looking above and below the face captures less of the listener's attention and can make the listener uncomfortable.

Avoiding eye-contact pitfalls

When speaking to others, avoid eye-contact behaviors that make your message less than assertive, such as:

✔ **Staring and glaring:** This kind of eye contact locks in and sometimes has a menacing feel to it. Such looks often are interpreted as aggressive, which is far too strong for any message. Staring and looking below face level at the same time, causes discomfort and may even offend your listener.

✔ **Looking away and all around:** This is the most common eye-contact pitfall for speakers. Whether they're searching for their thoughts or deeply absorbed in their messages, speakers who maintain little or no eye contact cause listeners to drift away.

Speakers who mostly look down while addressing someone else — especially when the message is about a sensitive issue — lessen the value of their messages. It puts you on the nonassertive track as if you can't stand firmly behind your own message.

✔ **Darting glances:** These are sudden looks going to and away from the listener. They make the receiver feel that you're looking at something else or avoiding something. Darting glances usually create a distraction for the listener, who then loses the focus of your message.

✔ **Blinking excessively:** Blinking is a normal function for your eyes. When they do it so rapidly and often that the blinking is noticed, however, it creates a distraction for the listener. It may make your listener feel that you're nervous about what you have to say. If you even hint of an appearance that you lack confidence in your message, in the blink of an eye, the receiver will, too.

✔ **Focusing in on one person, not everyone:** This behavior happens in group situations, like meetings. It's one thing to address someone who has asked you a question. However, when your eye contact stays with only one person, providing little eye contact to the rest of your audience, the other listeners feel isolated and left out, which usually creates resentment and keeps them from truly hearing your message.

✔ **Glazing over:** This is fine for donuts and hams but not for speaking. Sometimes this happens when you're overly absorbed in your own thoughts or when you lose your train of thought. Once is no big deal, but have it happen more than that during a conversation and you appear to have tuned out your own message. Don't expect others to tune in if you're not doing so yourself.

Your Body Is Talking; Make Sure It's Supporting Your Message

Body language refers to everything you do with your body to express your message, including facial expressions, posture, and gestures. The idea behind assertive speaking is getting these myriad expressions and cues involved in your message; that is, coming alive when you speak.

Using body language to effectively get your message across

You have to decide what to do with your face and body when you speak: You can use them or keep them dormant. In assertive speaking, you can use them in ways that positively engage others in your message and that enable you to come across as confident, animated, and relaxed.

Confident means a sense of certainty in what you have to say. Animated means you're alive while you say it. And relaxed means you're at ease while talking. No one wants to listen to an uncertain, stiff, and uptight person for long. Here's how you use the body-language tool:

✔ **Posture:** Posture is how you carry and position yourself. Sit up and face your receiver as a means of expressing your message assertively. It is sometimes helpful to lean forward a bit as well.

Most important interactions take place while you're seated — or should be if they're not. In fact, quite likely you're sitting down now as you're reading this book. If you would please, sit up in your chair right now. What do you notice? You're more alert. Lean a little forward with it and you have a more commanding presence to go with your message. Sitting up also helps put strength in your voice. And facing your listener straight on enables you to positively engage him or her.

✔ **Facial expressions:** Technically, you can't see your face when talking unless you carry a mirror and hold it up to yourself. Yet you can sense what your face is doing. You likely know when you're smiling, when you have a look of concern, or when you're showing a strong feeling about something. Your face communicates these emotions to others. The idea in expressing yourself assertively is to show positive life through your facial expressions.

You've probably heard an expression about putting a smile in your voice. It's about having someone sound more upbeat by smiling as he or she speaks. The muscles in your face change with a smile and help pick up the inflection in your voice. That's the idea here. Have your facial expressions match what you're saying in your message. Doing so gives your message confidence and sincerity — a double dose that positively engages people to want to listen to you.

Your facial expressions greatly influence how people receive your messages. In fact, try this out. Ask someone to receive your message twice and give it to them twice. Make it a short message of two or three sentences and start out by saying, "Something important to me is. . . ." First say your message showing a great deal of interest with your facial expression, and then repeat the same message with a blank look void of any expression. Ask your test subject to let you know which message evokes a more favorable response.

To which message will the other person respond more favorably? The message with interested looks best supports the verbal message. The no-expression look contradicts the message. You'll also probably notice that your voice sounds somewhat different each time from lively to monotone. Your intention matches your message when you confidently get behind your message with your facial expressions. So keep that chin up and get that face of yours to come alive when you express your message.

✔ **Gestures:** Gestures are what you do with your hands when you're talking. I know people who were told when they were younger not to talk with their hands. I, too, heard that message when I was a child and wondered if something dangerous was going to happen if you talked with your hands. What's wrong with using your hands to say something? Not a thing! In fact, you're more dangerous (in terms of boring other people) if you use no gestures at all when you speak.

Use gestures to come across assertively, to help your message flow properly, and in essence, to punctuate or emphasize key points when you're talking. People often do just that in casual and social conversations. Just apply that same effort to your important messages at work. You may also notice that your gestures have connections to your facial expressions, helping you deliver your message in an animated way within your own style. (The hand bone is connected to the face bone . . . sing along, now everybody.)

Everyone look into the mirror

Jan managed a large group of customer service representatives (reps). The nature of their work involved heavy telephone interaction. They received customer calls, answering questions and helping conduct transactions. While using her lead workers to help train staff regarding the company's products and services and hearing that the staff came across as knowledgeable, Jan thought something still was missing. After seeing some customer feedback surveys and hearing the sales reps on the phone herself, Jan noticed that many of the staff spoke in monotone and became almost robotic in explaining issues to customers.

Merely telling employees to sound livelier was not enough. The material they shared with customers often was quite technical, even when they put it in lay terms, so Jan decided to utilize mirrors as a remedy. She purchased the mirrors and placed one right next to each service rep's telephone. That meant when the reps picked up their phones, they saw themselves talking in the mirrors. With the mirrors in place accompanied by an instruction for the reps to put a smile in their voices, Jan soon noticed a change. After the staff got over the initial trepidation of looking at themselves in the mirror, they became more animated in their facial expressions and gestures. The boring material they talked about with customers started to sound more interesting. Conversations started to take on some friendly chatter, too. The service not only began providing better technical assistance but also increased its people value — something all customers want.

Avoiding body-language pitfalls

You want your posture, facial expressions, and gestures to come across as confident, animated, and relaxed. Certain behaviors, however, make you less than assertive and create emotions that range from disinterest to disgust.

✔ **Slouching:** Some chairs in offices are mighty comfortable, especially the big cushy ones you sometimes find in conference rooms. They make it easy to lean back and relax. Unfortunately when you do so, no matter what kind of chair you're in, you come across as too relaxed. Less energy gets behind your voice as well. Slouching, as you may have been taught as a kid, was no good at the dinner table. It's also no good if you want to assertively communicate and be taken seriously by others.

✔ **Invading space:** This pitfall occurs more when people are standing and attempting to engage in lively conversation. It's where you're getting too close for comfort to the other person. Certainly if that person is leaning away from you, that's a sure sign you've crossed the comfort zone of physical space.

You won't find a hard and fast rule defining what a safe space between people is in any given conversation. Riding crowded subways does not count here. Generally, you'll find the more the familiarity and rapport between two people, the more closely they can converse and still be comfortable. But you probably don't want someone right in your face. Sometimes such behavior happens when you're becoming too strong and agitated with your message — you're falling into the aggressive track (see Chapter 2). Getting closer, and often louder, is not going to better convince someone about your point of view. In fact, it generally does the opposite.

✔ **Hovering over the listener:** Quite often, the person to whom you're speaking is either much shorter than you or is seated while you're standing and talking. You may often be too close in physical space, as well. Hovering over the listener for an extended conversation may make you too close for comfort for that person. If you then raise your voice, you'll become intimidating.

Be sure to talk to people on a level plane. Level plane means physically at the same level, which can be done only when you're seated together. A conversation of a minute or two when you're standing with someone or when you're walking somewhere is different. But when you have important matters to discuss, have a seat with the person or persons with whom you're speaking. When both parties are seated, it gives a sense of ease to the conversation. It no longer matters how tall each of you is. In a chair, you're physically equal and more comfortable talking with each other.

✔ **Looking blank:** This is the facial expression with no emotion. While it's good to use when you're playing poker, it's useless when you need to express an important message to someone else. It conveys a lack of feeling, one way or another, for your own message. If you look disinterested, others will come to feel that way fast.

✔ **Looking stern:** This facial expression usually is displayed with furrowed eyebrows and a near frown or scowl. It has an uninviting, if not intimidating, feel to it and causes your listener, more often than not, to want to disengage. It has a tendency to increase or exaggerate the sharpness in your tone of voice as well — behaviors that put you on the aggressive track.

✔ **Displaying threatening gestures:** The most common examples here are demonstrative finger pointing at someone else or pounding a fist on the table. These gestures often are part of strong messages and have you coming across aggressively instead of assertively. They intimidate, if not disgust, your listener — not exactly positive motivators.

✔ **Showing no gestures:** Sometimes people tuck their hands in their pockets when speaking. Others keep them under the table. Some keep them folded tightly together or pasted tightly to their legs. When your hands look cut off and are nowhere in sight as you're expressing your message, you take away one of the strongest ingredients you can use for positively engaging the attention of others. Without using gestures, you can appear stiff or timid — behaviors that have you moving on the nonassertive track.

✔ **Folding your arms:** Folding your arms when speaking is different from folding them as you listen. When you're listening, as long as you don't look closed off, folding your arms helps you appear relaxed and receptive to hearing someone else's message. When you're speaking, however, folding your arms makes you come across as stiffer and less interested in your own message — signals that are the opposite of what you want to convey.

✔ **Exhibiting distracting habits:** Picking, scratching, twirling hair, and pulling on jewelry are a few examples of habits that people exhibit when they're talking to someone else. These habits distract your listener from hearing the message and bring attention to you rather than what you have to say. They either turn people off or make them want to laugh for all the wrong reasons.

Putting the Oomph in Your Voice

Your voice is a powerful tool for delivering your message in an assertive manner. When not used wisely, it can easily cause you to come across as nonassertive, passive-aggressive, or aggressive. When used wisely, however, it makes others pay attention to what you have to say.

Using your voice to effectively get your message across

The emphasis on the vocal tool for assertive speaking is not about the physical quality of your voice. You have what you have. And like everyone else, you never sound like you think you will the first time you hear your voice recorded on tape. No, the emphasis is on utilizing the richness of your voice in terms of volume, inflection, and tone, so that your delivery commands positive attention. Here are some tips for using this tool:

✔ **Project your voice.** Are you audible enough when you speak? The idea is to be heard loud and clear. This effort becomes even more important when you're interacting in group situations such as meetings. The tendency many people have, especially in group meetings, is that if they don't hear you well, they ignore what you're trying to say. They're less likely to ask you to speak up and repeat yourself.

Therefore, vary your volume for the situation. Go a little louder in group situations, and then turn it down slightly for one-on-one interactions. Always keep it at a volume that makes your voice easy to be heard.

Using the volume of your voice wisely can help you put a greater emphasis on an important point that you want to make. Increasing your volume at an important point commands attention, and sometimes softening your volume at a particular point of emphasis has the effect of drawing people's attention closer to you. In either case, the variation from your normal volume helps the point you're trying to make stand out — an effective and assertive way to get people to truly listen.

✔ **Show inflection in your voice.** Inflection deals with your pitch. If you're at a high pitch, your voice comes across as shrill, which nobody wants to hear. More common, if you stay at one pitch, and a rather flat one at that, you sound dull. Who likes to listen to dull-sounding people? The key to being assertive is to have variety — known as *modulation* — in your pitch. In particular, modulation makes your voice pleasant to listen to and conveys energy in your message.

Like volume, showing a greater variation in the inflection of your voice when you want to drive home a point helps you command positive attention. Exhibiting slightly higher or slightly lower levels of enthusiasm about the point you're trying to make draws your listener's attention to that point.

Knowing when you want something important to stand out, and then using variation in either volume or inflection to highlight that importance, comes across to the listener as confidence in your message — an assertive characteristic that tends to positively engage the attention of others. Therefore, it's a good idea to know what's vital in your message so that you assertively apply your voice to help convey that importance.

✔ **Display sincerity in your tone.** Tone wraps up the volume and inflection in your voice. It conveys the feeling of your message and, therefore, plays a huge part in what your message means and how others receive it. You want your tone to communicate a sense of importance in your message, greatly affecting whether the message is clear.

You also want your tone to communicate sincerity. When you're sincere, your message is better received. Sincerity certainly is impacted by the words you say, but it is greatly affected by the tone of your voice. In fact, a tone of sincerity basically says to the other person, "I mean what I say, I say what I mean, and I do so with respect toward you." When your tone communicates this kind of message, you're in control. When you're in control, you can have a positive influence in your interactions and thus assertively get your point across as you want others to understand it — productivity at its best.

Avoiding vocal pitfalls

Your voice can often be your greatest tool for communicating your message positively and effectively to others. However, when it isn't used assertively, your voice can be your greatest hindrance to being understood in the best possible way. Here is a list of pitfalls that make you sound less than assertive:

✔ **Sounding uncertain:** When your voice sounds shaky or hesitant, you sound unsure about what you're saying. If you sound uncertain of your own message, no one will have confidence in you or what you say. Your voice serves as a barometer of the amount of confidence you show in your message. For instance, when your voice lacks confidence, you're on the nonassertive track and you're not taken as seriously as you want to be.

✔ **Being too soft-spoken:** When you're not audible enough to be heard well, the likelihood that no one is listening to you increases. If you can't speak up to be heard, you come across as lacking confidence in your own message.

The emphasis here is on being *too* soft-spoken. Some people, as part of their communication style, tend to be soft-spoken, yet it isn't overdone. They're what I call E. F. Hutton assertive types. Like the old advertising campaign for the former investment firm ("when E. F. Hutton speaks, people listen"), these individuals command attention whenever they talk. Their voices may not overpower anyone, but they have just enough oomph, along with a sense of certainty, that they are heard quite well.

✔ **Mumbling:** Mumbling has elements of being too soft-spoken and sounding uncertain. Sometimes you mumble as you're talking out loud to yourself or as you're changing directions in your message. Because people can't make out clearly what you say when you mumble, some make the assumption that you're saying something negative under your breath. Others just get the impression that you're unsure about what you're talking about. Overall, mumbling detracts from a clear and confident message.

✔ **Being too loud:** When the volume in your voice is too strong, you're put on the aggressive track. You come across as overpowering and sometimes intimidating to others — especially when dealing with problem situations. If you sound too loud for what the situation calls for, you seem out of control. If you have to shout to be heard, generally no one wants to listen.

✔ **Dropping your voice at the end of a sentence:** This is a common pitfall for many people. You're hearing them fine but as they get to the end of a sentence or key point, the volume of their voices becomes almost silent. The sentence then sounds incomplete, as if a word or two were left out. When you sound like you lack the energy to complete your sentences, your receivers often lose your message and lose interest in hearing your message.

✔ **Sounding monotonous:** Monotone is the dreaded low-pitch sound in your voice, which when it is heard continually through a message, creates considerable disinterest in the message. No inflection in your voice usually translates to no attention gained from others. Think about it for a moment. If you sound disinterested in your own message, how can you expect others to take an interest in that message? It ain't gonna happen.

✔ **Putting people down with your tone:** Tones that sound like you're arrogant, patronizing, or condescending hit people quickly with a feeling of disrespect — regardless of your intentions. Any better-than-you sound in your tone of voice is a pitfall to definitely avoid.

✔ **Having harshness in your tone:** You communicate much of your message's emotional meaning through your tone of voice. When negative situations happen — welcome to the world of work! — and associated emotions enter into your message without any self-control, people may take your meaning far worse than you intended. For example, your frustration sounds like whining; your feeling down sounds as though you're defeated. Because most people haven't been trained to listen for and understand feelings, they don't pick up on your concern. Instead, when they hear negative emotions sounding out of control in your tone of voice, they feel defensive or turned off — usually the opposite of the reactions you want to have happen.

The key to adjustments to your tone is to manage the emotions and have seriousness enter your tone to join in with sincerity. This is what captures people's attention in a positive light and makes what you have to say worth listening to instead of dismissing it.

Your emotions greatly influence how people receive your messages. In fact, try this out. Ask someone to receive your message twice and give it to them twice. Make it a short message of two to three sentences and start out by saying, "Something that concerns me is. . . ." First say your message in a very frustrated-sounding manner. Vent with the best of them. Then repeat the same message in a serious and sincere tone.

To which message will the other person respond more favorably? The message that is serious and in a sincere tone evokes a response of interest. People will pick up more on your concern and want to deal with it. The first message sounds more like you're whining. Few people have the patience to listen to that.

Managing Your Pace

Pace is the rate at which you speak. It determines how fast or slow the words come out of your mouth and how clearly those words are heard and understood.

Using pace to effectively get your message across

Many people speak at the same rate in every interaction. Who they're talking to has little effect on their speaking pace. Within the United States, certain regions are often influenced by certain patterns of speech. If you're from the Southeast, you may speak at a slower rate than many people may from other parts of the country. Conversely, if you're from the Northeast, you may speak at rates faster than many people may from other parts of the country.

On the other hand, no hard and fast generalizations can be made based on where someone lives or hales from regarding the pace of his or her speech. In today's workplace, people often have grown up in places far different from where they're working now, including many from other countries around the world. Education and many other factors that affect their speech patterns have influenced them. In other words, a wide variety of people come into our workplaces with a wide variety of communication styles. That's why maintaining a steady pace of speaking so your words come out clearly and exhibiting a flexibility to relate to the people with whom you're talking are so important.

This tool is about finding the happy medium with your rate of speaking somewhere between too fast and too slow. A steady pace can help you speak effectively with a wide variety of people. At the same time, this tool tells you to sometimes vary the rate a bit, especially based on the type of audience you're addressing.

Here are some tips for applying the pace tool:

✔ **Enunciate your words clearly.** Enunciation is about saying words as they are meant to sound. Are you goin' to the meetin', or are you going to the meeting? Do you have some-un importin' to say, or do you have something important to say? These subtle differences (and the list is quite lengthy) are often noticed by your receivers and at times create confusion — exactly what did you say? — or a sense that you're not certain or knowledgeable about your own message. When people start judging how you use vocabulary, they're less tuned in to what you mean and you no longer have their attention.

Enunciating words clearly helps you greatly manage your pace. It keeps you focused on saying your words well so they'll be clearly heard, as opposed to rushing your pace and slurring your words in the process. When you enunciate clearly, your words and the meaning of your entire message are more easily understood and captured by your listeners.

✔ **Insert pauses occasionally in your message.** What's your hurry? Thinking before you speak and allowing yourself the chance to breathe comfortably enhances your message. That's what pauses do for you. Instead of racing ahead or thinking out loud with all sorts of filler sounds, pauses help you smooth out your pace, gather your thoughts, and enunciate your words clearly. Simply give yourself permission to think and breathe as part of your speaking habits.

Showing a variation in your pace adds flavor and significance to key words. It also helps those words to stand out more clearly to your listeners. Sometimes this means speeding up from your steady pace as you say a key phrase or sentence. Sometimes this means slowing down from your steady pace at these critical points. In either case, managing pace with this gas pedal and brake being applied adds an emphasis to your message that makes it more appealing to be heard.

✔ **Match your pace of speaking with your listener's pace of speaking.** This last aspect of pacing is close to but not quite the same as *mirroring*. The main idea with mirroring is that your communications matches what the other person in the conversation is doing — from body language to use of words and rate of speech. Sometimes that effort goes too far. You either try to mirror so much that you lose track of the message you're listening to, or you come across as mimicking someone else.

The idea is to tune in to the other person in the conversation and show some flexibility based on that person's communication style. For example, if you're talking with someone who is highly expressive and speaks at a fast rate, pick up your pace a bit. If you're conversing with someone who has a low-key, reserved communication style, slow down a bit. Focus on being on a similar pace level with your listener. When your pace is the opposite of the person to whom you're talking, your message often becomes harder for that other person to listen to — and that has nothing to do with how fast he or she is able to listen. People generally receive and take in messages at rates faster than they're being said.

Pace helps build rapport. Having good rapport with someone else is having a working relationship with mutual trust and respect. We normally work best with people who have those qualities. When you manage your pace to be at a level similar to the level of the person with whom you're speaking, you show that you relate well to others. When people think you understand where they're coming from, the likelihood of their understanding where you're coming from with your message is much greater.

Avoiding pace pitfalls

Four main pitfalls of speaking pace are highlighted here. You may see yourself in one of them, and if you do, welcome to the human race. Now go after correcting them and manage your pace to come across assertively.

- ✔ **Speaking too fast:** If you're familiar with the stereotype of the fast-talking used-car salesman, you'll immediately recognize this pitfall. When your pace of speaking is at a rate that's so much faster than your listener's speaking style, emotions are heard at an exaggerated level — you're too excited, you're overly anxious. As a result, your sincerity and confidence levels don't come across, so your listener isn't connecting with your message.

- ✔ **Slurring words:** Words sometimes are slurred because someone's speaking pace is too fast, but at the heart of the problem is the repeated unclear enunciation of your words that sometimes sounds like they're being combined together with the same effect as when someone drinks too much. When your message sounds less intelligible, you can guess how it is going to be received — or in this case, not received.

- ✔ **Speaking too slowly:** Kind of the vice versa of the pitfall of going too fast, speaking too slowly, saying one sentence in the time it takes someone else to say three, may cause your listener to lose patience in following what you're trying to say.

The point is to tune into your speech pattern and be aware of how you come across. If you're fast, but so is the person you're speaking with, you're fine. And if you talk at a slow rate, and so does the other person, you're fine too. The idea then is to look at your rate of speaking like driving a car. Sometimes you need to hit the brake and slow down, and sometimes you need to hit the gas pedal and pick up your speed. When you manage the brake and gas pedals of your speaking rate, you'll do just fine communicating with all sorts of people.

- ✔ **Using excessive filler sounds:** Frequent sounds that people make when they're talking, which often occur between sentences but also at times at the start and in the middle of thoughts, have the effect of chopping up and putting hiccups into your pace. They clutter your message and make it difficult to listen to and understand.

Filler sounds more often are heard in what are called *nonwords*. Nonwords are sounds or words that people say that aren't really words that attach to their messages. Here are common forms of nonwords:

Uh

Um

And (when it starts to create run-on sentences)

Like

Okay

You know

When used occasionally in a message, nonwords aren't that noticeable, but when they're used frequently, they distract the receiver's attention away from your message casting doubt as to whether you really know what you're talking about. For example, look at the following response given by this person when asked how his meeting with his team went yesterday:

"You know, uh, the meeting yesterday, um, went fairly well. You know, we, uh, had some like, uh, tough issues, um, to tackle, and you know, how some of the, uh, team members, like, can be, when you have, uh, sensitive issues to discuss, and uh, we put them, you know, on the table. You know um, what happened, uh, then. Okay, you know, it got, like, heated for a bit, and then, okay, people started talking, uh, about solutions, and uh, you know, we came out, um, in the end, you know, quite well."

Listening to such a message is torture. Yet people do this sometimes as they're formulating thoughts or searching for words out loud. The key to minimizing the nonwords is to make better use of pauses. As mentioned before, pausing allows you to think first and provides a smooth delivery to your pace — much more appealing to listen to. Contrast the previous message to the one that follows where the person spoke and had pauses between the thoughts:

"The meeting yesterday with the team went well. We had some tough issues to tackle and certainly some sensitivities came out initially. Eventually we were able to focus on coming up with solutions and got everyone involved. So the final outcome turned out well."

Maintaining the same pace

The following story helps illustrate the importance of communicating at the same pace as the person with whom you're speaking.

Allen worked for a Chicago-based company that had a manufacturing plant located in a small town in Arkansas. Allen was sent to the Arkansas plant on a month-long assignment to interview many of the employees and gather information about their jobs and job situations. Prior to leaving on the assignment, Allen's manager gave him one little instruction.

"Slow your pace of speaking down when you're working at the Arkansas plant. Don't be mechanical about it, but just be conscious of it."

When Allen asked why this instruction was important, his manager didn't give him a direct answer. He merely told him to give the suggestion a try. So the point stuck in Allen's mind. When Allen arrived at the Arkansas plant —

it was his first time being there — he soon discovered that most of the employees were native to the area and generally spoke at a slow rate. So in the course of his conversations during the month, Allen made a conscious effort to slow his sometimes fast-speaking rate, taking things at a slower more easy-going pace.

Allen's work went well and he was on schedule for completing his assignment as the month drew to an end. Just prior to his departure, one of the staff members supporting Allen's efforts at the Arkansas plant gave him a compliment. She said, "You're not like the rest of the damn Yankees who come down from the Chicago office. They're always in such a hurry that you can hardly talk with them. In your case, we can talk to you."

Allen's question about his manager's suggestion was answered.

Chapter 8

Speaking in the Positive

. . . .

In This Chapter

▶ Understanding positive language and how to show service and commitment with it

▶ Making your verbal messages clear and concise

▶ Using language that solves problems

▶ Avoiding words that hinder your messages

. . . .

*S*ticks and stones can break your bones but words can never hurt you. You probably heard this old nursery rhyme when you were a child growing up. Parents give this advice to their children so the children don't let something someone else says bother them.

Unfortunately, it isn't true. Words that you say to someone else can hurt. Although words don't create any physical bumps or bruises, they can hurt others emotionally. And quite often, people recover sooner from physical bruises than they do from emotional ones. In fact, you've probably met a few people in your life who can remember the stupid things you said, sometimes years ago. (We usually call these people "family.")

How you use language greatly influences how people receive and understand your verbal and your written messages. Chapter 7 focuses on nonverbal tools (how the message is said) for assertively communicating your messages. This chapter focuses on verbal tools for assertive speaking — the substance of what you say. In the work world, all style and no substance often doesn't go far. You need both of them to come across positively to others.

Yet language is a funny thing. Two people can be speaking the same language and not understanding one another. Or they can be aggravated by what others are saying even when intentions are meant to be good.

The idea, then, is to *speak in the positive*. This phrase summarizes the package of assertive tools for using language in your interactions. In brief, it's about saying your messages the best way possible.

Being Powerfully Positive: The Can-Do and Will-Do Uses of Language

If you're like most people at their jobs, co-workers, superiors, and subordinates are asking things of you all the time. They want you to provide answers to their questions. They want you to perform certain duties or functions. They want to know when you're going to get something done. The list of requests and inquiries you get goes on and on. In summary, people from internal staff to external customers have expectations, requests, and inquiries to which you can respond and act accordingly. Isn't that why you're being paid to do your job?

Much of how you manage and then meet these expectations ties into how you communicate about them with others. Communication starts by understanding how to use language in its most powerful and positive form. The package of positive-speaking tools is first defined in this section and is followed by two aspects of the tools that help you better manage the expectations of others — explaining what you can do and will do to respond to people's inquiries and requests.

Speaking in the positive

How you use language has great influence on others. When you speak in the positive, you're being honest, direct, and constructive. Take a look at what each of these ingredients means:

- ✔ **Honest:** That old expression "honesty is the best policy" nicely summarizes the first key ingredient of speaking in the positive. Communicating honestly means being straight and truthful with others, having nothing deceptive or insincere in your language. In my experience, most people are able to honestly tell what they think about an issue — as long as they feel safe in doing so.

- ✔ **Direct:** Direct means simply getting to the point and doing so with tact and respect. Sometimes people confuse directness with being blunt. In assertive speaking, you're direct. In aggressive speaking, you're blunt. Being blunt doesn't take the other person into consideration and often is hurtful in the way the speaker gets to the point. It also is less clear than direct speaking. Here is an example that contrasts direct and blunt speaking:

  Direct: "You have a spot on your shirt right by the pocket."

  Blunt: "Look at your shirt. Ever heard of napkins?"

✔ **Constructive:** Being *constructive* is being as objective as possible in the words you say. Sometimes, people tell it like it is and get right to the point, but then ruin their messages by using *destructive* words. That isn't speaking in the positive. Whether the issue is a sensitive one or you have good or bad news to report, being constructive means making your point with words that make the message clear and respectful.

The following examples contrast constructive and destructive uses of language to make the a sensitive point:

Constructive: "I had a chance to review the marketing plan that you submitted yesterday. It's going to need revision to meet our needs. Let's review what's needed and strategize on the corrections to be made."

Destructive: "That marketing plan you did just isn't going to cut it. If this is the best you can do, you've got major problems."

Avoiding sugarcoating or putting a positive spin on your words

You probably remember this message as a kid: *If you don't have something nice to say, then say nothing at all.* The meaning of speaking in the positive closely resembles this saying, but expands on it by adding that if a point is important to make, you must say it the best way possible. Sometimes, people think they are speaking in the positive (but aren't) by sugarcoating or putting a falsely positive spin on their words.

Sugarcoating

Sugarcoating is trying to sweeten a bad message, an effort to make tough news not sound so bad. It often involves trying to say something nice even though that nice point isn't necessarily relevant to the main issue at hand. The problem with sugarcoating is that it tends to make the message less sincere and direct, which in turn, can make a message more bitter than sweet for the receiver.

Compare these two messages:

✔ **Sugarcoating:** "Sarah, I know you worked hard on this report. Maybe I didn't make my directions clear to you. I know you want to do a good job. Next time, I'm sure you'll do even better when you have to do another report. Just let me know how I can help you."

✔ **Speaking in the positive:** "Sarah, I reviewed your report. A few parts need some revisions. Let me show you where they are needed and then talk with you about making the corrections."

In the sugarcoated message, the speaker tries hard to be nice and not hurt Sarah's feelings. An implication is made that Sarah's report needs improvement but that's as far as it goes. In this soft, nonassertive (as described in Chapter 2) approach, Sarah doesn't get a clear picture of what was done wrong. In instances like this, the receiver often dismisses the message because no sense of importance is conveyed.

In the second case, the message is spoken in a straightforward manner. The language is clear, indicating that parts of the report need to be fixed. The mystery is gone and no harshness is delivered. This is an assertive approach.

Putting a positive spin on the message

When you put a *positive spin* on your message, you make something sound better than it is. That is far different than saying something in the best way possible, as you do when speaking in the positive. In the latter case, you're not shying away from making an important point; you're just not saying it as harshly as possible. You're using language that combines tact and clarity.

Here are two messages from a manager to his group. Both are about the same point and deal with a tough situation. One attempts to put a positive spin on it and the other speaks in the positive.

- ✔ **Positive spin:** "This decision by management is really a good one for you. Remember that our jobs are about adapting to change and keeping this business moving forward. If you keep this in mind, the new strategies will work just fine."

- ✔ **Speaking in the positive:** "I recognize some concerns have been expressed about management's decision to change directions in our product development strategy. I know that affects what we have been working on the last few months. Our focus on this issue will be best served by gaining an understanding of the rationale behind the decision versus having an opinion poll about it. Therefore, I want to inform you of this rationale, and then have you discuss with me how we can implement this change within the team to make it work for us."

The positive spin scenario makes the situation sound like management's decision was in the best interests of the employees. No one is buying that message because it doesn't address the real issue about how change is affecting the employees' work efforts and direction. The comment, "Our jobs are about adapting to change," may strike some as condescending. Everything sounds fine and dandy, which brings the sincerity level of the message into question.

The speaking-in-the-positive response acknowledges concerns people have with the decision. It doesn't attempt to insincerely defend a questionable decision — yet, at the same time, it doesn't openly criticize it either. This message focuses attention on what's more important, understanding the rationale behind the decision, and then working on its implementation — an assertive approach to a tough situation.

Emphasizing what you can do instead of what you can't

Sometimes when people respond to the requests of others, they hit on only one or two of the three key ingredients for speaking in the positive. Honesty is the most frequently used ingredient followed by being direct. When they leave out the constructive ingredient, they sound less than helpful.

For example, suppose someone in another department asks you to research something in your area and report back with your information tomorrow. Check out the following two responses and identify the one to which you would respond more favorably and why:

> ✔ "I can't get that information for you tomorrow. I won't be around all day to do any of the research."

> ✔ "I am leaving shortly for an off-site meeting today. What I can do is work on that research when I return and have the information to you the day after tomorrow."

The same message is evident in both responses: The request can't be handled as quickly as was requested. The first response, however, doesn't let the requester know when the request can be completed. The second response does, and that makes it the one to which most people favorably respond. Not only is it honest and direct like the first response, but it's also constructive.

Emphasize what you *can* do far more than what you *can't,* especially in response to requests and inquiries. Using this language tool effectively often requires a shift in thinking. Like many people, you may be used to reacting to customer or co-worker questions with the first thought that pops into your head. When the request isn't something that you can do or that you know about, out pops that unhelpful response. Here are few common unhelpful responses that people often employ to start their replies:

> ✔ "I can't do that right now."

> ✔ "I don't know what happened to that item."

> ✔ "I won't know for at least two days."

When you lead your message with remarks like these, even if you communicate something helpful, the other person may not hear it that way. Because the first comments out of your mouth indicate how you can't be of any help, what possible good can come from listening further?

However, when you emphasize what you can do first and foremost, you lead with a positive rather than a negative statement. Quite often, if you can steer clear of what you can't do, you come across as honest, clear, and helpful, which evokes a positive feeling in return.

Here's how the unhelpful responses like "can't do," "don't know," and "won't know" sound after changing the focus to what can be done:

- ✔ "Based on a few other matters I need to handle now, I can take care of your issue by the end of today."

- ✔ "I can give you a status on that item by the end of tomorrow. I first need to check on what happened with it."

- ✔ "I can give you an update in two days. I'll know more about where that issue stands then."

The three revised responses essentially convey the same messages as the ones emphasizing the words can't, don't, and won't. The key difference is the revised responses emphasize and lead with what can be done to help. Yet the revised messages still make clear that the desire of the moment isn't going to be met right away. People can live with not having every desire or demand met right away, when the emphasis of your message is on how you can help meet them in due time.

Emphasizing what you can do is especially helpful in situations where what is requested isn't exactly — but is in some way related to — what you do. It's also useful when the request isn't something you can fulfill, but you have access to alternatives or options that still can be done which may be of help. Focusing first on options that can be done always is better than telling the requester that you can't do something.

Take, for example, a situation I have encountered at times: I've been asked whether I offer sales training as part of the services that I provide. I don't offer sales training in and of itself, but I do provide training programs that can relate to a client's needs in this area. Here is how I respond to the inquiries about whether I offer sales training:

"What I can offer is a two-day training program called *Communicating with Impact* that can be customized to address sales groups. Instead of dealing with how to sell, this seminar emphasizes interpersonal communication skills that deal with how you listen and present yourself effectively — both of which are important skills for sales people."

The listener gets something else to think about while still finding an answer to the original inquiry. That person can decide whether what I have to offer meets his or her needs.

Focusing on what can be done is extremely important when you're working in jobs that have regulatory responsibilities, such as those within public-sector organizations like government and education.

For example, instead of telling a citizen what can't be done because it violates some code or policy, why not provide information on the options the citizen can take to be in compliance. Suppose you're working in a building-enforcement capacity for a municipal government and facing a situation in which a citizen is attempting to do home construction without a permit. He has created a nuisance hazard in the neighborhood by leaving building materials and debris all over the front yard. You can say to the homeowner:

"You cannot do any more work on your house because you're in violation of the city codes on building and maintaining property neatly and safely."

Nothing in this message is helpful. It easily sounds like a bureaucrat standing in the way of some poor homeowner who wants only to do something to improve his property.

To speak in the positive, you can say:

"To do the home construction work you want, you have options you can follow before work can continue. You can come to our offices and get the permit you need for the building work you want to do. In addition, you can stack all your building materials together in your backyard and clean up the debris and nails in the front. Take these two steps and you can proceed with the work you desire and be in compliance with all the city building codes."

Mr. Can-do

Milt worked in a materials-handling role that involved shipping and receiving supplies and products and sometimes delivering these items to internal customers. The volume of work at times was high, making for a fast-paced, stressful work situation.

Milt often came across to others as somewhat agitated and stressed out in these more fast-paced, high-volume situations. He would get many requests for items to be delivered, sent, or processed, and often found himself saying he wouldn't or couldn't do what people were asking right away. He thus came across as stressed out and not very helpful.

Then Milt discovered the tool of emphasizing what he could do far more than what he couldn't.

His responses to people's requests changed, "I can have that item to you by noon tomorrow." Or, "I can look into what happened with that package and can give you a status on it within two days." So instead of replying that he couldn't deal with the request at that moment, Milt's responses focused on the actions he could do to help.

Over time, Milt came across to others as more in control and more helpful in getting things done. He felt that way too and seemed to exhibit more of a can-do attitude in his approach. In fact, at times you can hear Milt saying to himself and his team members as a reminder, "Tell them what you can do, not what you can't do."

The latter response makes it clear that regulations need to be followed and work can't be done without that happening. The focus is on informing the citizen about the steps to take to meet the codes and do the work he desires. Help is being given and responsibility is being clearly defined — an assertive approach in using language.

Emphasizing what you will do

In the workplace you're often asked to take action and make commitments, and the people doing the asking want to know when you'll be done with what they need.

For example, suppose you have told someone in another department that you can provide the information that person needs. This internal customer then asks you, "When can you get that information to me?" Which of the following two responses to that request would you respond to more favorably and why?

> ✔ "I'll have that information to you by the end of this week."

> ✔ "I'll try to have that information to you by the end of the week."

Most people respond more favorably to the first response. The second response sounds less certain; you're just going to *try* and maybe not actually do it. The first response says that you *will* get the response done. It communicates a clear commitment — and such communication evokes a positive feeling in the requester.

The old customer service maxim, *underpromise and overdeliver,* stems from situations that often involve the use of the will-do tool. Sometimes you see people do just the opposite in their jobs. They overpromise and underdeliver. In essence, what they say they'll do doesn't happen. They make commitments they can't meet.

The concept of underpromise and overdeliver deals with giving yourself a large enough cushion of time to get things done as you formulate your response to a client's *when* question, "When will you get that work done?" You know that trying to get everything done at once and making commitments without thinking about your own time and the time it takes to do what your clients request only invites trouble and disappointment. And if you say you'll *try* to do it, you communicate a lack of certainty that doesn't help either.

So when you underpromise and overdeliver, you pick a deadline that you can meet or beat. Therefore, when you say, "I can have that done and sent to you by Friday of this week," and you get the job done by Friday at the latest, then your actions have matched your words and you have managed others' expectations of you. Actions that match expectations are key to building credibility in your communications.

Emphasize what you will do, especially in response to questions asking for commitment or an action to be taken.

When you let others know what you will do to handle their requests or inquiries, you're speaking in the language of confidence and commitment. This is the language that has positive influence with others.

A good example of how positive and powerful this will-do language tool is was evident in *The Equalizer,* a television show that ran for few years in the 1990s. The premise of the show was that when you feel in trouble and don't know where to turn, call the main character of the show, the Equalizer. With that premise in mind, you're likely to picture the main character as some big strong macho type. In fact, Edwin Woodward, a short, gray-haired, slightly overweight actor who clearly didn't physically fit the part, played the main character. Yet the character's lines were full of strongly worded will-do statements:

- ✔ "I will help you."
- ✔ "I will ensure your problems are resolved."
- ✔ "I will take care of the situation once and for all."

Delivered with a confident voice, you believed him. Then the character would outsmart and out-tough the bad guys and do what he promised. (Remember this is television.) When actions follow your words, your expectations are met and you feel reassured — benefits for the receiver of the will-do tool.

Telling people what you will do to handle a situation or when you will deliver on a commitment removes uncertainty for the receiver and lessens the tug-of-war feeling that interactions can have. People want to deal with others who are reliable and who set and meet their commitments. When you don't sound fully certain of what you'll do or when you'll do it, the level of confidence people have in you goes down. When someone sounds uncertain, seldom do the actions that follow do any better than the level of uncertainty allows.

Just say no

On those occasions when what the other person wants you to do simply cannot be done, saying no is appropriate and is likely to be the best thing you can do. First, look to offer alternatives or options for the person to consider instead. When that isn't possible, say no to the request and briefly explain why it can't be done. This has you sounding firm and reasonable as opposed to unyielding and autocratic, the latter of which are aggressive characteristics as described in Chapter 2.

Say What? Communicating Your Messages with Clarity

By making your message short and sweet and avoiding jargon, you make your messages clear to others. Quite simply, the clearer your message, the more the listener tunes in to receiving it. The more the message is tuned in to, the more the listener understands it the way it was intended.

Making your message short and sweet

Sometimes people get in the way of their own messages. They say too much or keep talking too long and, as a result, lose the interest of their listeners or convince their listeners not to support their proposal or idea. This is the opposite of what you want to achieve in your interactions.

Concentrate on three efforts with every message you express to others:

✔ **Be direct.** This means *get to the point.* Get there as quick as you can so that your main idea comes out clearly.

Being direct also is about using "I," "me," or "my" rather than "we" or "our" when expressing your own thoughts and ideas. Use "I," "me" or "my" to own your ideas. For example, say, "My idea is about reducing costs," in place of, "Our idea is about reducing costs." "Our" or "we" work only when more than one person was involved in coming up with the idea.

When you're really talking about only one person, yourself or the other individual, use the singular and correct pronouns so that you're direct.

✔ **Be as concise as possible.** Make your points as briefly as possible. Fewer words are better than too many words when making an important point. As the old saying goes, "When I ask you what time it is, please don't tell me how the watch works."

✔ **Focus on main ideas first.** What important points do you want to say? Make sure they stand out when you speak by using details to support them. Don't focus on too many ideas. Having only a few truly main ideas, or sometimes just one main point, keeps your message short and sweet. Through what you're saying, let your listeners in on what's important. The details then make far more sense.

Less is more. Get to the point, concentrate on what's important, and say it as briefly as possible. As a result, you'll come across positive and clear. It all boils down to thinking before you speak — the secret to being an effective assertive speaker. So tune in and catch yourself the next time you think you're getting long-winded. Tell yourself to stick to the point and you will, and your listeners will appreciate it.

Less is more

Clear and interesting messages often stimulate people to engage in discourse about them. That's what less is more is all about. Therefore, stay away from the following traps that people often fall into when talking to others:

✔ **Beating around the bush:** This is about talking around a point as opposed to getting right to it. It tends to rear its ugly head more often when sensitive issues are being discussed. Of course, the more indirect you become with an important message, the less clearly it is understood. See Chapter 3 for assertive approaches to expressing potentially sensitive points.

✔ **Rambling and being verbose:** These two behaviors often go hand in hand. *Rambling* is talking on and on and on, often on tangential subjects. *Being verbose* is using too many words when fewer make the point just fine. Either way, the main point usually is lost.

Avoid starting your message with long prefaces, going off on tangents that take the listener away from your main points and thinking out loud to sort out your thoughts. All of these common habits add unnecessary verbiage to your message, making the job of listening much harder for your receivers.

✔ **Overloading on details:** Details have their place and importance. To resolve an issue, you sometimes need to work through the details. But when you overload on details, your message doesn't have a clear sense of importance. The listener is left with the job of figuring out how all these details fit together, if they do at all. Information overload like this usually turns off most receivers. Don't make them work too hard to figure out what you mean. Most won't bother to do so.

Speaking in terms your audience understands

Jargon is special terminology — usually technical in nature — that only those closely associated with a job or field of study really understand. Organizations often create their own languages, ranging from special terms to acronyms. When such a language is used with new employees, customers, and visitors who are unfamiliar with it, messages quite often become confusing. Because many people are uncomfortable speaking up and admitting they don't understand what some terminology means, they tend to nod and smile and then walk away baffled by such situations. Therefore, be sure to speak in terms you know your audience understands.

Recognize to whom you're addressing your comments and use language familiar to your audience so that it can easily understand your message. Here are some key points to keep in mind:

✔ **Speak in technical terms only when your audience understands the technical language of your job nearly as well as you do.** When technical language is less familiar to the other person, speak in common language or *lay terms*.

✔ **Give statistics or other supporting data relevance and meaning.** Use numbers in terms that are understandable from the listener's perspective. State them in ways that are commonly understood and familiar to persons outside your area of expertise.

✔ **Use acronyms correctly.** An *acronym* is the first letters of a series of words that go together to form a word, such as the FBI (Federal Bureau of Investigation), and NATO (North Atlantic Treaty Organization). At work, you probably have dozens of acronyms that have become part of the lingo of the operation — and even many that are particular to certain departments and not the entire organization. When you must use an acronym, translate it first for newbies or listeners who may not know the term. That way they can clearly follow your message.

✔ **Avoid figures of speech, idioms, and metaphors around people for whom English is a second language and is relatively new.** Language has many nuances and when someone has little experience speaking English, he or she may be confused with the various figures of speech people use. Therefore, express your points in common language rather than the many expressions native speakers often take for granted. For example, say, "Be direct," as opposed to saying, "Don't beat around the bush." Or say "We had a major success on that project," instead of "We hit a home run on that project." If there is an expression you truly want to use, translate what it means the first time you use it.

Employing the Language of Solutions

Problems are a part of almost every job. In fact, developing solutions to problems is what many employees get paid to do. So the fact that you may frequently talk about problems is to be expected.

How you talk about problems and the language you use when you talk about them are important. This section explores language that worsens problem situations and language that facilitates positive solutions and good working relationships.

Avoiding language that dwells on problems

Most problem situations at work involve people. Not talking about problems — a nonassertive approach — doesn't solve any of them. Blaming or pushing guilt onto others when problems arise — aggressive or passive-aggressive approaches — doesn't help either. (These approaches are discussed in Chapter 2.)

When you focus your discussion entirely on the problems and who caused them, negative language comes out and destructive reactions occur. The following messages cause people to dwell on their problems and push positive solutions out of the picture:

- ✔ "Who screwed up here?"
- ✔ "Whose fault is this?"
- ✔ "Why did you do that?"
- ✔ "You're wrong about what happened."
- ✔ "You never help when I need you."
- ✔ "You messed up big on this one."
- ✔ "Why are you causing such problems here?"
- ✔ "Why can't you get this right?"

The list can easily go on and on. The tone of these messages is accusatory. The questions don't really ask for answers but instead make statements of blame. Sentences that start with "you" and "why" in problem situations often create this blaming tone. They hinder constructive discussion from occurring and invite defensiveness or turnoff in return.

Using language that focuses on solutions

When you speak in the positive about problem situations, your language is quite different from that used in problem-dwelling conversations. Use terms and statements that encourage dialogue and focus attention on developing solutions.

When you use the language of solutions, you talk about problems long enough to understand them, analyze them as needed, and then spend more time talking with others about the actions to take to fix them. The following list provides some techniques that facilitate solutions-based language.

- ✔ **Own your message when describing a problem.** Lead your statements with an *I-*, *me-*, or *my-*focus as opposed to a *you-*focus:
    - • "As I see the problem. . . . "
    - • "What I've noticed is. . . . "
    - • "From my experience, the problem deals with. . . . "
    - • "To me, what is happening is. . . . "

✔ **State what you see or what you know.** In talking about problem situations, describe what you have seen or known about the situation. Avoid speculating or offering opinions without factual bases.

✔ **Invite dialogue with questions.** Problems are best defined, analyzed, and resolved as collaborations. The best way to get someone else to join in such discussions is to ask questions — using the active listening tool of probing as covered in Chapter 5 — that truly request constructive input. Remember to avoid the accusatory *why* questions:

- "Describe what you've seen happening here with this problem?"

- "What do you see as possible causes for this problem situation?"

- "Brainstorm with me some ideas to help improve this situation."

- "How would you propose implementing that idea?"

✔ **Focus on solution terms.** Here are solution terms that focus attention on working out solutions:

- Option: "Let's explore some options for resolving this situation."

- Idea: "I have an idea that can help solve this problem."

- Recommendation: "Here's what I recommend we do."

- Suggestion: "May I offer you a suggestion or two on handling that challenge?"

- Solution: "Let's take a look at some possible solutions that can help us."

- Proposal: "I have a proposal that can help resolve this issue."

Emphasize these words when you want to collaborate on creating solutions. They start people thinking about solving problems versus dwelling on them. When you use them, you assertively drive forward possibilities that create solutions — efforts that stimulate positive energy.

✔ **Disagree without being disagreeable.** When you discuss problem situations with others, you may disagree with how they see the problem or — even more so — how they think it can best be resolved. To say nothing when you disagree, especially on the solution part, does you and them a disservice and has you agreeing to plans you don't support. That won't work.

Instead, you want to speak up, but avoid problem-dwelling negative language that sometimes seeps into attempts to talk about solutions:

- "I don't know what we can do."

- "That won't work here."

- "I disagree totally with that idea."

- "We can't do that."

To stay constructive when you have a disagreement, keep your tone sincere rather than debating or attacking. Emphasize in your language what you disagree with and not merely the fact that you disagree. Then offer an alternative wherever you can. State your disagreements after you've heard an idea all the way through and ask questions to draw out the thinking behind the idea so that you fully understand the other person's point of view. In many such cases, you may be able to dwell on parts you agree with most and not on parts you disagree about — a positive approach.

For example when you disagree with a point someone makes, you can start out by saying any of the following:

- "Joe, I disagree with that point and let me explain the reasons."
- "Sue, let me give you another point of view on that issue."
- "Jose, let me suggest an alternative that may work even better."

Staying Away from Speaking in the Negative

The preceding sections of this chapter focus on how to use language to get your points across in the most positive way possible — being honest, direct, and constructive. This section aids that effort by reminding you of language that people often use that does the opposite of what is intended. Often this is language you may think is harmless, but it ends up muddying your message.

Avoiding language that hinders your message

In this section, you can find several categories of useless or negative language that prevent your message from being received as well as you desire. View these examples as language to minimize (if not rid yourself from using completely) so that you can fully speak in the positive.

Loaded language

Loaded language is comprised of words or comments that offend, insult, hurt, anger — or all of them together — or otherwise trigger a negative emotional reaction regardless of your intention. "Idiot" and "stupid" are some common examples. Calling someone an "idiot" or calling something the person has done "stupid" seldom gets a laugh or a smile in return.

Sexualized language

When you comment in the workplace about someone's anatomy or sexual activity, you're certain to offend that person (or friends of that person) without even trying. Harassment laws aside, I've yet to meet an adult who didn't know that language of a sexual behavior is unwelcome and offensive in the workplace.

Stereotypical and derogatory remarks of a personal background nature

When you make comments that deal with who people are — their color, ethnicity, religion, age, weight/stature, sexual orientation — with sweeping generalizations or other pointed comments, you're certain to offend and anger.

Profanity and vulgarity

I know that you need no examples here. An occasional cuss word among close associates is seldom a big deal. Frequent use of swearing soils a good message and calls your intelligence and education into question.

Gender-specific nouns

Saying *policeman* instead of *police officer, fireman* instead of *firefighter, foreman* instead of *supervisor, mailman* instead of *postal carrier* shows little consideration for people today, especially women: For the few who cry "political correctness," that's not what I'm talking about. Instead, this is simply about showing that you live and talk in the 21st century and can show respect to everyone with whom you interact on the job.

Trigger words

Trigger words aren't negative by definition but they often trigger negative reactions from listeners. Here are some common examples of trigger words:

- ✔ ***Always, never,* and *constantly:*** These words are the language of absolutes. No exceptions exist when you use them and, as a result, they seldom fit the receiver but create much harm.

 "You always make that mistake."

 "You never help me when I ask you."

 "You constantly interrupt when I try to make a point to you."

- ✔ ***Should, must,* and *need to:*** In the context illustrated in the following examples, *should, must,* and *need to* are used to order others around.

 "You should do this right now."

 "You must do it this way."

 "You need to correct that problem."

Issuing commands tends to work much less in the workplace than in the military. At work, such comments usually trigger responses that communicate "Don't you tell me what to do!" (Don't try these words at home either.)

✔ ***Not* and its cousins *can't, won't,* and *don't*:** These words become trigger words when they're heard initially in response to someone's request or inquiry. In such situations, the receiver hears a lack of helpfulness and openness — major turnoffs for most people.

Not also comes in the form of *un* attached to the front of words, such as unfortunately, and has the same negative effect.

✔ ***Try, maybe, perhaps,* and *may*:** As one participant in my seminars put it, these are *the wimpy words*. They communicate doubt and uncertainty and no sense of commitment.

"I'll try to get that assignment done this week."

"Maybe I'll get this assignment done this week."

"Perhaps I'll get this assignment done this week."

"I may get this assignment done this week."

✔ **Promise:** As the saying goes, promises are meant to be broken. Sometimes when you have to *promise* you'll do something, doubt and uncertainty are communicated instead. If you'd just do what you say, you wouldn't need to promise it.

"I promise, I'll have an answer to you by the end of the week."

✔ **Policy:** In this context, the word *policy* makes you sound inflexible and gives the impression that you're hiding behind a rule that you really don't understand. Explaining how a process works or the rationale for decisions is much better than giving a pat answer that has you hiding behind a policy.

"I'm just following the policy."

Trigger phrases

Trigger phrases are similar to trigger words: They're phrases that are unnecessary to say, add no real meaning to your message, and sometimes disengage your listener from hearing your message in a positive light. Here are few common trigger phrases and what runs through my mind when I hear them:

✔ "To be honest with you." (Were you being dishonest the rest of the time you were talking to me?)

✔ "You know what I mean." (Not really. You haven't explained yourself very well. Is that what you're telling me?)

✔ "Trust me on this one." (Now I won't and why should I, anyway?)

Mixed messages

Mixed messages are statements of contradiction in the same sentence. They usually contain the words *but, however,* or *although* in the middle of the sentence. They attempt to start the message by saying something nice like: "Joe, I know you've been working hard lately, but. . . ."

What follows the *but* usually is criticism — the main point of the message. The attempt to be nice in the beginning is wiped out and the sincerity and directness of your message are greatly diluted. When you use a word such as *but* in the middle of your thought, *but* communicates to your receiver that what you said before it didn't really count, and you couldn't convey your real point to him or her. Better to be direct and sincere.

Qualifier statements that negate your message

These are statements at the beginning of the message that prepare your listener to tune out the message that follows — the opposite of what you're trying to achieve. Here are a few examples:

- ✔ "Now don't take this personally. . . ."
- ✔ "I don't like to have to tell you this. . . ."
- ✔ "I don't think you'll like to hear this. . . ."
- ✔ "I'm not saying that you're not open to new ideas. . . ."
- ✔ "I don't think you'll understand this. . . ."
- ✔ "Now don't take this the wrong way. . . ."
- ✔ "This isn't probably a good idea. . . ."

As you see in these examples, these qualifier statements tell your listener not to listen to you. They communicate a lack of confidence in your own message or a fearfulness in approaching a difficult issue.

Let your receivers evaluate your messages for themselves. Delete these negating statements from your language. Chapter 9 touches on ways to open your messages to gain positive attention. In brief, give a message that starts out saying something to the effect that, "I have an important message. Please listen." Then get to the point.

Responding in the positive

This section gives you a few examples of responses to inquiries and requests. After first reading the less-than-positive responses, think of how you would revise them to speak in the positive — being honest, direct, and constructive in your language. Then compare your revisions with the sample revised responses that are provided.

Seeking an answer to a question

Requester says: "What's the part number on this item?"

Initial response: "I don't know the part number on that item. I wasn't working with that order."

Revised response: "Let me check the order book to familiarize myself with it. I can have an answer for you on this item by the end of the day."

The revised response removes the trigger words — don't and wasn't — from the initial response. It communicates an action to be taken as opposed to sounding helpless.

Dealing with a demanding request

Requester says: "Here's a change I need to make on my work order. I'd like to have it ready within two days."

Initial response: "My group can't get that work done in two days especially when you come to us with these last-minute changes. This job is going to take at least three days."

Revised response: "Based on the work that is involved with this change, my group can have what you need in three days."

The initial response sounds like a complaint. Comments like "can't get that work done" and "last-minute changes" are sure to irritate the requester. The revised response in a straightforward manner communicates a brief rationale and a commitment as to when the request can be met — a good way to manage expectations.

Forgetting about something important

Requester says: "I want to get your input on the issue we talked about briefly last week so I can go forward with my assignment."

Initial response: "I don't recall what your issue is all about. Unfortunately, I've been really busy lately with more important matters."

Revised response: "Please refresh my memory and bring me up to speed about your issue so I can give you some input to help."

The initial response communicates a lack of interest, perhaps even a dismissive tone — "busy with more important matters lately." It adds a couple of trigger words ("don't" and "unfortunately") that also hinder the message. The revised response lets the requester know that you need to be reminded about the issue and that you do want to engage with the person about it.

When you give positive messages as you intend, you're truly speaking in the positive and using language at its best to make your points.

Chapter 9

Keeping Your Listener Engaged

. . . .

In This Chapter

▶ Introducing issues and bringing them to closure

▶ Keeping your listener involved with your message

▶ Preparing a plan of communication for important situations

. . . .

*W*hen you have something to say to others — co-workers, your manager, a client, a vendor, or your staff — you want to be heard and understood. As mentioned in Chapter 1, however, people seldom are taught to truly listen effectively, so you can't count on your listeners to be attentive and interested even when you have something important to say.

Getting your listener's attention requires you to express your messages in a positive and confident manner. If you don't show interest and certainty in your own message, how can you expect others to want to hear it? You want your listener *engaged* (that is, tuned in and interested) with your message. When your listeners are engaged, the likelihood of your being understood and coming across well increases. Similarly, the opportunity to influence others to action when needed also presents itself.

When people are disengaged from you and your message, your communication with them is troubled. Listeners become disengaged for many reasons, but mostly from what they sense in you — disinterest, disgust, disrespect, and disillusionment. You can minimize disengaged reactions and maximize engaged reactions by helping listeners to sense your enthusiasm, enlightenment, and interest (which you can spell "enterest" if you want!).

This chapter helps you engage and influence your listeners. It gives you strategies to express your messages in an organized manner and tips for helping your listeners feel connected when you speak so that you can enhance their understanding of what you have to say. When your listeners are engaged, good two-way communication is a-happenin'.

Several nonverbal tools of assertive speaking also help you deliver your messages in a positive and confident way (see Chapter 7). Moreover, your language influences your listeners to tune in to your messages on the same frequency you're transmitting them. Being direct, clear, honest, and constructive with your language (see Chapter 8) are critical factors in helping listeners understand your message.

Making Your Conversations Open-and-Shut Cases

Have you ever felt lost for a while when someone just starts talking to you and reporting all kinds of information like gangbusters? You probably wondered what the message was all about. Have you ever conversed with another party about several issues, but when the meeting ended, everything still seemed left open or unfinished? You walked away unsure of who was going to do what or whether any resolutions had been reached.

These kinds of conversations, often about important matters, are common occurrences in every type of workplace. People sometimes dive into their messages before the listener is ready to follow them and other times talk about issues but don't think or work to bring the matters to some kind of closure.

In this section, I provide you with methods for assertively opening your conversations and bringing them to positive closure. The context, like the rest of this book, is when you have important messages to express and discuss with others — generally every day at work. Casual or strictly social conversations are not the emphasis here, but neither are formal presentations (covered in Chapter 14).

Staging the grand opening

The best place to start is at the beginning. Your important messages must come across in a clear and organized fashion as soon as you open your mouth to speak.

Take a look at the following two initial statements about the same topic. They're the first words that start a conversation with a co-worker. From which one do you get a clearer idea of what the main topic is about?

> ✔ "John, I want to talk to you about the proposed customer service training program. What I want to work through with you in our discussion is the length and content of the training."

> ✔ "John, I think a full day, at least, is needed if we are going to do justice to this training program. I also think the training should emphasize dealing with customers over the counter. We're asking staff to do more work at the counter these days and that has now become an important part of our service delivery. In addition. . . . "

I'm sure you'll agree that the first message is the clearer. The topic (proposed customer-service training program) is stated up front, and two points to discuss with it are identified. No details have been given yet, only the main topic for the discussion. As a result, John knows what you intend to talk about before you jump into the details of your message. He can easily follow along because he is aware of the main topic to which he can connect all your thoughts. You have set the stage well.

The initial statements of the second message are potentially confusing. They bypass the topic and go right into the details. If John listens carefully, he may realize these thoughts have to do with some kind of training, probably relating to customer service. It will likely take him some time, however, to catch on.

I remember an important meeting I had with a client. I was working on a project with the vice-president of human resources regarding a new change in her company's performance-review system. The purpose of our meeting was for me to play a support role to her as she presented the plan for the change to her boss, the company president. After our initial greetings and some small talk, the business of the meeting began. The vice president jumped right into the details of the plan. After about a minute — and I was cringing inside as the president had this confused look on his face — he interrupted and said, "What's this all about?"

The vice-president stopped and said, "Oh, we wanted to go over the proposal for the new performance-review system and how to roll it out into the company with you." The president said fine and the rest of the meeting went well.

To assertively open or introduce your messages, do the following:

> ✔ **State the topic.** Tell your listener the main subject of your message. What is this conversation going to be about? In a previous example, the speaker wanted to talk about the proposed customer-service training program. That's a topic.
>
> By stating your topic in your opening, you prepare your listener for how everything that follows in the message is related. It's like the frame in which you put a picture.

> When you state the topic of your message, do so in one sentence. In many cases, that is all you need for your opening and then away you can go into the details of your message.

✔ **Identify and introduce your theme.** The theme is the main idea you want your listener to think about as you express your message. It's the overriding point that you want to make. Here's an example:

"John, as I share some ideas with you about what we should do for customer service training, I want you to know that everything I'm going to suggest is about making the program hands-on and practical for the staff."

The topic is customer service training, and the theme of the message is to have a training program that is hands-on and practical. By stating this theme at the beginning, your listener gains an understanding of where you're coming from with all the thoughts or ideas you're about to express. Details make much more sense when they connect to a main idea or theme.

✔ **Provide context.** Context gives your receiver a brief picture of the overall situation or background of an issue. Providing it is like setting a scene for a movie clip you're about to watch. Here's an example:

"Steve, as you know, we on the executive team have discussed the need to create a more meaningful performance-review system for the company. I've worked with Marty during the last few weeks to design such a system. So in our meeting today, we want to review our plan for the new review system and how we can roll it out in the company."

In the first two sentences, the speaker provides Steve with some context — in this case, some background history — about the issue of the performance-review system. The plan for the improved system is the topic for the message to come. By providing this background first, the listener gains an understanding of what led to this point.

✔ **Tell your goal.** Explaining the goal of your message clues your receiver in on what you want to accomplish in your discussion, the outcome for which you're aiming. Here's an example:

"John, as I talk to you about a few changes I see we need to make for the proposed customer service training program, I want to reach agreement with you on those changes so that we're ready to go forward with starting the program."

The goal is clear in this opening — agree upon the changes to make to get the training program started. Stating this goal upfront gives your message a focus on results and prepares your listener to work with you to get something done out of the conversation.

✔ **Lay out the structure.** To help keep your discussion on track when you know it's going to be deeply involved, set the structure for your meeting right upfront. The structure is the agenda the discussion follows, a brief outline of where you intend to go with the conversation. Here's an example:

"John, as I talk to you about a few changes I have in mind for the pro-posed customer-service program, I want first to describe those changes and then get your feedback on them. From there, we can reach consen-sus on what changes to make and finish by discussing implementation of the training program."

As you see in this example, setting the structure of the discussion is a list of the areas to cover. You provide no detail on purpose, because you want to give your listener a clear, organized, start-to-finish picture of where your discussion is headed.

✔ **Set the tone.** When you have a sensitive issue, set the tone for what you want to discuss. The tone is the feeling and behavior you want to have with the other person. To be effective, the tone you're seeking needs to be positive. For example, in a serious discussion, you want constructive dialogue; an open and honest exchange. Your opening message also needs to set this tone in a positive way — what you want to see happen as opposed to what you don't want to see happen.

Contrast these two examples:

"Sue, I want to talk with you about some problems I'm having with the new procedure you recently asked me to use. As I talk to you about them, don't be defensive or rigid in our discussion about improvements."

"Sue, I want to talk with you about some problems I'm having with the new procedure you recently asked me to develop. I want an open and honest exchange to get your help coming up with ways that this procedure can be improved."

The first response includes the trigger word *don't,* which gives the mes-sage a negative focus. (See Chapter 8 for more about trigger words to avoid.) The second response states a *positive intention,* telling the lis-tener, Sue, that you mean well and want something good to come out of your discussion. (See Chapter 11 for more about what a positive inten-tion is.) It sets a tone that invites a positive discussion.

✔ **Prepare the listener for what he or she needs to do.** Sometimes you want your listener to do something constructive after hearing your mes-sage. Here's an example:

"Betty, after I describe how this system conversion project works, I would like you to take what you've heard, ask questions about anything that was unclear, and tell me the pros and cons you see in what I'm proposing."

In this example, the listener is asked to be ready to take actions on what she hears. Such requests when asked in a positive way with reasonable consequences, move your listener from a passive to an active state of listening, focus your listener's attention, and prepare your listener for constructive involvement in your conversation.

Be sure to focus the listener's actions on how to respond to your message, not on how to think about it. Avoid telling people how to think, which usually causes them to disengage from your message. Instead, let people formulate their own opinions but help them to tune in so they know what you want in terms of feedback.

Putting on the finishing touches

In old cartoons and movies, you knew when the show was over because the words *The End* came up on the screen. Because you probably don't carry a sign around with you when you talk, you find other ways to let your listeners know when your conversations are over.

You want your conversations to end with a clear result established. Rather than leave an issue still in doubt — what's going to happen next, who's going to do what action, has an agreement been reached — you want to make sure closure is achieved, giving you and your receiver a sense of completeness and accomplishment. It lets you know your work is done or what the future is for the issue. Clarity prevails over confusion, results over time wasted.

Dealing with defensiveness

Here's how a manager handled an employee who became defensive in problem situations.

Teri received a phone call from a customer with whom her employee, Ken, had dealt the day before. The customer, Don, complained to Teri about Ken's manner in handling his account. From the specifics given by Don, Teri knew she needed to address the issue with Ken. From previous encounters, she knew if she raised anything sounding critical to Ken, he would react defensively with tension in his voice, interruptions, comments of denial, or counter arguments. These behaviors made it difficult to resolve anything with Ken.

This time, however, Teri put into practice an assertive opening to her conversation with Ken. She said: "Ken, I want to share with you some concerns expressed to me by Don of the ABC Account you worked with yesterday. First, I'm going to share the feedback. Then I want to talk with you about what happened and get your help to work out a solution as to how to best address Don's concerns. In our conversation, please listen in an open and receptive manner the whole time and then take a solutions-oriented approach to help define steps to take to fix this problem."

Ken, squeezing the arms of his chair much of the time, avoided becoming defensive. He heard Teri's feedback, debated none of it, and came up with corrective steps to take to fix the problem with Don — the outcome Teri most desired.

In this story, Teri set the topic in her first sentence of the introduction. Then in the rest of the sentences, she outlined the structure for the discussion, set the constructive tone she wanted, and prepared Ken for what he should do — all in one paragraph. Short, sweet, and focused . . . those are the kind of openings you want to set when dealing with potentially challenging interactions.

Here are a few ways to assertively bring your conversations to positive closure:

- **Recapping:** A recap is a summary that leaves your listener remembering the main points of your message. Like opening statements, when you close with a recap you want to be brief. Generally, stick to summarizing a maximum of three main points, because if you talk about any more than that, you're probably getting into too much detail and not giving your listener a clear sense of closure. Here's an example of a good recap:

"To sum it up, the customer-service training program in what I'm proposing is one day in length and filled with hands-on practice and includes instruction on dealing with customers over the counter."

This example, in one sentence, recaps the speaker's message by briefly summarizing the three main points but steering clear of a boring, if not confusing repetition of the details. That's what an effective recap does.

- **Stating what you need:** Similar to recapping, this type of closure gives your receiver specific actions to take or support to give, thus meeting the needs of your situation. Although you're not making demands, you're closing by briefly summarizing what you desire to have happen. Here's an example:

"So Alice, to close, for my team to help your group get through this tight period, we'll need you to give us all your research plus options you've tried to solve the problems raised."

This closing comment invites acknowledgment from the receivers of what you need them to do. If you don't get that acknowledgment right back, then simply ask, "Will you do that?" This question erases any doubt of whether the other party is willing to respond to the needs you've expressed.

- **Setting next steps:** On many occasions, you may be collaborating with someone else on an issue where more work needs to be done. So as not to leave the "what's to happen next" implied or unclear, set the next steps to be taken as you work together. You can suggest these next steps or ask your receiver to help plan them all with the idea that you're not done with your conversations until the next steps are defined. Here's an example:

"Andy, based on ideas we have agreed on for this project, how about this plan of action? You test these ideas with your group, and I'll do the same with my team, and then we can meet again in a week to review their feedback and see if we need to make any changes. Does that sound good to you?"

This kind of closure sets directions for each party and enables the project to move forward positively and on the issues — important efforts for achieving productivity on the job.

✔ **Asking for agreement:** As you work through issues with others, you may think a conclusion that everyone agrees upon has been reached. However, unstated agreements often mean no agreements. Just because no one objects doesn't mean that everyone agrees. When conclusions appear to have been reached, bring certainty into situations by asking for agreement. Here's an example:

"Bob, to wrap this up, do you agree to support the marketing strategy I've outlined here today?"

This one-sentence close is asked as a direct question that seeks confirmation. If the other person says no, then you know you need to work through unresolved concerns by continuing the discussion. Leaving issues unconfirmed creates misunderstandings that result in opposition. Asking for agreement replaces doubt and assumption with certainty and support.

✔ **Asking for commitment of action:** Another good way to assertively bring closure to a conversation is to ask for commitment of action. This usually means asking when someone is going to take actions that have been discussed. Here's an example:

"So Julie, when can you get back to me with an answer to the issue that I raised?"

Sometimes asking for commitment to an action is making an effort to confirm what commitment has been made. Here's an example of this:

"To confirm, Bob, you'll handle all the research tasks associated with this project. Is that correct?"

When you're asking for agreement or for commitment of action to bring a discussion to closure — these two efforts sometimes go hand in hand — you want your questions to be close-ended. (See Chapter 5 for more about the two ways to ask questions.) By purposefully using close-ended questions, you're seeking short, definitive responses. You want to know if the other person says yes or no to what you've asked or when an action will occur. The definitive response pushes the other party to clearly agree or commit, leaving no uncertain issues.

Helping Your Listener Stay Involved

Now that you know how to set your messages up so they're focused and organized, and how to effectively bring them to closure so that issues are not left in doubt, you need to know what to do in between the opening and closing of your important messages. The emphasis on the in-between parts helps keep your listeners excited about listening and gaining a good understanding of your messages. The tips and strategies that help achieve these objectives build upon the nonverbal and verbal tools of assertive speaking as covered in Chapters 7 and 8 and describe what you can say, do, and ask to help your listeners stay actively involved in your conversations.

Adding meaning to your message

This section offers tips on ways that your message can be better understood and more interesting to hear. Use these suggestions to make your messages more appealing and easier to follow.

Using visual aids

Visual aids can help others see or read your message. They come in various forms:

- Graphs and charts
- Handouts
- Written reports
- Pictures
- Diagrams and drawings
- Articles
- Computer graphics
- Maps
- Slides

When you're expressing an important message, visuals provide data — pictorial or written — that support your key points. These aids help provide a clearer understanding of your message. If, however, they become the focus of the receiver's attention, they can distract and diminish the clarity of your message. The idea is to show and refer to visual aids when you make important verbal points. Here are a few examples:

- "You'll see on the front page of the handout the key recommendations that I'm going to explain to you in this discussion."
- "Look at the graph here (pointing) to follow the trends in customer responses to our advertising program that I am going to highlight for you."
- "This picture gives you an idea of the waste problem we've been having at the plant."

Showing what you mean

When you can, show what you're talking about to make your message clearer.

In my early work history, I had a job in which I had to write job descriptions. The best approach for doing so was interviewing the employees to find out what their jobs entailed. Because I didn't have the technical expertise to easily understand what their jobs were all about, I asked people to take me out to the manufacturing floor and show me what happened in their jobs. When we went back to the conference room and they started to describe their duties, I followed along more easily without being a technical expert.

Seeing is believing. More important, seeing helps your listeners understand your topic. Take the person to the scene of the event to explain what you mean. To describe how the equipment works, put the other person in front of it. To explain the features of a product, demonstrate it as you talk.

These showing-what-you-mean efforts familiarize your listeners with and establish a foundation for your message, thereby enhancing the ability of your listeners to understand what you mean. They often have the effect of encouraging them to ask questions along the way — all adding to the effectiveness of your presentation.

Telling stories and anecdotes

A characteristic common to people of all ages is that they like to hear stories. When you use a story or anecdote in your message, the key is to tie it to the point you're making. To effectively use a good story or anecdote, you want to be able to answer these questions:

- How does the story or anecdote connect to the point I'm making?

- How does the story or anecdote support the point I'm making?

- How will the story or anecdote help listeners to better understand my message?

When you tell stories or anecdotes so that they clearly support the point you're making and they're tied into and not isolated from that point, they make your messages much more interesting to listen to and easier to understand.

Don't read from your visual aids

Avoid reading to your listeners, especially when your visual aids contain written information. Reading what people can read for themselves has two major drawbacks. First, it insults people's intelligence. It isn't like you're reading a bedtime story to them; people can read for themselves. Second, reading information to others doesn't come across as well as telling people about the information, because reading generally results in less eye contact with your receivers and often puts you into a monotone voice — a boring look and sound that causes most people to tune out. Therefore, speak up and highlight portions of your visual aids so that they're truly aids to your verbal message.

The longer the story you tell, the less effective it is for illustrating your points. If you're testing people's patience to wade through the heavy details of your story, you may not have their attention when you want your story to connect to your point. Likewise, the less organized the flow of your story, the less your listeners can make sense of it.

Adding good sense to your humor

Humor often adds a nice touch to important messages. When done well, humor eases tension and relaxes people.

Humor builds rapport with the audience when:

✔ Your receivers laugh *with* you and not *at* you. They don't feel as though you're laughing at them.

✔ Making light of a situation relaxes your receivers but doesn't distract them from the seriousness of your message.

✔ Your receivers relate to your situation and laugh if they feel like it was fun, and not because they're expected to laugh at any certain point.

Steer clear of poor taste

The following are pitfalls to avoid with humor because they detract from the importance of your messages and usually turn off your listeners:

✔ **Sarcasm:** Sarcasm is different than wit. Wit is the clever remark that makes people chuckle. Sarcasm is the biting remark said in so-called jest that people more often take personally as a put-down. Saying, "Now don't take this personally," neither lessens the sting of sarcasm nor makes it sound more witty. Instead, it more than likely shows the speaker to be a dimwit.

✔ **Ridicule:** Ridicule sometimes contains sarcasm. It's kidding that goes too far. Some people aren't comfortable at all when you kid them, especially when your intent is to express an important message. Ridicule makes people feel that they're being laughed at and that they're the butts of your jokes — definitely the wrong feelings to evoke when you want people to connect to your messages.

✔ **Off-color jokes:** These are jokes of a sexual nature or about people's personal background such as race, ethnicity, religion, and sexual orientation. While some people laugh, others in a workplace situation are greatly offended. It doesn't fit into the workplace — in fact, it can get you fired.

✔ **Trying to be a comedian:** If you're trying hard to be funny, the sense of importance of your message often is lost and you won't be taken seriously. And if you're trying hard to be funny, you may be in the wrong line of work. When humor is forced, it tends to lose its positive effect.

Stories often work best for allowing humor to fit in the flow of your important messages. They recount life's experiences that others can relate to in different ways and cause people to laugh because they find familiarity in what they hear to be funny — the best way for humor to happen.

Getting your listener to respond

As a speaker, you can invite your listeners to more actively participate in your conversation and thus help your message be heard and understood in the ways you most desire. This is done by requesting feedback, encouraging questions and then answering them, answering questions with questions, checking for understanding, and tuning in to how your message is being received.

Requesting feedback

Did you ever have a conversation at work with someone who, after you expressed something important, just sat there with a blank look and had no comments, no smile, nor even a frown? Such experiences leave you wondering whether the person likes or dislikes your message, whether there is agreement or disagreement, and whether your conversation generated interest in your message. You don't know what impact your message had when you get a passive, no-feedback response in return.

Avoid repeating yourself in these circumstances. Finish your point and then ask open-ended questions such as the following:

- "What do you think?"
- "What do you see as the pros and cons of what I expressed?"
- "Tell me your view of the issue I've described."
- "Give me your evaluation of the recommendation I'm making here."

Open-ended questions, covered in Chapter 5, solicit responses that require the expression of thoughts, ideas, or feelings. They can't be answered in a word or two the way close-ended questions can. When you're talking to a passive listener, open-ended questions work well by allowing you to switch from the role of speaker to that of listener in the conversation. Sometimes you can tell your listener in the opening to your message that you want feedback. You can even explain toward what you want that feedback directed after you complete your message (see the "Staging the grand opening" section, earlier in this chapter). Then when you hit that point, directly ask for what you want.

Encouraging questions and answering them

When your receivers are asking questions about your message, your job of expressing it clearly gets much easier. Questions from receivers provide you the opportunity to clarify key points, address concerns, and persuade people to see another point of view. In simple terms, questions help you greatly.

Therefore, you have to take actions to encourage questions from your receivers. Here are a few ways that help:

✔ When you have a fairly long message, tell listeners up front that they're welcome to ask questions at any time.

✔ When you get a question, provide positive reinforcement, "That's a good question," or "Thanks for asking."

✔ When you finish expressing a point of considerable length, say, "What questions can I answer for you?" Open-ended questions like this work far better than the more commonly used close-ended questions, such as: "Do you have any questions?" or "Do you understand what I've told you?" Rarely does anyone say no to the latter question and only occasionally does anyone say yes to the former, but neither of these two questions sparks much response from your receiver.

✔ Answer the questions clearly and positively.

The best encouragement for prompting others to ask questions is for them to see someone who is receptive to questions and gives clear and direct answers. To effectively answer questions from your receivers, avoid the following comments, which cause receivers to disengage:

✔ Comments that express disagreement or suggest the other person is wrong right from the start of the answer.

✔ Comments that criticize the person for raising an issue.

✔ Comments that ramble and never get to the point.

✔ Comments that sound like an excuse, which usually contain a but in the middle of the initial thought (mixed messages as described in Chapter 8).

To effectively answer questions from your receivers, be direct and concise. In more involved conversations, use this three-step approach to handling questions:

1. **Open your response with a positive or an affirmative.**

   "Yes, I'm glad you raised that issue."

   If you're not fully certain of the question that was asked, paraphrase first to make sure you're clear. This effort also helps give you time to think of a response.

2. **Give your explanation in answer to the question.**

   Provide examples or anecdotes as needed to give specificity to your response.

3. **Close with a brief recap of your answer.**

   Make this recap a one-sentence summary.

Answering a question with a question

You occasionally can answer a question initially with a question. This tip is best to use when you're asked a challenging question and you want to gain more insight into the questioner's thinking. Here are a couple of examples:

"Sandy, I hear a concern about something in your question. What is that concern about?

"Bob, please help me understand; what prompted your question?"

As these examples point out, you're switching from a speaker to a listener in the conversation. Your purpose is to gain a better understanding of where the other party in your conversation is coming from. You may even want to paraphrase or reflective paraphrase (see Chapter 5) the explanation behind the question you hear. Thus, when you respond to the issue raised, you're more likely to address the real core of it, rather than give information that may not be the focus of the other person's need or concern. Therefore, even when you need to speak, listening first sometimes is the better strategy with which to start.

Checking for understanding

Sometimes a better way to find out if your message was clearly received is to ask your receivers to explain their understanding of your message. Slightly different than the request-for-feedback tip, here you're going after understanding alone, not after what the other person thinks about your message.

To check for understanding after you've expressed a lengthier message, use an open-ended question. You can sometimes preface your question by saying something such as the following:

"To make sure I'm clear, what's your understanding of what my message was all about?"

When you periodically check for understanding, you help avoid misunderstandings and encourage your listeners to speak up, letting you know when something isn't clear.

Tuning in to how your messages are being received

This last tip for getting your listeners to respond to your messages is about reading the nonverbal messages that your listeners sometimes express when they hear your message. Tune into tone of voice and body language and, in particular, their facial expressions. Sometimes you identify looks such as concern or confusion.

When you see looks like these, instead of proceeding with your message, respond to what you see. Sometimes you can do this by adjusting your vocabulary or pace to better connect to your listener. Even better, you can be direct and reflect back what you think you're seeing:

"You look confused by what I'm saying. Please tell me about it."

Such reflections invite your listeners to share what's going on in their minds and provide you opportunities to make adjustments or address listeners' concerns. They turn the nonverbally responsive person into a verbally responsive one, which makes your job of getting your message across clearly, concisely, and positively a whole lot easier.

Developing a Plan for Sensitive Issues

From time to time you may encounter situations in your job in which you need to deal with sensitive issues or important matters. You want these critical interactions to go well.

Quite often, people wing it — they just show up and start talking with little prior thought and organization about how they want the meeting to go. Do you know what happens in critical situations when you speak before you think? You may be misunderstood, or overreact to people's comments. Simply put, you're less likely to experience a successful outcome if you speak off the cuff.

Mapping out your strategy prepares you for these challenging situations and develops your communication plan of action for how you want a serious meeting to go. When you have a plan, you'll likely achieve the positive results you're aiming for much more often than when you don't have a plan.

Knowing when to map out your plan

In what situations is mapping out a plan of communication beneficial for you? This kind of preparation is something to do for special occasions; that is, critical situations in which important or sensitive issues need to be addressed, where being organized and careful in what you say are crucial for influencing positive outcomes.

Here are some special occasions for which mapping out your plans may prove beneficial for you:

✔ **Making proposals to management above you:** Sometimes you're wanting big things to happen and you know you need management consent for them. Maybe it's the purchase of major equipment, the addition of staff to your team, or a significant change in policy or strategy. In any case, you want your recommendations to sound thorough and organized — a perfect occasion for mapping out your plan first.

✔ **Addressing conflicts or concerns with others:** Suppose you have a problem with someone else; something is not going the way you want it to. Emotions are definitely involved. You know that not addressing the situation won't help it get any better. And winging it in sensitive situations usually causes emotions to get out of control — especially your own. Thus, this is another perfect occasion for mapping out your plan before entering a sensitive situation. (Chapter 12 provides you with problem-solving models for these kinds of conflict situations.)

✔ **Handling client meetings:** You have an important meeting coming up with a client or customer. You need to show what you can do to win the client's business or solve a critical problem with a customer. Preparation is going to be key to achieving positive results; therefore, map out your plan first.

✔ **Leading group meetings:** Trying to lead a meeting without an agenda, while common in many a workplace, is asking for trouble. A meeting agenda is a form of mapping out your plan. It helps you establish the structure you want to have for the meeting and maintain the focus of the participants — important factors for having productive meetings.

✔ **Reporting important news to others:** This situation presents itself when you're in a management role. You may be faced with telling about a significant change to come — personnel changes, business changes, or cutbacks in jobs. These are the kinds of changes that greatly affect other people in good and bad ways. You definitely want to be ready with your communication points outlined in advance.

✔ **Persuading others to support your major idea:** If you have an idea that needs the support of team members or staff from other groups to become reality, then mapping out your plan ahead of time may be helpful.

✔ **Delivering important presentations:** Many people need to make formal presentations to fellow team members, to management, to other teams, or to customers. These are critical situations when you want to come off well and definitely opportunities for mapping out your plan first. Chapter 14 covers how to effectively organize and deliver such presentations.

Mapping out your plan

The aim of mapping out your plan is to organize your communication effort for when you're speaking face to face with others. While you may do some pieces in writing, you're readying yourself for that in-person communication through which critical issues must be handled. When you're mapping out your communication plan, you're preparing the written outline, supporting documents, and visual aids that you need to have with you at these meetings.

The following sections outline key tips to follow in mapping out your communication plan to increase the likelihood for good results in your important interactions:

Doing your homework first

Know what research you do need to do, what data you need to gather, and what issues you need to understand better. Nothing is worse than communicating something important to a decision maker and leaving out vital information or not having your facts all in order to back you up.

Sometimes you do your homework by reading reports, articles, or other records of information; sometimes you do it by talking to others and getting answers from them. Other times you do both. When needed, homework also involves developing your visual aids and supporting documents to help make your case.

People often are quite impressed when you come to an important meeting and show that you've done your homework. The way you make your presentation shows preparation and thoroughness — efforts that increase the likelihood of your message being received in desirable ways.

Considering your audience in your plans

How you develop your plan depends on to whom you're going to present it. Here are some factors you should take into account:

- ✔ Who is your target audience and what's important to them?
- ✔ What are your audience's hot buttons (critical points you need to address and sensitive points you want to stay away from)?
- ✔ What's their level of understanding of your issue and the language to best use to discuss the issue with them?
- ✔ When is the best timing to discuss your issue and where is the best location to do so?
- ✔ What possible objections or negative reactions are you likely to encounter, and what's the best way to address those concerns, if they come up?

Planning for these factors often is part of the homework you do prior to preparing your plan. If nothing else, homework and planning get you ready to tailor your message best to your listener, emphasizing and generating favorable responses.

Outlining your communication plan

With homework complete and audience factors considered, you're ready to map out your plan in writing. Here are key factors you want your outline to address:

1. **Set the opening.**

   Set your topic and provide context as needed.

   State your purpose; that is, say what you're trying to accomplish in this meeting. Know and state the positive outcome you're seeking.

   Tell your listener(s) what you want them to do so they best receive your message.

2. **Organize the key points.**

   Determine the key points and the order in which you want to make them.

   Determine what stories and anecdotes will help illustrate your points and when to tell them.

   Determine, if you're using visual aids, when best to present them.

   You also need to determine when you're going to provide the positive punch to your message by showing your audience the benefits or positive gains from what you're proposing, the recommended solution for the problem you have defined, or the idea for change that makes the improvements desired.

3. **Get the listener's response.**

   Determine when you want your receiver to respond, at a certain time or at any time.

   Prepare a few questions to invite feedback.

   Prepare responses in anticipation of possible concerns you expect to hear.

4. **Bring the meeting to closure.**

   From a recap of important points to a confirmation of an agreement or an outline of the next steps, set how you want your closure to go.

Tasting a sample plan

Mike was a benefits manager who had been on the job at a large company for seven months. The third party vendor the company used to administer its health benefits programs was inefficient, error-prone, and unfriendly in its service to employees. Thus, what was otherwise a good benefit plan had been a great source of frustration for many employees in the company since long before Mike took on his responsibilities. His efforts to work with the vendor to improve administration and services yielded no tangible results.

Mike scheduled a meeting with his boss, the vice president of human resources, and the company president. While they were aware of the problems, he knew the two executives didn't know the extent of how bad the service had gotten. He prepared a two-pronged strategy: Add a new position to his group and contract with a different vendor he knew from his previous company. Having done his homework, Mike was aware of the hot buttons of the two executives: The vice president had chosen this vendor a few years ago and had a good relationship with executives of that company, and the president was reluctant, outside of the sales area, to add new positions in the company. Mike also knew that they wanted good morale in the company but that neither wanted anything to distract employees from performing their jobs well.

Here is the plan that Mike mapped out for this critical meeting:

1. **Open.**

   Set the topic and purpose: Correct the problem with the company's health-benefits administration and create a cost-effective solution that increases employee satisfaction.

   Ask the listeners to hear the proposal first, and then ask questions and give feedback on proposal.

2. **Make key points** (do so in less than 15 minutes).

   Outline problems over the last seven months and show how they have affected employees.

   Show stories to document and support patterns. Rather than criticizing the current vendor, place emphasis on the effect on employees and the volume of problem cases.

   Show which steps have been taken with the vendor. Emphasize that they have a high volume of clients and it's hard for them to make changes.

3. **Recommend a solution.**

   Highlight how current services can be better handled in two-pronged way — through an additional staff person and by a new vendor who focuses just on claims administration versus handling all service aspects, which can be handled by direct staff in-house.

4. **Show the benefits of the proposed solution.**

   - Show how costs for the new plan are nearly the same as for the current vendor.

   - Show track record reports of the new vendor.

   - Explain how the staff will be more empowered to help employees and how it currently spends much time trying to work through the vendor to do this.

   - Explain how software from the new vendor that will help the staff is included in costs.

   - Explain how the current vendor's contract runs out in less than two months, so transition will be easy.

   - Summarize what these benefits will do for employee satisfaction.

5. Get executives responding by asking the following questions.

- What questions can I answer?

- What aspects of the proposal do you find favorable?

- Can I address any concerns for you?

6. Close.

- Confirm agreement.

- Outline the next steps.

With this plan outlined, Mike felt well prepared to make his case. While he knew he had no guarantee that his proposal would be accepted by the executives, he went into the meeting confident that he could present his proposal well enough to gain their agreement This is the essence of what mapping out your plan aims to do.

Know your audience (especially when it's your boss)

I used to have a boss who was a key decision maker, and I sometimes had to get his approval to make the significant changes that I was proposing in the company. As I got to know him better, it helped me in how I mapped out my communication plan to address an issue with him.

First, I knew he was more alert and relaxed later in the day. Don't tackle critical issues until after 4:00. He also tended to be more relaxed when discussions took place in his office. While he had a general understanding of most of the issues I brought to him, he had a tendency to get bogged down in the details if I wasn't careful in what I presented to him. So I learned to stick to the highlights and give details only when I needed to support a key point.

I also learned that he wanted to hear how what was being proposed was going to help the company and not be a great burden to him or anyone else at the same time. So I focused less on how much something might cost and more on how it will benefit others, less on radical change and more on how the proposal would be a moderate improvement, and less on his involvement and more on how I could handle the implementation.

Part IV
Win-Win Conflict Resolution

"A large part of our success is based on our ability to resolve conflicts before we get to work."

In this part . . .

Conflicts are inevitable at work. The key is not whether you have them but how you deal with them. In this part, you discover how to approach conflict situations in a constructive way instead of turning them into major confrontations. You also add to your toolkit some communication tools that help you manage conflict effectively. Finally, I introduce you to problem-solving models that help turn conflicts into solutions.

Chapter 10

Approaching Conflicts Constructively

- -

In This Chapter

▶ Understanding what works and what doesn't in dealing with conflicts

▶ Looking at assertive and three other common approaches to effectively deal with conflicts

▶ Taking a consistently respectful approach to working relationships

- -

Conflicts are a part of life. Because much of your life takes place at work — as do many of your interactions — the workplace is an environment ripe with conflict. But conflict doesn't have to be all bad. Your approach to conflict situations is the key to whether it is.

Conflicts within the workplace generally involve two issues — those about business concerns and those about working relationships — but all conflict situations involve people. Because people are the source of problems and the key to creating the solutions, interpersonal communications, from listening to speaking, play a major role in the course that conflicts take.

This chapter discusses behaviors and ways of communicating that greatly improve conflict situations on the job. It also presents an assertive approach applicable not only to conflict situations but also to working relationships on a day-to-day basis.

Taking the High Road or the Low Road?

A *conflict* is a problem in which two or more people have a difference of opinions, methods, goals, styles, values, and so on. They are a normal part of most workplaces, and those differences tend to stir up conflict. They also involve situations in which two people rub each other the wrong way — generally referred to as a *personality clash*. But before you can apply communication tools that help you deal effectively with conflicts (see Chapter 11), and before you can apply problem-solving models to gain positive outcomes with conflicts (see Chapter 12), you must first be aware of the behaviors and communication efforts that make or break potential conflict situations.

In other words, whether the outcome you get out of a conflict situation is positive or negative is greatly determined by the approach you take. When your approach sends you down a destructive path — *the low road* — the likelihood of arriving at a good resolution with someone is slim to none. When your approach sends you on a constructive path — *the high road* — you increase the likelihood of achieving positive results. You're the driver; it's up to you what road you want to take.

While you don't control others, you do greatly influence them. When you take control, you have the greatest opportunity to assert positive influence with others. In conflict situations, using your positive influence is the secret to staying on the constructive track and achieving the outcomes you desire.

The low road: What not to do in conflict situations

Being aware of what not to do is an integral part of figuring out how best to resolve conflicts. The list of behaviors in this section put you on the destructive track; they make conflicts much more difficult to deal with and resolve. If you're like most people, you've probably had some experience with these behaviors: doing and receiving them.

In my communication seminars, I ask participants to brainstorm together in small groups answering the following question: Based on your experiences at work, what destructive behaviors should be avoided in conflict situations?

From your experience, what have you seen? Every group I ask to do this activity usually has no problem coming up with a bundle of behaviors to avoid. Compare your list with the following list that I've compiled from participants in this activity over the years — I call it the *destructive dozen*.

> ✔ **Yelling:** Few people respond well when you raise your voice loudly when you're trying to communicate with them. When this happens in a public setting, it comes across even worse. Yelling intimidates some, angers others, and begets yelling in return.

✔ **Blaming:** Blaming is the faultfinding approach. It is verbally attacking someone else and making the focus of the situation personal. When you focus on all that's wrong, you lose touch with the issue that needs to be resolved. At the same time, you discourage — not encourage — people from taking responsibility for their own actions and working with you to come up with solutions.

✔ **Reacting defensively:** This behavior — often the result of interrupting, getting louder, reacting with counterattacks — makes the speaker who raises the issue with you feel like a wall has been erected between you.

✔ **Focusing on perceived intentions:** When you focus on your perceptions of what someone else's intentions are in a problem situation, you're making assumptions. Assumptions prevent you from seeing people's actions and prejudice you into thinking the worst about those actions. They take your focus away from solutions and giving others the benefit of the doubt. See Chapter 1 for more on the problems with assumptions.

You can't see others' intentions, only their actions. When you deal with actions, not perceived intentions, you increase the likelihood of working out solutions for conflict situations.

✔ **Not dealing with the situation:** This is one of the more common behaviors in conflict situations. Conflict situations involve emotion — sometimes a high degree of emotion. Not surprisingly, they frequently evoke feelings of great discomfort. Unfortunately, when some people feel discomfort with something or someone else regarding an important issue, they avoid dealing with it. Yet, the situation won't change on its own. Quite often, the problem gets worse. As long as the other person is unaware that you have a concern with what he or she is doing, that person will never feel a need or have a reason to change anything.

The key in conflict situations is recognizing that comfort isn't part of the equation. Give yourself permission to feel uncomfortable. Then focus your attention not on your comfort level but rather on how best to resolve the issue with the other party. When you take this step, you can face up to these challenges and increase your chances of having a positive outcome.

✔ **Making subtle digs and sarcastic remarks:** These kinds of comments put others down or belittle them. They're hints containing snide remarks. The touch of supposed humor that sometimes come with these remarks has a tendency to heighten only the tension in conflict situations.

✔ **Making personal insults:** Nothing is subtle about this behavior. Insults are harsh and involve forms of name-calling. When you refer to the actions of others (and sometimes the people themselves) in words containing loaded language like *idiot*, *stupid*, and *dumb* (see Chapter 8), you tend to influence others in such a way that they don't want to work with you toward resolutions — to say the least.

✔ **Complaining constantly about the situation:** In conflicts, the difficulties you're having with someone about an issue certainly can be frustrating. But when one party continuously complains about difficult situations, what may initially have been venting turns into chronic whining — nothing anyone wants to listen to for long at all.

✔ **Issuing ultimatums:** Ultimatums have a tendency to be received as harsh demands or threats. They're the sounds of warning: "If you don't stop or do this my way, this is what I'll do to you." They push power, not reason, as the way to work out the differences. With customers, they cause business to suffer and even discontinue. With co-workers and staff, they create animosity and defiance.

✔ **Pushing harder and harder for your way:** Some people call this behavior *arguing*. It's certainly neither actively listening to the other person's point of view nor collaborating to generate ideas for solution. Generally, the harder you push for your way, with little consideration for the other person's view, the less persuasive you become.

✔ **Sending flaming e-mail messages:** When you use e-mail to voice concerns to others — especially if you copy additional people on the matter — you flame tensions; you don't spark solutions. In fact, what you'll probably get are harsh messages flaming back. When you have sensitive issues to deal with, explaining your concerns by using e-mail — despite your best intentions — usually results in messages that are read and interpreted far worse than you ever imagined. (See Chapter 13 about the good uses of e-mail and misuses to avoid.)

✔ **Going to others rather than the source:** For some people, this behavior is the most destructive one in conflict situations. Some characterize it as backstabbing, telling others about your concern with a particular individual but never saying anything directly to that individual. Telling others about your concern generally sounds like you're complaining or degrading that person. That kind of behavior, however, is great for stimulating gossip and rumors and stirring plenty of negative energy.

The destructive dozen does nothing to work out resolutions in conflict situations. Instead, they escalate tensions, strain working relationships, prevent important improvements from happening and destroy communication and information sharing. In short, they keep you away from resolutions and make animosity, rather than the issue, the focus of a conflict

The keys for driving on the high road

This section shows how to approach conflict situations constructively rather than destructively. Certain skills are necessary in implementing these behaviors (see Chapters 11 and 12 for these behaviors), but you first must know and incorporate the essential constructive behaviors into your approach so the tools in those two chapters can work. Here are the *magnificent seven:*

EXAMPLE

Stamping out the e-mail flame

Paul was a manager. He knew that his staff sometimes showed a lot of passion for their work, which he liked. He also knew that because of the passions that existed, his staff sometimes disagreed with one another about their work — Paul didn't mind that either. Disagreements stimulate thoughts and ideas and new ways of looking at issues. Paul didn't want a bunch of agreeable yes people on his team.

For Paul, the key was for these conflicts to be handled constructively and between the members of his staff. He had little tolerance when these conditions weren't met.

Sure enough, one day, a staff member named Matt sent a scathing e-mail to another team member, Joe, about what he viewed as Joe's incomplete work on a project. Matt copied Paul and the rest of the team on this message. Upon reading the message, Paul immediately went to Matt's office and without hesitation told Matt in a direct and firm manner how his use of e-mail was way out of line. Voicing concerns over an e-mail, copying others on it, and not talking to the person directly are not the ways to handle a conflict. (See Chapter 13 for more about the uses and misuses of e-mail as a communication tool.)

Matt came back to Paul a day later and told him he had talked to Joe and they had settled their differences. The flame wars had been extinguished.

✔ **Go to the source.** No invention can ever take the place of face-to-face interactions for resolving disputes and conflicts. E-mail can't do it; neither can voice mail. Telling others and not the source doesn't do the trick either. People need to meet directly with one another and use conversation to settle their differences. That old-fashioned, tried-and-true method works best for constructively resolving conflicts.

✔ **Stay in control.** The toughest person you have to manage in interactions, especially challenging ones, is yourself. When you're in control of your own emotions (versus them being in control of you), you're better able to influence the direction of a conversation toward achieving a positive outcome. Having an argument requires at least two participants, but when you're not participating because you're staying in control, the argument dies out. Similarly, making an agreement requires at least two participants, and when you're in control, you increase the likelihood that the other party will join you in reaching an agreement.

✔ **Stay focused on issues.** This action is related to staying in control. Your opponent may exhibit destructive behaviors that can distract your attention from the issues. Regardless of whether the issues at the core of the conflict deal with the behavior of others, different styles, or differences of opinion about how to do a job, the key is to focus on the issues, not on your or the listener's personal opinions, in your discussions.

Focus not on the person but on what was done. Stay away from engaging in behaviors that derail you and prevent you from resolving your issue. When you stay focused on the issues, you're far more able to keep your language and tone constructive.

✔ **Actively listen.** Chapters 4, 5, and 6 explain how to listen actively in your interactions. In conflict situations, your ability to listen to and understand where the other person is coming from is critical in achieving positive outcomes.

It isn't too far of a stretch to realize that sometimes the more you speak when differences flair up, the more you aggravate the situation; while, on the other hand, the more you listen, the more likely you'll gain understanding and diffuse tension. Active listening helps you manage conflict situations by promoting dialogue — a key to success in conflicts.

✔ **Be straight and sincere.** People sometimes worry so much about being nice to others that they can't be clear and honest when they attempt to address their concerns. Conflict situations are neither about being nice nor mean; they're about working out issues and differences to make positive results. Save being nice for social situations.

One of the nicest behaviors, nevertheless, is being honest with your fellow workers, especially when you're attempting to address problems and concerns. That means you need to be direct, respectful in your tone, and constructive in your use of language. In other words, present your message in the best way possible, but don't shy away from making the point — even if it's a hard one for the other person to hear.

✔ **Go for solutions.** When you're dealing with problems or conflicts, your whole emphasis must be to work out a solution with the other people involved. You want to be *solutions-oriented* so that your end result creates an improvement, corrects an error, or makes things better than they were in their previous state.

Being solutions-oriented means being able to define the problem and then develop a solution. Chapter 12 provides you with a couple of problem-solving models with specific steps to follow. If you approach conflicts by defining a problem and working out a solution with the other parties, you're on the high road to success.

✔ **Assume the other person means well.** Chapter 1 touches on the many problems that assumptions can cause: They often lead you to think and act negatively in your interactions. Assuming the other person means well is, however, safe because it takes your focus away from what you perceive someone intends and, instead, places it on the actions you see. What a relief to get rid of all your conspiracy theories! Rather than worry about what you *think* is the meaning of someone causing you concern, you can deal with the actions and the issues themselves and focus on solutions. When you make this shift in attention, your whole approach to your behavior with other people changes and you'll be on a constructive track.

Get Mad? Get Even? Get Over It? Oh, So Many Choices

People use four common approaches to express their messages to others — aggressive, nonassertive, passive-aggressive, and assertive (see Chapter 1). Because most people aren't taught, in basic education, to constructively express messages nor to constructively listen, many people find it difficult to handle stressful and challenging situations such as conflicts in positive ways. No need to feel bad about that, though: Welcome to the human race.

The assertive approach, which utilizes speaking and listening skills, is the most effective for dealing with the two main types of workplace conflict: those that involve business issues and those that involve working relationships. This section contrasts the four common approaches to resolving conflict situations and shows you how the assertive approach offers you the best choice for dealing with these potentially challenging interactions.

The four approaches for handling conflict

The following four sections give an overview of the four common approaches (patterns of behavior and communication) including some of the key actions that appear when conflicts arise. If you see yourself in some of the less-than-positive approaches, flip to Chapters 11 and 12 to uncover new tools and problem-solving skills. But don't feel bad: If conflict situations all were easy to deal with, life would be boring.

The aggressive approach

Aggressive is a hard-charging approach, often interpreted as hostile in manner, in which you come across as seeking to control or dominate. In conflict situations, you don't back down from the conflict; in fact, you go on the attack. The conflict is a competition to be won.

If you're in aggressive mode during a conflict situation, you're likely to do several of the following:

- **You blame.** Finger pointing and finding fault with others for the concern or problem dominate the interaction. When you're on the receiving end of this behavior, you may want to say, "I got my head bitten off" by so-and-so.

- **You interrupt and talk over.** Using the aggressive approach often turns into an argument or debate as you become a combatant, handling the interaction by getting louder, preventing the other person from getting a word in, and fighting for air space by talking more — all behaviors that tend to escalate tensions.

✔ **You push to get your way.** Compromising and listening to the other person's point of view? No way! The way to resolve the conflict is by pushing harder for your own view, being unyielding, and browbeating (verbally) the other person to get your way and what you want.

✔ **You demand and order.** With this behavior, your solution to the concern, without any hesitation, is telling the other person what to do. Directives that sound like orders to be followed usually are stated loudly and harshly — characterized by comments like, "What you need to do is. . . ."

Quite often, in the aggressive approach, all four of these behaviors come together at once — blaming, talking more and getting louder, pushing your way, and ordering. That ought to settle the dispute, right? (Don't try this at home!) The aggressive approach doesn't focus on solutions, nor does it seek to build agreements that both parties can feel good about. Instead, it invites defensiveness and resistance — not ingredients for resolving conflicts.

The nonassertive approach

If you're *nonassertive* in your approach to conflicts, you maintain a passive manner and do not express your rights or views. You let others dominate or control the situation, even if the result is not a positive outcome for you. When you fall into the nonassertive approach, conflicts are situations that breed great discomfort, and your comfort zone becomes the focus of the situation. As a result, the focus of the actions taken tends not to deal directly with the issue at hand nor work on what needs to happen to make something better.

Here are actions common to the nonassertive approach to conflict situations:

✔ **You avoid conflict.** In this behavior, issues of concern with others often are put off and not dealt with. Because such situations often create a great feeling of discomfort, they are commonly avoided even when the problem gets worse. A lot of reasons, which usually sound like excuses, can be given for not dealing with the concern.

✔ **You appease the other person.** In this action, you give in to the other person's demands just to go along and keep the peace — even if those demands aren't in your best interests. You don't want to upset the other person, so you try to be agreeable, hoping that everything will just be fine from here on out. Those who take an aggressive approach in conflict love dealing with individuals who take a nonassertive approach — just ask them to jump and they ask, "How high?"

✔ **You become hesitant and apologetic.** This behavior includes a lot of hemming and hawing. You sound uncertain and say a few "I'm sorry" comments along the way, because you don't want to hurt the other person's feelings. All this hesitancy, however, communicates a lack of confidence and importance in your messages and, not surprisingly, you're not taken seriously.

✔ **You ramble and beat around the bush.** As in the previous behavior, at least *some* effort is being made to discuss an issue with the other party. The problem with rambling is that the message has no focus; the problem with beating around the bush is that points of discussion are indirect and implied at best. As a result, nothing gets resolved and the other person walks away thinking there's been much ado about nothing.

More often than not, in the nonassertive approach to conflicts, an avoidance behavior emerges. The other common behaviors are reactions to challenging situations and usually appear when the conflicts are thrust upon you. Taking the initiative to get an issue of concern addressed seldom shows itself in the nonassertive approach.

The passive-aggressive approach

If your approach to conflicts is *passive-aggressive*, your communications and actions come across as subtle, yet negative, and implied, while manipulative. With the passive-aggressive approach, what appears quiet on the outside has underlying it (on the inside) actions that others receive as hurtful or deceitful.

Here are common actions that the passive-aggressive approach displays in conflict situations:

✔ **You tell others, not the source.** This is the classic passive-aggressive behavior in conflict situations. You engage in behind-the-scenes complaints about the source of the concern, telling everyone except that source. Such actions often stir much gossip, create negative energy around an office, and can become quite disruptive.

✔ **You withhold.** In this passive-aggressive behavior, you refuse to cooperate. You don't pass on important information the other party can use or give assistance that is helpful. You say, "You didn't ask me," when questioned about why something didn't happen. You give the source of your concern the silent treatment and refuse to talk to him or her. This also is a form of withholding — in this case, withholding civil interaction and courtesy.

✔ **You make subtle to not-so-subtle critical remarks.** Sometimes you display this behavior through little put-downs or sarcasm. Sometimes you make openly critical remarks in group situations about something someone else has done, although you never address these same comments to that person individually. In either case, the brunt of your remarks feels the criticism and experiences a lack of direct and constructive communication. Sometimes you communicate your criticism by hiding behind e-mail messages. Instead of talking directly to the source of your concern about an issue, you send him or her a harsh or flaming e-mail message (see Chapter 13).

✔ **You hold in for awhile, and then unload.** This behavior is the aggressive side of passive-aggressive. If you're the recipient of the passive-aggressive's ire, nothing visible is displayed for awhile about concerns with what you've been doing — at best, you receive subtle hints and sarcastic comments. Then one day the person verbally explodes at you and lashes out with personal attacks and blames you for pent-up woes. You may get an apology later, but it often is tinged with veiled remarks that everything still was your fault — a little pushing of guilt that kills the sincerity of any apology.

The passive-aggressive approach to situations where concerns exist tends to be indirect and often characterized by actions that have an *I-don't-get-mad, I-get-even* feel to them. Frustration is stored up and channeled into nonproductive behaviors that sometimes beget such behaviors in return. In the passive-aggressive approach, people shy away from addressing issues directly and constructively but are not shy about showing the negative emotions about the concerns.

The assertive approach

Being *assertive* in conflict situations is about expressing your rights and views in a positive and confident manner, and enabling others to do the same with the intent and effort to work out resolutions. If you need to address an issue of concern, you'll tackle it but do so respectfully so that you promote two-way communication.

When using the assertive approach, here are the common actions you can take in conflict situations:

✔ **Go to the source.** Not through e-mail, not through voice mail, not through a messenger . . . go to the source. In the assertive approach, you go to the other person with whom you have your difference to open up dialogue. This action takes place one-on-one and privately.

✔ **Be direct and constructive in language and tone.** Assertive people don't shy away from expressing problems and describing them as they see them. But language and tone are to the point and tactful (the opposite of being blunt) and focused on the issue — the *actions* of the other person, not directed at the *person*. The message is expressed with a sense of importance, with sincerity, and in the best way possible to clearly make the point.

✔ **Collaboratively problem solve.** This behavior is the big emphasis in the assertive approach to dealing with conflicts, focusing on talking and listening with the other person in an effort to work out a mutually beneficial solution — come up with agreements you both can support. The problem is stated but the emphasis from that point forward is to dwell on solutions (not on problems) and to work through the issues together as partners (not adversaries).

✔ **Stay firm yet willing to compromise.** Being firm means being strong in your convictions and confident in your manner, but not harsh in your tone or language. In this assertive behavior, the emphasis is to get your concerns and ideas across but also to show an openness to hear the other person's input. People compromise as needed because it's good for the solution. Your views and the other person's views are looked at together, along with what's good for the job at hand. No appeasement aimed at getting an uncomfortable discussion over with quickly. Yet no being inflexible so that other possible options are not considered.

When you're using the assertive approach, you're willing to deal with conflict situations regardless of the comfort level you feel. Emphasis is placed on working through the issue with the other person and, more important, to work out solutions. Treating others with respect and problem solving with them are expected — and that's the assertive approach, the most effective in tackling conflict situations.

Scenario #1: A bad idea

Sally is a staff member from another group that you have to work with on a cross-functional project team. Her efforts and yours need to closely coordinate for your areas of responsibility with the project. You have worked with her in the past and found her not too well focused in her communication and work efforts.

Now, as the two of you meet to plan how you're going to handle your project work together, Sally expresses an idea that isn't fully clear to you and that sounds nearly the opposite of what you think should be done.

Take a look how each communication approach would respond to Sally in this small conflict situation:

✔ **Aggressive response:** "Sally, why do you have to waste our time with your off-the-wall ideas! I can't make sense out of half of what you say anyway. Sally, here's what you need to do. Just follow my direction and don't question anything, and we'll be just fine for this project. Got it?"

This response attacks Sally personally and harsßhly and gives her orders about what she should do instead. It shuts her right out of any useful discussion.

✔ **Nonassertive response:** "Uh, Sally. Maybe that idea can work here. I don't know but if you think so, I'm uh open to what you have to suggest. Well anyway, let's talk about this project some more."

The nonassertive response attempts to sound nice; it doesn't want Sally to feel bad for her idea. On the other hand, it leaves the matter unsettled and may give Sally the wrong impression that her idea is indeed acceptable to you.

✔ **Passive-aggressive response:** "Another brilliant idea, Sally (chuckle, chuckle). You just have a way with words that just inspires me so (rolling eyes as remark is said). Just kidding around. If you think your idea can help us, then don't look at me if it doesn't work."

In this response, Sally's ideas are met with snide and sarcastic remarks. Then it finishes with what I call the *whatever-remark* — whatever you want to do is fine but don't count on me for any support for it. This kind of remark is indirect and disapproving. It doesn't invite dialogue to collaboratively work through the issue.

✔ **Assertive response:** "Sally, your idea here is not fully clear to me, and I don't see how it ties into our objectives for this project. If you would, please address these concerns."

Unlike the other responses, the assertive response invites dialogue to collaboratively work through the issue. It doesn't mislead Sally into thinking her idea is a good one but, at the same time, doesn't put her down for expressing an idea. Instead, it clearly and directly states the concern seen with her idea but enables Sally to explain herself. In many cases, this response allows her to leave the thought alone because she then sees that it doesn't pertain to the task at hand. In either case, the choice is hers and nothing is wrong with having made a suggestion.

Scenario #2: The disagreement on who's to do what

You've been working on a critical assignment with Don, a member of your team. As the assignment nears deadline, you realize an important task has not been completed. Your understanding is that Don was supposed to handle this task. But Don has just sent you an e-mail message asking if you got the task done. So you know his thinking was not the same as yours about who was to be responsible for the task.

How would each communication approach address this potential conflict with Don?

✔ **Aggressive response:** You walk down to Don's office and say: "Don, what's wrong with you here! You were supposed to get this key task done for our assignment and now you send me this message asking if I did it. Don't give me this crap. We had an agreement for you to do this task, so don't shirk away from your responsibility. You better get this task done right away and not put us in jeopardy with this assignment!"

As you see in this example, the aggressive response gets right into Don's face, so to speak, and blames him for the problem at hand. Don is under attack and told what he better do right away in no uncertain terms. If Don isn't intimidated by this action, a messy confrontation will ensue.

✔ **Nonassertive response:** Even though you strongly feel this was Don's job to handle and you know that you have a good deal of other work to do right now, you respond to Don via e-mail and don't speak to him directly. Here's what you say in your e-mail response, "Don, I'm sorry. It must've been my mistake. I'll do my best to get this task done."

In the nonassertive response, the speaker doesn't speak directly to Don and, in addition, burdens himself or herself with handling the task and gives an unnecessary apology on top of it — appeasement at its best.

✔ **Passive-aggressive response:** You reply to Don's message with this strongly-worded e-mail note: "Nifty move, Don. Think you can pull off this I-don't-remember stuff at the last minute? You know you were supposed to do this task. All right, maybe this was just an oversight on your part. I can forgive you this time. But please don't let this happen again; it really makes you look like a screw-up when you do."

In the passive-aggressive response, you lash back at Don's hiding behind e-mail. Then you forgive Don with a dig at him in the process, while still not talking to him to gain any kind of agreement. Look out for the flaming e-mail you're likely to get in return.

✔ **Assertive response:** After seeing Don's e-mail message, you pick up the phone and ask Don if he has a moment for the two of you to chat right now. When he says yes, you walk down to his office and initiate your conversation by saying, "Don, I got your e-mail message regarding whether I had done this key task for our assignment and I was worried by it. My understanding was that you were to handle the task and, judging by your message, you thought I was to handle it. So apparently we have a misunderstanding. I think it best if we focus together on what we can each do to help get this task done on time. What do you think?"

Like the aggressive response, the assertive communication goes directly to Don. Yet the assertive way is constructive. It states the problem at hand in a matter-of-fact manner without blaming anyone and then invites Don to collaborate on a solution — solutions-focused at its best.

Using the Assertive — and Best — Approach

Being assertive takes the most constructive stance in dealing with conflict situations. A big part of handling conflicts assertively is exercising judgment and choosing the best course of action for dealing with an issue.

Now or later? When to deal with the problem

Here are three of the better choices of assertiveness and descriptions of when they work best in conflict situations:

- **Dealing with the matter now:** Sometimes, as the expression goes, no time is better to do something than the present. The concern is upon you and addressing it right away with the other party is better for turning the problem around and preventing it from building up and becoming a bigger problem. You feel in control of yourself and ready to speak up and know your emphasis is on resolving the conflict. You're also in a setting, or can create one right away, in which you and the other party can talk privately in a one-to-one interaction.

- **Dealing with the matter at a later time soon:** You know you have a problem you need to address, but now isn't the best time to do so. Emotions may be too high — yours, the other person's, or both. Trying to resolve conflicts in the heat of the moment is often the worst of timing. You may not be ready. You may not have a plan thought out to express your concerns. You may be in a public setting void of any opportunity to talk privately. Sometimes, the present time simply isn't the right time to work on a conflict.

  If you can't address a conflict right away, set a time to meet with the other party while the issue is still fresh. When the matter is important enough not to let go, delaying for a brief time can be helpful, because you have time to prepare and then meet in the near future to resolve the problem. Putting off an issue that you know you need to address (procrastination at its worst) doesn't help and only makes issues harder to handle.

- **Leaving the matter alone:** This third option works only when the matter at hand isn't really that important — emotionally, you can let go of it and not be troubled. Assertiveness isn't about addressing everything that bothers you. It is about picking and choosing your issues. Some matters are small in nature and are easy enough to tolerate and let go. Choosing to act, however, is quite assertive. Showing tolerance for the little issues usually results in your being taken more seriously when you're seen focusing on the big issues. That's true to the old expression: Avoid making mountains out of molehills.

Should I talk about this now? Assessing your own readiness

When using the assertive approach to handle conflicts, you evaluate the best course of action to take before you act. You think before you speak. Here are some factors to evaluate in determining the best choices:

✔ **Your own readiness:** How in control of yourself are you? How well ordered are your thoughts? What are you positively seeking to accomplish? When you have answers to these questions, you know you're ready to address the concern. When you're in control of your own emotions, you're in position to constructively deal with, and not be deterred by, strong emotions from someone else — an assertive action.

✔ **Your need for preparation:** Generally speaking, the bigger the issue involved, the more prepared you want to be to deal with it. Preparation means getting your thoughts in order, setting your objective for a positive outcome, and outlining your agenda for managing the meeting — mapping out your plan as described in Chapter 9.

✔ **The state of readiness of the other person:** People have an easier time addressing problems when they're not stressed or emotional but are in a calmer frame of mind. Mind you, some people may never appear to be in a calm state; nonetheless, you want to choose the moment closest to when this can occur.

Avoid situations with tight deadlines or heated arguments to work out conflicts. Catch people at quieter times of day or set appointments when both of you can get away from the work area and talk more peacefully.

✔ **The impact that the problem or conflict is having or will have:** The greater the negative impact of a problem or conflict, the greater the need to address it sooner rather than later. Although the impact may not appear that great at the moment, you can see the potential for a negative impact in the near future if nothing is done. In these situations, take action and address the issue with the source. Only matters of small importance and little impact — the ones you encounter on a day-to-day basis — are the ones that you can let go and not worry about.

If the issue you've attempted to put aside keeps gnawing at you, it's probably a problem that needs to be addressed. Not doing so is a nonassertive approach. Put your focus on the importance of the problem and its potential impact rather than your comfort level at the time. No one expects conflict situations to be times for great comfort. Conflicts aren't the same as vacations, but they'll ruin a vacation when they're left unaddressed and are still bothering you.

Becoming Assertive: A Guide for Those Who Aren't

You can build foundations, or roadbeds, that make assertive approaches to future conflict situations possible and effective. Such foundations serve as a basis for the way you approach working relationships that you create with staff members, peers, managers, customers, and vendors — everybody that you frequently to occasionally work with.

This approach is one that I refer to as being *consistently respectful*. The following sections explain what this approach means, key principles to follow to make it work, and the benefits you can get from using it. When you have it working, you're in position to handle any conflict that confronts you and thus keep the molehills from turning into volcanoes.

Paving the road to productive working relationships

Being *consistently respectful* is an approach to working relationships that relies on the following two points about how you interact and work with others:

- ✔ I should do those actions that are good for me, considerate of you, and good for the relationship overall and the job we have to do — regardless of whether you reciprocate.

- ✔ My approach is to be constructive in all interactions and focus on getting the job done well — regardless of whether I like you personally.

The *regardless* parts of this definition are aspects that give many people lumps in their throats. Who can argue with a constant desire to have consistently respectful working relationships? But others sometimes act or behave in ways that make it hard to maintain a constructive relationship with them. That's the challenge of being consistently respectful, but that's what makes it so powerful.

Being consistently respectful is not about putting conditions on working relationships, such as "I'm going to help you only if you help me," or "Because you didn't help me once, I'm not going to help you now." It isn't about deciding to treat with respect only those whom you like or with whom you get along and to heck with the rest. It also isn't about avoiding issues of concern because you're afraid of how the other person may react.

In fact, being consistently respectful follows a *win-win* approach in working with others, especially in conflict situations. Win-win means working out issues as best as possible for the parties involved, while maintaining the dignity of the relationship. In other words, mutual benefit with mutual respect is upheld. This means dealing with issues, but doing so in a respectful and solutions-oriented manner with a focus on the job at hand to be done — actions that keep conflicts on a constructive high road.

Being consistently respectful helps you avoid what I call *foot-in-mouth disease* — saying things that you'll later regret. Actions you take out of frustration or anger may cause you to say things you wish you hadn't. When you operate with the consistently respectful approach to working relationships, you increase the likelihood that you'll think before you speak and thereby gain control of your own emotions.

Consistently respectful means thinking before you speak

A few years back, I had an opportunity to start an exciting assignment with a new client. The company vice president with whom I was dealing wanted to make a major investment in training for his people and had reached agreement with me on what services would be provided. A third party then entered the picture and caused the momentum to get the training program running to come to a halt.

The third party was a manager new to the company and out of the corporate office located in another state who had oversight responsibility for the company's training efforts. We had talked briefly over the phone because I worked with the vice president in putting the program together. As we were ready to start, the corporate manager wanted to further evaluate the program to see if it was the right thing to do. In this case, the vice president didn't want to push the issue and, if he had to, was willing to wait. He was fine with my talking to this corporate manager if needed.

After waiting a few weeks, having a few conversations with the corporate manager about the proposed training, and hearing about more steps to be taken to continue the assessment and put in place some kind of mechanism for establishing company training initiatives, I grew quite frustrated. I felt a bureaucratic approach was being used for something quite simple. I saw people being cautious and sitting still rather than making progress and moving forward.

I was ready to pick up the phone at this point and give this corporate manager a piece of my mind. At that point, however, the concept of being consistently respectful entered my thoughts, and as I do in such challenging situations, I asked myself this question: "If I say what I feel right now, how will that help?" When my conscience told me that it wouldn't help, then I knew to rethink my actions and make an adjustment. After I did exactly that, I had a constructive and frank discussion with this corporate manager in which I not only was able to speak under control but also to listen and be consistently respectful. A short time later, the training program got started and went on to become well received throughout much of the company, more so than I originally anticipated.

Keys to being consistently respectful

Being consistently respectful paves the way to a strong foundation for tackling issues and especially conflicts with others. The following key principles make this approach to relationships work in your day-to-day interactions on the job:

> ✔ **Operating collaboratively:** This means people you interact with are viewed as partners, not adversaries. They don't have to become your friends; you don't have to take anyone home for dinner. On the other hand, they aren't your enemies whenever you have a disagreement with them. It also means that you work with, rather than against, others in a

cooperative rather than competitive manner to get the job done. When you operate collaboratively, issues of difference or disagreement become issues to settle, not battles to fight.

✔ **Working to understand others:** This means making as much of an effort to understand where someone else is coming from as you do when you're letting the other person know your own point of view. It means actively listening so that you can show a true understanding what others have to say, especially in conflict situations. You listen and show understanding first, instead of pushing your point of view harder — a key to diffusing tension and reaching resolutions and a skill that is explored in Chapter 11.

✔ **Building relationships for long-term potential:** *Long-term* is the key word in this third principle of being consistently respectful. Remember the saying that cautions you not to burn your bridges before you've crossed them? In brief, don't do things that make others feel hurt and disrespected, because sooner or later you're likely to run into those people again, and they won't forget acts that they view as unprofessional conduct directed toward them. Treating them in ways they find respectful makes your job a whole lot easier and builds allies for you today and in the future. This principle is about seeing relationships as investments for long-term growth.

✔ **Fixing problems rather than blaming:** Recognize that people are a part of every problem. Blaming them for problems solves absolutely nothing but creates animosity and distrust. Working with others to solve problems is the best way to get solutions that work and that others will support.

The benefits of being consistently respectful

Each of the four principles for taking a consistently respectful approach to your working relationships (covered in the previous section) goes hand in hand with the others. Together, they develop the consistency that others appreciate and respect and build a solid foundation in your working relationships.

We're all human, and humans make mistakes. But when you deal with others in a consistently respectful fashion, you build trust with them. When others respect and trust you, they're more forgiving of your occasional mistakes. And when problems of difference, disagreement, or other concerns come up (sure sounds like a conflict to me!), they're more willing to resolve these problems with you in an emotionally-controlled manner.

In fact, conflicts can then be dealt with in manageable sizes and kept on the constructive track. Best of all, conflicts can be positive and not thought of as terrible and tense situations.

When relationships operate on this constructive level, the positive benefits include the following:

- ✓ **Sparking creativity:** Good conflict resolution explores ideas and options for making something better, challenges the status quo, and enables you to listen to others' perspectives to reach outcomes — great endeavors for stimulating creative thinking.

- ✓ **Opening lines of communication:** When people deal with conflicts constructively, they're talking face to face about the issues and maintaining respect while doing so. Such behavior does wonders for enhancing communication and creating the likelihood that people will take the initiative to go talk to one another about issues. Open communication builds relationships, which stimulates familiarity, which stimulates more communication. Aha, the new math!

- ✓ **Building teamwork:** In the consistently respectful approach, people are pulled together to work through conflicts. They must collaborate — promoting and laying the groundwork for more teamwork — to reach resolutions.

- ✓ **Making things work better:** The ultimate focus when you constructively deal with conflicts is on reaching solutions. When you collaboratively fix problems, as opposed to fixing the blame, you make a situation work better than it did before. Getting people going in the same direction and focusing on doing the job often results in improvements and increased productivity — something your boss prefers to pay you for.

You can thrive on conflict. Conflicts can have a positive connotation, especially when you use an assertive approach and build working relationships to be consistently respectful as you resolve them. So if you go for a job interview and meet a hiring manager who wants conflict in his or her group, ask what approach is used. When the approach is constructive, sign on and be ready to join in the lively discussions.

Chapter 11

Communicating to Keep Conflicts Cool

In This Chapter

▶ Setting a positive tone for conflict situations

▶ Using active listening skills to diffuse tension

▶ Expressing your concerns constructively

▶ Stating your feelings and thoughts so that you're understood

As Chapter 10 points out, successfully resolving conflicts at work starts with taking a constructive approach to them. In particular, you want to take actions that are assertive: Go to the source, listen, focus on the issue, state your views directly and sincerely, and collaboratively come up with solutions. Quite often, however, this is easier said than done. Assertive action doesn't just happen because you want it to happen. It requires skill.

Although people sometimes make the right effort in conflict situations, they often run into trouble because they don't know the right tools to apply. They go to the person who is the source of the conflict and attempt to work something out, but as soon as they speak, they rub the source the wrong way and end up in a heated debate that goes nowhere. After one bad experience like that, many people become leery of addressing their conflicts with others. However, avoiding the issue (the nonassertive approach) doesn't help, nor does venting your frustrations behind the scenes to others (the passive-aggressive approach). And trying to win an argument with the other person (the aggressive approach) doesn't resolve conflicts at all and usually aggravates working relationships.

Taking an assertive approach works best for resolving conflicts; therefore, assertive communication tools are what must be applied. This chapter reinforces the active listening and assertive speaking tools discussed in Parts II and III of this book and explains how to apply them in conflict situations. It also adds a few more tools to your toolkit that help keep conflicts on the constructive track.

More often, the toughest person to manage in these interactions isn't the other party; it's you. While you don't control another person, you can influence him or her; for instance, how well you keep yourself under control influences how well the other person stays under control. How you speak, verbally and nonverbally, and how you listen affect your own control. People react to you and how you communicate with them.

When you express yourself clearly and sincerely, and listen with empathy to truly understand where the other person is coming from — regardless of whether you agree with the point of view being stated — you're under control. That puts you in a position to influence or change conflicts from problem-dwelling to solutions-building discussions. The tools provided in this chapter help to positively and assertively arm you for conflict situations. You know conflicts are challenging interactions, so you may as well have all the tools at your disposal and ready for use.

Getting Started on the Right Foot

Why don't they ever say to get started on the left foot? And if you put your best foot forward, is it all right if it happens to be your left foot? Well, in conflict situations, you definitely want to put your best foot forward — whichever one it happens to be — and you don't want to put your foot in your mouth at the same time.

Anatomy aside (okay, I'll stop pulling your leg here), you need to start your discussions on a positive track when you address conflicts or concerns with others. Introductions are important for managing discussions involving conflicts, especially when emotions run high. Regretfully, people quite often skip this critical step. You may have even done it yourself. You get up the nerve to sit down with the source of your conflict, and then you dive right into your issue. Unfortunately, the other person (the source of your conflict) reacts defensively to what you're saying. What you intended to happen and where you wanted to go with the discussion weren't made known to the other person, and as a result, you find yourself getting off track.

The following sections focus on how to begin communicating when you're addressing conflict situations (see also Chapter 9 on how to assertively begin communicating in a way that positively engages your listener). They concentrate on setting the right tone and structure to promote constructive dialogue.

Letting your positive intentions be known

People have intentions and they have actions. Which can you see? You guessed it: You can see only someone's actions. Of course, people make assumptions — usually negative ones — about someone's intentions, but the truth is, intentions are invisible. To let good intentions be known, they must be expressed. When you address concerns with others, you want to express a *positive intention* as part of a strong opening statement before you get into the specifics of your issue. A positive intention is one of the most important tools to have in resolving conflicts.

Stating a positive intention

A positive intention is a statement that says you mean well. It tells the other person in your conversation that the discussion and actions that follow are meant to be good. Such statements hold you accountable to actually match your actions with your intentions as the discussion ensues and help the other party refrain from making any negative assumptions about your intentions.

Stating such an intention as part of your opening for a conflict discussion sets the positive tone you seek for the discussion. Here's an example of a statement of positive intention:

"George, as we address this issue today, I want you to know my whole focus here is on helping us clear the air and getting back on track toward having a working relationship in which we support one another."

Try arguing with or getting defensive about that statement! The statement of positive intention often helps to put the other person at ease and sets the tone for a constructive dialogue to follow, which, in turn, increases the likelihood that you can steer the discussion toward achieving a mutually beneficial outcome.

A good statement of positive intention meets the following criteria:

- ✔ It's said in one sentence in most cases. Rambling messages tend to lose their impact.

- ✔ It's expressed in a sincere tone. Without sincerity, your statement has negative intentions!

- ✔ It's stated in positive language, and trigger words such as *but* or those containing *not* are avoided. (See Chapter 8 for more about trigger words.)

- ✔ It defines the positive outcome you're seeking.

You must know what you're trying to accomplish before having the discussion with the other party. Until you recognize the positive outcome you seek to achieve, you're not yet ready to address the conflict. Figuring out this answer first puts you on a constructive track. Avoid initially thinking of specific solutions; you want to work them out with the other person. Instead, look for the positive outcome in the broader sense.

Understanding the my and you types of positive intentions

In your introduction to a conflict resolution discussion, you can use one of two types of positive intentions, or you may even want to use both. One type of positive intention is your own; the other type is the one you state for the other person.

As you can see in the *my* emphasis of the following type of positive intention, you *own* the statement. Words like *I, me, my,* or *mine* show you have possession of the message. It is coming from your perspective:

"Sue, my emphasis with you today is on working out solutions that help us do our jobs well."

Here is an example of a positive intention you give to the other party:

"Sue, one thing I want you to know is that I greatly appreciate the passion you bring to your work and regardless of what we come up with, I want to see that continue for you."

As you see in this second type of positive intention, the emphasis is on the other person. Its intent is to communicate your respect for the other person and acknowledge your understanding of his or her good intentions. The conflict to be worked out can, therefore, be more about the issue on which you differ than on the people who are involved.

When you provide someone with a positive intention as your introduction to addressing a conflict situation, make sure it meets the following criteria:

✔ The language used is positive.

✔ The statement is said, in most cases, in one sentence.

✔ You sound sincere in language and tone.

✔ The statement is relevant to the issue being discussed.

This last point is important, because you want to avoid saying something about the other person just to be nice. Doing so without any relevance to the matter at hand causes you to lose all sincerity and sets the opposite tone of what you want. In essence, you're recognizing the skills and attributes of the other person, which in spite of your differences make you realize that he or she means well.

Sometimes, of course, you can't think of anything positive about the other person. Don't force it! If that's the case, then just stick to stating your own positive intention. You won't go wrong by doing that.

Diffusing tension with a positive intention

Chris was a team leader who had to coordinate efforts for a project with another team leader, Norman. At times, when members of both teams needed to work together, Norman lost his temper. He had outbursts in which he raised his voice loudly and criticized others — often publicly — for mistakes.

Chris hadn't personally experienced the brunt of Norman's outbursts but had seen them on occasion. He was aware that they intimidated some team members and most were just plain fed up with Norman's behavior. For this project to succeed, Chris decided he'd first see if he could address the issue with Norman by himself rather than getting their manager involved. He knew Norman wanted the project to succeed.

In his opening for the meeting with Norman, Chris stated his own positive intention and one he knew reflected Norman's strong desire for the project to succeed. This effort helped the meeting get off to a good start. As the discussion proceeded, Norman, at times, began to get defensive. When he did, Chris reminded him of the positive intention that he, Chris, was after. Every time Chris did so, the tension was diffused. When they got to the solution stage of the discussion, Norman offered some good ideas about what he could do to better control his temper with team members. He thanked Chris for meeting with him, and the project got back on track from there.

After you've stated the positive intentions, especially your own, you can sometimes repeat similar comments during the discussion to help diffuse tension and keep the other person on a constructive track with you. Occasional reminders that you mean well and want to achieve positive outcomes often help in keeping people focused and working with you to reach resolutions.

Setting an agenda

In addition to setting a positive tone, you want to establish a structure (organization) for the meeting, so that it doesn't wander aimlessly. Conflict discussions that have no structure are less likely to reach a resolution.

To set a good structure when you initiate a conflict resolution meeting, do the following:

✔ **State that you have an issue.** The point of the issue statement is to let the other person know you have a serious and important matter to address. Do this right at the start. It is a general statement that either names the overall subject you want to discuss ("Sue, I want to discuss some challenges I see happening with our ABC project.") or simply states that you have an issue of concern that you want to address with the other person.

Limit this opening line to one sentence and keep it general in nature. You want to avoid getting into the specifics at the start. Otherwise, you pull the other person's attention into details, making it much harder for you to have an organized flow to your discussion.

✔ **State your positive intention.** Make sure your listener is aware that you mean well by stating your own positive intention, by stating the positive intention of the other person, or by stating both as you deem necessary. (See previous section.)

✔ **Outline your agenda.** Another good thing to do when setting the structure for your meeting is to briefly highlight your agenda. As a general rule, the more sensitive the issue and the more its potential for strong reactions, the more you want to verbalize an agenda in your introduction.

The agenda outlines the flow of your meeting. When you do it right, it describes the problem-solving process you're going to use to guide the discussion. It's a list of headings, as opposed to specific topics of discussion. For example:

"Sue, in our meeting today, I want to first share with you my concerns about what's been happening recently and then hear your point of view. From there, I want us to brainstorm ideas of how we can make things work better, evaluate which of those ideas will be mutually beneficial, and then close by finalizing our plan and even setting a follow-up time to review our progress."

This agenda overview gives your receiver a verbal outline of what's intended to happen at the meeting. It sounds like bullet points you'd actually see on a written agenda and moves from discussing problems to working out solutions — a logical, focused, and positive flow.

By having a set track to follow for your discussion, you and the other party know what to expect. If, during the course of the discussion, you and the other person veer off track, you can use the agenda to steer the other person back on course. The agenda also reinforces your positive intention by letting the other person know that working out a solution is your aim.

No matter what problem-solving process you choose to follow in the meeting (Chapter 12 provides you with a couple of models), this is the kind of introduction you want to have for initiating conflict-resolution discussions. It gives you an organized flow with a constructive tone — a winning combination for getting started on the right foot.

Sometimes, people ask whether they should provide the other person with a written agenda when the meeting begins. Generally speaking, for one-on-one discussions, verbalize your introduction instead of handing out notes. Having notes for yourself is a good idea because they keep you focused, but you want an informal feeling for the meeting, and giving someone a written agenda for a sensitive discussion may make it seem more formal.

On the other hand, if your conflict resolution situation involves a group discussion, providing a written agenda is a good idea since group dynamics are more challenging than one-on-one discussions. In fact, prior to the meeting, let the other people involved know that you'll set an agenda and get it to them a little in advance of your meeting. This is an assertive tactic that helps you focus everyone toward having a positive outcome.

Be First in Showing Understanding

If you're a competitive person, conflict situations aren't the right opportunities to show off your competitive spirit. Being competitive may invite adversarial and aggressive reactions between you and your listener — then you both lose.

If you want to compete at anything during a conflict situation, compete at demonstrating the ability to listen and understand the other person. Listening, especially active listening, sets the tone for collaborative discussions, which are a key for success in resolving conflict situations. When you win as a listener, you help the other person win too, as you increase the likelihood that the two of you together can hear each other out and reach a satisfactory resolution.

Being an active listener isn't always easy because conflict situations can spark a high degree of emotion. The tool that helps you listen actively is what I refer to as the *shift and show understanding* tool. The following sections explain what the tool means and how to use it in conflict situations.

Making the shift and showing understanding

When a conflict situation generates an especially high degree of emotion, both parties spend a lot of energy trying to outtalk each other. As the great debate ensues, you end up with two or more people sometimes vehemently talking and no one really listening. The more the tension rises, the further you get from reaching any kind of solution.

The *shift-and-show-understanding* tool places an emphasis on active listening that includes two main efforts:

✔ Shifting your attention off of your own message and onto capturing the other person's message.

✔ Responding by showing understanding of the other person's message before continuing any efforts to express your own views.

This shifting of your attention from your own message to that of the other person brings your emotions under control. When you're in control of your own emotions, you increase the likelihood of influencing the other person to control his or hers. On top of that, responding with verbal feedback to show understanding of a point, regardless of whether you agree with it, lets the other person be heard.

When you get yourself under control first and verbally show that you're listening to the other person's message, you often diffuse the tension in an interaction. Tensions don't escalate when people are listening to understand each other: Someone has to start the process, so you can take the lead by shifting and showing understanding.

As you may have guessed, this listening effort is extremely important when you see the tensions rising in the conflict discussion. But it also is a good tool to apply periodically throughout the conversation to maintain two-way, controlled dialogue. You may also notice that even in simpler conflicts that come up in everyday conversation, when you and another person start to debate with each other, shifting and showing understanding helps diffuse the tension.

Shifting into gear with the tool

To make shifting and showing understanding work, follow these key steps:

✔ **Mentally focus your attention on the speaker.** Stop speaking and put your attention into capturing what the other person is saying. (Sometimes I'll mentally say the word "shift" to myself just as a reminder to listen.) Then focus on seeking out the meaning of the person's message.

✔ **Give verbal feedback to show understanding.** After you get a sense of what the message means, paraphrase or reflective paraphrase what the speaker has said to you.

Paraphrasing and *reflective paraphrasing* (covered in Chapter 5) are two important tools of active listening. Through your own words and observations, they help you show understanding of the message you've heard.

In paraphrasing, generally in one sentence, you summarize the content of the message you've heard: "So your point, Sue, is that doing further research is only going to slow us down and it's time for us to move ahead and finish the project. Is that right?"

In reflective paraphrasing, usually expressed in one sentence as well, you capture and reflect back to the speaker the emotional meaning that you hear and the content that supports it. For example: "Sue, you're feeling frustrated because the research has taken longer than expected and you don't see how spending more time on it is going to help us get this project done. Is that correct?"

✔ **Gain confirmation or clarification of your verbal feedback.** You want to invite a direct response from the other person to find out if you're hearing the message correctly. To make sure your speaker knows that you need a response, you can either raise your sentence-ending tone to make your feedback message sound like a question or simply ask, "Is that right or correct?"

When you're not accurate about what the speaker means (as you give your verbal feedback) and you're given a clarifying explanation, you may find it helpful to paraphrase or reflective paraphrase again to make sure you truly understand.

✔ **Ask questions when you need more information to understand the message.** Before you can provide verbal feedback to check your understanding, you sometimes need to get more out of the message. In addition, after you've given feedback and gained confirmation, you may need to get more information to further understand why the person thinks or feels the way he or she does. When you find that you need more information or background, ask for it. Use the probing tool (covered in Chapter 5) to ask highly effective, open-ended questions.

✔ **Stay nonjudgmental.** When you're looking to show understanding of the other person's message, your role is to understand it as that person meant it. Avoid interpreting and adding your own spin to the message. People become aggravated, especially in conflict situations, if they think you're putting words in their mouths. Likewise, avoid judging the speaker's view as right or wrong. The other person's view is merely *different* than yours, which is why you're having a conflict. You don't have to agree with it — just understand it.

Occasionally, you may actually find out that the other person's viewpoint is quite similar to your own. Perhaps no one was listening before, so neither of you realized it.

✔ **State your view as needed or just move forward.** When you've shown in a nonjudgmental manner that you understand the other person's message, you then have the opportunity to get your point across next in the conversation. In essence, you actively listen first and speak second.

When you state your view on an issue, do so only to provide background and information. Don't dwell on the fact that you disagree with the other person. In fact, avoid saying that you disagree, because that can trigger conflict situations. Trigger words, discussed in Chapter 8, although not negative by definition, often cause or trigger negative reactions from your receiver. It is perhaps better to start your message by saying something like the following: "Sue, let me give you another view to consider on this issue." Then you can state your view with constructive language and a matter-of-fact tone. See the "I've Got a Thought and a Feeling to Share" section later in this chapter for more on how to constructively express your views.

Sometimes after you've gained confirmation of the other person's message, you can simply move forward into the solution stage of the discussion. Adding more to your point may cause the two of you to dwell only on your differences, which usually is pointless.

In conflict situations, it isn't the problem you need to agree on but rather the solution. The best direction for any discussion is to work out solutions. If you've already made your point, rehashing it will probably take both of you off track. Keep your focus on a far more positive endeavor to undertake — gaining agreements around solutions.

Taking the tool for a spin

Now it's time to let you try out your abilities to shift and show understanding in a stressful, challenging situation. Here's one scenario:

You're a project manager who is expected to lead cross-functional teams to deliver services for clients. As part of this role, you coordinate efforts with a variety of department managers ranging from creative services to engineering, assigning staff resources from their groups to help you do the projects.

In your last few projects, you've had difficulty with the engineering manager. Getting fully committed assistance from his group has become an obstacle. When telling him about this in a meeting that you set up, he responds with this argument: "Hey, I've got resource demands myself. In fact, a month ago you were given two of my engineers to help you on a project. The deal was they'd help you on a full-time basis for a couple of months. Yet what I saw happening was they were only being utilized on a half-time basis at best. They told me they had some time on their hands. So if you're not going to fully utilize them, I've got other work they can be doing."

Shift and show understanding by paraphrasing or reflective paraphrasing the engineering manager's message. What would you say?

Showing that you get the message

A few years ago, I was in a meeting with the three senior executives of a client company for which I had just started doing some work. The internal coordinator for the client company had been working for awhile to have me come in and work with her company's managers. Because outside consultants rarely were used, she started by having me conduct a one-day workshop as an elective for her managers. As she had hoped, the workshop was received positively, and soon enough training was offered so that every manager in the organization could attend. In fact, the entire management staff — except for the three senior executives — attended. The workshop created a buzz in the organization that the company needed to do better at showing positive leadership. So the three senior executives asked the internal coordinator to organize a meeting with me to give them an overview of what may have seemed to them to be a controversial workshop.

Part way into this meeting, as I was briefly explaining the content of the course, one of the executives reacted to a single word on one of the pages in the participant manual. That word was *empowerment,* something the workshop had spent all of two minutes reviewing.

This executive started getting louder and sharper in his tone and firing questions at me: "Don't you think sometimes people don't understand the responsibility that goes with empowerment?" and "Why is it that people want autonomy but don't want accountability with it?"

As I tried to respond to his questions with explanations, he interrupted me, and his volume and speaking pace increased. At the same time, the two other executives were growing stern looks on their faces. I felt like I was facing a hostile mob.

Then I said to myself, "Shift," and stopped talking. I soon realized I wasn't really being asked questions but was having a concern expressed to me. So I fed back that message with a reflective paraphrase, "So you become frustrated sometimes that some managers in your company take the concept of empowerment the wrong way and don't understand the accountability that goes with it. Is that right?"

With an emphatic response of, "Exactly!" he started to smile and so, too, did the other two executives. The tension diffused immediately. Did I agree with his point of view? No. Was it worth telling him so? Not really. I moved forward and the rest of the meeting went on with much positive energy. The company became a client that I ended up doing a great deal of work for and the relationship led to wonderful opportunities. The shift and show understanding tool is a handy one to have, especially in tense moments.

Here's a sample response: "So what you're telling me is you thought your two engineers were available and thus able to do other work to be kept fully utilized. Is that right?"

Here's another scenario:

You were able to get a staff member from another team to help you with a heavy workload you've recently been facing. In the first couple of weeks, this other person, Tina, has been a big help to you. Now over the last week or so, you've seen a dip in her productivity. She is slow to get work done and curt when you ask her to do things. As you attempt to address this concern with her, she reacts, saying, "I was asked to help you out with some of your work-load nearly a month ago. The deal was that I was supposed to support you on a half-time basis for approximately one month. Yet, you keep asking me to do more than a half-time load of work, and I don't see any end in sight to what was suppose to be a temporary arrangement. You know, I've got other work to do that's getting backed up right now."

Shift and paraphrase or reflective paraphrase Tina's message. What would you say? Compare your response to this sample: "Tina, you're feeling upset because you see that an arrangement is turning out quite different from your understanding of what it was meant to be. Is that correct?"

As these examples show, you don't have to agree with the other person's viewpoint and feelings, but you do need to understand them. By showing that you understand the other person's views, you can better get yours across when you take your turn to speak, and you can ask him or her to show understanding of your message.

Remember, you're not trying to win a debate; you're seeking a constructive dialogue in which both people can hear each other's differences and find a solution to make things work better. When you show you can actively listen, you end the debate and increase the likelihood for the constructive dialogue — a key to success in conflicts.

Give Me a Description of the Suspect

A big part of a police officer's job is writing reports about the incidents he or she deals with while on duty. The best officers write reports that cover, as Sergeant Joe Friday of the old television show *Dragnet* used to say, "Just the facts." You can read such a report of an incident and see the scene in your mind as if you were watching it on videotape. That's the idea of the *describing tool*. The following sections explain what the tool is and how to put it to use when you're dealing with conflicts.

Describing describing

Don't worry! Your eyes are fine. You're not seeing double or hearing an echo. But if you know what the word *describe* means, you probably have a good idea of what the describing tool does.

Describing is reporting behaviors that someone displays in observable and objective terms. It's telling what you see, not giving your opinions about what you see. It's telling what someone has done, not stating your assumptions about the person's motives. It's what you've seen versus why you see it. To clearly understand what describing means, keep the following points in mind:

✔ **Behavior, not attitude:** Describing focuses on behaviors but not on attitudes. People often confuse these two words. Behavior involves someone's actions. You can see them and hear them. Attitude, on the other hand, is how someone thinks or feels about something. You can't see them (although people often make assumptions about others' attitudes); they're locked away in the individual's mind. Certainly, attitudes influence behavior, yet they aren't the same as behavior. In fact, a person can have a lousy attitude about an issue but still manage to keep it in check by displaying respectful behaviors in any interaction.

For example, Kim has one customer she deals with whom she finds distasteful. That's her attitude about the one customer. Yet when she interacts with this customer, she remains courteous and respectful in her behavior, as she does with all her other customer interactions.

✔ **Substance, not generalities:** Describing, sometimes referred to as *constructive feedback,* is providing substance to your message so the stated observations are clear and concrete. Sometimes, people comment on your behavior in general terms. For example:

- "You did a good job at the team meeting today."

- "You were not constructive at the team meeting today."

In both cases, receivers of these messages don't get a clear picture of what was done well or badly. At best, the messages are implied.

When describing, the receiver gets a clear picture of what you saw in that person's behavior. Here are a couple of examples of describing:

✔ "As I facilitated today's team meeting, I want you to know that I found your contributions to be helpful. I noticed that a few times you directed questions to some of our quiet members, and this drew them out and got them involved. In fact, I saw you using paraphrasing skills, checking your understanding of what was said. In addition, I noticed you raised a couple of ideas that helped the teamwork out solutions to the shipping delays. Thanks for your contributions today."

✔ "As I facilitated today's team meeting, I was concerned about the behaviors you displayed that were different from your usual positive participation. On three occasions, I noticed you interrupted other team members before they were done expressing their points. On one of those occasions, I heard your voice get loud and you told Joe that his idea to solve the shipping delays was "a waste of time." As the exchange between you and Joe started to escalate, I then asked you to stop. What I saw happen for the rest of the meeting was that you sat quietly, had your arms folded, kept your chin down, and gave no response when asked a couple of times for your thoughts to help on other ideas."

As you see in these examples, describing gives you a clear, specific and concrete picture of the events that took place as if you were watching them again on videotape. In conflict situations, describing is an important skill for expressing the concerns you have about what someone else is doing. Describing is much better than general criticism.

As the first example shows, describing can be used to express appreciation for certain behaviors. By going beyond the standard *good job* and describing the good behaviors seen, the message has greater impact to the receiver, who knows that the positive actions have been recognized.

Reviewing the guidelines for the describing tool

Now that you have a picture of what describing is and how it may come in handy in conflict situations, you must discover how to use it. Here are guidelines to follow when describing:

✔ **Focus on the issue and use *I*-messages to help.** General praise and criticism tend to make the focus personal. *You* is the subject of the sentence and little else of substance is said beyond that. And if you start out by saying in the critical situations, "Now don't take this personally," you make the message even more personal in a negative way.

In describing, your focus is on the issues in your message. You're commenting on the person's actions versus commenting on the individual. Leading the key points of your description with I-messages helps you do this. *I-messages* are phrases such as the following:

  • I've noticed . . .

  • I've observed . . .

  • I've seen . . .

I-messages have you owning your observations. They help you focus on what the person did, the actions that have been seen, the issues, and not the person.

✔ **Give specifics.** Without specifics, you end up with a description of general praise or criticism. Specifics give your descriptions substance, replaying the behaviors in concrete and matter-of-fact terms. Giving examples of what was done and sometimes using quotes or paraphrases of what someone said are the best ways to improve your description from generalities to specifics.

✔ **Report observations, not interpretations.** Observations are different from interpretations, and knowing the difference is a key to effectively using describing when dealing with behaviors. An observation is what you have seen. An interpretation is what you think or feel about what has been seen. Take a look at these examples:

- **Interpretation:** "I noticed you were in a bad mood at today's meeting."

- **Observation:** "I noticed you sat quietly and said nothing at today's meeting and even when asked a question, you replied with a one-word answer."

An observation reports the actions of another person that you've seen, but you're drawing conclusions when you interpret what you've seen the other person do (like in the first example above). "Bad mood' is an interpretation. What you must ask yourself when you reach these conclusions is: "What did I see in the actions of this person that led me to draw this particular conclusion?" Usually, the answer is your observations. Observations make your description come across as concrete and constructive. And the neat thing about observations is they aren't right or wrong, they're just what you've seen. As a result, they often stimulate constructive dialogue as opposed to the defensive sparring that interpretations often spark.

An observation is matter-of-fact. It's the replay of the behavior, not the analysis or characterization of the behavior. People often are experienced in characterizing what others do in their behavior — meaning they're good at interpreting! That's why people often struggle with addressing conflicts in working relationships. Their characterizations and conclusions leave the recipients of their messages anywhere from confused to defensive . . . and rightfully so.

✔ **Be direct.** Quite simply, get to the point. Don't beat around the bush, ramble away in your message, or talk around a point. Such forms of communication cause confusion and apprehension. In describing, especially when addressing your concerns about the behavior of others, being straightforward is the most effective way to make a message clear to someone else.

Now don't confuse direct with blunt. Being blunt is an aggressive behavior, while being direct is an assertive behavior. When you're blunt, tact is tossed aside, the message usually has a personal sting to it, and as a result, the purpose of your statement sometimes is less than clear. When you're direct, you get to the point and say it with respect (see Chapter 8).

✔ **Show sincerity in your tone and language and avoid mixed messages.** Sincerity is expressing the message with care, respect, and a degree of seriousness that's appropriate for the issue at hand. In addressing conflicts or concerns, you want to show a level of seriousness that exhibits the importance of the message and maintains respect so that you prevent your tone from moving from sincere to harsh. If anger and frustration drive your message, the harshness is heard and the receiver misses your point. When you stick to sincerity, you're in control of your emotions and your message is expressed with concern and respect.

Avoiding mixed messages helps you maintain sincerity. Mixed messages, as explained in Chapter 8, are those *yes, but* types that are attempts to say something nice in the first part of your message, followed by a *but* or *however* that introduces criticism, which the recipient understands to be the real point of your message. For example, "Jim, I know you were trying hard on this project, but the report you did missed the mark and was poorly written."

The *but* after the positive message negates what was said before it, making you sound as though you didn't really mean it and lessening the sincerity of the real point you're trying to get across. When describing, therefore, remain sincere and direct. Mixed messages take you off track with both guidelines.

Keep in mind that part of being sincere is expressing appreciation when people show good efforts in their work and behavior. Expressing appreciation to co-workers, bosses, and others in specific terms about their good actions — referred to as *positive feedback* — adds to your credibility and your effort to build consistently respectful working relationships (the importance of which is discussed in Chapter 10). If you regularly express appreciation to people when they make good contributions on the job, you already have a high level of respect for and from them.

Describing tool scenario

Following the guidelines about how to use describing, try it with the following scenario.

You're a project manager. Your role is to lead project teams in the technical implementation of the services that clients order. Business development completes the sales side of the deal and is supposed to close the deals before handing them to you to coordinate the work for the client. Your concern is with what Sandy, one of the specialists in business development, is doing. Instead of handing off the client service work to you on a new order with the XYZ account, she's getting involved and in the way.

The initial meeting to introduce you to the client's main contact earlier in the week was canceled at the last minute by Sandy without explanation. Then today she sent you an e-mail message asking you to give her some sample work-order forms, which you normally use to scope out the work with the client. The last straw is a second message, "just to let you know," that she's having dinner with the client tonight to work out some issues regarding this major order and will keep you informed on what happens.

Using the describing tool, what do you say to Sandy? Remember, stick to observations not interpretations and go directly to Sandy to speak with her.

Compare your answer with the example that follows:

"Sandy, I want to share a concern that I have regarding the transition of the XYZ account. At the end of last week, I was informed that a deal was made and that I was to lead the project team in servicing the client. What I've seen happen this week regarding the handoff from you in business development to me as the project manager has led to my concern. First, the meeting with the client to introduce me was canceled at the last minute without any explanation given to me. Today, I received two messages from you about wanting sample work-order forms and scheduling your meeting with the client tonight to work out some issues. These functions are my responsibility, and I haven't yet seen the needed handoff support."

Certainly in this scenario, you could've said something like: "Sandy, you're getting in the way and trying to take over the project management role for this account. You don't trust me to do the job. Well, by getting in the way and doing something you don't know how to do, you're just going to mess up the service the client needs."

Unlike the example of a good description, this second version is full of interpretations and sounds like the speaker is venting at Sandy. When you stick to observations, however, reporting the specifics of what has happened, as you know it, you keep the tone sincere while letting her know you have a concern. Perhaps Sandy has a good reason for doing what she is doing. Jumping to conclusions as to what she is doing will only aggravate the situation. Not telling her clearly where you're coming from with your concern will only make her confused and apprehensive.

A description that is focused on the issues, is specific, direct, sincere, and based on observations gives the other person a clear picture of what you're seeing and experiencing in the conflict situation. It reports rather than attacks and sets up the opportunity for a discussion in which you can hear what's going on with the other person and then work out a solution. In fact, in many cases, if you provide a description of your concern when the incident occurs, you can work out a solution and keep the conflict from escalating into a more tense and frustrating situation. In other words, the sooner you act, the easier you can effectively settle the issue.

I've Got a Thought and a Feeling to Share

Conflict resolution is a matter of problem solving. In this section, I share two communication tools that help define and solve problems by getting your points across so the other party can understand where you're coming from. These two tools, are the stating-thoughts tool and the stating-feelings tool.

Stating thoughts

Sometimes in the course of a conflict-resolution discussion, you need to offer an opinion. This primarily happens in the course of examining the problem situation but also can occur during dialogue about the solution. So as not to come across as opinionated, use the *stating-thoughts tool*.

Definition and purpose of the stating-thoughts tool

When stating thoughts, you indicate your views about a situation in two key ways:

✔ You tell how the situation is impacting you.

✔ You respond to the person through comments with constructive feedback.

In either case, this tool provides perspective and clarity for the other person in the conversation and enhances the issue's importance.

When you explain the impact or respond to someone's point of view, you do so to stimulate dialogue, not to provoke an argument. Not saying what you think prevents you from getting across important points that can lead to better understanding and, it is hoped, a solution. At the same time, however, putting others down or blaming them with your viewpoint takes you down a destructive path.

Using the stating-thoughts tool

When stating thoughts, you can usually use up to a few sentences. Don't be long-winded or you'll sound opinionated, but be sure to place your emphasis on being constructive and providing views supported by factual reasons. Here are some guidelines:

✔ **Own the thought.** Use the words *I, me,* or *my* to indicate the view is yours.

✔ **Tell your thought in positive terms.** Use language constructively, presenting the message in the best way possible and avoid words (as discussed in Chapter 8) such as *not* and *but.*

✔ **When defining impact, clarify the effect the problem is having on you.** Give facts to support your views or conclusions. Usually this form of stating thoughts is done right after you've used the tool of describing to state observations about your concern. For example:

"Based on the concern I just described to you, not getting the information I was expecting at the agreed-upon milestone dates has caused delays for me on this project and is affecting my ability to meet the final target date for the project."

✔ **When responding with feedback, focus on issues and behaviors.**
Explain, as needed, the basis of your feedback in response to the other party's thoughts. Focus your explanations on observations and facts, avoiding interpretations or analysis of other people's perceived intentions.

For example, say, "I'm having difficulty understanding your explanation of the circumstances. Your dates and events aren't coming across in a clear or sequential fashion to me." Don't say, "You're not making much sense here. You don't explain things very well."

As both examples show, you as the speaker own the message. Your emphasis is on your own thoughts, using words such as *I, me,* and *my.* You're also providing a rational explanation about where your views are coming from, which sets the constructive tone of the message.

In the earlier "Describing tool scenario" section, I describe a scenario in which you're in a project-management role with clients, and Sandy in business development causes you concern with a new client by taking charge of the account service after the deal is made. After you you've described your concern, use the stating-thoughts tool to explain the impact of Sandy's actions to her. What would you say?

Here's an example: "I see you continuing to work with the client after the deal is closed, and because you're doing so without my being involved and without the important handoff of the client to project management, the assignment of a project team to supply the services the client desires has been delayed. This doesn't help with what we both want to see happen — the client receiving the desired services."

Feelings, nothing more than feelings

Conflict situations evoke emotions. Your ability to control your own feelings has great influence on what happens with the other person's emotions. On the other hand, to act as though no emotions exist isn't realistic. The key is to express your emotions rather than show them, and this is where the *stating-feelings tool* comes in to play.

As discussed in Chapter 4, people show their emotions more often than they say them. They do this through nonverbal communication — body language and tone of voice. When people show strong, rather negative, emotions like anger or frustration, others react defensively or are turned off. These strong emotions — which you often feel in conflict situations — provide, in most cases, too much noise for others to be able to listen with understanding.

Remember that most people have never been taught to truly listen as active listeners. You therefore can't expect them to understand where you're coming from when you show strong emotions and they're struggling to maintain control over their own emotions at the same time.

Talking about your feelings, rather than putting them on display, is the key to maintaining self-control. That's where stating feelings comes in handy.

Definition and purpose of the stating-feelings tool

With this tool, you say the emotion that you feel about a situation in a direct manner to increase awareness and understanding for the other person and to lend importance to your concern or issue within the conflict.

Stating your feelings isn't intended to make others feel guilty or sorry or to blame anyone for any problem. Pushing guilt or blame on others creates negative energy in a discussion and usually stimulates adversarial reactions, both of which greatly diminish the likelihood of reaching a satisfactory resolution. Don't go after confessions or expect grand apologies in return for telling someone that you feel hurt. People are more willing to accept responsibility for their actions than they are for taking on blame or being humiliated. By stating feelings, you're looking for understanding and dialogue that can lead to a solution.

Using the stating-feelings tool

The stating-feelings tool often is used right after you use the tool of describing (see "Give Me a Description of the Suspect" earlier in this chapter). Describing outlines your concern or problem, after which you can state feelings in a few sentences that let the other person know how the situation has made you feel. Here are some guidelines for constructively using the stating-feelings tool:

- ✔ **Show ownership of the feeling message.** Use words such as *I, me,* or *my* to indicate that you own the feeling.

- ✔ **Name the feeling you have.** Directly identify the emotion you feel from the experience.

- ✔ **Use positive language and a sincere tone.** State the message in the best possible tone, with the most accurate meaning, while maintaining respect for the listener the entire time. Avoid trigger words (see Chapter 8) or any other harsh language or tones. Avoid showing your feelings. Here are contrasting examples:

  - • **Stating feelings:** "I was upset by those actions."

  - • **Showing feelings:** "I hate when you do that."

✔ **Give constructive reasons to explain the basis of your feelings.** Keep your explanations brief and focus on issues and behaviors you've seen. Avoid giving interpretations or making assumptions about the other person's perceived intentions. Spare them the psychoanalysis. Stick with what has happened as you've experienced it, and don't guess about the meaning behind it.

In the "Describing tool scenario" section earlier in this chapter, I describe a scenario in which you're in a project-management role with clients, and Sandy in business development causes you concern with a new client by taking charge of the account service after the deal is made. After you you've described your concern, use the stating-thoughts tool to explain how Sandy's actions affected you. What would you say to Sandy? Here's an example: "Sandy, based on the observations I've stated about your continuous involvement with this new client, I am feeling excluded and frustrated about the lack of a smooth transition into my project-management responsibility."

As this example shows, you're seeking to create awareness and understanding when you use the stating-feelings tool. You're not accusing anyone of willfully hurting you. Therefore, keep your language constructive and your tone sincere. But don't shy away from letting the other person know how the situation has made you feel. Much better than letting the feelings just grind and get in the way. Expressing what you're feeling constructively and sincerely puts you on the road toward the solution of the conflict by opening up the dialogue. Working together to achieve a solution is the essence of what conflict resolution is all about.

Chapter 12

Bringing the Conflict to Resolution

· ·

In This Chapter

▶ Preparing yourself to focus on solutions

▶ Resolving interpersonal conflicts with a problem-solving model for success

▶ Reconciling differences over business issues with a problem-solving model for success

▶ Handling challenges in the conflict-resolution discussion

· ·

*T*his chapter builds on Chapters 10 and 11, which provide you with the foundations for dealing effectively with conflict situations: Chapter 10 highlights the assertive approach and Chapter 11 provides you with communication tools that help make the assertive approach work in conflicts. This chapter introduces you to problem-solving models that help you bring conflicts to satisfactory resolution.

One problem people face when they attempt to deal with conflicts on the job is that they have no problem-solving plan in mind. They talk to the other person but lack a direction to go in and, as a result, have a difficult time of reaching any kind of agreement. You have to know where you're going in such challenging meetings to reach the desired destination — a mutually beneficial solution. Aimless discussions tend to be unproductive.

In many cases, conflicts that occur one or two times but aren't recurring can be solved with the tools provided in Chapter 11. You can state your concern by using the *describing tool*, add the tools of *stating thoughts* or *stating feelings* to let the other person know how the situation has affected you, and then collaboratively work out a solution.

This chapter provides two problem-solving models that help you for larger-scale conflicts, when patterns have formed and incidents have built up enough over time to cause the tension that now impedes your work. One model, called the *resolving-concerns model,* helps you work through conflicts that deal with differences or clashes in working relationships. The other problem-solving model, called the *needs-based model,* helps you work through differences over business issues such as differing ideas on methods and strategies. As you develop your problem-solving skills, you can mix and match with these two models or even add pieces from other problem-solving models.

This chapter also covers a few of the challenging reactions that can occur in conflict discussions and gives you tips on how to handle them assertively. Included are tips for times when you take on the challenge of being the third-party facilitator of conflict resolution with others.

Preparing for Solutions and Success

The conflict-resolution models outlined in this chapter are effective for situations you're having with peers, staff members, vendors, clients, or customers with whom you want to build long-term relationships, and even with your boss, making these models help you to assertively manage in any direction.

When you're dealing with a problem that follows a pattern, you want to come prepared. Shooting from the hip is likely to result in your saying things you'll regret and triggering adversarial reactions as a result. Preparation not only helps you stay in control but also helps you develop a plan of action so you know precisely where you want the discussion to go. The following sections review the importance of organizing a plan for the meeting and of readying yourself to have the right mind-set to constructively handle the conflict constructively.

Crafting the plan

When conflict situations turn into a pattern rather than an incident, you must arrange a special meeting with the other party for the situation to improve. Anxiety and tension certainly enter the picture for both parties in this kind of meeting, but a special meeting can serve as a turning point for putting the conflict on a constructive rather than destructive track.

For such meetings to be successful, you must come ready with a plan. Chapter 9 outlines how to map out your plan. Planning is extremely helpful in meetings that address conflicts and gives you a sense of organization. It helps you stay focused and thus increases the likelihood you can keep the other person focused too. Planning also enables you to be flexible, so that if you must veer off track for a good reason, you'll have an easier time getting back on track when you have an actual track to follow.

Planning means thinking through what you're going to do and how you're going to do it when you meet with the other party. In fact, for people I coach on handling conflict situations, I recommend they outline their plan or agenda for the meeting. Life is not a closed-book test. Having a few notes or an outline to guide an important discussion is helpful; the notes keep you focused. Use them as a reference — not as a word-for-word script — so that you come across as conversational. But don't hesitate to use your notes. That way, you don't need to memorize your plan nor do you speak off the cuff.

In outlining your plan for the conflict-resolution meeting, find the key points by answering the following questions:

- ✔ **Objective:** Overall, what do you want to accomplish in this meeting? What is the positive and reasonable outcome you desire that will be mutually beneficial and still maintain a respectful working relationship?

- ✔ **Introduction:** What will you say up front when you kick off the meeting to set a constructive tone and an organized structure? Chapter 11 talks about *stating positive intentions,* a useful tool for setting the right tone for the meeting.

- ✔ **Strategy:** What problem-solving model do you plan to follow to guide the flow of the meeting? Depending on whether the conflict situation is more relationship-oriented or business-issue oriented, which model will work best? (The two models are covered in-depth in the "Using the Resolving-Concerns Conflict-Resolution Model" and the "Understanding the Needs-Based Conflict-Resolution Model" sections, later in this chapter.)

- ✔ **Objections:** What challenging reactions or other objections do you anticipate? How do you plan to assertively deal with them when they arise in the discussion?

- ✔ **Message:** What key points do you plan to make when you state the problem? What are the ideas you have for the solution in terms of what the other person can do and what you can do?

The plan works best when it revolves around the problem-solving model you intend to use. Prepare yourself by filling in the blanks on what you'll say on each point that helps you work through the problem-solving model during the meeting. The questions on this list don't have to have a right answer; they just need an answer.

Thinking with a solutions focus

The opposite of focusing on solutions is dwelling on problems, but that polarity represents the two more common mind-sets (or ways of thinking) that people use when they deal with problem situations. Conflicts, of course, are among the more challenging types of problems.

These mind-sets form the attitude that you bring with you into discussions. They serve as the generator for your behavior and attention. They influence the dynamic of the interaction between you and the other party. With a *solutions-focused* mind-set, more of your attention is on working out solutions. With a *problem-dwelling* mind-set, more of your attention is directed toward the problem.

While you don't control another person, you can control your own behavior, and your behavior can have a great influence on what behavioral response you get from the other person in return. Put your emphasis primarily on working out a solution, and you'll see a particular set of behaviors in return. Put your emphasis in the conflict discussion on the problem, and you'll see a completely different set of behaviors. In short, the behaviors you most want to see from the other person are greatly determined by where you put your attention — on the problem or on the solution.

Take a look at the two mind-sets and examples of behaviors that each commonly exhibits in conflict situations.

Problem-dwelling behaviors include the following:

- Focusing constantly on what's wrong
- Making accusations or blaming the other person for the problem
- Pushing guilt or looking for the other person to admit all wrongdoing
- Debating every contrary point heard
- Expressing concerns over e-mail instead of through face-to-face discussions

The use of e-mail in conflict situations can often be as effective as putting gasoline on a fire. It doesn't work at all and usually aggravates the situation. E-mail messages can be ignored and most often are misinterpreted. People often react to what you say far worse than the way you actually mean it. E-mail isn't live discussion — and live discussion is the only way conflicts can be resolved. Chapter 13 covers more about the good uses and misuses of e-mail on the job. For conflicts, avoid it at all costs.

Solutions-focused behaviors include the following:

- Stating a positive outcome that you're seeking for the discussion
- Brainstorming ideas and conducting the solution discussion as a two-way conversation
- Defining the problem in factual terms as the first step toward solving it
- Listening to the other person's concerns and then moving ahead to work out a solution together
- Evaluating ideas against a set of criteria, such as goals or business interests, and developing a solution that meets this criteria to the benefit of both parties
- Requesting what you need the other party to do to help resolve a situation and asking or offering what you'll do to help as well

Now contrast these two sets of behaviors in terms of the dynamics or energies they create with the other person in conflict situations. With problem-dwelling behaviors, you're more likely to see the following:

- ✔ Defensive reactions
- ✔ Emotional outbursts
- ✔ Accusations flying back and forth
- ✔ Withdrawal and silent treatment
- ✔ Heated debates, with each person trying to talk over the other one

Problem-dwelling behaviors more often focus people's attention and energy in counterproductive directions. They don't point attention toward solutions.

The solutions-focused set often stimulates such actions as the following:

- ✔ Listening and two-way conversation
- ✔ Creative problem solving
- ✔ Working to make agreements that both parties can live with
- ✔ Clearing the air and moving forward to enhance communications

The solutions-focused actions often focus people's energy and attention in positive and productive directions — a different dynamic than what happens with the problem-dwelling behaviors. What's in common with both sets of behaviors is that they often stimulate high energy in return: With problem dwelling you get energy that adds tension and drains people, while with a solutions focus, you get energy that is uplifting and motivating.

Therefore, a significant part of your preparation is more than just outlining your plan for guiding the discussion. By preparing the mind-set you want to take into the discussion, reminding yourself of the behaviors that influence the solutions-focused mind-set, and reminding yourself to be determined to work out a solution, you're more likely (drum roll please) to work out a solution.

You're not going for world peace; you're merely working to resolve a conflict on the job. (Of course, after you do such a good job with this conflict resolution, the government may want to draft your assistance to help negotiate worldwide conflict situations.)

Using the Resolving-Concerns Conflict-Resolution Model

This section covers the first of two conflict-resolution models presented in this chapter. The *resolving-concerns model* provides a problem-solving plan to use in situations in which the working relationship, for one reason or another, isn't working as well as needed.

The following are the key steps to follow in the problem-solving plan:

1. **Introduce the meeting.**

2. **Describe the concern.**

3. **Express your feelings or explain the impact from the concern.**

4. **Let the other person respond.**

5. **Work out the solution:**

   • Set the goal desired.

   • Develop ideas to meet the goal.

   • Evaluate the ideas and reach consensus.

6. **Close by confirming the agreement and clarifying the steps for implementation of the solution.**

The following sections walk you through each step and explain how the model works. I also provide you with a case study that helps you see the conflict-resolution model in action.

Going through the model step by step

The time has come to take a stroll through the resolving-concerns conflict-resolution model. Step 5 is the part you want to spend the most time on in your discussion with the other party. On the other hand, you want to keep Steps 1, 2, and 3, during which you talk, as concise as possible. You want this meeting to be a good two-way exchange as opposed to a one-way lecture, so you want to spend more time focusing on the solution than dwelling on the problem. That's what Step 5 is all about. But before you can solve a problem, you first must explain what it is.

The following sections provide a step-by-step analysis of the resolving-concerns model.

Step 1: Introduce the meeting

Before you dive into the details of an issue, you first want to give your meeting a solid opening. Your introduction sets a positive tone and organizes the structure for the meeting. In particular, using the communication tool of stating positive intentions (see Chapter 11) in your introduction is important. In short, a positive intention is a statement that says the actions that follow are meant to be good. You can also state a positive intention that the other person can have, a statement that says, "I sincerely know that you mean well, too."

The following are the key points to express in your introduction to the meeting:

1. **State a one-sentence general purpose for the meeting.**

   For example, "Jack, as you know, I called this meeting to address an issue with you that has been affecting our working relationship."

2. **State a positive intention, either your own or one the other person can have, along with your own.**

   For example, "Jack, I want you to know my focus in this meeting is about working out ways to determine how to get the job done well when we work together. I also know and appreciate that you want to have good results when you take on a job."

3. **Announce your agenda or plan for the meeting.**

   Keep it brief and tie it to the steps you intend to follow in the conflict-resolution model. This focuses attention and lets the other person know where you intend to go in this discussion. For example, "Jack, in this meeting, I first want to cover the concerns that I have as I see them and the impact they've had, and then get your take on the situation. This part is meant to be rather brief. I then want to spend the majority of time exploring solutions with you about how to strengthen our working relationship and then close by confirming an agreement to follow through on what we decide."

Step 2: Describe the concern

In many respects, this is the most critical step in the whole process. You can't solve a problem unless you can clearly define it. On the other hand, if you dwell too long on defining the problem and offer too many details, you may never move forward to work on a solution.

Your purpose in this crucial step, therefore, is to let the person see what you view as the problem in a constructive manner. This is where the communication tool called describing (highlighted in Chapter 11) comes into play. The following guidelines can help you describe your concerns clearly and constructively:

- **State your observations not interpretations** — actions you've seen, not your characterizations or assumptions about the actions. For example:

    Observation: "Jack, one concern I've had deals with your responsiveness to my requests for information. The pattern I have noticed is that usually two or three reminders are given on my part before I hear an answer from you about my requests."

    Interpretation: "Jack, the concern I have is that you ignore requests for information I make of you. You act like you're too busy to bother with me."

- **Be direct and sincere** without any mixed messages.

- **Be specific.** Summarize the pattern of behavior you have seen that has caused you concern. Use a representative example or two to illustrate your points clearly, but avoid using too much detail. Be specific yet as concise as possible.

Quite often, you can communicate the problem coherently by organizing the concerns you've experienced into topics or categories that you'll explain one at a time. For example: "Jack, I have three main concerns that I want to share with you." This tells the other party what to expect and allows you to provide the necessary specifics to make each of the three points (in this case) clear.

People often ask me whether it's possible to describe the good behaviors of the other party when describing the concerns that you have? In many cases, doing so is helpful. If, however, you'd avoid stating something positive to soften the blow, you'd only be diluting the sincerity of your message. Don't send mixed messages either — "Jack, you're good at doing this and such, *but* you cause a problem when you do this and such." Stay away from these contradictory statements. When you raise positive behaviors of the other person, do so to provide a full context of the situation, recognizing the positives with specifics in the same way that you acknowledge concerns and stating them as points that stand on their own.

For example, here is the start of such a message: "Jack, I've outlined three concerns to you. At the same time, I want to outline a couple of actions you do that I find helpful and that I want to see you maintain as we work together. They are as follows . . . ."

As this example illustrates, describing positive actions works best when they're seen as relevant to the entire situation, and you want to recognize them so that they continue. Describing positive actions tells the other person that you see everything and you're not focused only on what looks negative. They're also points that stand on their own, but they're not any kind of contradiction to the problems you've raised. In fact, when you go to the solution stage, you may want to bring them up again so they're incorporated into the agreement because they're behaviors you want to see continued.

Step 3: Express your feelings or explain the impact (optional)

This step is optional, and you either express your feelings or explain the impact (see Chapter 11). This step heightens awareness, which helps you gain a sense of importance for your issue of concern. If you don't think you can do this step constructively and with sincerity, skip it. When you use Step 3, you do so to help the other person see where you're coming from.

Remember to hit the following basics with each tool:

- ✔ **Own the message.** Use the words *I, me,* or *my* as opposed to *you* to indicate that you own the statement.

- ✔ **When stating feelings, identify the emotion** you've felt over the situation.

  Stating feelings: "Jack, because of the reminders involved in getting answers from you, I often feel annoyed that I need to keep asking."

- ✔ **When stating thoughts, explain how the situation has affected your getting the job done** — conclusions supported by rational points.

  Stating thoughts: "Jack, because of the reminders involved in getting answers from you, my work gets delayed as the information I need does not arrive as timely as needed."

- ✔ **Keep the messages brief,** one to a few sentences at most.

Step 4: Let the other person respond

For some people, this is the toughest step. Almost never do you describe the concern so well (as constructively as possible) that the other person hugs you and apologizes profusely. As concretely and constructively as you've stated the problem, people still need to process what they've heard and respond to it as they desire. That starts you down the road to having two-way conversations. That's why you want to cover Steps 1, 2, and 3 quickly.

Your role in this step is to let the other person have his or her say for a bit. You, therefore, want to listen and not debate what you hear. Employ the active listening tool of probing (discussed in Chapter 5) to convince the person to explain the specifics of his or her thoughts or concerns. Employ the effort called shift and show understanding (highlighted in Chapter 11), providing verbal feedback with the active listening tools of paraphrasing or reflective paraphrasing to demonstrate your understanding of the individual's messages.

Keep in mind that you both don't have to see the problem the same way. You're working toward an agreement on a solution, not on anything else. You both want to be aware of each other's concerns so that you can take them into consideration when you collaboratively work out the solution. Your showing an openness to hear the other party's concerns increases the likelihood that your concerns also will be heard. And by your showing an understanding of those expressed concerns, you can thereby ask the other person in return to give you feedback showing an understanding of your concerns. When you have two people receptively listening to one another, you manage tension and resolve conflicts.

Step 5: Work out the solution

This is the step with which you want to take the most time. The two of you crafting a solution is the key to success with conflicts. In this meeting, as in others, stay focused on solutions and don't dwell on problems.

Three main pieces highlight the solution stage. When applying these three pieces, you often need a transition from the problem-discussion phase to the solutions-discussion phase of the meeting. The best transition is a one- or two-sentence statement of positive intention that tells the other person where you want to go in the meeting at this time. For example: "Jack, as mentioned at the beginning, my intent here is to develop solutions that help us work productively together. How about moving ahead now and focusing on doing just that." From there, follow through on the three key steps for working out the solution.

1. **Establish the desired goal.**

    Make this a one-sentence, positive statement that defines the picture you want to see for the working relationship when it is functioning well. Offer the goal statement as *your* recommendation and let the other person then respond to it.

    Hold firm to the idea of the goal but be open to how it is worded. The goal statement defines the *what;* that is, what the target for the relationship should be. It doesn't define how to reach the target. That comes next. Usually when you define this goal in a clear and positive sentence, you seldom find disagreement. Some kind of positive working relationship is what both parties most often want. If the other person has a better way to state this goal, by all means, go with it. Here's an example: "Jack, how about this as the goal to shoot for in our working relationship: Establish a working relationship where we work together in a cooperative, respectful, and responsive manner. What do you think?"

2. **Develop ideas to meet the goal.**

    This element defines the *how;* that is, how you two are going to reach the goal. It defines the actions both parties will take to achieve the goal of the working relationship. This piece can be made to fit by one of three methods:

    • Recommend your ideas and ask for any other ideas the person may have.

    • Solicit ideas first from the other person and add yours into the mix.

    • Brainstorm in turn.

Tips for brainstorming

If you choose the brainstorming approach, set ground rules for it upfront. Here are some tips for how to run an effective brainstorming session:

✔ Go with one idea per person per turn.

✔ When someone has a turn but no idea ready to offer, that person *passes* to keep the momentum going.

✔ Refrain from making judgments about any of the ideas until after the brainstorming is done. Thus, you have no bad ideas at this stage.

✔ Record the ideas as they're presented so that they are visible. Record what the other person says, not your interpretation of what is said.

✔ Keep going until you both run out of ideas.

Whichever of the three methods you use to develop ideas to meet the goal, be prepared to come up with specific actions for the other person, as well as an idea of what you're willing to do. Both parties must contribute and make commitments if the conflict is to truly be resolved. Be sure to discuss all potential ideas before beginning to evaluate them. Setting ground rules upfront before starting on the next element in the problem-solving process helps bring out all the possibilities so the discussion about a solution isn't bogged down.

3. **Evaluate the ideas and reach consensus.**

Evaluate the ideas together, trying to determine which will best meet the stated goal. Go after ideas first that are more in common so that consensus can easily be reached. With *consensus,* you're asking this question, "Can you support this option or idea?" While people don't generally agree to every idea, they're often willing to support something for the good of the cause.

Starting out with the ideas you have in common builds momentum toward reaching an overall agreement. For ideas in which differences exist, explore the rationale behind the thinking, listening to one another's points of view and explaining the benefits — that's how you get constructive two-way dialogue. If necessary, propose alternatives to work through the differences by continuing the emphasis on problem solving as you develop the solution.

Step 6: Close

After all of the ideas are evaluated and consensus is reached on the ones you both plan to go forward with for your solution, you're ready to bring the meeting to a close. Here are the steps to take in this final stage:

1. **Confirm the plan and all the actions agreed upon by both of you.**

2. **Clarify which steps need to happen for implementation of the solution.**

3. **Close on a positive note, thanking the person for working with you to craft this solution.**

Here are a couple of other tips to cement a strong close for this meeting.

✔ **Commit to typing up the agreed-upon plan and providing a copy to the other person.** Sometimes people are nervous about writing something down. Writing the agreement down as it is formed helps clarify it for both parties and gives your solutions discussion a focus. Otherwise, you'll go around in circles. Writing down the plan also helps you both avoid having to rely on memories when honoring your commitments.

✔ **Set a date for the two of you to get back together in the near future, such as a month out, to review your progress with the plan.** This effort builds accountability for you and the other person and increases the likelihood that the agreement will stick. Sometimes, doing a second progress-review meeting down the road maintains the good efforts you both have started.

Case study: The case of the overzealous boss

In this section, I put the resolving-concerns conflict-resolution model into practice through a scenario in which the source of your conflict is your boss. Put this conflict-resolution model into action and compare what you would say and do with the sample provided.

The scenario

You're a manager of a group that performs project work in service of internal customers — employees within the organization. During the last few months your boss's actions have formed a pattern that causes great difficulty for you and your group.

Your boss, Jim, has been making commitments to assignments and their deadlines for your group without consulting with you first. He leaves you notes about the assignments or has a short conversation while on the run to tell you about them. Attempts to discuss the projects and their effects on other priorities usually are met with the statement, "I've got to go right now. I know you and your group can handle it. Keep me posted on how things turn out."

Just yesterday, as a matter of fact, he told you to incorporate another project as a top priority without discussing a reason for it or adjustments to make with your current priorities. You realize that your boss doesn't have to consult you on every decision he makes, and you know some of these decisions are policy-type matters decided at top-management levels. Nonetheless, this hit-and-run approach to making assignments without consulting with you on what's possible, at least a half-dozen times over the last three months, has affected your and your staff's workload and morale.

The conflict-resolution discussion

You schedule a meeting with Jim to address this conflict at a time on his calendar when he has enough time for a discussion. Following the resolving-concerns model, how will you constructively address this issue? Samples are provided in the following sections.

Introducing the meeting

"Jim, thanks for meeting with me today. As mentioned when I set this meeting, I want to address an issue that is affecting me and my group in our work." (The general purpose of the meeting.)

"I want you to know that my emphasis in this meeting is on problem solving. As you've told me before, you appreciate when people speak up about a concern or problem as long as they come ready to work on solutions. That's my focus for this meeting." (Statement of positive intention.)

"Here's where I'd like to go in our meeting. I want first to have you hear me out as I describe the concern I'm having and its effect, and then to hear your thoughts about it. From there, I would like you to work with me on developing a solution that works well for both of us." (Announcing your agenda.)

At this point, Jim says, "Fine" and asks you to proceed.

Stating the concern

"Jim, my concern deals with a pattern I've noticed in how you've made assignments regarding my group over approximately the last three months. About a half-dozen times during this period, I've received projects from you for my group to do without any consultation with me about their feasibility. The assignments have been given either through a note you send to me via e-mail or through a quick conversation as you are on the run to another meeting. Therefore, the chance to discuss the rationale for these projects or how they're to mesh with our current workload has not been available when you've made the assignments. I'm also concerned that when I've been given these projects, I recall in your statements that commitments with target dates already have been made with internal customers, again without consulting with me first on what's possible."

"I realize I haven't said anything to you directly before today and that my group has worked hard to continue meeting the commitments, but the project you assigned yesterday, the ABC Project, isn't going to work for us and is causing a major strain on my group. So I recognized that I'd better speak with you now so we can create a better way to handle these situations." (The tool of describing.)

Expressing the impact

"Jim, this current situation with how assignments are being made has been causing me much strain and frustration. I feel caught in the middle and not in a good position to explain the rationale for the decisions to my group and, at the same time, I'm frustrated because I see the effect this process is having on staff morale." (Stating feelings.)

Letting the other person respond

You: Jim, thanks for hearing me out. Before we move ahead into talking solutions, I'd like to hear your thoughts about what I've had to say to you.

Jim: Well, I want you to know I'm not trying to put any undue stress upon you and your staff. I get a lot of pressures put on me for us to move ahead quickly to meet the demands of our internal customers. And you know me, giving excellent customer service is a high priority for me and one I want to see throughout all my groups.

You: So what you're saying is you've been focused on how best to meet our customers' needs, which can be quite demanding sometimes. Is that right? (Paraphrasing to show understanding.)

Jim: Exactly. So if there's a better way I should handle these requests, I'm open to some ideas as long as we are responding quickly to meet what our customers need.

You: Good to hear. Let's talk about some of those ideas then.

Working out the solution

You: I'd like to work with you now on developing a solution that helps you, me, and my group make this process of fulfilling customer requests a workable one for all involved. (Statement of positive intention as transition into solution discussion.)

Jim: Sounds good. What do you have in mind?

You: First, I want to recommend a goal for the situation as our target and then to offer some ideas of what you and I can do to meet this goal. How's this for our goal? We need to develop a response process to customer requests that meets the needs of my group's workload capacity while providing our customers with realistic project deadlines.

Jim: I see what you're getting at with this goal statement, but I don't like that word, *realistic*. Realistic to whom?

You: Balance is what I'm after. It does none of us any good if commitments are made that we can't really deliver on or that nearly kill us to do so. How about this? Develop a response process to customer requests that balances customer needs with my group's workload capacity level. (Setting the goal desired.)

Jim: That sounds good.

You: I want to make some recommendations on what you can do and what I can do to help make this goal happen. My ideas are going to center around you and I communicating and consulting with one another as a regular practice.

Jim: Go ahead. I do like when people make their recommendations for a solution.

You: I have two options in mind regarding when customer requests come to you. One is when you receive requests for projects, talk with me first before making any commitments. Within two days of the initial request, a definitive response can be given to the customer regarding how we'll handle their project Option two is to delegate the handling of customer requests related to my group's work to me. I then inform you of the commitments I'm making to keep you in the loop. In addition, regardless of which option you prefer, you and I maintain our one-on-one weekly meetings that we used to have. At these meetings I'll provide you status on how we're coming with the projects while you share any plans in the pipeline for future work coming our way. I'll also commit to letting you know right away if any difficulties are happening for my group, so that we can make or adjust plans accordingly to keep morale high.

Jim: You're right, we've gotten away from our regular meetings. I like the idea of how you propose to have them. I also favor option two. You can handle the responses as long as you let me know the commitments you're making in our one-on-one meetings.

You: Great. I'd also like to draft a memo coming from you to inform our internal customers that they should contact me directly with their needs relating to what my group does, thus enabling smoother communication flow and timely responses to their requests.

Jim: Good thought to help the customer service.

Closing

You: To recap, we've agreed the best response process that balances customer needs with my group's capacity is for me to be the first line of response to customer requests and to keep you informed about them. We'll strengthen that by getting our weekly one-on-one meetings going again. That'll provide you status on where the projects stand and me status on possible work coming down the pipeline. Have I captured it correctly?

Jim: Sounds good.

You: How about I'll recap this plan in writing and copy you on it. I'll send you a draft of the communications memo to go out to our customers by next Monday. Are you available next Wednesday morning to start our one-on-one's at the time we used to have them?

Jim: "Next Wednesday at 9:00 looks good. If you get me the draft of the memo by Monday, I can have it ready by our meeting date to show you what I'm sending out. Let's stick to maintaining these meetings.

You: Jim, thanks for working with me today to resolve this concern.

Analysis of the case

You handled yourself well in this meeting with your boss. Up front, you set the tone and structure for the meeting — solutions-focused and organized. Then you followed through on the plan and worked out a solution with your boss. You kept the description of the problem short and sweet. If you had recounted each incident, you likely would've aggravated Jim. Even when he reacted somewhat strongly to the concerns you described, you stayed in control and listened, and then moved forward to the solution stage. That created dialogue rather than debate. The fact that you focused on the issue and not on Jim as the total problem helped as well.

Then at the solution stage, knowing that your boss likes people to bring recommendations to their problems, you led with the ideas. He responded well to your putting forth options that pointed toward the goal that you were trying to reach. The ideas also focused on how the two of you can manage customer requests well instead of telling him how he should do his job. Then you assertively recapped the agreement, defined how it can be implemented, and showed him your initiative in helping to make positive actions happen.

Understanding the Needs-Based Conflict-Resolution Model

The second of the conflict-resolution models works well when resolving differences that are more work-issue related (as opposed to the relationship-related issues that the resolving-concerns model addresses). As you become familiar with each model, you can often mix and match what you think will result in the best problem-solving plan for handling the conflict. Work issues and relationship issues certainly get tangled together in conflict situations.

This second model is adapted from work originally done in the Harvard Negotiation Project by the folks who wrote the series of books that included *Getting To Yes, Getting Past No,* and *Getting Together* — William Ury, Roger Fisher, Scott Brown, and other authors. In this section, how the model flows is explained first, followed by a sample case to show you how it is applied. The following outlines the problem-solving process of the model:

1. **Introduce the meeting.**

2. **Define the problem.**

3. **Identify the needs of the stakeholders.**

4. **Work out the solution:**

   • Brainstorming ideas to meet the needs.

   • Evaluating the ideas to meet the needs.

   • Reaching consensus on what is mutually beneficial.

5. **Close by confirming the agreement and clarifying the steps for implementation of the solution.**

Going through the model step by step

The following sections take you through the five steps of the needs-based conflict-resolution model.

Step 1: Introduce the meeting

This step works as follows:

1. **State your general purpose for the meeting.**

2. **Provide a positive intention to set the tone for the discussion.**

3. **Briefly outline your agenda for the meeting to give it a logical and organized structure.**

Step 2: Define the problem

In this step, you want to do two main things with the other party:

✔ **Develop the problem statement.** This is a one-sentence statement that identifies the issue to be resolved. It isn't the conflict you're having but rather the issue over which the conflict stems.

✔ **Clarify the source of the conflict and briefly analyze where the differences are coming from.** Differences on business issues often are around such areas as the following:

- Different ways or methods to get a job done.

- Different ideas or views on how to solve a problem or what strategy to follow.

- Different values or styles in how you approach work.

- Different goals or expectations.

- Different understandings or information about a situation.

To keep the discussion constructive as you define the problem and the source of the conflict, you must recognize that differences aren't right or wrong. The differences help identify why the conflict exists. Understanding the source of those differences often starts to help both of you to focus on issues rather than on people alone.

Here's a brief example that sets up how you work out Step 2: Deb and Sue are managers whose groups have to work closely together to fulfill customer orders. Currently, a fairly high number of orders, approximately 25 percent, go out incomplete or with the wrong items in them. This, of course, leads to the orders being returned for correction and a great amount of rework that slows everybody down.

Deb has proposed that work should be done to streamline the order-fulfillment process to make it simpler and more efficient. Sue has proposed implementing a formalized training program for all employees because many tend to just learn on the job. Because they disagree on which approach to take, they have a conflict.

✔ **Problem statement:** Customer orders aren't being fulfilled accurately on a consistent basis.

✔ **Source of the conflict:** Different ideas and views on how to solve this problem.

Step 3: Identify the needs of the stakeholders

This is a critical step in the problem-solving process. *Needs* are what drive people; they're your important interests and motivations as related to the business relationship. *Stakeholders* are the key parties affected by the business relationship and by what gets worked out in the conflict resolution. Usually this involves more than just the two parties having the conflict: customers, vendors, investors, other internal groups, your team, the other person's team, management above, or the company or organization as a whole.

In this step, along with the other person, you want to identify the key stakeholders and then list the most critical needs each one has in the business relationship. Prepare the list together. You're looking at their needs, not at their positions on the issue. Focusing on positions, such as your way versus my way, perpetuates a situation trapping you both in the conflict. Looking at needs helps both of you take a broader perspective to see what's really important.

For example, in the conflict over the order-fulfillment problems in Step 2, Deb and Sue list the key stakeholders in this issue and their main needs:

- ✔ Deb's team:

  - Has accurate customer orders delivered consistently.

  - Maintains high levels of customer satisfaction.

  - Maintains cooperative working relationships with Sue's team.

- ✔ Sue's team:

  - Has accurate customer orders delivered consistently.

  - Maintains high levels of customer satisfaction.

  - Maintains cooperative working relationships with Deb's team.

- ✔ The company:

  - Maintains high levels of customer satisfaction.

  - Ensures long-term relationships with customers.

  - Provides customers with value for what they buy.

  - Maintains an efficient operation.

- ✔ Customers:

  - Consistently receive on-time and accurate shipments of product consistently.

  - Have vendor relationships marked by reliability and high-quality service.

  - Pay a reasonable price and get value in return.

This is what you want to do in your conflict-resolution discussion: List each main stakeholder related to the issue and itemize its important needs in the business relationship. As this example points out, the needs of each group often have similarities and sometimes complement one another. For example, the company's need to provide customers with value because what they buy complements the customers' need to pay a reasonable price for getting that value in return.

By identifying key needs, you begin moving the conflict away from two people and their own positions on an issue toward a broader view of the big picture — who is really affected by this issue and what's really important to them. This is the key. Avoid focusing on positions and shift toward looking at everyone's needs or interests.

Step 4: Work out the solution

Now the problem-solving effort kicks into high gear. The following are the three main elements to work through in the solution stage:

1. **Brainstorm ideas to meet the needs.**

   Take turns throwing out ideas to meet the needs that were identified. Remember to have those needs as your visible guide and to refrain from making any judgments about the ideas until after the brainstorming is done. Don't forget to record your ideas as they're stated.

2. **Evaluate the ideas against the needs.**

   This is the beauty of identifying the needs first. It establishes the criteria for evaluating your ideas. Therefore, the discussion no longer needs to dwell on your position versus the other person's position, or whether your idea or his idea is good or no good. You evaluate the ideas together based on how well they meet any and all of the needs you've listed.

   By brainstorming before attempting to evaluate, you also expand the realm of possibilities. This helps the discussion move past thinking that only one right answer exists — a reason conflict discussions often get bogged down and go nowhere. Seeing the multitude of ideas and combinations set against a list of needs that must be met is what sparks creativity and builds the best agreements.

3. **Reach consensus on what is most mutually beneficial.**

   Step 2 often rolls right into Step 3. You're looking to reach an agreement on the ideas that best meet needs of all of the stakeholders involved in or affected by the conflict.

Step 5: Close

After you reach agreement on the ideas to act upon, confirm this understanding with the other party and clarify what needs to happen to implement the solution — who's going to do what and when.

Setting a follow-up date to review progress often is a good idea. Doing so means that both of you are serious about making the agreement work. You're reinforcing accountability. Consider planning the follow-up meeting about a month in the future. You want to give the solution time to be implemented, but at the same time, you don't want to go so far out that you forget about the agreement. Sometimes, doing a second follow-up a little further into the future, when progress is going well, maintains the positive momentum you're building.

Case study: The case of the staffing dilemma

In this section, you see the needs-based conflict-resolution model in action. The scenario is a challenging situation. As you follow along, think about how you would apply each step and then read the samples provided.

The scenario

Sandy manages a large technical group. She has a special project coming up for which she needs a team of seven people, with one of those people serving as project leader. She has had some initial conversations with the people she wants for this critical project. Her dilemma and conflict centers on Rob.

Rob is one of the brightest and most innovative technical performers in the whole company. No technical problem is too complex for him to solve. In fact, he can work hours — if not days — on end to solve a problem or get a project done. On the other hand, Rob often rubs people the wrong way. His callous remarks and lack of sharing information and knowledge make him difficult for others to work with.

Rob wants to be project leader for the upcoming special project, the Big Ben Project. He's hinted about leaving the company and "taking his talents elsewhere" if he doesn't get the role he wants working on this juicy project. He says that his technical expertise is why he'd be the best person to serve as project leader. On the other hand, the team members Sandy wants for this project already have let her know they'll not work with Rob if he is named team leader because of what they view as his poor interpersonal skills. For this project to be successful, Sandy greatly needs Rob's contributions, and she certainly doesn't want to see him leave the company over this.

The conflict-resolution discussion

Sandy decides to facilitate a meeting to resolve this conflict by involving Rob and two key team members, Stan and May, whom she views as better qualified to be team leaders. Applying the needs-based conflict-resolution model, here is how that discussion flowed:

Step 1: Introduction

Sandy kicks off the meeting be covering three points:

"I've called this meeting today to address a conflict affecting the upcoming special project, the Big Ben Project." (General purpose for the meeting.)

"My focus for this meeting is on reaching solutions that work for all of us involved and for the company, and I look to the three of you as people whom this project most needs to involve." (Statement of positive intention.)

"Where I want to go with you in this meeting is first to define the problem we're facing and then to outline the needs that key parties have as related to this project. From there, I want us — all of you as well as me — to work out a solution that meets the needs of these parties." (Announcing the agenda for the meeting.)

Defining the problem

Together they defined the problem statement in this situation: Who should be project leader for the Big Ben Project and how best to involve the key people needed so the project is successful.

As the discussion explores the source of the conflict and the reasons for it, sparks fly between Rob, Stan, and May. Why Rob should or should not be team leader is the focus of a tense discussion. Sandy recognizes that talking about this much more may derail the meeting, yet at the same time, she's beginning to gain some insight about what Rob's needs are. So she pushes ahead with the agenda.

Identifying the needs of the stakeholders

Sandy gets Rob, Stan, and May to focus on outlining the needs of the stakeholders for this project and move away from the positions they were arguing about. Some of the points she hears Rob raise in talking about the conflict lead to a discovery about his important personal needs. Here are the stakeholders they identified and each one's needs:

- Rob:

    - Recognition for his contributions.

    - A chance to take on new challenges in his work.

    - A successful project.

    - Good working relationships with fellow team members.

- Team members:

    - A successful project.

    - Positive and organized project leadership.

    - Good working relationships with fellow team members.

- Sandy:

    - A successful project.

    - A smooth-running project with good teamwork and leadership.

    - Retaining staff and having them feel valued for their contributions.

✔ Company management:

- A successful project.

- A smooth-running project that meets its deadline.

- Retaining staff and having them feel valued for their contributions.

By outlining the needs of the key stakeholders with Rob, Stan, and May, the dynamic of the meeting shifts away from its adversarial tone, and everyone is then ready to map out a solution.

Working out a solution

The group brainstorms a number of ideas and then evaluates those ideas against the key needs that were identified. In the end, here is what they agree to do:

✔ May will serve as project team leader.

✔ Rob will serve as chief architect for the project and lead all the design efforts and as lead troubleshooter for the most critical problems.

✔ May will handle the project-management side of the project, tracking the team's progress and keeping it on schedule with Stan to assist her in this effort.

✔ Rob will attend and constructively participate in all team meetings, as will be expected of all team members.

✔ The team will undergo training a couple of hours every week on interpersonal communication skills, enhancing its members' ability to work together effectively. Sandy will arrange for the training.

✔ Sandy will meet with team's core leadership, May, Rob, and Stan, once a week to review progress and help tackle any problems.

✔ Sandy will conduct one-on-one mentoring meetings with Rob about what he's getting out of the communications training and how he's doing on the project.

✔ If the team meets its deadline and deliverables for the Big Ben Project, Sandy will ensure recognition for the whole team with upper management and help organize some kind of celebration of the success.

Closing

The meeting closes with May, as project leader, taking the responsibility of writing up the agreement, setting target dates, lining up the team, setting up the training with Sandy, getting the project off and running, and scheduling the first progress review meeting with Sandy. Implementation of the solution is ready to go.

Analysis of the case

Rob's needs for challenge and recognition helped explain why he wanted to be the project leader. By creating another role on the project that is just as significant, Rob's needs were met, as were those of the other team members. Stan thought May had the best temperament to work well with everyone on this project, so he supported her taking on the lead role, as did Rob.

Rob surprised Stan and May by expressing a need for good working relationships, which was something they also desired. Conflicting parties often find that they have similar needs. In addition, Rob didn't want to be singled out as the only person needing work on interpersonal communication skills. Everyone then agreed that learning these skills would be beneficial for the whole team — an example of the value of outlining the needs and evaluating the ideas to meet the needs of the stakeholders. Such discussion also led the group to look not only for ways to recognize Rob but also everyone else on the team. The discussion helped Sandy realize that Rob needed some one-on-one mentoring time from her as a good way to help meet his need for challenge and recognition.

As this case points out, more time was spent on identifying needs and working out a solution to meet those needs than on dwelling on the problem and the reasons for the conflict. Sandy recognized that taking a solutions-focused approach would be the key to success. By looking at a variety of ideas, as opposed to a single answer, the group expanded the discussion and developed a much more creative win-win solution.

Dealing with the Challenging Reactions

Like anything in life, the best-laid plans don't always lead to smooth actions. Coming in with a problem-solving model that provides you with an organized plan to resolve the conflict, however, increases the likelihood that you'll reach a mutually beneficial solution. This plan helps your meeting have a focus and reach a positive outcome.

Nevertheless, challenging reactions do arise sometimes, and you have to be able to deal with them constructively when they do. If you get caught up in these reactions, you may get derailed from your plan and no solution will be worked out. Remember that you're not done until an agreement has been reached that both parties support.

The following sections cover two challenging reactions that can come up in conflict-resolution discussions. You get helpful tips to work through these challenges so that you can reach the agreement you seek.

Handling the defensive blows

When people react defensively, trying to get your point across is difficult. A loud voice, anxious body language, interruptions, and verbal counterattacks are signs of defensive reactions. In a conflict-resolution discussion, these behaviors often start right when you bring up the problem.

First, here's what to do when faced with these defensive hurdles:

✔ **Avoid debating.** If you counter every attack or contrary point with an argument, the great debate will rage on. Such debating tends to fuel more defensiveness and has you sounding defensive, as well. The more you try to out-argue the other person, the more you create an adversarial interaction — a lose-lose strategy.

✔ **Avoid abandoning ship.** This is the nonassertive way of dealing with difficult behavior. End the conversation the minute the other person becomes defensive and you've reinforced a counterproductive behavior. If the other party verbally browbeats you once when he or she doesn't like what you're saying, the person will do it again if you do something in the future that he or she doesn't like. If you walk away with little effort made to address the concerns, you're walking away from any opportunity to work through the challenge with the other person and to ever reach resolution.

Therefore, here are a few tips to help you manage a challenging reaction:

✔ **Shift and show understanding first.** Using this active-listening effort (as described in Chapter 11), you let the other person have his or her say. Probe to get the point(s) fully explained. The more you try to cut the other party off and debate, the more off track your meeting goes. After you've heard the person out, paraphrase or reflective paraphrase to check your understanding of the message. Say your response in an inquisitive manner so you invite a confirmation or clarification in return.

Remember that you don't have to agree with what you're hearing; you have to work only to understand the message from the other person's point of view. Showing that you've heard what the other person has to say greatly diffuses the tension in your interaction.

✔ **Speak to clarify, not to counter.** After, not before, you've paraphrased or reflective paraphrased to show understanding, speak only to clarify, add useful information, or address a concern that you've heard. You can start out by saying such comments as the following:

- "Let me clarify something for you."

- "Please allow me the chance to add something that will help clarify my point."

- "I'd like to briefly address a concern you raised."

Avoid speaking if it does nothing more than show that you disagree or you think the other person is wrong — those actions only fuel more defensiveness.

✔ **Ask the other person to check understanding of your message.** In essence, you're asking the other party to paraphrase what you've said. It, too, is best done after you've shown understanding of the other person's message. Avoid asking for this with a close-ended question, such as, "Do you understand what I said?" That question gets answered with a "yes" or "of course" and tells you absolutely nothing. Instead, ask an open-ended question such as the following:

  • "What did you hear me say?"

  • "Can you please feedback your understanding of what I was telling you?"

What you may find when you do this is that other person is unable to capture your message at all or at least not accurately. When people get defensive, they often aren't listening to your whole message. What this tip does is push the other person to listen as well. When you show you can listen and ask the other person to do the same, you've influenced dialogue rather than debate and you've diffused the tension. Two people truly listening to understand each other leaves no room for defensiveness.

If the other person is unable to accurately show understanding of what you meant, briefly clarify your point but don't dwell on it.

✔ **Provide the reminder of your positive intention.** By stating a positive intention in the introduction of your meeting, you're helping set a constructive tone for your dialogue. Giving a reminder of this intention when a challenging reaction occurs, helps ease tension and refocus both of you on making something positive happen, as opposed to dwelling on the problem. When you give this reminder, you may find that it helps to be patient and in control, which keeps the other party from staying defensive for long. You aren't offering anything to fuel further defensiveness. In fact, when you take away the air, you extinguish the fire.

✔ **Move forward to the solution stage.** Remember what you're doing — working out a resolution to the conflict. After you've heard the person out, move ahead as quickly as you can toward working on the solution. The meeting is about making efforts work better for both of you, not about dwelling on what's wrong. Keep your focus moving in this direction and the other person's attention will go with you.

Dealing with the reluctant solution-maker

Sometimes the obstacle comes as you are attempting to work out the solution to the conflict. Your ideas are met with criticism and the other person offers little in return to help. You feel as though you're going nowhere and an agreement never will be reached. Here are a few tips to help you work through this challenge:

✔ **Probe to uncover concerns.** When your ideas are met with responses like, "That won't work," stick with the discussion. Ask open-ended questions (discussed in Chapter 5) to get an explanation for the concerns the other person has with your idea. By understanding that someone else's concerns can help, you can respond with ideas to address them or explain how the ideas offered actually help alleviate those concerns.

✔ **Brainstorm together.** Take the pressure to come up with all the ideas off you by setting up a brainstorming effort in which you each take turns coming up with ideas. Remind the other person of the ground rules for brainstorming, especially that no judgment or discussion is permitted until after the brainstorming is complete. After you begin, throw in a stupid idea or two. That often gets a reaction and a little humor going and sparks some creativity.

✔ **Talk benefits.** What are the positive gains from the ideas suggested? Sometimes, people need to hear the benefits to be convinced that the solution is a good one. Benefits are the gains that can be made from the ideas, not how the ideas work. Benefits can be saving time, saving money, improving communication, and increasing efficiency, to name a few.

Talking about benefits works best when you've heard the other party's concerns first. You want to talk benefits in terms of how the ideas for the solution help you, the other person, and any other party affected by the conflict.

✔ **Explore consequences.** This is a last resort. When every other option fails to come up with a solution, explore what can happen if the conflict is left unresolved. Ask open-ended questions to get the other person to think about this:

- "If we leave this issue unsettled, what happens for us?"

- "If you were in my shoes and you couldn't get the issue worked out with you, where would you go next to get support?"

Firmly let the other person know that you don't plan to leave the matter unsettled, and then ask questions like these examples, which often move people out of their state of reluctance into exploring options for a solution.

This step also lets the other person know that you'll go forward to get others — usually management above you — involved to resolve the situation. If you do involve others, it then comes as no surprise and takes place after you've made a good-faith effort to resolve the conflict directly with the source. Getting support from others then becomes much easier to do. This kind of message provides the source with an incentive to work out the situation with you rather than face the consequences of inaction.

TIP

Facilitating conflict resolution

On occasion in conflict situations, a *third party* (not directly involved) is needed to help the two conflicting parties come together to reach a resolution. If you're that third party, your knowledge of the assertive approach, the communication tools, and problem-solving models for effective conflict resolution covered in this chapter (and in Chapters 10, 11, and 13) is critical for helping bring about a positive outcome. To achieve success as a third-party facilitator, follow these tips:

✔ **Make sure both parties agree to have you facilitate.** Going in, you want both parties agreeing that having you facilitate the conflict resolution is fine with them. Get involved only if both parties want you.

✔ **Understand your role.** Your role in this situation is that of a facilitator. That means you help guide the meeting toward reaching a solution. The responsibility for the resolution of the conflict belongs to the parties involved. You aren't there to make an agreement for them or impose one on them. If you do, you become an easy target to blame when something goes wrong. You're there to help them help themselves.

✔ **Set your plan.** Determine the problem-solving process you'll use to guide the conflict-resolution effort. Know the agenda you want to follow. This is one meeting for which having structure is critical.

✔ **Prepare the parties individually before bringing them together collectively.** Meet with the individuals involved separately first. Have them write notes to prepare themselves for the upcoming conflict-resolution meeting. Have them write notes that follow the problem-solving model you'll use so they know to bring their key concerns and ideas to the table. Allow them to work through their strong emotions with you too. Then when they come to the meeting with their notes, they're focused and ready to engage in constructive dialogue.

✔ **Manage the meeting.** Assert yourself from the start at the conflict-resolution meeting. Set ground rules to encourage constructive behavior. Follow through with your agenda, having each person expressing his or her concerns one at a time through the problem-solving process. Actively listen to help clarify messages and periodically have each party paraphrase what the other is saying to keep the dialogue constructive.

✔ **Develop a working agreement.** Make the outcome of the conflict-resolution meeting a written working agreement that the two parties develop together. It spells out the solution and what actions each person will take to make the solution work.

✔ **Conduct a follow-up meeting.** End the meeting by setting a date when the parties can meet to review their progress on the working agreement. Give the initial agreement enough time to take effect and then meet with the two parties in a month or two to evaluate progress. In many cases, let them further follow-up on their own from that point.

Part V
Tackling Communication Challenges

The 5th Wave   By Rich Tennant

©RICHTENNANT

...which reminds me of a story about a dyslexic mathematician...

Oh no. Not the perturbation of transient time-independent theory joke again!

QUANTUM FEST

In this part . . .

Having some communication challenges at work? Who doesn't? This part explores some of the common communication challenges that people face in their jobs and gives you tips and strategies for conquering them. From making formal presentations to conducting interviews, from running a sales call to dealing with a difficult customer situation, from coaching your staff to managing your boss, this part covers them all and then some. It even has some important messages about communicating via e-mail.

Chapter 13

You've Got Mail: Managing E-Mail Communications

In This Chapter

▶ Making good use of e-mail to enhance communications

▶ Avoiding the misuses of e-mail

▶ Writing e-mail messages that keep communications positive

Most offices in the United States today have e-mail and Internet access as standard features. With these tools, you can not only talk electronically to everyone within your company, but you can also communicate online with people outside your organization. More and more people have computers in their homes and are able to send e-mail messages to their friends, family, and work associates. Now, when people ask for your address, they quite often mean your e-mail address.

Although technology has provided new means for person-to-person communication, it is not without pitfalls, and it has created many challenges for people as they do their jobs. This chapter can help you understand how best to use e-mail and how best *not* to use it when communicating on the job.

Note: Documents and reports that can be sent via e-mail as attachments aren't the focus here; they are work products in and of themselves. Rather, the focus of this chapter is on direct communication through e-mail.

To E-Mail or Not to E-Mail, That Is the Question

You may be like some people I run into these days who literally can spend their entire workday reading and responding to e-mail. Even for people who don't use e-mail to that extent, receiving and sending messages can take one or two hours per day. E-mail has become a standard part of communication in today's workplace. Like any form of communication, you need to use skill and judgment to maximize e-mail's value.

Knowing when to use e-mail

One of the major factors that have led to the popularity of e-mail is its speed and ease of use. Just type away on your keyboard, and in no time, you can send a short message to someone — a message that person receives soon after you send it. Using e-mail is much easier than writing a letter and putting it in the regular mail (or *snail mail*). As a result, e-mail can be a tool for many useful communication purposes, such as the following:

- **Sending interoffice memos:** Written communication in the office is nothing new. Many workplaces used to live and die by the interoffice memo. Today, you can send memos giving news and announcements about business, personnel, and policy matters via e-mail. Type the message and hit the Send button, and you can reach as many people in the organization as you want, at one time — a much more efficient process for distributing the news than the old interoffice memo method.

- **Making requests:** E-mail works well for making requests. Perhaps you need assistance on a project or you want to set up a meeting. People often respond quickly to these kinds of requests.

- **Making inquiries:** Sometimes, the quickest and easiest way to find an answer to a question is to ask in an e-mail. If the inquiry isn't overly involved and doesn't require a great deal of explanation, e-mail is a handy communications vehicle for getting an answer.

- **Keeping in touch:** Letters and cards aren't going away; they make for a nice personal touch in communications. On the other hand, e-mail enables you to drop quick notes to clients, staff in other departments, and other business associates. A simple here's-what's-been-happening-with-me, how-goes-it-with-you communication lets key businesspeople whom you may not see often know that you care about how they're doing.

- **Conducting routine business transactions:** Some business relationships, such as customer-vendor ones, run under established processes. In such cases, e-mail helps transactions run efficiently. For example, you (the customer) need so many parts from your vendor. The vendor tells you the price and when he can ship them, you confirm, and away you both go. When transactions and negotiations require little discussion, e-mail helps you exchange information and get the deal done.

- **Providing status and news:** If you're a manager who, for example, has salespeople in different locations or who oversees the work of field-service technicians — employees you don't have the opportunity to see very often — you can use e-mail to find out the status of their work efforts. If you want to keep your boss in the loop on your latest project or on what happened with that important customer issue you tackled today, e-mail is a great option for passing on the news and highlights. These kinds of updates and status communications help keep fellow staff informed and can usually be handled via e-mail.

✔ **Recapping agreements and discussions:** One of the best uses of e-mail is to reinforce verbal interactions, especially when decisions or agreements are made or when action items are established. Instead of leaving what you worked out in a meeting to your memory, you can recap these important points in an e-mail to team members. When minutes of meetings — the absolute essentials, such as decisions and agreements — need to be recorded, e-mail works well. By not leaving these important items to memory, you enhance productivity.

✔ **Seeking ideas:** E-mail can be useful for generating ideas. Maybe you're working on an assignment or planning an event for which you need assistance in brainstorming ideas. Using e-mail to solicit this input, which often doesn't require a thorough discussion or a meeting, enables you to save time.

✔ **Giving simple feedback on others' work:** *Simple feedback* means that the comments you write aren't long, aren't controversial, and have been requested. Many an occasion arises in which people want your feedback or thoughts on their plans, proposals, or other work. If that feedback doesn't require a great deal of explanation, e-mail can be a quick and easy way to pass along your comments.

E-mail can be an effective vehicle for sending and receiving various forms of news and information when live interaction isn't really needed.

Recognizing when not to use e-mail

Many of the problems connected with e-mail communication result from people using e-mail when they should be talking — and listening. Remember that e-mail is one-way communication and isn't usually live. You have less opportunity with written messages to be understood clearly than with live conversation because you can't use your tone of voice and body language to convey sincerity. In fact, on sensitive (or even some not-so-sensitive) matters, people often interpret your e-mail messages in a far worse light than you ever meant. Relying on e-mail when engaging in live conversation is more appropriate tends to increase the tug-of-war in working relationships.

To keep working relationships on a constructive level and to enhance productivity, here are some situations in which you should not use e-mail.

When you need to give constructive feedback on performance

There are two types of constructive feedback: positive feedback for good performance and negative feedback for performance that needs improvement. Although positive feedback given in an e-mail message may be well received, it still has less impact and seems less sincere than feedback given in person. And the less frequently positive feedback is given in person, the less sincere any attempts at giving positive feedback seem.

The recipient of negative feedback often interprets that feedback as far worse than was ever intended, and may stew about what was written. When the feedback is given via e-mail, the receiver doesn't have the opportunity to discuss the matter and work out solutions. Verbal, face-to-face communication allows the giver of feedback to explain his or her messages and to help the other person understand them, as they were intended, and then to listen to and understand the recipient's perspective.

The nature of giving constructive feedback — positive and negative — is verbal and informal. It works best when it's part of a two-way conversation.

After your previous e-mail messages get little or no response

You may encounter situations in which your inquiries made by e-mail get no response, or your questions are met with partial answers. When you send follow-up messages, you still get little or no response. The reasons for this lack of response vary: disinterest in your issue, too many e-mails to pay attention to yours, poor follow-through skills. Just because you think that you write the message clearly doesn't guarantee that the receiver thoroughly reads and acts on it.

Continuing to send follow-up e-mail messages after a couple of tries may turn you into an irritating pest and give those who want to ignore your messages even more reason to do so. Instead, talk to the person to find out what has happened and determine when you can get an answer to your inquiry. Although reaching the person, either by phone or in person, may take a few attempts, it's well worth the effort. The truth of the matter is that only live conversation can get an unresponsive person to respond.

When you address sensitive issues

Suppose you have a co-worker who wants to act on an idea that you know from experience will lead to problems, or you have reservations about your boss's proposal for a business change, or you've received a message from a customer who is unhappy about service. In these kinds of circumstances, attempting to share your feedback, thoughts, or feelings via e-mail often exacerbates an already touchy situation.

With e-mail, you don't have a chance to listen to what the other person is thinking. When you choose one-way communication to communicate about sensitive matters, you increase the risk of misunderstanding and tension, which is the opposite of what you're trying to achieve.

When you want to elicit support and understanding for important changes and initiatives

Organizations are going through so much change that, in many companies, change is the only constant you can count on. Written communications can help reinforce announcements and updates about changes or new initiatives, but as the sole communications for these matters, e-mail messages can create anxiety.

Only live and ongoing face-to-face communication about significant changes helps get people on board. The chance to explain the company's rationale, answer employees' questions, seek input and involvement, and address concerns is lost when this kind of communication is handled by e-mail. Rumor and innuendo — key ingredients in resistance to change — often fill the voids that are created.

When you need to resolve concerns and conflicts

Want to aggravate a conflict? Attempt to address it in an e-mail message. Trying to resolve conflict via e-mail is one of the major abuses of e-mail communications.

New terms from this technology have entered into the communications arena — *flaming e-mails* and *nasty grams.* A *flaming e-mail* or *nasty gram* is an attempt by one party to voice a concern to another party through an e-mail message that's harsh in language and tone. What often results is that the other party, hurt by the nasty gram, shoots one back through e-mail. Then, as the terminology goes, the *flame war* is on as the warring parties send negative e-mail messages back and forth — sometimes copying others on them as well. All this negative communication escalates tensions and brings no resolution to the conflict.

Voicing concerns and expressing disagreements involving strong opinions — which is what conflict is — through e-mail messages tends to be interpreted as far worse than you ever meant it. Attempts to address conflicts in this way come across as hiding behind e-mail — a passive-aggressive form of communication approach that's covered in Chapter 2. The only tried-and-true method for resolving concerns and conflicts is live, person-to-person interaction — face-to-face or by telephone when you and the other person are in different locations. Technology can't do it for you.

If you find yourself getting worked up or rewriting much of what you want to say when you're drafting an e-mail, you shouldn't send that message. If you have an important issue or problem that involves a high degree of emotion, go directly to the source to talk and listen — the assertive approach that's introduced in Chapter 2.

Staying on the Right Track When Writing E-Mail

Use care when communicating your messages via e-mail. Here are a few tips that will enhance rather than hinder your electronic communication:

- **Go for short instead of long in your messages.** The same adage applies with e-mails as it does with office memos: If you write more than a page, nobody wants to read it. In other words, the shorter your message, the more likely people will read and comprehend it. If you find your e-mail exceeding a page in length and you can't edit it to be much shorter, paste the information into its own document, attach the document to your e-mail, and use your e-mail message to briefly introduce the information in the attachment. In most cases, you want to stick to short e-mail messages.

- **Make your points directly and concisely.** Get to the point and say what you need to say as briefly as possible. Give the highlights (not all the details) and make the point relatively simple (rather than rambling). Go with the main point first and give supporting information next as needed. Verbosity in writing creates more confusion and less interest than face-to-face conversation, where at least you have the chance to adjust your message and help your listener understand it.

- **Keep your language constructive.** Say — or rather, write — your messages in the best way possible. Keep the words respectful rather than harsh. Avoid anything that sounds blaming or threatening: "You didn't do what you said you would do" or "If you don't do this, I won't do that for you." Also avoid words that can trigger negative reactions, such as *always, never,* and the not-words (*don't, won't,* and *can't*). Here are a few such examples:

  - "You always forget to follow the procedure."

  - "You never help out when I request your assistance."

  - "That idea won't work."

  - "We can't do that on such short notice."

In many cases, you can rephrase your message to be more constructive. And in some instances, you may be better off talking to the other person rather than sending an e-mail. The idea is to keep your language straight-forward and to focus on the issue rather than the person. Say what you mean while sounding matter-of-fact and positive. (See Chapter 8 for more on how to use language to have a positive impact.)

When people use all caps for some or all of an e-mail message, others interpret it as shouting at them. Stick to the standard practice of using caps only at the start of your sentences.

✔ **Watch the humor.** Having a sense of humor is a great attribute, especially in the workplace. Displaying that humor is much harder to do in writing than it is in person-to-person interactions, where you can gauge how the other person is reacting to what you're saying. The receiver of an e-mail message may interpret your attempts at clever wit as biting sarcasm.

If you can add an occasional lighthearted touch to your e-mail messages, great. The key is to focus on the content rather than the delivery.

As stated in Chapter 9, off-color jokes and ridicule are offensive to readers of your e-mail. Even if you think the other person wants to read the risqué joke you're forwarding, such messages can be forwarded to others via e-mail. Sending off-color or demeaning e-mails — even in jest — generally invites more trouble than fun.

✔ **Write for your audience.** As you do when speaking, consider whom you're addressing when sending an e-mail message. Understand who your audience is. If they respond best to brief highlights, keep the message short and sweet. If they like detail, give them explanations. If they speak in technical terms, use the jargon they understand (and vice versa — keep the language in lay terms when your audience does not know the jargon). Keeping your audience in mind helps you keep your messages clear, concise, and respectful.

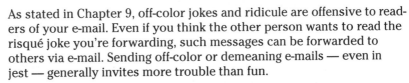

Copying others not involved with the issue

People sometimes copy others in conflict situations, which can stir up negative energy around the office. Upper-level managers often receive too many e-mail messages as it is and don't need more messages about matters in which their involvement isn't really needed. In addition, the other party in your discussion becomes aggravated by the move to notify others who aren't involved in the matter — sometimes this is viewed as a violation of confidentiality, too. And when other people are copied on the news, they may get involved (sometimes referred to as *butting in*) and make the situation worse.

If you see the need to copy others on an e-mail message that contains potentially sensitive information, make sure the other party or parties you dealt with on the issue agree that the need exists. Very simply, you should avoid other people's time and attention with unnecessary e-mail.

A message about voice mail

Voice mail is another form of technology that has become a big part of people's daily communication on the job. *Voice mail,* the verbal message you leave when someone doesn't answer the telephone, is often a much more efficient way to leave someone a phone message than to relay it to a receptionist, a secretary, or any other live person. You can say what you want without wondering whether the other person wrote down your message, let alone your name, correctly.

Using voice mail is like using e-mail. It works best when its purpose is to make a request, briefly share news, or pass on basic information. It does not work for raising concerns or addressing issues of a sensitive nature. Venting on voice mail, for example, tends not to increase understanding or excite others to help you. Voice mail can be used to request a discussion but should not be used to present details about an issue.

Like e-mail, voice mail is one-way communication and doesn't work when two-way interactions are needed. Also like e-mail, the shorter your voice mail messages, the better. Briefly tell the other person the nature of your call and what you want the individual to do, such as call you back, and then make sure that you slowly enunciate your name and phone number. Repeating your name and phone number helps the person you're calling write down and double-check your information. The faster you say your number, the less likely the recipient will understand it and return your call.

Be sure, too, to be responsive. When people leave you voice mail messages asking you to call them back, do so on a timely basis. When you are responsive and follow through, you build credibility. Credibility enhances your ability to communicate effectively so that others respond to you in the ways you want.

Chapter 14

Oh, No! I Have to Do a Presentation!

In This Chapter

▶ Recognizing the factors that lead to effective presentations

▶ Organizing your content to communicate clearly from start to finish

▶ Delivering your presentation with positive impact

▶ Making good use of visual aids

▶ Managing the audience and your own composure

For many people, one of the most frightening and nerve-racking experiences they encounter at work is being asked to give a *formal presentation:* speaking in front of a group of people and conveying some kind of important message for a period of time in an organized and interesting way. If you're part of this crowd, you can probably think of 100 other things you'd rather do than take on an assignment involving public speaking.

Yet try as you may to get out of it, if you've been asked once to give a speech to a group, you're likely to be asked again. So instead of fighting it, a better tack is to learn how to give presentations so that you come across well and live to tell about it the next day. And even if you're one of those rare types of people — those who don't mind speaking in front of groups or even enjoy it — giving an effective presentation is no small feat.

Formal presentations can be one of the great challenges of communication at work. You're called upon to speak in front of a group — sometimes to a handful of people and sometimes to a bunch of them. You have a limited amount of time to talk — sometimes a few minutes, other times an hour or more. You're expected to give the audience what it wants, from information to inspiration — an audience you may know or who may be totally new to you. So if such challenges strike a little fear in your heart, welcome to the human race — your feelings are normal.

Your ability to channel this anxiety and deliver a successful presentation can be a ticket to success in your career. Sales and marketing presentations, technical presentations, community presentations, and other types of business presentations go on all the time in many job situations. Doing well in such situations is your opportunity to shine; that is, to show what you can do and to connect with other people. Therefore, you may as well learn how to make the best of these situations if you're going to take advantage of these important opportunities.

That's the emphasis of this chapter: taking one of the greatest challenges of communication — giving formal presentations — and helping you prepare for and deliver them effectively. In particular, you'll find out how to organize a presentation from start to finish and how to speak assertively so that you come across clearly and connect positively with your audience.

Hitting the Essentials of Effective Presentations

You've probably seen many formal presentations at various business meetings within your organization, as well as at various events you've attended outside your organization, such as seminars, conferences, and professional association meetings. From observing these various meetings and events, you can learn a great deal about how to give an effective presentation.

You've probably noticed that some presenters are organized and confident and, as a result, really engage your attention. You've probably seen others who were a chore to listen to and didn't seem to know what they were doing up there on the platform. You may have seen professional speakers — those who get paid to talk to audiences — who ranged from highly effective to ineffective.

As you find out in the following sections what others do, you discover not only what to do but also what *not* to do. Learn from successes and mistakes about the essentials that make for effective presentations. In doing so, you'll come to recognize the importance of preparation and the steps that go into it, which increase your likelihood for success.

What breaks a presentation

To understand what makes an effective presentation, you must be aware of what breaks or detracts from a good presentation. In my seminars over the years, I have asked groups to name the reasons that technical or business presentations are ineffective. Here are the answers that come up most often — the pitfalls to avoid:

✔ **Looking or sounding nervous:** Sometimes nervousness is apparent when the presenter stands stiffly in one spot with his hands tucked in his pockets. Other times you see the presenter constantly pacing back and forth or scratching or fidgeting with her hands. Sometimes you detect nervousness in the quiver in a person's voice or his constant hesitation in delivering the speech. Even worse, sometimes speakers tell their audiences that they're nervous, which, along with all these nonverbal behaviors, tends to focus the audience's attention on the high anxiety level instead of on the talk.

✔ **Sounding monotone:** Nothing sounds duller, regardless of the content of the speech, than a presenter's voice that has no emotion or enthusiasm to it. The flat sound of a monotone voice is as bad as a singer singing off-key.

✔ **Speaking too softly:** When speakers are barely audible past the front row, audiences tend to barely listen. Restlessness and disinterest generally take over.

✔ **Making little direct eye contact:** When the speaker looks down, away, or over the audience during a talk, people feel disconnected. They question the speaker's confidence level and credibility. Quite often, the audience wonders why they should listen if the speaker can't look at them while speaking.

✔ **Reading slides or handouts to the audience:** Supporting materials and visual aids can add much value to a presentation. But when speakers read nearly every item on the slides or handouts, they insult the intelligence of their audience and render their materials nonsupportive. People come to hear speakers talk, not read. And often, when you start reading to the audience, you sound monotone.

✔ **Using overloaded slides:** Whether the technology used is a PowerPoint file or overhead transparencies, when the slides are crammed full of too much information, they lose their value. When people can't see all the tiny charts and data on the slides, they stop focusing, especially if the presentation depends heavily on slides.

✔ **Using too much jargon:** When the audience is less familiar with the specialized terms and language of the speaker's organization or field of expertise and the speaker uses this jargon frequently, a major disconnect with the audience occurs. Such language creates an audience of disinterested souls, many of whom take on that deer-in-the-headlights look.

✔ **Overloading with data:** This speaker is full of details — so much so that what's important in the message easily gets lost in the minutiae. You walk away confused or bored with no key points to remember.

✔ **Tinkering with the AV equipment:** When speakers look like wannabe mechanics with no skills — that is, when they become preoccupied with trying to get their audiovisual equipment to work — they tend to occupy the audience's attention with everything but the speech.

✔ **Sounding like a know-it-all:** This pitfall occurs when sounding authoritarian replaces sounding authoritative. An arrogant tone and overconfident voice and language come into play. Sometimes speakers act this way in response to audience questions — responses that, in effect, say, "Didn't you know this already?" or "That's a stupid question."

✔ **Being vague:** This is the opposite extreme of having too much detail. When the speaker is vague, all you hear are generalizations and platitudes with no specifics and no substance — a talk about a whole lot of nothing.

✔ **Rambling:** A rambling speaker just won't quit. The speaker's points are lost as he or she talks on and on. Verbosity and redundancy replace clarity and conciseness.

✔ **Coming across as disorganized:** This type of presentation has no flow or direction. The speaker jumps back and forth with various points and sometimes ends up rambling. Put this mix together and you usually have a presentation that does not maintain the audience's attention for very long.

✔ **Trying to be funny too often:** Humor in a formal presentation can be a nice touch, but with forced humor or just too much humor, the seriousness of the message gets lost, or worse, wisecracks alienate the audience. You see this sometimes when speakers make ongoing attempts to be funny or laugh at what they've said well before the audience does (if the audience laughs at all). In these efforts to be funny, the joy that humor can add is lost.

✔ **Having no closure:** I close this list with the pitfall about no closure. In some presentations, the only way you know it's over is that the speaker stops talking. The speaker offers no wrap-up and makes no other effort toward closure. When the speaker does nothing to end on a positive note, the audience walks away with less of a feel for what they heard — the presentation is incomplete.

Let these 15 common pitfalls serve as your checklist of what *not* to do when you need to give a formal presentation on the job. They not only lessen your effectiveness as a presenter but also lessen your audience's confidence in you as a competent professional. In many cases, speakers behave in these ways because they're unaware of their own actions. But you can use this checklist to tune in to what you're doing. When you know what not to do, you have a better understanding of what *to* do to make your presentations effective.

What makes a presentation

Now for the flip side. I've also asked groups in my presentation seminars to identify from their experiences the characteristics that effective speakers display. Here are the responses most often stated. Consider them tips to follow:

- ✔ **Being well organized:** Presentations should flow in a logical sequence. The points expressed connect in an orderly fashion. Thus the presentation is easy to follow.

- ✔ **Getting to the point:** The speaker is direct, clear, and, most important, concise. You walk away understanding and remembering the key points because they are stated succinctly and in language that makes sense to you.

- ✔ **Displaying confidence:** The speaker sounds authoritative as opposed to authoritarian, knowledgeable but not a know-it-all, and definitive rather than hesitant. In both voice and demeanor, the speaker expresses his or her points with certainty and credibility.

- ✔ **Showing sincerity:** Often going hand in hand with confidence, the sincere presenter's tone and language come across with care and respect. He or she conveys a certain believability and genuineness that engage others to want to listen.

- ✔ **Giving you a message:** You walk away from the presentation knowing exactly what was important. You grasp the main ideas or themes clearly and don't get lost in detail. You walk away with a message or point of view to remember.

- ✔ **Sounding positive:** The speaker's verbal and nonverbal messages match and have an upbeat feel. Points are expressed in the best way possible. Even when talking about tough issues, the speaker makes key points in a positive way.

- ✔ **Relating well to the audience:** The presenter understands your issues, speaks to them, and does so in language you can understand. You get information that's useful and relevant.

- ✔ **Having enthusiasm:** In their own style, whether low-key or full of energy, these speakers come across as animated. They sound alive and interested in what they have to say and, as a result, make their topic interesting and worth hearing.

- ✔ **Using visual aids to support the presentation:** Visual aids serve to enhance and work in tandem with the oral message. The speaker uses them as points to talk from or to help make a point.

Use this list as your guide — the to-do's for giving effective presentations. What this checklist points out is that effective presentations involve three key ingredients:

- ✔ **Substance:** The content of the presentation.

- ✔ **Style:** The delivery of the presentation.

- ✔ **Supporting materials:** The visual aids that enhance the talk.

On your mark, get set

Formal presentations are quite different from informal work-related conversations. In day-to-day interactions, you respond to the situation at hand. Preparation is often not needed or impossible. But with formal presentations, you're scheduled to speak in a group setting for a longer period of time with the communication going mostly one-way: You talking to the audience. Thus the expectations that you come across effectively — clear, organized, positive, interesting, and informative — are much higher. People want their listening time to be well spent. Winging it in formal talks — that is, coming in unprepared and talking and talking — is usually a recipe for disaster.

Preparation is the hard work you do before going live with your presentation, taking steps to increase the likelihood that you'll deliver a winning speech and to decrease the feeling of stage fright you may get when you're put in front of an audience. When you know what you want to say and how you want to say it, you're in a much better position to be confident and in control.

Here are the key elements of preparation to help put you on the road to success. Use the questions or comments listed under each step as your guide for what to figure out and do so that you're ready when speech time comes.

1. **Consider your audience and the time you have with them.**

   Think about the following:

   - To whom are you presenting?

   - What are the group's interests and issues?

   - What are the group's *hot buttons,* those points of sensitivity to address or stay away from in the talk?

   - How long do you have for your presentation?

2. **Determine your purpose.**

   Ask yourself these questions:

   - What's your goal for this talk; why are you giving this speech?

   - Overall, what do you want to achieve with this audience?

3. **Conduct your research.**

   Determine what homework you need to do for this talk and what answers you need to get.

4. **Develop your core message.**

   Decide on the key message or theme(s) you want to get across.

5. **Set your introduction.**

   Think about how you'll grab the audience's attention.

6. **Organize the body of your presentation.**

   Consider the following:

   - What are the main points you want to cover?

   - In what order will you present these points?

   - What supporting data and anecdotes do you want to use?

7. **Set your conclusion.**

   Decide how you want to bring the presentation to a close.

8. **Develop your visual aids.**

   Consider what materials — slides, charts, handouts, and so on — will best support your main points.

9. **Rehearse.**

   Practice your presentation often before the big day.

Some of these steps for preparation will need more attention than others, depending on the circumstances of your talk. But when you follow through on these steps, you'll be ready to deliver a confident and engaging presentation. Preparation helps you hit the essentials for an effective presentation.

Becoming Content with Your Content

You may have heard about what you need to do to deliver an organized presentation — tell the audience what you're going to tell them, tell them, and then tell them what you told them. In other words, in terms of content, an organized presentation contains three critical parts:

- The introduction
- The body
- The conclusion

The content of a formal presentation is *what* you're going to say. It is the verbal component, the information to be expressed. When you present the content in these three critical parts, you are more likely to come across to your audience in a clear and organized fashion. The following sections walk you through each of these critical parts, helping you understand their purpose and how to craft them effectively.

In the beginning: The introduction

Developing an organized presentation starts with your *introduction*. The introduction opens your speech. The common way in which many presenters start their talks — "My name is . . ." or "Today I'm going to talk to you about . . ." — is not much of an introduction. The purpose of a good introduction in a formal presentation is to achieve three goals:

- Grasp the audience's attention.
- Identify the topic and the purpose or core message of the talk.
- Provide a brief overview or agenda of what you will cover in the talk.

Speakers often overlook the part about grasping the audience's attention. They just start talking without creating any interest for the audience to want to listen. The key point to keep in mind here is that if you don't grab your group's attention up front, you may not have it for the rest of your speech.

The following are useful opening techniques that gain the audience's attention in a positive way:

- **Quote someone else.** A quote is a line said by someone else that helps set up what you're going to talk about. When using a quote, you want to accomplish two things: Cite the source of the line and tie the quote to your topic. Here's an example that a company president might use to talk about major changes happening within the organization:

  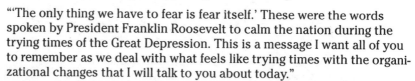

  "'The only thing we have to fear is fear itself.' These were the words spoken by President Franklin Roosevelt to calm the nation during the trying times of the Great Depression. This is a message I want all of you to remember as we deal with what feels like trying times with the organizational changes that I will talk to you about today."

- **Tell a joke.** A touch of humor in good taste is a great way to break the ice with an audience; that is, to ease the tension and relax everyone. The key, as with a quote, is that the joke must be tied to the topic you're going to talk about. Otherwise, it serves as a distraction and can turn an audience off regardless of its humor.

If you have the touch to tell jokes well, a joke can be a great tool for kicking off a presentation on a high note. My father was just such a person and often did this in his working career. He worked himself up into an executive role and as part of his job gave many presentations at company meetings. He established himself as a great joke teller in these presentations. Nearly every speech he gave started with a joke, such that his audience came to expect that a joke was coming. Quite often, the audience began chuckling the moment he started his speech with a line like, "What I'm going to talk to you about today reminds me of the time . . . ." After the joke came his deft transition tying the joke to the topic of his talk. Being told the jokes later and having the chance to sit in on a few of his presentations, I saw that sometimes the greatest laugh from the audience occurred when my father made the tie-in from punch line to topic.

If you're not comfortable as a joke teller, go with another introduction technique. There's nothing worse than watching someone fumble in trying to tell a joke.

✔ **Share a story.** A short story — with the emphasis on *short* — is another clever way to kick off a presentation. To work, the story needs to make a point or contain a message that you can tie to the talk that follows.

✔ **Make a bold statement.** This introduction technique involves a brief, thought-provoking statement that sets up your topic. Say it with a strong voice and it commands attention and gets the group ready to hear what will follow. Here's an example I've used in talking to groups in government organizations about customer service:

"Keep this in mind: Service in your jobs is far more than what you do. More important is how you do it."

✔ **Get the audience to participate.** With this technique, you start your presentation by having the audience do something, from a brief exercise to responding to questions. This technique gets people's energy levels up. By using the activity as a message to relate to your topic, you really capture the group's attention. The caution is to not do an activity that creates such a ruckus that getting the audience to focus back on you becomes difficult. Manage with care.

✔ **Ask a rhetorical question.** A *rhetorical question* is a thought-provoking question that you ask the audience but for which you don't expect an answer out loud. When you ask the question, you want to answer it either within your introduction or a short time later in your talk. Otherwise, the question serves only to confuse people. Here's an example for a talk on customer-focus group findings:

"If you were a customer doing business with your company, what would most frustrate you in this effort? As I share my findings from the customer focus groups, I'm going to tell you what these frustrations are and what you can do to address them to increase the quality of the service you provide."

✔ **State noteworthy facts.** With this type of introduction, you provide the audience with some interesting statistics or other facts that stimulate thinking and help set up your presentation. This technique works well when the facts you report are not common knowledge yet are relevant and stimulating. Just be sure to keep the statement brief so that you don't clutter your opening with too many easy-to-forget details.

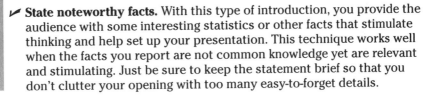

✔ **Make a list of common items.** This introduction involves using a short list of at least three items that have something in common. It usually works best to say the list and then state what the items have in common with one another.

"Joe Davis, Sue McGee, and Jose Martinez are three people you all know well in this department. They are also three individuals who have used the communication techniques I'm going to tell you about today and have seen their success double in the last year."

✔ **Give an interesting example.** In this technique, you start with a demonstration, showing something or telling of a situation that illustrates what your topic, and especially its core message, is about. To be effective, the example must be relevant and fairly brief. The example isn't the actual talk, but it sets up the presentation that will follow. A good example of this technique is the showing of before-and-after pictures from the use of a product or service. I remember a talk in which the speaker started out by showing a picture of two sets of lungs — one with no history of smoking and the other with a long history of smoking. Boy, did that get a message across!

As you prepare your introduction, carefully plan the opening technique you want to use to grab the audience's attention. Whether you start with this technique or with the component identifying your topic briefly doesn't matter. Just go with what works. Then follow these two components with a quick overview of what's to come to get your talk off to a strong start.

Shaping up: The body of a presentation

The *body* is the part of the presentation between your introduction and your conclusion. It's the longest part of the presentation. Its purpose is to get your key points across.

In preparing the body of your presentation, you have two main efforts — determine the key points you want to make and organize the sequence of these points. Here are some effective ways to determine the order or sequence of your body:

✔ **Problem to solution:** In this sequence, you first describe the problem. Then you give the recommended solution, emphasizing how it helps correct the problem.

✔ **Chronological:** In this sequence, you explain a series of events from past to present. It follows the element of time and moves the audience from event to event up to current times. You want to make the dates of the events stand out clearly so that the audience is not confused as to what occurred when.

✔ **What once was to what needs to be in the future:** In this sequence, you describe how things once were and how they need to be in the future. You use this sequence to recommend a new direction or course of action and to highlight how the future will be different from and better than what once was — the success to aim for. Sometimes this technique is also used to highlight the dangers of staying with the status quo and describe what will happen in the future if no changes are made now.

✔ **General to specific:** This type of presentation flows from general information to a few key points explained in detail. Sometimes it works by starting with a main idea and then detailing how to make the main idea work.

✔ **Less important to most critical:** This presentation builds to a climax. Each piece of information or topic serves as background for the one that comes next, and the importance of each subsequent topic gets greater and greater, right up to your climactic conclusion.

✔ **Logical topic flow:** Sometimes the various topics in a presentation just go in a certain order that makes the most sense. Presentations that center around processes (how to do something) work well this way, taking people through each step in the process.

✔ **Benefits and features:** *Benefits* are the gains to be made or the things that are good about your idea, product, or service. *Features* are how the idea, product, or service works. Benefits are the highlights; features are the details that support the benefits. Sometimes you want to cover all the benefits first and then explain the features; sometimes you want to go vice versa. Sometimes you want to go one at a time, describing each feature and the benefits it brings. Go with the order that works best for your subject and stick to it throughout the body of your presentation. When you do, the audience sees what's important and gets enough information to understand why.

✔ **Persuasive flow:** Some presentations try to persuade others to a point of view or convince them to take action. Here are three ways to organize a presentation where persuasion is your primary purpose:

- In a sales presentation in which you want the customer to decide to buy what you have to offer, describe features and then highlight their benefits to the customer.

- For other situations in which you're looking to persuade, such as when you're making recommendations to solve a critical problem, give the background of the issue first and then highlight what needs to happen and why.

- In still other persuasion situations, such as when you're convincing people to support a new process, provide the idea followed by its benefits and your recommendation for next steps.

Transitions and stories in a presentation

Transitions and stories are two of the finer touches that help make for a smooth flow and a more interesting presentation.

Transitions are segues, moving from one topic to the next in a presentation. They create the bridges that help move a presentation forward and connect points. Transitions are one to two sentences long. The best ones refer to the topic just discussed and point the audience to what's coming next. For example, "Now that we've looked at the main causes of the problem, I want to outline a solution that can help."

Stories are the sharing of life experiences, yours or others', that highlight or illustrate a point you're making. To make stories work

effectively in a presentation, keep these tips in mind:

- Determine the story's purpose and message.
- Plan when and where you will tell the story — when leading into a point or as an example after you have made the point.
- Have a sequence to the story. The best order to use is either chronological or building up to a climax.
- Tell it briefly — the highlights version.
- Connect the story to your key point with a sentence or two at most.

Organizing a sequence to your presentation helps give it a smooth flow. Start by determining the key points or topics you want to cover. After you determine these key points, think of the supporting data you need for each point and any relevant stories and examples that can help.

Give highlights with supporting points but avoid overloading your presentation with too many details. Also speak in the positive, as covered in Chapter 8, so that you're using language in the best way possible to get your message across.

That's all, folks: The conclusion

In the old cartoons, you knew that the show was over because the words "The End" came up on the screen. To utter such phrases as "The end," "I'm done," or "That's it" is not really a *conclusion* to a formal presentation. These phrases say nothing and stop your speech rather than finish it. A good conclusion brings closure to a presentation and also seeks a lasting impact. Because the conclusion is the last part of the talk, it is often the part the audience remembers best. So you want to leave them with a bang.

Here are six techniques that can help you bring positive closure to a presentation:

- ✔ **Recap:** A *recap* is a summary of the main points covered in your talk. You want it brief, generally covering no more than three or four points. If you cover more than that, you're probably going to get too detailed, lose your audience, and sound like you're repeating yourself.

- ✔ **Repeat of core message:** This technique ends your presentation by briefly emphasizing the theme that you have carried throughout the talk. It works really well when your introduction raised this theme and you want to wrap it up in the end.

- ✔ **Call to action:** With this closing technique, you finish by requesting that the audience take some kind of action. That action can be implementing an idea that they have gained from your talk or doing something to support a cause.

- ✔ **Quote:** This technique works best when you can come up with a witty or interesting line that wraps up your presentation nicely. As you do in an introduction, you want to identify the source of the quote and tie it, in this case, to what you said before it.

- ✔ **Rhetorical question:** In this technique, you leave the audience with a thought-provoking question. Most often, you don't answer it for them as you would in an introduction; instead, you leave them to ponder the question for themselves. As with an introduction, make sure that the question is relevant to what you've said so it has them walking away thinking, especially about possibilities or opportunities.

- ✔ **Story:** A story often makes for a nice close to a presentation. To make a story work in a conclusion, you want it to be relatively brief and to illustrate a point that ties to what the whole presentation was about.

Special Delivery: It's a Presentation Given with Impact

The preceding section dealt with the substance of a presentation, the content of what you say. This section focuses on style, which deals with the *delivery* of the content. Here is a reality that comes to pass in formal presentations: What you say is important, but how you say it carries more weight. Delivery is the *how* side of a presentation.

Delivering a presentation involves nonverbal communication. It is how you express your messages. The following sections explore five nonverbal behaviors of delivery and show you how to get the best out of them in your presentations. You can see that the nonverbal tools of assertive speaking, as described in Chapter 7, come into play when you give formal presentations.

Here's looking at you, kid: Making eye contact

One thing you can usually count on when you're giving a speech is that everyone in the audience is watching you. What are you doing with your eyes when the audience is looking at you?

In a formal presentation, your eyes serve as the nonverbal mechanism to connect you with your audience. As they watch you, you want to look at them. Here's what to do to achieve this objective:

- ✔ **Look at their faces.** More often than not, when you're giving a presentation, you're standing while the audience is sitting. Therefore, you're taller than they are. If you look straight ahead, you see no one directly, and the people in the audience wonder what you're looking at. Instead, look at the faces of the people in the audience. Your eyes give your message credibility and also serve as a magnet to draw people's attention toward you.

- ✔ **Include everyone.** As you look people in the eyes when you talk to them, scan the audience to reach everyone. Avoid locking in on a few faces and not seeing the rest of the group. Spend a few seconds on everybody and your eyes will reel everyone in to you — right where you want their attention. When you're making a point that pertains to a certain individual in particular, look at that person. Doing so makes the person feel included and important.

Getting your hands up: Using gestures

Gestures are what you do with your hands while you talk. Cling to the podium the whole time and you look like a tin soldier. Flail your arms around the whole time and you look like you've taken some strange drugs. For most people, the problem with gestures is usually not too many but rather too few. They don't recognize what gestures can do for a presentation.

The objective of gestures in a formal presentation is to give life to the talk and to emphasize key points. Gestures help you look relaxed and animated. In other words, talking with your hands is actually good to do, especially when giving a presentation. Here are a couple of tips to get the best from your gestures:

- ✔ **Go with the flow.** Gestures work best when they go with the flow of what you're saying. When they help give a visual picture of your words or help punctuate a point, gestures add energy to your message and greatly engage the audience's attention.

> ✔ **Vary your gestures.** If you stick with the same gesture or two throughout your speech, they will lose their positive effect. People will walk away remembering that particular gesture like it was a nervous habit and not remember what you said. Using a variety of gestures that show you getting into your message as you speak is the key to sparking positive attention from your audience.

Atten-hut: Paying attention to your posture and body position

You're more likely to be standing than sitting when giving a formal presentation. What do you do with your body? And what kind of posture should you show?

Slouching over a podium or leaning on a table as you talk makes you look too relaxed and lessens the seriousness in which your presentation is received. At the same time, standing still in one spot the whole time makes you look extremely stiff. So what do you do with yourself?

The objective with your posture and body position is to show alertness and confidence, to come across as relaxed yet with a sense of importance. Here are a couple of tips to help achieve this objective in a presentation:

> ✔ **Stand tall.** Stand at your full height. No leaning down or hunching over. Use good posture and, like your mother told you when you were a kid, don't let your shoulders slump.

> ✔ **Stand steady and comfortably.** Move your body in ways that fit with the flow of your presentation. No need to stand tightly in one spot the whole time; moving around in a general area can add a feeling of positive energy to your talk. On the other hand, don't race around or get into what looks like dance steps or rocking motions with your legs. Don't make people seasick.

> ✔ **When seated, sit up.** If you are expected to sit while you present, sit up. Slouching in a chair is really easy to do. At the same time, lean forward a bit as you look at and address your audience. This motion helps you command attention and puts confidence behind your message and in your voice.

I can't hear you: Using your voice

Your voice provides the volume, inflection, and tone of your message. It's one of the most powerful instruments you have to give the best of you in your presentation.

The stumbling president

I had a group a few years back that took my communications seminar in segments over the course of a few weeks. I covered in the course the importance of avoiding nonwords so that you come across assertively when speaking and delivering presentations. Shortly after this segment, the members of the group attended a major presentation given by their company's new president.

The new president, based in another state, had flown out purposely to meet the few hundred employees in the location where I was doing the training. He gathered them all together for a company meeting so that they could meet him and get an idea of the leadership direction he wanted for the company.

The next week in class, nearly everyone in the group reported that the new president had come across poorly in his presentation. They said that he used more than 100 nonwords in his talk of 15 to 20 minutes. They couldn't stop counting them. He left an unfavorable impression on almost everyone in the audience. The general sentiment was that he was a nice guy but had little confidence — not exactly the inspirational leadership you'd like to see in your company president.

When using your voice in a speech, your objective is come across with positive energy and sincerity. Your voice helps put you firmly and confidently behind your own talk, which has the effect of pulling the audience with you. Here are a few tips to follow to get the best out of your voice:

- ✔ **Project loud and clear.** In a formal presentation, you want the people at the far edges of the room to hear you easily. When you achieve that goal, everyone else will hear strength in your voice. This doesn't mean that you should shout; just pump up your volume so that no one has to strain to hear you.

- ✔ **Convey a tone of respect and importance.** Your tone of voice carries a tremendous amount of the emotion of your message and therefore greatly affects the message's overall meaning. Sound frustrated or upset and you turn an audience against you; sound insincere and you turn the audience off. You want your tone to say what you mean and mean what you say, and to do so with care and respect for your audience. That tone captures and holds people's attention.

In particular, think about the feeling you want to convey in your message — the feeling you want your audience to walk away with after hearing your presentation. Then speak with that feeling in mind, and you'll connect well with your audience.

✔ **Show a little enthusiasm.** In your own style, you want enthusiasm for the talk to come across in your voice. This deals with the pitch or inflection that you use. Avoid the monotone; have some life in your voice.

✔ **Vary at times for emphasis.** Your voice can serve as a powerful tool to emphasize key points in your talk, especially when you vary it from its normal volume and inflection. At times, get a little louder or softer on a key word or phrase, or put a little extra oomph in your voice at these critical moments.

Whoa, Nellie: Pacing yourself

Pace is your rate of speech when talking. Go too fast when you're giving a presentation and you may slur your words and confuse your audience. Go way too slowly and you may torture the group, who can't wait that long for you to make a point.

In a formal presentation, the objective of pace is to manage the flow of your delivery so that the audience hears your words clearly and leaves feeling comfortable. If the pace doesn't match what the audience is comfortable with, you lose their interest. Here are a few tips to help you manage your pace:

✔ **Go at a steady rate.** You're looking for a happy medium between too fast and too slow. If you concentrate on enunciating your words clearly and easily, you'll be right where you want to be.

✔ **Vary your rate at times for effect.** A little variation when making a key point — sometimes speeding up and other times slowing down — adds spice to your talk. The slight exaggeration in your pace helps grab the audience's attention.

✔ **Use pauses.** *Pauses* are those moments of breathing and silence that occur in the midst of speaking. They work well between thoughts to help you formulate how you want to make your next point. They help you stay on top of your pace instead of racing ahead of it.

Best of all, pauses help you minimize nonwords, talked about in Chapter 8. *Nonwords* are words that aren't words but are said aloud — the most common being "uh," "um," "you know," and "like." They often come from thinking out loud or searching for that next word. When uttered frequently in a speech, they make your pace choppy and distract your audience. Pauses enable you to stop and think and then speak; no useless noises are needed.

For Best Supporting Actor, Your Supporting Materials

Visual aids — the slides and graphics you show as you talk — are the supporting materials in a presentation. Their objective is to supplement your spoken message and add clarity and value to it.

The key here is to use visual aids to supplement your message rather than letting them be the focus of the presentation — a common mistake that some speakers make. The following sections make you aware of additional mistakes to avoid when using visual aids so that you get the best out of them.

Avoiding the pitfalls

The following are common mistakes presenters make when using visual aids in their talks:

- **Using visuals that are too small for the audience to read:** When the information on the slides is too small for the audience to see well, the visual aids tend to distract from your talk rather than support it. Visual aids that require magnifying glasses to see them clearly aren't aids of any kind.

- **Cramming too much information onto the visuals:** Beyond the size of the print, the volume of the information on the slides is sometimes too much to follow. The objective for each slide is not to cram as much data as you can onto it, but to highlight only one concept or idea that's explained in a few keywords or phrases and printed in large, readable type.

- **Including more than one concept per slide:** A slide or other visual aid starts to lose its value when it contains more than one key point or concept. The information is less organized and does not have a clear goal. Bunching and scrunching on visual aids doesn't grab an audience's attention in the least.

- **Handling the visuals or equipment for them awkwardly:** If you're not comfortable with the equipment you're using to show your visuals, consider either not using them at all or practicing their use so you don't look clumsy when your presentation goes live. People come to hear a speaker, not see a klutz.

- **Focusing on the slides or graphics and not the audience:** If you enjoy the visual aids you're using for your presentation, great. But if you look primarily at them and not much at your audience, people notice. You're usually better received when you face and talk to the live people and not to the inanimate objects.

✔ **Not having a clear connection to the main points of the talk:**
Sometimes you see speakers who have interesting graphics or slides but
don't explain how they support the talk at hand. When the audience
wonders what the point is of the visual aids you're using, using them has
no purpose.

✔ **Reading the points instead of providing the highlights about them:**
I save the best (or actually the worst) for last. This is the cardinal sin for
presenters. When you read your slides to the audience, they no longer
add value. People *can* read. They come to hear what you have to say, not
see how well you can read aloud. If you can't expound on the points of
your visual aids, your *presentation* will work better as reading material.
No need for anyone to attend the talk.

Preparing useful visual aids

Supporting materials can add value to your presentation. After you're aware
of what not to do with visual aids, use the following tips to prepare them so
that they supplement your presentation:

✔ **Include one idea or concept per slide.** Have each slide or graphic make
its own point so that it stands on its own. Doing so makes it easier to
determine where the visual aids fit in your talk, making their support for
the verbal message much clearer than when multiple concepts are put
on a slide.

✔ **Develop a title or heading for each visual.** This tip reinforces the point
that each visual should stand on its own. Give each one a title or heading so that it tells the audience what the points on it are all about. This
effort organizes your presentation and helps you know why you're using
a particular visual aid and where in the talk to use each one.

✔ **List key words or phrases.** This tip gets at two important points about
visual aids. One is that they work best as points to talk from and
expound upon, which is what key words or phrases help you do — like
talking from an outline. Second, by limiting the visual to a few words or
phrases, you make it much easier for the audience to see. No more sentences that crowd the slide and make it hard to comprehend.

✔ **Follow the rule of six.** This point reinforces the importance of making
visuals easy to see and read for the audience and of keeping them brief.
Thus the rule of six — no more than six words per line, and no more
than six lines per visual.

✔ **Use upper- and lowercase letters.** Capitalize the first letter of words,
but not entire words. For example, for a slide for a talk dealing with customer service, here is one line that follows this tip:

"Underpromise and Overdeliver."

Contrast this line with one in which the whole phrase is in capital letters.

"UNDERPROMISE and OVERDELIVER."

The combination of uppercase and lowercase letters on a slide tends to be more aesthetically appealing. Remember that you want the audience to see your visual aids easily when you talk from them.

✔ **Design visuals to be seen by the back row.** If the person in the back row of the audience can see your visuals clearly, so can everyone else, and thus they're not fuzzy-looking scribble that you ramble about. They truly become visual aids.

✔ **When in doubt, leave it out.** If you question whether you need a slide to help cover a point, or whether you should add more information to a particular slide, most often the answer is no.

Less is more. Being direct and concise with visual aids works best. Remember, you can fill in the gaps or add other information when needed simply by talking. Overall, effective supporting materials are brief, clear to see, and work to highlight your verbal message.

Live on Stage in Front of an Audience

Sometimes the biggest challenge in doing a presentation is not the presentation itself but contending with the audience's issues and your own fear. The following sections explore how to handle questions that come your way and how to stay composed while on the platform.

Responding to audience questions

In many business presentations, the recipients want a chance to ask questions. Allowing time for questions is to your advantage as a speaker because it gets the audience involved and gives you an opportunity to clarify key points and address concerns.

In some cases, the effectiveness of your presentation is evaluated more on how well you handle the questions that come your way than on the talk itself. Although you can anticipate some of the questions you may be asked and prepare responses to them, you won't know every question that people may ask. Yet in order to give a successful presentation, you need to be able to handle any and all questions that come up. Here are a few tips to help you respond to an audience's questions:

✔ **Determine when you want to receive questions.** Some presenters like to field questions from the group as people have them. This way, they can address matters as they arrive at points in the talk. Others like to hold questions until the speech is over. They don't want their flow interrupted, nor do they want to contend with an audience that may dwell on one issue for a while.

Go with the timing that's most comfortable for you. Just communicate in your opening when you want to take questions so that your audience knows what to expect. Then, if you've asked the group to hold questions until your talk is over, you can respectfully defer a question if someone interrupts along the way.

✔ **Listen closely to the questions.** Before you respond to a question, make sure that you understand what the asker is asking. Applying active listening tools (see Part II) helps you achieve this understanding. If you need to, ask questions to clarify and paraphrase to check your understanding. After the asker confirms your understanding, you're ready to respond to the question.

✔ **Be direct and concise in your answers.** Some people speak well when they have a prepared speech. But the minute you ask them a question where they have to talk off the cuff, they become verbose and vague and say a whole lot of nothing.

After you clearly understand the question asked of you, answer it as briefly as possible. Your listeners want answers to their questions; they don't want to be frustrated by rambling responses that give no clear answer.

✔ **Use your answers to reinforce key points or your core message.** Sometimes, questions from the audience give you the opportunity to re-emphasize key points you've made or to further promote a theme from your presentation. Take advantage of such opportunities. Emphasizing a point or core message as part of an answer to a question makes that concept more memorable for an audience.

✔ **Be positive in your responses, both verbally and nonverbally.** Just as you do in the body of your presentation, avoid coming across negatively in your language, tone of voice, and body language when you respond to questions. The tenor of your presentation needs to stay positive and sincere throughout, including the question/answer period.

Also, avoid sounding annoyed with the person asking the question. Show patience and receive each question with interest. Annoyance and arrogance are major turnoffs to audiences.

Speak in the positive, not only during the presentation but also as you answer the questions you field — be honest, direct, and constructive. In particular, avoid trigger words, mixed messages, and qualifier-type statements that negate your message (see Chapter 8). Translate terms that the audience may not be familiar with so that you keep jargon out and clear language in. Using a brief story to illustrate a point you're making when answering a question can also be very helpful.

✔ **Positively reinforce the asking of questions.** People need to know you're receptive to questions. Sometimes simple remarks such as "That's a good question" or "Thanks for asking" or "You've raised a good issue" go a long way to encourage questions and make people feel appreciated for raising them. This positive reinforcement adds to your sincerity level and helps you create a connection with your audience.

✔ **Don't make it up if you don't know the answer.** You may be asked a question to which you don't know the answer. Trying to fake an answer isn't a good ploy. People don't want to hear misleading or inaccurate speakers. On the other hand, you may be able to give a good answer if you give yourself time to think. Sometimes paraphrasing to check that you understood the question helps not only to clarify the question but also to give you time to think of the appropriate answer. In addition, sending the question out to the audience for their thoughts on the issue allows others to help provide an answer and gives you time to think. If you still aren't sure, tell the person that you'll check it out and get back with an answer shortly. Then follow through and do so.

Overcoming stage fright

Perhaps the biggest challenge in giving a formal presentation is yourself: You know the subject well and you're articulate in expressing it, but you're incredibly anxious about the presentation. *Stage fright,* a feeling of anxiety or nervousness that arises when a person is expected to perform in front of others, is a normal occurrence for people, especially when they have to get up in front of a group to give a speech. If you have such feelings, the key is to recognize that they are normal and then take steps to deal with them.

Here are some tips that help you move from high anxiety to relative composure:

✔ **Come prepared, come prepared, come prepared.** Know your stuff before the big day. Be in command of your material and how you want to present it. Winging it (just showing up and trying to talk off the cuff) increases the pressure you feel. Practice does help make perfect. Use preparation as a primary method of preventing stage fright.

✔ **Recognize that nervousness can be a positive motivator.** When I mention this tip to people, they often are surprised. They think that feeling nervous is a negative. Being nervous is a normal feeling that many entertainers and athletes experience before going on stage or into a big competition. It serves to drive them and spark energy. I know that I worry if I don't feel nervous when I give presentations because I want to have my energy up and not feel flat. When you think of nervousness as something that's not only okay but also stimulates positive energy, it becomes a motivator rather than an inhibitor.

✔ **Use notes to help.** No need to memorize your presentation — doing so adds undue stress, especially if you lose your place. On the other hand, having a written script of your whole talk may lead you to read the script, losing eye contact with the audience and sounding monotone.

Having note cards or an outline often works best. These materials serve as a reference to glance down at periodically and to then talk from to your group. When you develop simple notes as part of your preparation, they become useful aids that help keep you on track and composed.

✔ **If you stumble, move ahead.** Musicians make mistakes all the time when they perform. In most cases, they're the only ones who know that they didn't hit a note just right. People in the audience generally don't notice because the musicians just keep on playing. The same principle applies when you're giving a presentation. If you don't say that word just right or make the point as clearly as you wanted, keep going. Taking time to freeze up because you think you made a mistake or were less than perfect is a waste of time. No one expects perfection from you; they came to hear what you had to say, so keep your focus on the next point in your presentation.

✔ **Don't point out that you're nervous.** When you bring attention to anything that has nothing to do with your presentation, you take your audience's attention away from your talk. As in the preceding point, don't dwell on it if you stumble, because doing so will make you more nervous. Keep your focus on your talk and move forward with it.

How you feel on the inside often has little to do with how you're seen on the outside. People often don't know that you feel nervous unless you tell them. Remember that they came to hear your presentation, not to put you on the spot or make you uncomfortable.

Chapter 15

Hurdling Customer Challenges

. . . .

In This Chapter

▶ Managing sales interactions successfully

▶ Giving service that keeps customers coming back

▶ Handling difficult customer situations

▶ Gaining support from internal customers

. . . .

Sales isn't just the responsibility of sales representatives and account executives, although professional salespeople can benefit from the tips in this chapter. As used in this chapter, *sales* means getting someone to buy the product or service you're offering. Many people who don't carry tradi-tional sales-related titles still perform sales-related functions in their jobs. If you work in a service business such as a law firm, a public relations firm, an accounting firm, a construction business, an advertising firm, a financial ser-vices company, or a staffing services agency, part of your work is to help bring in business. That's sales.

Likewise, customer service is a responsibility for more than just the people who work in customer-service departments. *Customer service* in this chapter is defined as work performed that is of help, use, or benefit to someone else. In fact, whether you work in the private sector or the public sector, customer service is a part of your job — and everyone else's — to some degree. Whether your customers are primarily *internal customers* (those within your organization to whom you provide service) or *external customers* (those out-side your organization whom you serve) applying the tools of active listening and assertive speaking is critical for providing high-quality service to your customers.

In many jobs, sales and service go hand in hand. You may sell a product or service, but you also take care of that customer after you make the sale. Without good service, you won't get any more sales. And without serving your internal customers, the service needed for the external customers to whom you're selling your wares won't be effective.

Providing quality service and sales to customers is quite a challenge in many jobs. Customers can be demanding and, at times, even unreasonable. Also, problems sometimes affect your customers, many of whom let you know their dissatisfaction when they're unhappy. Yet without customers to serve and sell to, you have no job and no business. Like them or not, you need satisfied customers. Therefore, knowing how to handle the challenges of servicing and selling to customers is the focus of this chapter.

You're Selling, but Are They Buying?

Many people think that the key to success in sales is how well you can persuade a potential customer to buy your product or service. They imagine the stereotypical image of a used-car salesperson — pushy and talkative — and think that's the way successful sales are made. It isn't.

Your sales success more often lies in remembering this point: You have two ears, two eyes, and one mouth, not one ear, one eye, and two mouths. In other words, your ability to listen effectively is as critical, if not more so, than your ability to talk. When you listen effectively, you discover what's important to the customer so that when you talk, you say what the customer needs to hear. This section explores two main issues in this process for successful sales: how to uncover customer needs and how to negotiate a business deal. In the following sections, you see how active listening and assertive speaking become great selling and service aids for you.

Identifying needs and selling to meet them

One of the common mistakes that people make in sales situations is to focus on the product or service they have to sell. Doing so leads them to talk more than they listen and to say things that the prospective customer may not be interested in hearing. They overlook two important aspects of why people buy:

- People buy to fulfill a need.
- Buying is often an emotional decision first; a rational decision (to justify the purchase) comes second.

If you don't know or understand a customer's need, or if you don't make the buying experience satisfying for them, the likelihood of your persuading the customer to buy anything is slim.

As opposed to selling to consumers, you may be involved in business-to-business selling, in which you sell fairly high-priced products or services. If you're going to make a deal in this situation, you probably aren't making the sale on the spot. A sale often involves a few meetings, sometimes with a variety of people, over a period of time — a longer sales cycle than in a one-shot situation. Thus a big part of what you're doing is *relationship selling* — building positive rapport so that customers buy what they need from you rather than someone else.

Regardless of what you're selling, the following tips can help you identify customer needs and build a positive relationship so that you meet those needs. Keep in mind that all of the following tips can be summed up as, "Listen first, talk second."

Probing to uncover customer needs

Probing, as covered in Chapter 5, is a tool that utilizes questions to listen actively. You ask open-ended questions (as opposed to close-ended questions) so that the speaker expresses thoughts and ideas freely. And those thoughts are expressed as sentences instead of one- or two-word responses.

Because customers often don't express their needs upfront, you want to probe to find out what those needs are. You also may find that what customers say they want isn't what they really need. To get at what they really want, you have to ask questions. Here are a few open-ended questions that you can adapt to your sales situations to help uncover these needs:

- ✔ What are you looking for?
- ✔ What are the reasons for what you're asking to have done?
- ✔ What issues or challenges are you facing?
- ✔ What led you to want to explore the product or service I have to offer?
- ✔ What questions can I answer about the product or service I have to offer?
- ✔ What's been your experience with this type of product or service?
- ✔ With what you're looking for, what would you like to see happen?
- ✔ What does your business do?
- ✔ In a business relationship with a vendor or service provider, what's important to you?

Confirming that you understand what the needs are

Your probing for specifics draws out your client's or customer's needs. After you get a picture of what these needs are, give feedback to check your understanding of what you've heard. Use the active listening tools of paraphrasing or reflective paraphrasing to do so: In one sentence, they help you check your understanding of the client's main idea in the message — paraphrasing — or the content and emotional meaning heard in the message — reflective paraphrasing. See Chapter 5 for more information on these two tools.

Here's an example:

"So you've been frustrated by a lack of reliable service, and if that service is backed in actions, not just words, that's what you really need. Is that right?" *(reflective paraphrasing)*

"What you're telling me is that you're looking for some kind of training program that can show your employees how to serve and satisfy your customers?" *(paraphrasing)*

As these examples show, in one sentence you capture the essence of the message you heard. And you check your understanding: Thus the sentences end with a question mark that invites a direct response to confirm or clarify your feedback on the speaker's message. In this way, you can avoid misunderstandings.

Understanding objections before you attempt to address them

Sometimes you hear concerns or objections from a customer about what you're offering — from the price to the quality. If, when an objection comes up, you react by speaking first without fully understanding what the concern is all about, you risk alienating the customer. Speaking without a true understanding can make you sound like a pushy salesperson, and the customer may not want to do business with you.

Instead, shift and show your understanding of the customer's concerns first — the active-listening effort described in Chapter 11. This effort involves using paraphrasing or reflective paraphrasing in a potentially conflictive situation to check your understanding, and may also involve probing first to gather background on what the client's issues are. You may say, for example, "Please tell me what your concerns are with what I've been explaining to you." Ask questions to get specifics and then give verbal feedback to check your understanding. Sometimes, what customers say on the surface isn't the full extent of the concerns and issues they have. Asking the customer for suggestions on what would help them overcome their objections can provide helpful input.

Emphasizing what you can do to meet the needs or address the concerns

When you understand first what customers' needs are and any objections or concerns they have, you're in a good position to address those needs or concerns when you speak. Focus on what you *can* do as opposed to what you *can't* do (see Chapter 8). In particular, tell how what you have to offer directly benefits the customer.

After you've heard and understood the objections, overcome them by showing how what you can do helps alleviate the customer's concern — tie the message to how you can benefit the customer. For example, if a customer has concerns about your price, explain how your product or service can help solve problems, increase efficiency, or provide some other benefit to meet the person's needs. By doing so, you help the client see value in the money spent.

Keeping your messages concise and clear

In Chapter 8, I discuss how less is more and explain that you must speak in terms your audience will understand — this tip ties in with that tool. Avoid being verbose, overloading on details, and using the latest buzzwords and jargon. Get to the point and use language that means something to your clients. Translate terms you need to use so that your client understands your points. You build credibility and rapport when you speak on your client's level.

Speaking with sincerity and confidence

This tip encompasses many of the nonverbal tools of assertive speaking covered in Chapter 7. Sounding sincere and confident means first doing your homework and knowing your products and services well enough to explain their features and benefits to customers. You don't have to know the product as well as, for example, the engineers who designed it, but you at least need to know how the product works and how it can help meet a customer's needs.

Then, when you speak, do the following to help you come across sincere and confident:

✔ Make direct and steady eye contact.

✔ Project your voice and speak with certainty.

✔ Use a tone that communicates knowledge and respect.

✔ Let gestures go with the flow of your message to add enthusiasm.

✔ Sit up and look alert.

Leaving issues hanging

Martha was involved in helping to start up a consulting services business. She did well at finding potential customers and had resources lined up and ready to serve those customers. Her challenge came when she met with the prospective clients.

Martha could explain fairly clearly the services her firm offered, and she could do so in a friendly manner. She could listen to what the clients' issues were, if expressed to her. Her biggest difficulty in these sales calls was that her conversations ended without definitive closure. Whether or not clients were interested was not flushed out clearly. What was to happen next, and when, were not discussed. In the end, what essentially occurred was a nice presentation with little impetus for clear action on the client's part. As a result, Martha seldom walked away with business, and seldom did she get calls back asking to do business with her firm.

Coming across sincere and confident engages your client and helps you build a sales relationship. When you listen to gain an understanding of a customer's needs and you speak directly and clearly about how you can help meet those needs, you couple persuasion with credibility without being pushy — and that's the key to success in sales.

Closing conversations

Check the customer's interest level. Asking for feedback as simple as, "What do you think?" helps you gauge whether you have a potential business deal and also helps you draw out any concerns or objections.

End every sales-related conversation by knowing what's going to happen next. Because many sales situations require further discussion, finish by outlining the next steps with the customer. Determine what needs to happen and when you will talk again. Use primarily close-ended questions (see Chapter 9) such as, "When should we talk next to explore these matters further?" Also, remember to check your understanding of any agreements reached so far. In this case, you recap and ask for confirmation.

If the time is right, ask for the order: "How about I make you a proposal and we talk next week to finalize it. Will that work for you?"

Negotiating to seal the deal

Sooner or later in any sales-type situation, you have to talk money. The customer wants to know how much your product or service is going to cost. In many cases, however, especially in business-to-business sales, one price doesn't fit all situations. Volume of business, complexity of an order, and the time involved to fulfill the order are just some of the factors that come into play in how much a product or service will cost the client. Nonetheless, you have to talk dollars for the deal to close. No customer says, "Charge me whatever you like and I'll gladly pay it."

When you need to talk money in a sales situation, avoid the approaches of nonassertive negotiators and aggressive negotiators.

✔ The *non-assertive negotiator* sounds hesitant and even sometimes apologetic in stating how much something will cost and lowers the price quickly at the slightest look or sound of consternation from the client. In the nonassertive approach, you sound uncertain and, as a result, decrease the value of what you have to offer.

✔ The *aggressive negotiator* pushes hard, comes on strong, and shows no willingness to compromise when talking dollars. In the aggressive approach, you come on as overbearing and, as a result, convince the other party to avoid doing business with you.

Instead, the *assertive approach* works best in negotiating deals. What this means is the following:

- ✔ Business negotiations are treated as a collaborative discussion rather than a game or a battle of wills.

- ✔ Business deals are worked out to be good for both sides to the greatest extent possible.

- ✔ The focus of discussions is on meeting needs, not solely on money.

- ✔ You express yourself confidently and listen actively.

- ✔ You conduct negotiations so that you build relationships for the future, not just the present.

As these points demonstrate, an assertive negotiator follows the principle of being consistently respectful, as outlined in Chapter 10. The emphasis is not only to make the deal now but also to lay the foundation for future business should opportunities arise again.

Here are the key steps to follow to negotiate sales deals assertively:

1. **Know the customer's needs before making your offer.**

   As much as you can, find out what the customer's needs are before you begin the actual negotiations. During phone calls and sales visits, listen to uncover these needs. Knowing the client's needs helps you craft deals that are designed to meet those needs without focusing on just money. This information is what I call "the gold." Once you gain the gold, you have the opportunity to make the deal. In addition to wanting a reasonable or affordable price, business customers have such needs as the following:

   - Gaining solutions to their problems

   - Building long-term relationships with their vendors

   - Receiving responsive, timely, and user-friendly service

   - Getting reliable products

   - Developing stronger staff or more efficient systems

2. **State your offer firmly and confidently.**

   Don't hesitate. Know that you're giving a fair price for the value of your services and products, and sound that way. As needed, give the business reasoning on which your offer is based — the time involved, the complexity of the work, or the volume requested, for example. Keep your explanations brief.

3. **After making your offer, wait patiently.**

Let silence be your ally. Sometimes customers go through the *hemming and hawing phase* as they ponder an offer. Stay out of the way. The more you talk at this time, the more you get in the way of their thinking, and the more doubt you create in their minds. Often, after the hemming and hawing is over, the client comes back and accepts your offer, and the deal is done.

4. **If the client expresses concern with your offer, explore the reasons for it.**

Listen first, speak second. Probe to find out the reasons for the concern and then paraphrase or reflective paraphrase (see Chapters 5 and 11) to confirm your understanding. Avoid talking and making any effort to address the concern until you gain this information definitively. Talking before then can make you sound like you're making a rebuttal in a debate, which can turn you into an aggressive negotiator.

5. **Address concerns on the basis of worth and benefits.**

People need to see that they're getting value for what they buy. You may be able to persuade a customer to accept your original offer by empha-sizing the worth of what you're offering — not your wants or demands — and explaining its benefits to the customer. When you show that what you have will meet their needs, customers are reassured that spending the money is worthwhile.

Here's an example. A client is seeking temporary high-tech labor help for a project. Your staffing firm provides such labor. Here's how you over-come the concerns you've identified with an assertive message:

"To recap, your critical needs are to get this project done on schedule and to acquire talent who can come in and get the job done with little guidance. Based on these needs and the market value of such skills, you'll find $100 an hour a cost-effective rate for these services."

6. **If the concern about price still exists, explore other options.**

You don't want to provide a lesser offer before this point, but sticking to your original offer now makes you look stubborn and aggressive. Explore options together for mutual gain. Sometimes you can negotiate longer terms for a service or a higher volume of product for a lower price. Sometimes you can agree to a lower price now and come back and look at a higher rate a few months down the road after you have estab-lished a positive track record for the client. Other times you can agree to reduce the scope of the service or product to meet a reduced price.

Ultimately, if the client demands a price that isn't reasonable for your business, say, "No, thank you." You're out to make deals that meet the needs of both parties. Thanking the client and saying no firmly and politely leaves the door open should the client reconsider and, more important, you leave the relationship on a respectful level.

7. Confirm the agreement.

After both you and the customer agree to the deal, recap and confirm the understanding you reached — use close-ended questions (see Chapter 9) to ask for commitment or agreement. Then talk about the next steps for implementation and get the order rolling.

Quality Customer Service Is Not an Oxymoron

You've probably seen statistics that say the cost of attracting and gaining new customers is far greater than the cost of keeping them. But if you don't provide customers with quality service, they may not come back for more.

I define *quality customer service* as adding value to the product or service a business offers, especially people value. This valuing (or not valuing) of people occurs more often at the points of contact, the interactions during which a customer seeks service. If the customer finds the help at those points of contact to be consistently respectful, responsive, accurate, efficient, and reliable, quality service is achieved — the people value shows and satisfies the customer.

The following sections provide you with the thinking and communication actions that help you deliver quality customer service consistently. If customers get good service only some of the time, the service isn't good at all. When customers can count on every interaction being positive, you have quality service working well.

Following the Golden Rule

The tools of active listening and assertive speaking play a major role in delivering quality customer service. You begin the effort by thinking like a customer. Actually, doing so shouldn't be hard because you've been a customer for many years yourself.

In workshops I've done on customer service, I ask participants to list the behaviors they've experienced as customers that they consider to be examples of good service. Here are some of the more common examples mentioned:

- Displayed a friendly and courteous manner.
- Acknowledged my presence and sometimes even my name.
- Followed through and did what they said they would do.
- Made the effort to understand my needs.

✔ Directed me to the resource who can best help me.

✔ Offered assistance when I was wandering around but didn't pester me.

✔ Had a patient and caring manner and listened to what I had to say.

✔ Responded to problems empathetically and corrected them in a timely fashion.

✔ Helped me get things done or find what I needed.

✔ Gave recommendations that helped me make decisions.

✔ Spoke to me in lay terms and made good sense in doing so.

✔ Responded in a timely and helpful manner to my requests or inquiries.

These dandy-dozen service behaviors are the experiences customers may have at the point of contact with you. When they have these experiences, they tell others and come back to do more business when future needs arise. When the opposite of these behaviors occur, customers also tell others, and they don't come back to do more business with you. If they do anything, they file complaints with your management. When I ask workshop participants to describe their experiences with poor customer service, the volume in the room goes up and the stories get longer. Emotions tend to run high when people have negative experiences.

When you remember what you've experienced when receiving good service and use this thinking in your job, you increase the likelihood of your using the *Golden Rule* — do unto others as you would have them to do unto you. You also increase your awareness of your own communications and are in a better position to use the tools of assertive speaking and active listening in customer interactions.

Part of thinking like a customer or making the Golden Rule work for you is putting the focus of your *points of contact* (live interactions with customers), whether they occur over the phone or in person, on understanding and satisfying customer needs. Here are seven common needs that customers bring to business interactions:

✔ **Receive courtesy and respect.** From your nonverbal demeanor to the words you speak, what customers need from you in every interaction is to be treated with care and consideration.

✔ **Receive attention and responsiveness.** Customers are looking for listening and understanding — someone who acknowledges their presence and their issue.

✔ **Get prompt action and timely service.** Customers need to avoid unnecessary delays. Act as quickly as possible in providing the service.

✔ **Have commitments met.** This need is about doing what you stand for and doing what you said you would do.

> ✔ **Get assistance.** Customers come to you because they need some form of assistance from you. They need that help so that matters are handled properly and efficiently.
>
> ✔ **Be given accurate information.** Customers want you to know your stuff and provide information to help them make decisions, complete transactions, and get answers that make sense.
>
> ✔ **Resolve problems.** Sometimes this need arises when the other needs aren't met. It's about fixing problems, not blaming; about taking responsibility, not making excuses.

Customer needs often come in clusters. In one interaction, three or four needs may come into play. The neat part of this is that sometimes one or two actions on your part can satisfy a whole cluster of needs. A critical element that helps you satisfy these customer needs comes down to how you communicate.

Communicating with impact to deliver quality service

As you begin to focus on meeting customer needs, you're ready to begin acting in a way that satisfies those needs. In particular, this section gives you six communication tips that lead to quality customer service:

Identifying the customer's needs

What is the customer looking for; why is your service being sought? Probing (see Chapter 5) helps you discover the answers to these questions. Often, the effort starts with a simple question asked in a courteous manner, such as, "How can I help you?" Follow this question with further probes that provide you with the specifics of the customer's situation, and then use the active listening tool of paraphrasing to confirm your understanding.

In brief, listen before you act. The effort is often quick, but it saves you much time and the customer much aggravation. After you correctly identify the customer's needs, you're ready to act accordingly to meet them with your service.

Sounding definitive and genuine in how you can help meet the needs

You can do so with your language and your manner. In terms of your language, speak positively, as covered in Chapter 8. In particular, emphasize what you can and will do in response to customer requests and inquiries. The assertive speaking tools of can-do and will-do language communicate helpfulness and commitment — music to a customer's ears. Avoid the trigger words such as *try, maybe,* and *not* in your messages. They communicate doubt and uncertainty about whether you can help.

Quality service even in enforcement roles

I have done customer-service work with those who work in the public sector — that is, in government jobs. Many roles in government are designed to enforce regulations and laws. Yet what often gets overlooked is that following the Golden Rule can and should apply in public-sector jobs. You'll find that complaints about these employees often have little to do with anything they did technically and more to do with the abrasive or disrespectful manner shown to the customer during the interactions. The customer need of receiving courtesy and respect can still be met even if the customer would rather not see you enforcing a particular code or law.

I tell the story to public-sector groups that one of the best examples of quality customer service I've ever received was from a state highway patrol officer in New Mexico who gave me a ticket for speeding some years ago. In the whole interaction, he explained to me what he was doing and why. He spoke to me by name and gave me his name. His manner was courteous, and he did his work in a timely fashion — two important customer needs were being met. His objective, as he said, was for me to drive safely while I was visiting New Mexico. Although I didn't like getting a ticket, his communication was reasonable and professional the whole time — nothing I could be angry about. Instead, I drove away wishing that more police officers and government employees could learn to give quality service like this patrol officer did.

If you do need to say no, briefly give the reasons. Wherever possible, offer alternatives on what you or the customer can do or where the customer can find help. Doing so keeps you positive and helpful in both words and actions.

Avoid using the word *policy* as your primary reason for saying no. Quoting company policy makes you sound like a rigid rule enforcer, not a helpful service provider. Explain the policy in lay terms, how it works, and why it's needed.

To sound definitive, speak loudly and clearly. Avoid the hesitation that comes from using nonwords like "um," "uh," and "you know." Use pauses to help you breathe, and think before you speak so that you sound certain. If you're face to face with the customer, make direct and steady eye contact.

In addition, sound sincere and match your tone to that of the customer speaking to you. Consider using two ranges of voice tone based on what you hear coming from the customer:

- ✔ Customer sounds neutral to lively — you sound upbeat.
- ✔ Customer sounds worried, angry, or upset — you sound concerned.

No one wants to hear a bubbly, happy-go-lucky voice when they are greatly bothered by a problem.

When in doubt, check it out

One of the least useful initial responses to a customer request or inquiry is "I don't know." Saying "I'm new here" is no help either. These trigger phrases make you sound incompetent and unable to help. Of course, making something up when you don't know the right answer is even worse.

Instead, if you don't know the answer to a customer's question, give a response such as, "Let me check that out." Then indicate when you'll follow up with an answer and do so. This kind of response makes you sound resourceful. No one expects you to have all the answers; just communicate that you'll find out the answers, and you're meeting important customer needs — especially for accurate information.

Translating: Stick to lay terms

Talk to customers in plain and simple terms. Hold the technical jargon, keep the acronyms out, avoid citing regulations, and stay away from sounding like a policy manual. Customers don't need to be experts in your field — that's why they come to you. Let your language make them feel welcome by communicating in terms that make sense to them or by explaining the terminology they need to find out in clear, understandable language.

Underpromise and overdeliver

This customer service idea (covered in Chapter 8) is about making time commitments that you can meet, if not beat. Sometimes you're asked when something can be done or when you will have an answer to a question. Giving a vague answer doesn't help, nor does saying that a date isn't reasonable just to give an answer.

When you underpromise and overdeliver, you first estimate how long fulfilling the request will take you and factor in a cushion of time to be on the safe side. Then, in definitive language, you say when you will be done. For example, when you respond to a client's request for an assignment to be done by confidently saying that you'll have it ready within one week, that means you'll get the work done in less than a week, or by one week at the latest. If an unexpected variable comes up that will delay your completion time, notify the requester in advance of the due date you set and then set a new deadline.

The idea in this communication effort is twofold:

- ✔ Truly think through how long a request will take to complete before making a commitment.
- ✔ Follow through and do what you said you would do.

When you consistently underpromise and overdeliver in language and actions, you manage customer expectations and enhance customer satisfaction by providing reliable service.

Handling problems with the language of solutions

Problem situations are a real test of the quality of your customer service. They are a big part of why customers seek your assistance. How do you deal with such challenges? If you use the assertive speaking tool of the language of solutions (see Chapter 8), you communicate the steps that you will take to resolve the problem. For example, you explore options and ideas with the customer. Your language focuses on actions to occur to rectify the situation — efforts that greatly relieve customer anxiety when problems come up.

Say, Mate, Your Customer Is Irate

Probably the greatest challenge in providing customer service is dealing with a difficult or irate customer. A *difficult customer* is a person to whom you're providing service who is emotionally charged and very concerned about an issue. Anger, frustration, and distraught feelings are the strong emotions that the customer may display — and these aren't easy emotions to deal with.

Reasons vary as to why the strong emotions exist, but from the customer's point of view, there is a big problem. Don't use only volume as an indicator of these kinds of hard feelings; look at tone and body language to tune into emotions. For example, someone seething at you may speak at a low volume, but you may hear a sharp tone coupled with a wicked stare.

The following sections provide a problem-solving model to guide your communications through these difficult customer situations. They also give you a few other key tips to help you manage yourself so that you're in control and you can best help the customer.

Problem solving with difficult customers

The key to handling difficult or irate customer situations is to look at them as problem-solving challenges. Therefore, you need to have a problem-solving model to follow and at the same time emphasize that you care at each step along the way. Here is a useful model to follow:

1. **Show empathy.**

   In simple terms, listen with care and respect and show that you understand what you're hearing from the customer. Because interactions with difficult customers often begin with strong emotions, don't be afraid to acknowledge the emotions you're hearing. This effort involves using the active-listening tools of reflecting feelings or reflective paraphrasing (see Chapter 5).

"Sounds like everything so far has been one frustration after another for you. Is that right?" *(reflecting feelings)*

"You're feeling inconvenienced because of a process that has not gone as quickly as expected?" *(reflective paraphrasing)*

The key to diffusing the tension is to show the person that you care. When people have problems that make them upset or angry, they connect best and feel better when they're dealing with professionals who show that they sincerely care. Part of this sincerity comes from acknowledging the emotions you're hearing, because if you're not truly listening, you're not fully caring.

If you get a strong response in return, such as, "Darn right, this has been frustrating," don't be alarmed; you're actually making progress. The emotion has been identified and verbalized and is less likely to keep grinding in the conversation.

Avoid making the common mistake of passively listening in these situations and letting the customer vent endlessly. Eventually, the person may run out of steam and stop venting, but the customer won't feel understood. The likelihood of that customer feeling that he or she has gotten a satisfactory resolution from you greatly lessens when genuine care seems lacking.

Remember, too, your emphasis as you start out in a difficult customer interaction is to show empathy, not sympathy. (See Chapter 6 for more about empathy and sympathy.) Customers don't need you to feel sorry for them (which is sympathy). Some people view sympathy as condescending; others see it as misleading, that you agree with everything they say and you will do anything they want, even though it may not be what's best for your company. You want to show understanding of where the customer is coming from in a respectful manner. That's empathy, and that's the best way to begin to handle this challenging situation.

2. **Gain an understanding of the problem.**

   Gather information from the customer about the problem at hand. Probe for an explanation of what has happened, and then paraphrase to verify that you understand the problem as the customer sees it.

"What you're telling me is that no follow-through has occurred to get this damaged product repaired or replaced, despite your repeated efforts?" *(paraphrasing)*

Sometimes, you'll need to diagnose further to get a full picture of what has happened. This means probing with the customer to explore further the circumstances or causes of the problem. If you have worked in a technical support role, you know that this may mean walking the customer through different steps of a computer application to determine exactly where the problem is in a system.

3. **Develop alternatives for a resolution.**

   After you gain a full understanding of the problem, you're able to work out a solution. Don't move ahead to do so until then.

   Wherever you can, develop the options for the solution with the customer. You can ask something like, "What would you like to see happen here?" Sometimes, what a customer wants for a resolution is far less than what you had in mind. On the occasions that the customer answers with something beyond what can be done, simply say, "We'll need to look at some other options that are more feasible."

   Avoid trigger words in your language, as covered in Chapter 8. Focus on what *can* be done; don't dwell on what *can't* be done.

4. **Decide on the best resolution.**

   After exploring all the options, bring the discussion to a close by recapping what you decided or the best way to go under the circumstances. Clearly outline the steps you will take and when. When action needs to be taken, underpromise and overdeliver as to when it will happen.

5. **Follow through.**

   When action is needed to implement the solution, follow through and get it done by the time you set. As an extra touch that can go a long way in enhancing customer satisfaction, check back with the customer to ensure that everything worked out fine. This proactive move puts you in a position to fix any problems that still exist.

The great eight for dealing with customers who are irate

When everything is running smoothly, service can look good. But what happens when you have a problem that has created a difficult customer situation? How you handle these situations is the true test of how good your service is. Handle these challenging situations effectively, and you can win a customer for the long-term.

 Following the problem-solving model described in the preceding section gives you an organized approach to work through these challenging situations. This section provides you with eight tips to help increase the likelihood that you can work out satisfactory resolutions in these situations.

   ✔ **Stay in control.** When a customer has strong emotions, getting defensive in return is easy to do — and is not helpful for either you or the customer. Your defensiveness will serve as a spark to escalate tensions. Instead, shift your attention from how you're feeling to what the customer is feeling and saying. (See Chapter 11 for information on using the tool called *shift and show understanding*.) With this focus, you increase your ability to listen effectively, and when you do so, you eliminate the reactive need to become defensive.

✔ **Listen for facts and feelings, not delivery and manner.** Building on the preceding tip, focus on what you really need to listen for and understand — the content of the customer's message and the emotions being expressed. If you get stuck on how the message is being delivered, you're certain to lose what the message really means. Make your objective in the conversation to show understanding of the whole message you're hearing — that is, the facts and the feelings.

✔ **Be collaborative, not adversarial.** Sometimes in difficult customer situations, the service provider sees the customer as the problem and therefore shows little understanding or care for the customer's problem. Such a view tends to promote adversarial interactions — you against the customer.

Instead, look at the situation with this formula: You + the customer against the problem. With this focus, you work with the customer to solve a problem — a far more collaborative, positive approach.

✔ **Follow problem-solving guidelines and be flexible with them.** Follow the problem-solving model outlined in the preceding section. Recognize that the problem-solving steps go in a general order, but adapt to the situation. More important, you often repeat Step 1 (providing empathetic responses) throughout the conversation based on how the customer is coming across. The tools to apply consistently in these interactions are the following:

- Active listening with empathy.

- Assertive speaking in the positive.

- Problem solving with a focus on solutions.

✔ **Personalize the interaction.** Get the customer's name and use it periodically in your interaction. Give your name too. Now you have two people who know each other by name working on a problem together, as opposed to two relative strangers stuck in an emotionally charged situation. This personal touch goes a long way in helping diffuse the tension and in creating a comfortable atmosphere for discussion.

✔ **If you need help, ask for it.** Don't put undue pressure on yourself if you're not sure how best to resolve the customer's problem. You don't want to make the wrong commitments — then you'll really upset the customer. On the other hand, you don't want to be an obstacle who can't help solve a problem because you're saying no because you don't know what to do.

Let the customer know that you need to check things out, and set a time to call back. Seek the support you need so that the best possible resolution is worked out for the customer.

✔ **Apologize for others' mistakes, but don't criticize them.** When the cause of a customer's upset feelings is another staff member's mistake, sincerely apologize as if you were the one who made the mistake. Then focus your attention on initiating the most positive and corrective action you can as soon as possible.

Avoid criticizing another staff member or department for what went wrong. To the external customer, you represent your whole organization. If you're heard as critical of your own organization or people in it, you convince the customer to avoid doing business with your company again. Keep your focus on getting the problem resolved instead.

✔ **Utilize positive self-talk.** If you're like most people, you talk to yourself. When I ask people in my seminars if they ever talk to themselves, many nervously raise their hands as if they're afraid to admit that they do so. If you do it out loud on a frequent basis, others will question your sanity. But talking to yourself is a normal human action — it's called thinking.

In stressful, challenging situations, the self-talk racing in your mind may be full of negative messages: "Oh, what a pain to deal with" or "Why does this customer have to bother me today?" Many other, more colorful messages may also run through your mind in such situations.

With positive self-talk, you give yourself messages that help you stay on a positive track in the interaction. You have to find your own messages — such as "Stay focused" and "Listen" — and make them positive. These kinds of messages help you be more in control and more ready to help work on a solution — keys to resolving difficult customer problems.

Remember the Alamo and Your Internal Customers

The primary focus of this chapter so far has been how to communicate effectively for quality service and sales results with external customers. They are the ones you are in business to sell to or serve. Yet most everyone in their jobs has internal customers too. They are those people inside your organization to whom you provide some form of service or from whom you need support. If you're in human resources, information systems, office services, finance and accounting, and other administrative support functions, your primary customers are internal. To serve them well, you often need them to carry out certain responsibilities or provide you with support — from filling out forms to following established processes and policies.

Even if your main focus in your job is on dealing with external customers, you still may need support from internal staff in order to serve external recipients well. Sometimes, getting other staff people to cooperate with you and trying to satisfy them with the services you provide can be quite a challenge.

Seeing the internal customers

Kim was a dynamic sales rep. She worked well with her external customers, who liked dealing with her. She was positive, upbeat, and very responsive with them. Not surprising, Kim generally produced some of the top sales results in her branch. Yet sometimes she would get upset with her fellow staff when problems occurred in their work. They performed functions that affected her external customers — in particular, the processing of orders that Kim had sold.

Her outbursts were usually characterized by yelling, complaining, and debating with her fellow team members. They often responded defensively and told her that the information she provided about the customer orders was not always clear. From these sometimes-raging debates, nothing tended to be settled or improved.

Over time, Kim discovered that the more upset she got with her fellow team members, the less responsive they were to her. In fact, the staff generally viewed Kim as a talented sales rep but a difficult person to deal with. When Kim had the opportunity to find out more about the tools of assertive speaking and active listening, she began to see the use of these tools beyond providing good service to her external customers. She saw that her fellow staff members were her internal customers, as she was theirs.

Kim took steps to deal with her fellow staff as internal customers. Cooperation and responsiveness increased with her team members as she began communicating with them as she did with her external customers. Although she had moments when her stress level got a bit too high, Kim recognized that when she saw her team members as customers and responded positively to what they needed from her, they tended to give her much better service in return.

The key to gaining the support and cooperation you need from employees and managers in other groups is to see them as important customers to whom you provide quality service. This means that you communicate and act in much the same way as you would with your external customers:

✔ Identify customer needs.

✔ Focus on how you can help meet the needs.

✔ Speak in lay terms.

✔ Handle problems with the language of solutions.

✔ Underpromise and overdeliver — that is, communicate your commitments and meet or beat them.

In addition, to make your internal customer service effective, build working relationships on the principle of being consistently respectful (as defined in Chapter 10). In these working relationships, you give respect without conditions attached and build a track record as someone others can count on to deliver when your services are needed. In terms of applying the tools of active listening and assertive speaking to deliver this quality internal customer service, here a few tips:

- **Take initiative.** Assert yourself and be the one to take the first step to make something positive happen. Make that call, set up that meeting, go talk to that internal customer with whom you need to work something out. Don't wait for others to act first. As the expression goes, get the ball rolling.

- **Educate your customers so that they understand what to do.** Quite often, internal service providers want their fellow employees to follow certain processes or policies so that they give them the right services. But sometimes these processes or policies aren't followed very well, and the service providers feel frustrated. Prevent the frustration through face-to-face communication in which — and this is key — you show the internal customers what they can do to receive service from you. In other words, let them know how they benefit from taking the right actions that help you deliver quality service to them. Don't assume that they already know what these actions are.

- **Listen to concerns and feedback.** When your internal customers have issues or concerns with the service you provide, or they just want to give you some feedback, listen first. Avoid reacting defensively. Probe to get them to explain their messages and paraphrase or reflective paraphrase to check your understanding. You may even get a few good points that you can use to improve the service you provide. At the least, when you show that you can listen to someone else's issues, you increase the likelihood that they will listen to yours — the way to build a positive give-and-take in a working relationship.

- **Share what you know.** You have expertise, experience, sometimes-helpful insider tips, and knowledge of useful resources — all forms of information that internal customers need to do their jobs well. Respond to requests for such information and openly share it without being asked when the need is apparent. Gaining accurate, timely, and useful information is a critical need that all types of customers have.

- **Ask for what you need.** Sometimes you need your internal customers to do something, or you need help from them for yourself. In such cases, make your request assertively. Don't demand it, because employees in other groups generally don't respond well to orders, but don't shy away from asking either. Instead, confidently, sincerely, directly, and with a sense of importance ask for what you need.

Working relationships involve expectations, usually unstated, of give-and-take cooperation. The expectations are that if I help you with what you need, in time you will help me with what I need in some equivalent fashion. When you work to identify and meet the needs of your internal customers as a regular practice, you have a positive influence on others. To then ask these customers to respond to a need you have — assertively so — greatly increases your chances of getting that need met.

> ✔ **Express appreciation.** The practice of saying thank you to external customers when they receive or buy your service is common. No reason you can't do the same thing as you serve your internal customers. Especially when they do something that shows support for your efforts, thank them profusely. Even put in a good word with someone's boss for special occasions of assistance to you. Displaying common courtesy, with a touch of gratitude mixed in, makes for a very nice dose of quality customer service.

Making processes better

The main emphasis of this chapter is on how to apply communication tools and tips to meet the challenges of providing effective sales and service to customers. Quality customer service, however, is not affected in the points of contact only by the manner and communications of the service providers, but also by the processes used in carrying out the services.

Processes are the systems, practices, and written and unwritten rules used to get work done. When processes are inefficient, cumbersome, and not very user-friendly, they create a lot of the problems that impact the quality of the service you're seeking to provide to both external and internal customers. You can often take some assertive steps to help improve the processes in your work area by doing the following:

✔ Tune in and listen to what causes customer problems and frustrations so you can pinpoint where the process issues most are.

✔ Take a customer perspective in analyzing the efficiency of the service provided. Ask yourself — if I were the customer, what would I think of this service?

✔ Wherever possible, give your customers insight and guidance that can help them better navigate through your organization's processes.

✔ Bring ideas, not just problems, to your manager and to your team to help improve processes that result in better customer service.

Chapter 16

Interviewing from Both Sides of the Table

. . . .

In This Chapter

▶ Defining what you're looking for in the candidate you need to hire

▶ Preparing the right questions for your interviews

▶ Organizing your hiring interviews and getting the best from your efforts

▶ Preparing yourself for an interview as a job candidate to win the job

▶ Selling yourself positively in an interview and asking the more useful questions

. . . .

A job interview is like a test drive with a new car: It's a limited experience from which big decisions come. The interview is a point of live contact between the seller (the job candidate) and the buyer (the hiring manager). In many respects, both are taking each other for a test drive in the interview to see whether they want to forge a working relationship with one another. Thus the interview involves as much emotional appeal as it does rational decision making. In fact, most major purchases that people make are emotional decisions that are rationalized afterward in order to justify them. ("Honey, why did you buy such an expensive outfit?" "Because it was on sale.") Therefore, in the interview, if the situation doesn't feel right, the hiring manager isn't buying. And if the feeling isn't right on the other side of the table, the job candidate doesn't want to sell his or her wares to the prospective employer.

What greatly influences whether the job interview turns out to be a positive experience for both sides is how each party communicates with the other — speaking and listening. In fact, an interview, whether you're the hiring manager or the candidate seeking a job, is one of the best forums for applying the tools of assertive speaking and active listening. How you present yourself and how you listen to understand greatly influence how others evaluate you — and because interviews involve a relatively short time for the two parties to be together before decisions are made, you need to make your communication count in order to be successful.

While managers decide whether they want to hire an applicant, applicants decide whether they want to accept a job offer from the new employer. Both parties have to connect well for the manager to make an offer and the applicant to accept it. When labor markets are tight and finding highly qualified employees is a challenge, hiring managers need to promote the job and the organization during the interview process as well as explore the candidates' employment backgrounds.

This chapter delves into the communication efforts that make the interview process a success for both the hiring manager and the job applicant. From the hiring manager's side, you find out how to define what you're looking for so that you increase the potential for getting the right employee. The chapter also shows you how to ask questions and which types of questions are best to use, as well as how to organize your interview and promote interest for job candidates. From the candidate's perspective, you find out how to come prepared for an interview, how to present yourself positively, and how to ask the best questions to help you evaluate whether the job situation is right for you.

Knowing What You're Looking For

For hiring managers, a major emphasis of the applicant interview is on fact-finding. To help you make important hiring decisions, you want to find out as much as you can about a candidate's work background and qualities. While the person's resume gives you a sneak preview of this background, you need live discussion to get the fullest picture of what that person can do and what that person is like — thus the importance of the interview.

A common mistake I see among hiring managers is a failure to first define the factors they're seeking in the potential employee. These factors are usually in the backs of their minds and, therefore, aren't fully explored in the interview process. A hiring decision is one of the more important decisions a manager makes. To leave it to chance because you haven't fully thought through what you need for the job is risky business — but common.

Begin an organized and thorough interview process by formulating the job requirements for the position. The *job requirements* are a written list of the important hiring factors. The typical job description usually defines the worker's role and the job's main functions. The job-requirements list goes one step further, defining the qualifications and qualities of the ideal employee.

From a job-requirements list, you can formulate the right questions to ask and guide others who will assist you in interviews. It also serves as the foundation for developing your recruiting announcements and advertisements, as well as the criteria you'll evaluate more in your decision making. The best job-requirements list outlines two sets of factors — can-do factors and will-do factors — which I cover in the following two sections.

Can-do factors

Can-do factors answer this question: Can the person do the job? These factors define the job-related qualifications you need for the position. Here are the more common can-do factors:

- **Education:** What level of education do you expect or need in this position? In which relevant fields of study should the person have an educational background? Should the person have some specialized training for this job?

- **Job-related technical skills and knowledge:** Every job has certain skills related to performing the functions of the position. Those are the job-related technical skills, the essential skills people need to have to do the job at hand. Candidates may also need a certain body of technical information.

- **Computer skills:** Many positions need employees who are proficient at various computer applications, from word processing to spreadsheets. Include whichever computer skills you need someone to perform when carrying out the duties of the job.

- **Written communication skills/language capabilities:** Some jobs require excellent writing skills. In some positions, getting someone who, for job-related reasons, can speak more than one language is helpful. If either of these skills is needed for the position you're trying to fill, include a point about it in your can-do factors list.

- **Physical requirements:** If the job requires lifting abilities or other physical demands, clearly spell out the requirements for these duties. Only do so, however, when physical labor is a regular part of the job.

- **Industry knowledge:** For some jobs, you may want someone who has acquired certain knowledge related to the industry or sector in which your business operates. If you're a hotel, you're in the hospitality industry; if you're a phone company, you're in the telecommunications industry, and so forth. For some positions, having someone with deep knowledge of the market in which you do business is an important can-do factor.

- **Experience:** Experience is one of the more critical can-do factors to spell out. You want to look at all the key areas for the role in which having previous job-related experience is important — job skills, certain work situations, management responsibilities held, and so on. Spell out not only the types of experiences you're seeking but the level of experience as well — quantify that in years as best as possible. Other than entry-level positions, most jobs have two or more points in the experience category among the can-do factors.

Can-do factors define the essential qualifications for a job. They are the tangible factors that you use to screen resumes. When you write up the can-do factors that are important for the job opening you have, you want to write each point in a sentence that specifically defines the need, as the following example for a director of human resources shows. Make sure that your factors cover what truly is essential and aren't so narrowly defined that the pool of candidates who can fit the requirements is slim to nonexistent.

Position: Director of Human Resources

Position manages two staff members and administers the major human resource (HR) functions for a company of 120 employees, including recruiting, compensation, benefits, employee relations, policy administration, and training and development.

Bachelor's degree in business, HR management, or related field; master's degree is a plus.

Five to ten years experience in all facets of HR.

Two to four years experience in a management role.

At least five years experience in recruiting for technical and nontechnical positions.

Strong oral and written communication skills.

Thorough understanding of labor laws and compliance issues.

Will-do factors

The other factors to include on your job-requirements list are called *will-do factors*. Will-do factors answer this question: How will the person do the job? These are the personal attributes or qualities that make a good employee for the job you're trying to fill. As you know, many people are capable of performing a job; that is, they fit the can-do requirements. But whether those people will do the job *well* is another story.

The following are the more common will-do factors that are important in many jobs:

- **Team player:** Will the person work well with others in teamlike situations? Does the person take a cooperative and helpful approach in such situations? These are important questions to answer, especially in today's work world, in which people often have to work in teams.

- **Track record:** Experience tells you only how *long* someone has done something, not how *well*. A *track record* is the history of the accomplishments or contributions a person has made on the job. Defining the track record you're looking for is one of the more important will-do factors to have on the list.

✔ **Service orientation:** If having an aptitude for customer service is an important part of your job's functions, include this will-do factor on your list. You'll have more success if you hire people who view serving others well as important, rather than training people who haven't figured that out yet.

✔ **Interpersonal skills:** Does the person in your open position have to interact with others to get the job done? Does the position require someone who can verbally communicate clearly and constructively with others? If the job you want to fill requires these skills, this is an important will-do factor to include.

✔ **Organizational skills:** Many positions require attention to detail and the ability to deal with much data and keep it all organized. If that's the case for the position you're trying to fill, include this factor on your list.

✔ **Flexibility:** More and more jobs need people who can adapt to change — who can, as the old expression goes, roll with the punches. Rigid rule enforcers and those who cling to the status quo rarely make their way onto the will-do factors list.

✔ **Openness to learning:** Few jobs exist in which you can expect every person walking into them to know all they need to know. You probably don't want know-it-all types to apply anyway. You need people who are curious and eager to learn, and not everyone is. If the job situation you have is ever evolving or has a long learning curve to it, this is an important will-do factor to include.

✔ **Initiative:** Many companies need people who are self-starters. After they've acquired the essential skills, they can act without constantly being told what to do. They can step forward to help make things happen without a manager pushing them to perform.

✔ **Problem-solving ability:** The nature of some positions involves dealing with problems. People who can tackle such situations with analytical abilities and a solutions-focused mindset are critical to have in such roles.

✔ **Creativity:** Some roles need people who are full of ideas, who can think of new or different ways to get a job done. If creativity is important for the job you're seeking to fill, add it to the list of desirable factors.

✔ **Reliability:** This factor deals with employees who follow through, who meet deadlines, who are there when you need them, and whom you can count on to get a job done. Most jobs need people who regularly demonstrate this work ethic.

✔ **Motivation:** Many managers want to have self-motivated employees in their groups. These are the people who show effort and willingness to do a good job; they don't need constant prodding or pushing to perform.

✔ **Enthusiasm:** Some jobs require that people show a high energy level and an upbeat demeanor. Often, these jobs involve a lot of public contact. If enthusiasm is important for a job-related reason, add it to your job requirements list.

✔ **Effective management style:** This factor deals with how a person leads others and what behaviors and judgment they demonstrate in a management role. For management positions, put this factor on your list.

This list of 14 common will-do factors isn't meant to be all-inclusive. The idea is to make such a list for each position you're seeking to fill, including all the important factors for it. As in the following example, you want to specifically define what each will-do factor means to you and why it is important for the job at hand. Doing so takes the factor from being vague to being clear, a useful tool to guide you in formulating the questions you'll use in your interviews.

Position: Director of Human Resources

Position manages two staff members and administers the major human resource (HR) functions for a company of 120 employees, including recruiting, compensation, benefits, employee relations, policy administration, and training and development.

Track record of making HR a positive impact in the organization.

Strong interpersonal skills so as to relate well to all levels of employees and management.

Problem-solving skills that show judgment and sensitivity in handling personnel issues.

Organizational skills to implement and manage both employee programs and personnel record-keeping functions efficiently.

Management skills that demonstrate the ability to coach and develop staff.

Track record of bringing a customer-service orientation to HR.

Ability to assertively deal with issues and present ideas and recommendations to management.

Demonstrate creativity that shows progressive approaches to HR and organizational-development issues.

Asking Your Questions

Defining the job requirements for the open position — the can-do and will-do factors covered in the preceding section — helps you determine the questions to ask in your interviews. This section demonstrates two methods of asking questions and also shows you how to develop the best types of questions to ask so that you do a thorough job of fact-finding in your interviews.

Ways of asking questions

In Chapter 5, you discover that questions can be asked in two ways —
close-ended and open-ended. In interviews, you want to use open-ended
questions far more often, but you also use close-ended questions. The following sections can help you figure which to use when.

Close-ended questions

Close-ended questions solicit short, definitive responses — usually one to a
few words. Here are a few examples:

- ✔ When did you work for ABC Company?
- ✔ Did you work on projects that involved system conversions?
- ✔ You're saying that you've enjoyed working on your own more than in
  teams?
- ✔ How long did you serve as a manager?

In interviews, close-ended questions work best when you need to verify information, to clarify something said, or to get a specific piece of information.

Open-ended questions

Open-ended questions solicit an expression of thoughts, feelings, ideas, opinions, and explanations. Here are a few examples:

- ✔ What did you like most about working for ABC Company?
- ✔ Tell me about your role in that systems conversion project.
- ✔ Explain what your experience in working in teams was like in your last job.
- ✔ How did your last work experience help you grow as a manager?

In conducting interviews, open-ended questions serve to gather information —
a depth of information. You want to prepare these questions ahead of time,
whereas you can ask close-ended questions on the spur of the moment when
you need to verify or clarify something.

Remember that your tone is a very important part of how you ask questions.
You want to sound inquisitive — that curious and interested sound in your
voice that invites people to talk to you. You're conducting an interview, not
an interrogation. You want people to feel comfortable opening up to you.
Therefore, your tone is as critical as the wording of your questions in an
effective fact-finding interview.

Types of questions to ask

In conducting successful interviews, knowing how to ask questions is just part of the effort. Knowing the right types of questions to ask is critical too. In this section, you discover three types of questions to use in interviews — behavioral, informational, and introspective.

Behavioral

Behavioral questions ask a job candidate to draw upon past experience to demonstrate a point. The idea behind these types of questions is that past experience is often a way to predict future performance. Here are a few examples:

- ✔ Specifically, please tell me about a time when you had to resolve a customer problem under difficult circumstances.

- ✔ Describe a time when you had to sell an idea to your boss or another key member of management.

- ✔ Tell me about a situation that demonstrates you were a good team player.

- ✔ Give me an example of a critical project or assignment you had with a tight deadline and how you handled it.

Behavioral questions are especially effective for fact-finding on will-do factors. Through behavioral questions, you explore the key personal qualities you're looking for by having the candidate draw upon past experiences in which the behavior was demonstrated. If the experience occurred, a story can be told.

The key to discovering whether someone has a quality or will-do factor you need for a position is to shape your question around the factor and ask the person to tell about an experience in which it was demonstrated. For example, if your factor is the ability to solve problems, have that be the focus of the question, asking for an example in which the candidate demonstrated problem solving: "In your last job experience, please describe a challenging situation you handled that demonstrates your problem-solving abilities."

Informational

Informational questions gather detail and information about a candidate's job background. They are especially useful for learning more about can-do factors or qualification issues. Here are a few examples:

- ✔ What were the main responsibilities you held in your last position?

- ✔ What were the reasons you left that position?

✔ Tell me about the kind of technical projects you worked on in your previous job.

✔ Describe your experience specifically in utilizing programming languages.

✔ What are your key achievements in your current job?

Informational questions tend to be helpful in walking through a candidate's work history and in gaining a picture of someone's technical skills and knowledge. They challenge interview subjects to tell you about their work capabilities and experiences and help you gain greater depth into what the resume tells you.

Introspective

Introspective questions ask candidates to assess themselves and indicate their preferences about a job situation. They are useful for learning more about both can-do and will-do factors. Here are a few examples:

✔ In your technical background, what do you see as your strengths?

✔ What qualities do you have that make you a good fit for this position?

✔ How would your co-workers describe you as someone to work with?

✔ Describe the best manager you ever worked for and the worst manager, too.

✔ How would your former manager describe your performance and conduct as an employee?

Introspective questions cause interview subjects to reflect on themselves and their experiences. They give you an indication of people's awareness of their own work habits. You can discover a lot about job candidates by asking them to provide insight on themselves.

 In a good interview, you use all three types of questions. Using the active listening tool of probing (see Chapter 5), make many of your questions open-ended so that they draw out good information. Keep the questions clear and direct and, in most cases, focus on asking one issue or point. Only on occasion can you ask two things at once and still keep the question clear, and that's when the items relate to one another, such as, "Tell me what you liked and disliked about your previous job."

Avoiding common interviewing pitfalls

The combination of behavioral, informational, and introspective questions works best when you're conducting a thorough job interview. This section looks at questions managers sometimes ask that aren't effective, some of which are illegal. These are the pitfalls to avoid:

- **Long-winded questions:** This technique, which shows no skill, involves asking multiple questions at a time with no clear question coming through. By the time you stop talking, the candidate is often confused as to what to respond to and ends up rambling just as much as you did. The longer the question or the lead-in to the question, the less focused the answer tends to be.

- **Guessing-game questions:** I sometimes refer to these questions as *leading the witness* questions. Often said in a closed-ended fashion, they almost telegraph the answer you want to hear to the interview subject. Here are few examples:

  - Are you a team player? (Yes.)

  - How do you handle pressure? (Well.)

  - Do you think it's a good idea if . . . ? (Sure I do.)

  If people think you're looking for a right answer to your questions, they'll do their darndest to tell you what you want to hear. You'll learn nothing about what they can do and will do in a job, but you'll feel good that they know how to sing your tune.

- **Vague global questions:** These questions are so broad and vague that what the candidate should address in response is anyone's guess. A common example is the question, "Tell me about yourself." What exactly the interviewer wants to know is a mystery to the person receiving the question.

- **Hypothetical questions:** These questions often seem quite clever. They start out with, "What would you do if . . . ," or, "How would you handle a situation in which . . . ." They ask the interview subjects to tell how they would deal with a make-believe, although lifelike, situation. Although such questions require thought and knowledge to answer, they don't show what the person would actually do in such situations. Someone can easily know a *good* answer from attending a seminar or reading an article, but what he or she has done in actual experience is often quite different. That's where a behavioral question that asks the person to draw upon examples from past experience is far more effective in gauging reality than a hypothetical question.

- **Personal questions:** An interview isn't quite the same as meeting someone at a social function. You do want to have friendly conversation, but getting into personal matters beyond someone's job background is illegal in an employment-decision situation — which a job interview is. If the focus of a question gets at someone's personal background, such as gender, age, race, ethnicity, religion, marital status, family matters, disabilities, or sexual orientation, you've crossed a legal line.

Even if the job candidate mentions items of a personal nature in the interview, don't engage or explore them further, and leave them out of your notes and your evaluation afterwards. The key is to shape your questions so that they go after job-related issues. Contrast these two questions:

- Does your religion prevent you from working weekends?

- This position does require some work to be done on weekends. Can you meet this requirement?

The first question focuses on religion; as a result, it's illegal. The second question focuses on the job requirement of being able to work weekends. That's the focus you want for all your questions.

✓ **Talking too much, asking too little:** This is the most common pitfall: having few questions to ask and doing more talking than your interview subject does. Fact-finding, a main focus of your interview, is done mostly by listening. Throwing out a few questions to candidates and then talking at them most of the time doesn't get this done.

I've trained candidates on how to present themselves well in job interviews. The type of interviewer many worry about — the one who talks too much and asks too little — is actually the best kind to get. I teach job candidates that what you do with such interviewers is show interest and ask questions to really get them rolling. Because the interviewer is doing most of the talking, every now and then throw something in about your strengths and accomplishments and you'll have this interviewer walking away feeling pretty good about you. Your flaws and weaknesses won't be uncovered, but the fact that you showed interest will be remembered.

All Aboard: Conducting an Effective Interview

Knowing how to ask questions and the right types of questions to ask puts you well on your way to an effective interview. But making the interview go really well also involves being organized and promoting goodwill. The two following sections explores these issues. You'll see how the tools of active listening and assertive speaking maximize your efforts when conducting an interview.

Stay organized; don't wing it

The wing-it approach to conducting an interview is quite common among hiring managers. They show up to an interview, talk a lot, and fire away with questions that come to mind. Forget about having any sense of order or flow to the interview.

An interview is far too important to approach haphazardly. An organized interview allows you to be thorough and consistent with every candidate you meet. It also presents *you* well to job candidates. You come across looking like you know what you're doing (even if you don't when you're managing your group!).

Here are a few tips to help you conduct an organized and thorough interview:

✔ **Categorize your questions.** So that your questions fall into some kind of logical flow, group them into a few main categories. For instance, here are a few categories I commonly used to organize my questions:

- Work history.

- Technical background.

- Job-related personal qualities.

I like to take candidates from past to present in their work history to review the positions they've held and the track records they've built. I then like to explore their areas of expertise, which I call their *technical background,* in greater depth. I explore their management experience, too, if the role involves managing. Exploring the will-do factors (their personal qualities important for the job) helps round out a thorough interview.

✔ **Set and follow an agenda.** This is just like the communication skill called *mapping out your plan* (see Chapter 9). Determine the order of your questions, when you want to ask your questions, when you want to receive the candidate's questions, when you want to present information, and how you want to open and close the interview. You won't find any set answers for these issues, so answer them for yourself so you have an agenda to follow. Here is a sample agenda I frequently use and train managers to follow:

- **Open.** Set a relaxed tone and introduce the plan for the meeting.

- **Explore the content.** Ask your questions of the candidate.

- **Provide information and answers.** Present company information and the selling points of the job, and answer the candidate's questions.

- **Close.** Inform the candidate about the next steps in the hiring process and express appreciation to the candidate for meeting with you.

✔ **Have important materials ready.** Part of being organized in an interview is having materials on hand that give the candidate a good picture of your organization and the job. Consider showing or giving such items as a job description, company literature, benefits information, products or services information, and products that you sell or manufacture.

✔ **Know the salary and the hiring process.** Candidates want to know two things when they interview: the salary range and the process or steps in your hiring decision. As the hiring manager, you must know the answers to these issues before you begin your interviews, and communicate these essentials during the interview. Although the interview isn't the time to negotiate an offer or to make your hiring decision, giving candidates some idea of the salary range for the position and the steps and time frames for your decision shows professional courtesy and a sense of organization — a positive image to present to applicants.

✔ **Take notes of key points.** Don't rely on your memory when conducting interviews. Taking notes along the way is quite all right. Organize the standard set of questions you're using for each candidate into categories and allow space to write underneath so that taking notes along the way is easy and focused. The key in taking notes during the interview is to function as an active listener; that is, maintain eye contact and glance down to write quickly, capture main ideas (not all the detail), and paraphrase periodically throughout the interview to make sure that you're accurately understanding the main points.

✔ **Stay nonjudgmental.** It's best to stay away from reacting overly favorably or unfavorably to any responses by a job candidate during an interview. You don't want to give any wrong impressions. Function as an active listener (see Chapter 5) in which you probe to draw out information, check the subject periodically if the topic of the person's message becomes unclear, and paraphrase or reflective paraphrase throughout to verify your understanding. In this way, you show interest and objectivity, which stimulate a thorough interview.

✔ **Stay tuned in and follow up.** By having an agenda and a set of questions to follow for your interviews, you're in a better position to listen and ask the questions you can't prepare for in advance. Sometimes candidates give you signals that you need to go deeper — surface-level answers, vague responses not getting at the point of your question, rambling and rationalization, or sudden nervousness in the voice or change of pace in the rate of talking. In such cases, you want to dig deeper to get a clearer answer before going on to your next question. Here are a few active listening techniques that can help you do so:

- Probe by asking such questions as "How specifically?" or "Please explain further" or "Give an example to explain what you mean."

- Use *echoing,* in which you repeat a key word or phrase the person said and then wait patiently and silently to let the person explain further. Follow it with, "Anything else?" and you usually draw out a more complete picture.

- Occasionally, you can use the tool of reflecting feelings when you see discomfort or an unusual reaction in the interview subject's tone of voice or body language. For example, "You seem hesitant to describe what happened. Please tell me about it."

Your identity begins with your name

A big part of what promotes goodwill in a hiring situation is treating people with respect. Respect begins with your using your name, as the following story illustrates.

Wail (pronounced "WHY-ill") grew up in the nation of Oman, came to the United States as a young adult, and became an American citizen and a software engineer by trade. When the economy slowed, Wail found himself unemployed. One day he got the chance to interview with a hiring manager at a well-known company for a job that seemed to match his qualifications.

When Wail was directed to the manager's office, he knocked on the door and introduced himself. He initially got no response in return, as if Wail was not the person the manager was expecting to see. On his second try, Wail was asked to come in and sit down.

As the manager pulled out Wail's resume, he asked him to pronounce his name again. The manager stumbled in trying to say Wail's name and then said that he would call him Wally since that would be easier for him to say. Then for the rest of the interview, the manager referred to Wail as Wally. Toward the end of the interview, the manager became quite interested in hiring Wail. The position had been open for a while, and Wail's technical background looked like a good fit. When the manager asked Wail if he was interested, Wail responded as follows:

"The position does sound like a good one. I'm going to decline it, though. When I arrived, you initially did not acknowledge my presence when I introduced myself, and I find that discourteous. Then as the interview proceeded, you called me a name that is not my own and that I did not give you permission to use. For my own sense of dignity, no thank you." He then got up and left.

Tune in to the questions candidates ask of you. These questions help you gauge people's interest and capability levels. Do you hear enthusiasm or uncertainty, curiosity or demands in their questions? Tune in and take note as part of your fact-finding effort.

Promoting goodwill

Promoting goodwill is also important for conducting an effective interview. In this situation, each candidate interviewed walks away feeling that he or she got a fair chance, was treated with respect, and has a positive view of your organization — regardless of whether the person was hired. Promoting goodwill involves a few important communication actions, such as the following:

  ✔ **Greet candidates by name and use the name.** When you start the meeting with an applicant with a friendly greeting that includes the person's name, you help that person relax. Interviews aren't a natural conversation for most people, so you want them to be as relaxed as possible. Referring to a candidate by name periodically throughout the interview gives the interview a conversational rather than a grilling-session feel.

✔ **Listen responsively.** An interviewer who asks clear, thought-provoking questions, maintains eye contact, is patient, and periodically provides feedback to check understanding of what was said gives people the feeling that they are allowed to express themselves and to be heard doing so. Listening actively not only helps you find facts but also creates a positive experience for the recipients of your questions.

✔ **Highlight the selling points of the organization and the job.** What makes your organization a good place to work? What are the interesting challenges of this job you're seeking to fill? What successes has the organization had? These are the kinds of issues you want to address without even being asked. You want to present these points assertively (directly, confidently, and positively) so that people have a good reason to come work for you (besides getting a paycheck). Provide literature and other pieces of information that highlight these positives.

✔ **Allow for questions and answer them sincerely.** Promoting goodwill involves giving candidates a chance to ask you any and all questions and responding to them in an open and receptive manner. Speak in the positive, as covered in Chapter 8, so that the language you use in your answers is honest, direct, and constructive. People want to get a realistic view of the job situation, so tell it to them straight in the best way possible. If you sound positive but insincere, candidates will be turned off by what they perceive is a lack of honesty. On the other hand, if you come across sounding negative about everything, you'll convince them that you're not the person to work for.

✔ **Let the decision-making process be known and give timely responses.** Candidates appreciate knowing your process for making a decision, such as how many rounds of interviews you plan to conduct, estimated time frames when things will happen, and so on. More important, you promote goodwill by following through and responding to everyone you interview. This courtesy is part of good customer service. Nothing is worse for a candidate than wondering what the result of a job interview was. As part of underpromising and overdelivering as covered in Chapter 15, meet your commitments on communication, even if you haven't yet reached a final decision.

The Other Side of the Table: Preparing Yourself to Win the Job

This section looks at how the tools of active listening and assertive speaking can help you in job interviews when you are a *candidate* seeking the job. Presenting yourself effectively in an interview starts with preparation. In many respects, for candidates, a job interview is akin to giving a formal presentation (see Chapter 14): You need to present information — this time about yourself — coherently and positively to be successful.

Like a formal presentation, preparation is a key to success. Just showing up for the interview and winging it lessens your chances of communicating effectively. The following two sections provide you guidance as you prepare for your interviews.

Say it and prove it

What makes you a good candidate for the position you're seeking? Fundamentally, this question sums up everything you want to get across to the prospective employer when you interview. Answer it well and you may be the one to get the job offer.

To answer this essential question effectively, you need to communicate your best skills and accomplishments. That means you need to know thyself. Completing the Say It, Prove-It Chart in Table 16-1 helps you come prepared to communicate these vital points. Under the "Say It" column, list your strongest skills and accomplishments. In the "Prove It" column, give examples and stories that illuminate them.

Table 16-1	Say-It, Prove-It Chart
Say It	*Prove It*

As you outline the stories of proof, you want to be able to describe the situation at hand, the action taken, and, as applicable, the results gained from your actions. Here's an example about one skill following this say-it, prove-it method:

✔ **Say it.** "Self-taught computer troubleshooter."

✔ **Prove it.** "Used skill to solve problem of downed computers facing many people on my team at Company X. In one day, I had every computer up and running before MIS could even come help."

As you outline the stories on the prove-it side, practice saying them concisely and giving the highlights so that they make your points with impact. As you complete Table 16-1, make it as long as possible. When you have a bag full of skills and accomplishments with appropriate stories to go with them, you can pull out the ones that help you best respond to the question at hand — you are armed and ready.

The Say-It, Prove-It Chart helps you handle many of the common, sometimes difficult questions that interviewers ask, even if they aren't the best questions your interviewer can pose. Here are a few such questions for which you want to prepare answers, along with some recommended responses:

✔ **Tell me about yourself.** Respond with your 30-second commercial. This is a brief highlight of your background — three to four points at most, each said in one sentence, that summarize your strengths and qualifications. In particular, summarize your related experience and technical skills, your education, and something that characterizes your track record.

✔ **Why are you interested in this position?** "Because I need a job" is not the best answer to this common question. Emphasize how the opportunity fits with your career or job interests. Then list some of your strengths or skills and how they meet the needs of the job situation. This assertive response gives the hiring manager a strong picture of how you can be a good fit for the open position.

✔ **What did you like most and least about your last (or current) job?** Emphasize the most over the least. On the least side, give one or two points with brief explanations and constructive language. Go for items that sound realistic but don't have you coming across as harsh, bitter, or a slacker. On the most side, talk in terms of the accomplishments you made in that previous experience. Pull a couple of examples from Table 16-1.

✔ **What are your strengths?** Pull two or three from your completed Table 16-1. Choose strengths that connect to the employer's needs for this position and tell stories that back up the strengths.

Eve is applying for a position as a customer service manager. Here is how she answers the four challenging questions following the tips outlined:

Q: Eve, tell me about yourself.

A: I bring ten years of customer-service related experience, plus five years in management roles. I have a bachelor's degree in business and bring a solid track record of training and developing staff to be service oriented in their roles.

Q: Why are you interested in this position?

A: You've mentioned you have a growing company with the need to establish a strong customer-service orientation in the way you support your customers. That kind of challenge is what I'm seeking. In management roles over the past five years, I've helped organize and develop teams to provide top-notch customer service. To do this in a growing company that taps into this strength is appealing.

Q: What did you like most and least about your last position?

A: I had a lot to like in my last position, which is why I was there more than five years. I had a good team to work with and enjoyed having the chance to develop them into a strongly performing team. I liked the services we provided that made customer service something I could do with real sincerity. The dislikes centered on what happened with the company. As it suffered a downturn in business, it got away from providing perks and services for both employees and customers, which is why being part of a growing company like yours is of much interest to me.

Q: What are your strengths?

A: First, my management skills. I bring a track record that shows I can develop a strong team and help people become service oriented in their roles. Second, I bring excellent written and verbal communication and interpersonal skills that have helped me not only motivate my staff but also work cross-functionally to build a strong customer service presence in the organization. Finally, I'm a self-starter who can take initiative and develop strategies to solve problems. When I took on my management position in my last company, our customer-service function was somewhat dysfunctional. I worked with both employees and management to establish procedures and a training program that turned us into an organized and service-oriented function.

Handling your dark-cloud issues

Dark-cloud issues are potential liabilities. They are the flaws and shortcomings that everyone has to one degree or another about capabilities and work history. The fact that you have flaws isn't a flaw; the key is how you talk about them. If you talk about a weakness or mistake in an anxious or panicked mode, you convince people that your shortcomings are not short but are very big, and thus scare off your potential suitors. When you handle these issues matter-of-factly, you're a regular person who's not so bad after all.

Preparing for your dark-cloud issues is like taking an umbrella for a potentially rainy day. Have it with you and it doesn't rain. The day you forget to bring the umbrella is the day buckets of rain come pouring down. Prepare by identifying your potential liabilities. Here are some common examples:

- ✔ One job for a long time
- ✔ Too many jobs
- ✔ Experience in a different industry
- ✔ Unemployed
- ✔ Once got fired
- ✔ No experience in a company of this size
- ✔ Unrelated or insufficient education
- ✔ Overqualified

After you list all the liabilities or shortcomings that a prospective employer might see in you, practice how you'll respond to questions about them. Here is a good three-step process to follow to address your dark-cloud issues:

1. **Pause briefly and evaluate what can-do or will-do factor the question received most relates to.**

   Don't rush out with an answer; instead, think it through. If you rush out with many answers and then stumble or hem and haw, your confidence and credibility will be questioned. You want a consistent manner of being calm and confident in the way you answer every question in an interview.

2. **Respond briefly with the facts.**

   The emphasis here is on brief. Long explanations may sound like rationalization or defensiveness. Also, avoid remarks that go something like, "Well, but . . . ." Such comments make you sound like you're making excuses or reacting defensively. Speak in a straightforward manner.

3. **Redirect to your assets.**

   Assets here means something positive and relevant, such as what you learned from the experience, what improvements you've made, or what you've gained and now have to offer. As much as possible, when you redirect to a positive, tie your comments to the needs for the job you're seeking.

Raining on her own parade

Some years ago, I was conducting interviews for a new management position in the company for which I worked. Of all the candidates I interviewed, one in particular stood out because of her skills and strong background for what we needed. As I explored her work history, I asked on each job experience what her reasons for leaving the company were. On the job experience most closely related to our position, this candidate became quite flushed and gave me a vague and rambling answer. I followed up twice more, even rephrasing the question to try to get a clear explanation from her. Beyond "You know how it is, sometimes you just got to move on," I could get no real information. On the third try, I got an abrupt and agitated response, so I made a note of it. When I asked for references from her, I wanted one from this experience because it was quite relevant to ours. She reluctantly gave a reference on this experience.

What did I find out? She had been fired, for reasons that were understandable. Her former employer said that she would probably do well in a situation where she could create on her own and operate with little supervision. They had clashed because she did not want to follow the close direction this manager wanted.

Even though she was the leading candidate, we didn't hire her. Even though the reasons for which she was fired were factors that would make her a good fit for our company — we wanted someone who could create on her own and run with it — we didn't hire her, because she wasn't honest. Employers want honesty. We didn't fault her for what happened to her, but she wasn't honest in dealing with it. Had she sorted out how to handle this dark-cloud issue by being forthcoming and straightforward, we would have hired her.

In your preparation, define a positive asset to redirect to with every liability you have identified for yourself. Here's an example of handling a dark-cloud issue with this three-step process. The potential liability here is too many jobs.

1. **Consider the will-do factor dealing with reliability or stability.**

2. **Answer with something like the following:** "Layoffs and chances to grow and gain new skills have been the main reasons I've had such a variety of experiences."

3. **Redirect to assets by stating something like the following:**

   "What this has done for me is help build a multitude of skills that help me in roles like the one you have available. In addition, my experience has taught me to be adaptable to change. You've talked about the need to have changes occur in your work environment, and that is one of the factors that has attracted me to this position."

Part of handling potential liabilities means being able to handle these two commonly asked and sometimes challenging questions:

- ✔ **What are your weaknesses?** Usually asked right after the question about your strengths, the worst approach in response is to say that you have no weaknesses. (Or "My weakness is trying to answer this question.") The best approach is to follow the dark-cloud process. Pick a couple of items to talk about and redirect to positive assets in your response.

- ✔ **What are/were your reasons for leaving the job?** Give a brief explanation to answer this question in a way that provides the facts but not great detail. If you have sensitivities around a job experience, as you would if you were fired, follow the dark-cloud formula. Give the circumstances of the situation and say "terminated" instead of "fired," which is often a trigger word. Avoid sounding bitter, angry, or defensive.

People make mistakes, and things go wrong in their lives. Although being terminated involuntarily isn't something most people are proud of, sounding like you've grown or learned from the experience makes you sound human and genuine. People are often willing to give you a second chance. But if you sound bitter, angry, or defensive about what happened, you tend to take away a prospective employer's comfort with giving you another shot.

Scoring a Big Hit in the Interview

Your resume is your marketing piece. The interview is your sales call. During an interview, you're selling yourself, paving the way for a job offer in return. Much of what it takes to manage a sales call in a business situation (see Chapter 15) applies to presenting yourself well in a job interview. This section provides you with guidelines for being successful in an interview, along with pitfalls to avoid. You also get tips on how to present yourself effectively in a job interview.

Winners and losers

No matter how well you present yourself in an interview, there's no guarantee that you'll get the job. It's a competitive situation, and even at your best, you may not be the right match. Nonetheless, certain factors can increase or decrease your possibility for success. You want to be aware of the following pitfalls — in particular, the communication behaviors that have doomed some job candidates:

✔ **Being a distraction:** The interview is not the time to chew gum, twirl jewelry, squirm in your chair, smoke, fidget, or bite your nails. These inappropriate behaviors leave lasting impressions and cause hiring managers to hear little of what you have to say.

✔ **Rambling or being evasive:** When interviewers ask you questions, being verbose and not answering them directly are mistakes. Long-windedness and unclear responses are tickets for rejection.

✔ **Being critical of former employers or bosses:** To have a work experience that did not go well isn't unusual. To sound bitter about it after it's over doesn't usually sit well with prospective employers. When you sound critical of past bosses, regardless of how right you may be, you sound negative. Ever met a manager who wants to hire a negative employee?

✔ **Showing little interest or enthusiasm:** Looking stiff and sounding monotone give the impression that you don't care or have the energy to do a good job. Asking few or no questions also raises a concern of whether you have a real interest in the job. If interest and enthusiasm don't come across in the interview, you make the decision not to hire you an easy one.

✔ **Communicating no track record:** Experience tells how long, but not how well. If you can't articulate what you've done well in your experiences and the contributions you've made, you don't give a prospective employer a good reason to hire you.

In my years of conducting interviews, when I explored applicants' work histories, most could explain the job responsibilities they'd held. When I asked them to tell me about their significant accomplishments in each job, only one-third could clearly answer the question.

✔ **Sounding distasteful:** Sounding defensive, arrogant, condescending, or insincere are big turnoffs to those who hear them. Sounding confident isn't the same as sounding cocky. Sounding smart isn't the same as sounding like a know-it-all. Being sincere and genuine in your tone still carries the day — especially in a job interview.

Here are some guidelines to follow to be a winner in an interview. Look at them as the criteria to use to evaluate your own efforts.

✔ **Express yourself in a clear and concise manner.**

- Did you answer questions directly?

- Did you give answers in language that made sense to your interviewer instead of being full of jargon?

- Did you answer questions with enough specifics to make them clear, yet not so overloaded on detail that you were wordy?

✔ **Sound positive and confident.**

- Did you express your points in constructive language?

- Did you give steady eye contact to your interviewer when you spoke?

- Did your voice show expression and come across loud and clear?

- Did you use gestures to enhance your key points?

- Did you smile at times when sharing experiences?

✔ **Communicate your skills and accomplishments.**

- Did you clearly articulate what you're good at and what you've done well in your experience?

- Did you provide examples to back up your track record?

✔ **Learn about the job, the company, the people.**

- Did you get a picture of what the company is like?

- Did you get a sense of what your potential boss is like, as well as your would-be team members?

- Did you get a good understanding of what the job entails and what challenges it involves?

- Did you ask questions to learn about these issues?

If you can answer yes to nearly all the questions in these four areas, you know that you did well in your interview. Regardless of whether you get a job offer, hitting the mark on these items means that you gave the interview your best shot. If you evaluate yourself on these factors after each interview, you'll be able to improve and be tuned in to how to present yourself assertively.

You're on: Succeeding in the interview

Your success in an interview is ultimately based on what you do when the live performance happens. You know that you want to be clear, concise, positive, and confident in the way you present yourself — all-important parts of assertive speaking. Here are seven communication tips that help make these results happen and help you get the best out of your interviews:

✔ **Make a good first impression.** Impressions form quickly in interviews, so get off to a good start. Give a warm greeting, get your interviewer's name up front and use it, speak up with energy, and engage in conversation. Like giving a formal presentation (discussed in Chapter 14), you want to use your nervousness as adrenaline to stimulate energy. Show this energy from the get-go and you're an engaging person to listen to for any interviewer.

✔ **Truly listen to the questions.** One of the best ways to give clear and direct answers is to first truly understand the questions being asked of you. Listen patiently. Ask for clarification if a question is confusing to you. When necessary, paraphrase what you've been asked to make sure that you understand the question correctly. These active listening efforts not only help you understand the question clearly, but also give you time to think. And when you think before you speak, you increase your chances of coming across assertively.

✔ **Ask for the needs early on.** Find the gold. The gold is what the needs for the position are, the job requirements most desired in the right person. Early on in the interview, ask for it: "What are you looking for in the right candidate for this position?" Or "What are your needs for this position?" Gaining this information helps you know what's important for the hiring manager and, therefore, helps guide you to draw on what's more relevant from your background.

✔ **Tell how you can meet the needs.** After you discover the needs, such as communicating effectively on a sales call (see Chapter 15), confidently tell what you can do and have done to meet these needs at every opportunity throughout the interview. Use the positive language of can-do and will-do, as highlighted in Chapter 8, to do so. Keep these needs the focus of your answers.

✔ **Back up your key points with stories.** As you explain important points in your answers, pull real examples from your Say-It, Prove-It Chart (Table 16-1). Stories not only add substance to your points but also often give them a touch of humor. They help engage others' attention and make your examples come alive.

✔ **Check for concerns near the end.** As the interview with the hiring manager or recruiter winds to a close, tactfully find out whether he or she has any concerns about you. After you leave the interview, you seldom have an opportunity to address any concerns the interviewer may have. To do so, ask a question like the following:

"Based on our discussion today, please tell me any concerns you have regarding my background that I can address for you."

This polite invitation often brings out a concern or two that you can address. Do so in a straightforward manner. If you need to, first probe to get a deeper picture as to the basis of the concern, and then address it. Again, keep your manner patient and your tone sincere so you don't put your interviewer on the spot.

✔ **Do fact-finding.** The best hiring decisions are a two-way street — they are a match between the needs of the employer and the employee. Therefore, evaluate the job opportunity and the organization as much as the hiring manager evaluates you. Of course, this means arriving at the interview prepared to ask questions and asking them throughout the interview with everyone you visit.

Through various means of research, find out what you can about the organization and the job situation prior to the face-to-face meeting, and then use the interview to build on this information and get an insider's perspective. The questions you ask are best if they're open-ended and inquisitive in tone, using the active listening tool of probing (see Chapter 5). Identify the key issues you want to learn about and formulate open-ended questions around each one. Bring your notes with you — no need to memorize your questions. Keep in mind that asking questions shows interest.

Here are some important issues to ask questions about:

- Job duties

- Job challenges

- Needs for the position

- Performance expectations

- Where the position fits in the organizational structure

- Reasons the position is open

- Hiring manager's management style

- Each interviewer's history with the business

- Company history

- An overview of the company's business

- Future outlook for the company

- Growth opportunities

- Organizational culture

- Compensation and benefits package

- Training and support resources available

- Next steps in the hiring process

When you present yourself clearly and confidently in both delivery and content and ask good, thought-provoking questions, you come across as a positive and motivated candidate — and that's what employers like to hire.

Chapter 17

Conquering the Challenges of Management

In This Chapter

▶ Coaching employees to perform productively

▶ Facilitating meetings effectively

▶ Managing upward to work well with your boss

▶ Building cross-functional relationships that work

*R*egardless of where you work within a company, when you serve in a management role, you have a very challenging job. Managing means that you're responsible not only for your work, but also for the work of others who report to you. Managing also involves leading your staff and being able to manage upward and sideways across the organization to make results happen. No wonder that, in spite of bigger bucks, you get bigger headaches.

At the core of managing effectively is interpersonal communications. Your technical expertise is no longer enough in a management role. If you can't work and interact effectively with other people, you're a poor boss and a liability to your organization. In fact, if you're an effective manager, you most likely find that you spend more time talking with people than on doing the tasks or work that your group needs to get done. Most managers at all levels in an organization find their greatest challenges related far more to people and communication issues than to technical matters.

In my management seminars, I sometimes ask the participants to share experiences about positive and negative characteristics they've seen in managers. In both lists, many of the characteristics have to do with interpersonal communications. For example, on the positive side, I get examples such as the following:

✔ Communicates directly and clearly.

✔ Gives honest and constructive feedback.

✔ Listens openly and receptively.

✔ Shares information and keeps everyone well informed.

✔ Asks for input in dealing with issues and problems.

✔ Is calm under pressure.

On the negative side, I get examples about the lack of these same communication behaviors or about how the behaviors are sometimes exhibited in a harsh manner. This activity shows that management is most about influencing those who report to you. And how you influence others, whether positively or negatively, starts with how you communicate and interact with them.

This chapter looks at four areas of management challenge and how plugging in the tools of active listening and assertive speaking helps you hone them. These challenges deal with getting your staff to perform, running meetings that function productively, managing upward with your boss, and managing across the organization so that you build bonds and don't let turf issues get in the way.

Coaching Your Staff

In management, *coaching* is about developing and maximizing your staff resources so that they perform to their best. It's about working with your people to help them perform not only effectively but also self-sufficiently. That's why the nature of coaching in management is collaborative and involves two-way conversation. Dictatorial and one-way conversations tend to stifle self-sufficiency and fail to motivate high levels of performance. To delve deeper into details about coaching, check out my book *Coaching & Mentoring For Dummies* (Hungry Minds, Inc.).

At the foundation of the coaching skills that drive employee performance are interpersonal skills. Managers who can be assertive speakers and active listeners have the tools to be collaborative and two-way in their interactions. They can be firm when the situation calls for it (as opposed to reacting harshly); they can be patient when the situation calls for it (as opposed to acting stressed out); and they understand when to get involved when the situation calls for it (as opposed to being passive and hands-off).

The following are six communication tips that you can apply in your coaching efforts to motivate employees and gain good performance results.

State performance expectations and emphasize results over methods

When you delegate and make assignments, let your staff know what you expect from their performance. Focus your messages on the results that you expect, not on methods for doing the job. Let people figure out for themselves how to do their jobs. Instead, focus their attention in terms of the good results you want to see from their work. To clearly define expectations when you make assignments, outline the following:

- ✔ The *deliverables* you want; that is, the pieces or products of work to come out in the end.
- ✔ The *quality* of the deliverables; that is, what good performance looks like.
- ✔ The *manner* you expect; that is, if the assignment or project involves much interaction with others, the positive behavior you expect to see.

To state your performance expectations clearly requires using the assertive speaking efforts of being direct, concise, and confident. When you communicate performance expectations and then let your employees do the job, the likelihood of your staff producing the results you desire goes way up. The mystery has been taken away; the target to hit for good performance is clear.

Delegating isn't telling people how to do the assignment. If they don't know, show them. But after that training is complete, focus on results not methods: You can do a job in more than one way. When you concentrate on telling employees how they should do their jobs and check up constantly to seeing if they're doing them the right way, you're a *micromanager*. You're so interested in details that you'd be better off doing the job yourself.

Delegating works best when you spell out the results you expect based on progress reviews along the way and then let the employee handle the responsibility from there. Doing so in this empowering way is what coaching is all about — and that's the opposite of micromanagement.

Ask more than you tell

The habit of telling employees how to do their jobs and of giving them answers for every question they have is easy to develop. This may have been what other bosses have done to you and what you experienced from your parents and teachers. In coaching, you seek to have employees think for themselves so that they perform self-sufficiently. The idea is for you to be a mentor and a resource that stimulates this thinking.

Instead of answering every question, determining every course of action, and solving every problem your employees raise, you ask them for their ideas. Then ask them to evaluate the different options and determine how to implement the desired course of action. Provide them with the answers only when they really don't know what to do; otherwise, ask questions to get them to think their way through the situations they encounter in their jobs. This means being able to use the active-listening tools of probing for the questions and usually paraphrasing and reflective paraphrasing to confirm what you're hearing, which also aids them in thinking through their plans of action. See Chapter 5 for more on these tools.

Give ongoing feedback on performance

As a coach, you must, as a regular practice, let your staff know where they stand in their performance. Whether they perform well or they need to do something better, giving feedback means acknowledging what was done. It involves applying the tool of describing, covered in Chapter 11.

When you give feedback on performance, you want to do the following:

- Focus on the issue.
- Use "I" statements to own what you say.
- Provide observations, not interpretations.
- Be specific, not vague or general.
- State your messages directly and sincerely.

Letting your staff know frequently — through clear and straightforward feedback — where they stand in their performance provides recognition for what's been done well and stimulates improvement for what can be done better.

Listen first and give advice — framed as suggestions — when asked

A common pitfall that many managers fall into is listening in *advice mode* — that verbal barrier of listening that Chapter 6 describes. The moment they hear a hint of a problem, these managers start telling people what to do. This approach to managing can turn off your staff and convince them that you're not a resource they can use to share concerns. Sometimes that's all you need to do — use active-listening tools to draw out the message along with the tools to confirm the emotion and content you're hearing — and you leave employees feeling satisfied that you were a useful sounding board for them.

Advice is best received when it's asked for. When employees seek your advice, provide suggestions rather than edicts. Suggestions sound something like this to start: "Let me give you a couple of thoughts to consider." Edicts or dictates are like orders to be followed; they require obedience, not thought, and often are rejected because employees don't like their managers telling them what to do. Suggestions, on the other hand, stimulate thinking and dialogue, leading to two-way conversations. They give employees something to consider and leave it to them to decide how best to use it for themselves. Keep your suggestions positive and sincere, and you'll influence decision making, while helping employees perform for themselves.

Invite feedback and input in return

As a manager, you often need to give direction, share information, or provide explanations. Employees can become quite passive in these situations, showing nothing more than a nod and a smile in response to what you say. Instead, keep your listeners involved when you're speaking (see Chapter 9). Rather than doing nothing or asking close-ended questions such as, "Do you understand what I was saying?" (which nearly always comes back with an affirmative nod and a smile), use open-ended questions to get employees responding to you with input or feedback:

- ✔ "What do you think?"
- ✔ "Just to make sure I was clear, please recap your understanding of what I'm asking for on this assignment."
- ✔ "Give me the pros and cons of the plan I'm suggesting."

Getting this input helps clarify your communication, assists your getting insight on issues, and stimulates employees' listening and thinking.

Address issues directly with a focus on solutions

This communication effort involves using an assertive approach, much like you use in resolving conflicts, as Chapter 10 describes. Unfortunately, managers often take an aggressive approach when problems arise, as the following story shows:

Jill was a manager who found that she didn't always get the cooperation she wanted from her staff. When she asked them to do an assignment, they agreed but often didn't complete the tasks within the deadlines she established. Jill found herself taking a confrontational approach with her staff — usually raising her voice and loudly telling them what to do. Work then got done, but the pattern of not meeting deadlines continued. The aggressive approach wasn't working.

The nonassertive approach — to avoid dealing with unsatisfactory performance — wouldn't have worked either. Problems not addressed tend not to get better.

With an assertive approach, you do the following when performance isn't going as planned:

- ✔ Give feedback directly on the concerns you have.
- ✔ Clarify in positive language your expectations of the results you need.

> ✔ Ask the employee for ideas on how he or she is to meet those expectations. The questions need to be *you*-oriented; you want to be direct so the employee thinks of what he or she needs to do. This is the solution that gets worked out together.
>
> ✔ As needed, set a follow-up time to review progress.

Here's how Jill can use an assertive approach, encouraging employees to take responsibility for their own actions and solve their own problems:

"Here's the concern I've been seeing lately in your performance. When I ask you to take on assignments, I've seen your agreement to do so, but the work isn't completed by the deadlines set. My expectation is that agreed-upon deadlines are consistently met. Please tell me what steps you will take to ensure that you meet that expectation."

Managing Upward

One of the biggest challenges that managers face in their jobs is not managing staff but dealing with their bosses. Bosses are somewhat like families — you don't usually get to pick them. They have all sorts of qualities, some that make them effective and others that make them ineffective. Some are good role models, and others are role models for what *not* to do.

Regardless of what kind of boss you have, you still have to work with that person. In fact, leading your staff often requires that you manage upward effectively. To sit back and complain about your manager's shortcomings sets a tone with your group that griping about one's boss is okay. The goal in managing upward is to forge a relationship in which you work well with your boss without problems or conflicts, and your boss has confidence and no concerns about your performance. The two sections that follow give you communication tips to help you deal with problem situations and build confidence from your boss.

You have a problem — so what?

Problems come in all sizes and shapes. Many are the operational and personnel kind that happen within your group. Some are issues that stem from other groups. And sometimes the problems are concerns you have about your boss. A good rule is to handle as many problems as you can by yourself, especially those within your group. But when you need to take problems or concerns to your boss, use these tips to communicate them.

Bring solutions when you come with problems

If you go upward with a problem, bring a recommended solution as well. Put this statement on a bumper sticker or carve it into your desk. Just do something so that you always remember to do it when you feel the need to bring problems to your manager. The language of solutions in problem situations, as discussed in Chapter 8, engages people far more positively than the language of problem dwelling. It's the difference between sounding thoughtful and constructive and sounding like a whiner.

Give the data to explain the problem as opposed to venting about it, and then provide your recommendations for making the situation better. Bosses want to hear that you have ideas, that you don't just see problems but that you also see ways of fixing them. Assertive language also tends to give you a sincere tone as opposed to a frustrated one.

When you need support, ask for it clearly

Sometimes, to resolve problem situations you face, you need support from your manager. Think of what you need and ask for it directly and confidently. Don't hint at it and hope that your manager will guess what you mean and respond accordingly. If you need your boss to call someone, indicate that need and provide the phone number. If you need your boss to approve an expenditure, indicate that need and say for how much. Starting out with, "Here's what I need from you that will help," is a good way to clearly request your need.

Keep your requests simple and concrete so that your boss can meet them. Avoid asking for something that amounts to a change of personality or character from your boss. That's too much to ask for.

If you don't agree with decisions that come to you, ask questions first

Your boss may make decisions without consulting you and then announce them for you to implement with your group. Complaining about the decision to your group breeds misery and undermines the decision. Challenging your boss in the next staff meeting, an aggressive tactic, generally breeds confrontation, and you'll lose. Instead, use probing (see Chapter 5), go one-on-one, and ask a couple of questions like the following:

- What is your rationale for this decision?
- What are you seeking to accomplish with this decision?

When you understand the reasoning behind a decision, you'll have an easier time supporting it and explaining it to others. Sometimes, when you know the rationale that led to the decision and the objective being sought with it, you can influence a change in the decision. This information helps you understand your boss's needs. If you then assertively suggest other ways to meet these needs (an effective sales method that's discussed in Chapter 15), you may be able to convince your manager to make a change — especially if what you suggest involves your taking care of the situation and giving your boss less work and worry.

Address concerns about your boss constructively to your boss

Pick and choose here; don't make a big deal out of every issue. But if you keep getting worked up over something your boss is doing or not doing, it's probably time to have a one-on-one conversation. Complaining at the water cooler to everybody who comes by — the passive-aggressive approach — stirs up gossip and tension and does not solve problems. E-mail messages to your boss outlining your concerns can be even more explosive. And stewing about your concerns and talking about how there's nothing you can do — the nonassertive approach — leaves you moping around like a hopeless lug.

The only assumption to make about your boss when you address concerns with him or her is that your boss means well. You want to keep your emotions in control and to focus on working out a solution. Making this assumption prepares you to do so and to be assertive. Then follow the conflict-resolution model outlined in Chapter 12, in which, most important, you state your observations (not interpretations about your concerns), you listen openly in return, and you collaboratively seek a solution.

Don't worry, be happy boss

In addition to handling problem situations effectively, you want to build your manager's confidence in you through other important communication actions. This means that you deliver results in your performance. Nothing causes bosses to get in your way more than not seeing results being delivered.

If you deliver in your performance and add the following communication actions to your repertoire, you'll manage upward effectively.

Speak in the language of commitment

Bosses ask you to do things all the time, from carrying out assignments to providing them with information. Answer every request with an affirmative "Can do" or "Will do" in your response — the tools of assertive speaking that show action and commitment, as described in Chapter 8. Such answers inspire confidence. Follow through and meet your commitments and your boss will consider you a reliable manager on whom he or she can truly count.

Emphasize what you *can* do, not what you *can't,* in response to these requests so that you're helpful, not an obstacle. Remember, too, to assert yourself and negotiate deadlines you can meet — underpromise and overdeliver (see Chapter 15). If you agree to deadlines you can't meet, all you do is frustrate your boss. If you argue against the deadline your boss wants without offering what you can do, you still frustrate your boss. Think, state firmly what time frame will work best to deliver what your boss needs, and then follow through and meet your deadline. This assertive manner, combined with actions, make negotiating deadlines in the future much easier.

Maintain the information loop and focus on highlights

Bosses want to be kept informed of what's happening in your area of responsibility. Operating self-sufficiently as you manage your job doesn't mean being disconnected from your boss. In particular, talk about the successes and results you are achieving — bosses like to hear good news. Also, keep your manager in the loop about any critical problems or issues — bosses don't like surprises either. Give them a heads-up when an issue may draw their attention. Whether you do this informing in writing or in a face-to-face conversation (or both), do what fits your boss's needs. But by all means, if your boss keeps wondering what's happening in your area, use that as a signal to get the information flow moving upward. By focusing on reporting results and key issues, you give your boss the highlights — the "what's important" stuff. Avoid providing too much detail. Many bosses have no time to hear or read about it and will think that you don't know what's important. Others, like the micromanaging types, will delve into the details with you and end up telling you how to do your job.

The idea here, too, is to keep in touch with your boss. Whether or not you like or value your boss isn't important. Out of sight for many bosses doesn't mean out of mind; instead, it implies that something is wrong, and that's when bosses get in your way. Keeping in touch on a periodic and mostly informal basis builds confidence.

Ask questions in bunches and about what's important

View your manager's time as valuable. Avoid coming in and out frequently with one question after another. A lot of interruptions aren't a good use of time for either of you. Take time with your boss in concentrated chunks, say a half-hour to an hour periodically, and ask the handful of questions that you save up for the occasion. Doing so enables you to drive the meeting and makes life a little bit easier for your boss.

In addition, ask questions about what's important to your boss: company direction, department direction, priorities, key expectations, and past experiences with challenging situations. Stay away from asking questions that get at how you should do your job. You're being paid to know those kinds of things. Also stay away from asking questions that others (your staff, peers, or administrative support people) can help you with. Keep your focus on the big picture areas and you'll make good use of your boss's time and attention.

Taking charge of managing upward

Managing upward is about taking an assertive approach to your working relationship with your boss. You take the initiative and take charge of your own group and circumstances.

For example, Pat was a manager who did well with her staff. Her greatest source of frustration centered on her boss. He was not a mentor, nor did he offer her much support. He tended to be distant and hands-off, and she usually heard from him only when he reacted strongly to a problem or something she did that he didn't like. As a result, Pat found herself complaining and stewing over this relationship and feeling stuck.

She got some coaching on how to assertively manage upward and applied a few tips that changed her working relationship with her boss. She took the initiative to schedule a one-on-one

meeting with him once every three weeks. She drove the agenda and highlighted successes and key issues. She asked questions to seek his experience and direction for the department and sometimes to get feedback on the issues she was planning. Outside the meetings, she informally dropped by periodically to say hello or chat briefly. She also e-mailed brief status reports on key activities and results in her group from time to time.

For the first time in a few years, Pat found value in her boss. His insights and experiences were helpful to her, as was the feedback she asked for at times. The tension she felt with him disappeared, and her frustrations greatly decreased. Best of all, her initiative with her boss helped her manage herself even better and thus stay more positive with her own staff.

Give feedback and seek it when needed

As discussed in the "Coaching Your Staff" section earlier in this chapter, you can and should give feedback upward by using the skill of describing. When your boss does something well and/or helps you out, give positive feedback. Bosses like positive strokes too — it can be lonely at the top.

On the other hand, if your boss doesn't handle a situation particularly well, you can give more critical feedback. Pick and choose when you give this feedback, and keep all your feedback interactions on a one-on-one basis. If you have been consistently giving positive feedback, pointing out the negative on occasion lessens any potential tension you or your boss may feel. Make sure that you're giving constructive feedback, sharing observations in a helpful manner. Whether the feedback is heard or acted on is your manager's choice, but at least hearing it straight from you in a nonthreatening manner allows him or her to make that choice.

If you want more feedback from your boss on how you're performing, periodically ask for it. Seek feedback on visible events so that your boss has something specific to respond to. Doing so helps you get more substance about your performance. Listen openly to the feedback regardless of whether it's favorable. Remember that this person evaluates your performance, so you'd rather know now whether something needs to be improved than to be surprised later.

Managing Outward

For more and more managers, the job requires more than just managing their staff members and working well with their bosses. Today's managers often have to manage across the organization with other groups and managers to get work done — sometimes referred to as *matrix management:* coordinating and working with others who don't report to you in order to produce results and help your own group perform productively. Trying to push authority — the aggressive approach — won't work, nor will moving forward in a timid manner, pleading and begging (the nonassertive approach).

People cooperate because they trust you, and trust comes from how you interact with them. Collaborate in your interactions, and you gain respect. Be competitive in your approach, and you build adversaries. Sometimes, people cooperate because they have the expectation, usually unstated, that if they help you when you need it, you will help them in some equivalent fashion when they need it.

How you build relationships and interact with staff and managers from other groups greatly affects the cooperation you get from them when you need it. Use the following communication tips to help you in these endeavors — they reinforce an assertive, respectful approach to working relationships (see Chapter 10).

- **Make sharing information a normal practice.** If you have information that someone may need, take the initiative and pass it on. Don't wait to be asked. Don't hesitate to share experience, inside tips, contacts, and any other valuable information from which others can benefit. When you're a good information source, people find you a valuable manager to work with.

- **Listen and find out about their needs.** The secret to building cooperative working relationships across an organization is understanding who people are. When you spend time together, you ask questions and show interest about their work situations. You find out about *their* issues and needs; you don't just focus on your own.

- **Respond timely to others' requests and inquiries.** When you make timely turnaround a regular practice in responding to your boss, staff, and external customers, you can easily respond in the same way to others within the organization — thus you see them as internal customers. As Chapter 15 mentions, you should underpromise and overdeliver when you make commitments to allow yourself time to meet the requests.

- **Talk about the greater good when working on issues.** As a manager, when you're working with peers on issues from problems to coordinating workflow, talk about the greater good. The *greater good* is the organization, the goals of the project, and the needs of the customers. When the greater good becomes the focus, the discussion moves away from your way versus my way to what we need to accomplish together to make something happen for the good of others.

✔ **Bring closure to discussions.** As you work on issues and assignments cross-functionally, make sure that everything from one-on-one discussions to group meetings have closure. Listen actively to clarify what's been agreed to or what the points of view are. Ask about next steps. Recap action items and even write them up and distribute the notes so that everyone remembers what was agreed to. This way, you prevent misunderstandings and rehashing of old issues.

✔ **Show gratitude.** Make saying thank you a regular part of your routine when people from other groups provide assistance and respond to what you need. You can even put in a good word for what others have done for you to their bosses. A manager's efforts on behalf of others often carry a lot of positive clout. Showing sincere appreciation and recognition can go a long way in building bridges of understanding and cooperation.

✔ **Request help with rationale.** When you make requests of people outside your group, explain your needs and the reasons you need the assistance. Be brief, but give people the reasons you made your request so that they don't have to guess at its importance. Express your request with a sense of importance in your voice, and you help make that request a priority.

If the experience of assisting or working with you on an assignment will help someone grow or take part in a significant venture, highlight these benefits along with your request. Be sincere; otherwise, you convince others that helping out isn't worth their while.

✔ **Resolve problems with peers person to person.** As Chapter 13 mentions, e-mail doesn't work to resolve conflicts or problems. Running to your boss or the other manager's boss first to work out your differences tends to escalate tensions as well. When concerns arise, as they often do when you're coordinating and working on issues with other managers, take the initiative to go to the other manager and start the dialogue. Select whichever conflict-resolution model from Chapter 12 works best for resolving the situation. When you go to other managers directly to constructively settle differences and solve problems, you build credibility and command respect — key ingredients for eliciting cooperation from others.

Many managers do fairly well at working with their direct reports but sometimes run into difficulty when they have to deal with managers from other groups. Turf wars flare up, and differences surface over desires for resources and assistance from others or over opposing views of how to get work done. These differences sometimes lead to destructive conflicts. Many managers fail to see that cross-functional relationships are important and that collaboration is the key to making them work.

In my management seminars, I sometimes emphasize the importance of managing collaboratively across an organization. I share, as an example, a story about two managers who were assigned to co-lead a project between their two groups. Along the way, they developed disagreements over certain directions in which the project should go. As the disagreements grew, the direct communication between the two managers decreased, and they began criticizing one another behind the scenes. Sniping among the team members also ensued. I then ask my participants to be one of the managers and tell me what he or she should do to rectify this situation. What would your suggestions be? What usually comes out of the discussion in the seminars is a strategy such as the following:

Have the two managers meet one-on-one. At the meeting, they need to put their concerns on the table constructively and be willing to listen to each other openly. They then need to clarify the goals for their project, work out a plan to meet them, and agree to end the behaviors they've been engaging in. They then should work with their teams to implement this plan to get the two groups working together, and set a follow-up meeting to review progress.

After these points (or similar ones) are outlined in the discussion, I ask the seminar participants to tell me what they just did. What they don't realize at first is that they have outlined an effective approach to resolve conflict — an approach of two-way constructive communication and problem solving. This example serves as a reminder of the examples they need to set as managers in their own jobs.

Part VI
The Part of Tens

The 5th Wave   By Rich Tennant

"Excuse me, but you've had me on hold for so long I've forgotten who you are."

In this part . . .

The short chapters in this part provide you with extra tips and ideas for communicating effectively at work and for applying what you've learned from this book in your daily practices on the job.

Chapter 18

Ten Ideas for Effectively Handling Telephone Interactions

In This Chapter

▶ Understanding basic telephone interactions

▶ Getting the most out of your phone calls

*B*ecause the telephone is one of the major ways that people communicate at work, you must be able to handle yourself well on it so that customers, colleagues, and everyone else you work with will want to call you and receive your calls.

Because you don't have visual contact in telephone conversations, you don't experience the nonverbal cues from body language (the way you do in face-to-face interactions) that help you better understand and connect with others in your efforts to listen and speak. This chapter helps you overcome this difference and provides you ideas and tips for getting the most out of telephone interactions.

Start with a Smile in Your Voice

You've probably met someone who's warm and friendly in person but sounds like a drone on the phone. Some people aren't aware of their demeanor when talking on the phone, and this comes across with the person's voice.

Starting every call, whether you receive or initiate it, with a *smile in your voice* means sounding upbeat with some life in your voice. Bringing out the pleasant side of your voice at the beginning of the telephone interaction helps you set a positive tone for the call and makes others feel more relaxed with you.

Give a Professional Greeting

In some jobs, people are required to follow a four-step telephone greeting:

1. **Answer with a salutation such as, "Good morning" or "Good afternoon."**

2. **Identify what organization or department the caller has reached.**

3. **Identify yourself, the receiver of the call.**

4. **Offer assistance such as, "How can I help you?"**

Steps 2 and 3 in this process provide information. Steps 1 and 4 make the call sound courteous and friendly. While using all four steps may not be applicable to your job, at least use two steps, one that gives information and one that establishes a friendly tone. This starts your calls on a professional and positive note.

Direct People to the Right Resources

Nothing is more frustrating to a customer than giving a long explanation of his issue, only to be told that he's not talking to the right person. When answering calls from such a caller, you need to do the following:

1. **Listen carefully to quickly discern the caller's need or issue.**

2. **Before allowing the caller to go on for too long, paraphrase to confirm that what you're hearing sounds like a matter that doesn't relate to your area.**

   Briefly explain that a more suitable person can help and provide the name and number of that person.

3. **If your phone system allows you to transfer the call, do so and give a heads-up to the person to whom you're sending the caller.**

   This helps the person who is receiving the caller to be ready to handle the issue, which gives the caller confidence that he or she is going to be served by the right resource. .

Of course, when you transfer a caller to the right resource, you need to know how to work the transfer arrangements with your telephone system. If your system allows you to put the caller on hold first to see if the best resource is available, you can avoid sending the caller into a voice mail black hole. Before making the transfer, let the caller know the name and phone number of the right resource and give your name and number too, in case something goes wrong.

Put the Caller on Hold Smoothly

Want to aggravate callers quickly? Put them on hold abruptly and leave them holding for a long time. Even if you're receiving a high volume of calls, follow these three steps to courteously put someone on hold:

1. **Briefly explain the reason for putting the caller on hold and request it.**

   Do all this in one sentence such as, "I have another call, can you please hold?"

2. **Get the acknowledgment from the caller and then place him or her on hold.**

3. **Return to the holding caller by saying, "Thank you for holding."**

If you're putting someone on hold to check on something, don't leave that caller on hold for more than a minute. Any longer than that, even if music is playing while your client is on hold, and callers begin to feel forgotten and may hang up in disgust. If while a caller is on hold you find that you need more than a minute to find information or otherwise provide the requested assistance, return to the caller within that minute and explain that your task will take longer than expected. Then, give the caller a choice of waiting longer or having you call back when you have the answer.

When you're putting people on hold because of a large volume of incoming calls, and you know some calls may take you awhile to deal with, let the caller know as you make the request to put him or her on hold that you may be a few minutes. By doing so, the caller doesn't have to wonder where you went and why.

Sound Alive, Not Scripted

If the nature of your telephone interactions involves selling, avoid sounding scripted. Even if your role is to get information across to the people you call, as those in telemarketing must do, *saying* rather than reading your points is more likely to make you sound alive and thus avoid sounding monotone or robotic. More important, it also makes you sound as though you know what you're talking about and creates conversation, especially if you follow up your message with a question that invites dialogue (see Chapter 15).

When I receive scripted telemarketing calls, I sometimes interrupt the sales person with questions to see if they know what they're talking about. When they operate by rote, they're thrown for a loop; when they know their stuff, they can carry on a conversation.

Converse with Patience

Telephone conversations increase the tendency for you and the person on the other end of the line to talk at the same time. The visual cues that allow face-to-face conversations to flow more freely without interruptions are missing from conversations on the telephone.

For a two-way conversation to flow smoothly, you must show a little patience and slow your pace a bit, making sure that you hear the other person's entire thought before you speak. You may also want to paraphrase it first to ensure that you've captured the point being made. Then the transition for you to speak next is a natural one. Even if your waiting leaves a little silence, that's fine. Better for people to be heard than to be stepped on.

Tune In to Your Speaker's Tone

When you're listening on the telephone, you can't see (much less understand) your speaker's body language. As I discuss in Chapter 4, the nonverbal part of a speaker's message (body language and tone of voice) communicates much of the emotional meaning in that message. When you can't see nonverbal messages, then you must focus on what you're hearing, not only in words but also in tone.

When emotion is a significant part of the message, remain calm and use the active-listening tool of reflecting feelings (see Chapter 5) to unearth the cause of the emotion. When you confirm the message, then use the active-listening tool of probing (also in Chapter 5) to retrieve a better explanation of the emotion. Then follow up with a reflective paraphrase (discussed in Chapter 5) to capture an understanding of the entire message — the content and the feeling.

If Your Time Is Short, Say So

Have you ever been caught in one of those phone conversations when you have only a few minutes and the person on the other end has a whole lot to say to you? You don't want to (or maybe can't) cut the person off, yet at the same time, you're struggling with trying to end the call.

In such situations, be direct and courteous instead of trying to be nice and, in the process, adding unneeded stress to your life. Announce at the beginning how much time you have and then hold to it. In cases when you thought you had the time and the call went longer than expected, give the caller a heads-up warning so that you can break away in a couple of minutes. "Jim, I have to go shortly. Let's try to wrap up this call in the next two minutes."

If more time is truly needed, you can end the call by setting up a time for the next call. Quite often, by announcing the time limit, you encourage people to get to the point and get business taken care of on the spot.

By the way, when you're in a face-to-face conversation and your telephone or cell phone rings, don't answer it. Let it ring into voice mail. Unless you've said in advance that you're expecting an important call, respect the time you've spent with the person in your present conversation.

Close the Call before You End It

Saying goodbye may end a telephone conversation, but it doesn't necessarily bring it to a close. The nature of telephone conversations, even if they are scheduled meetings, tends to be informal, so it's easy to forget to close the call.

Closing the call is remembering to check agreements made or to confirm commitments set. It sometimes involves setting up the next steps and determining who's going to call whom and when. This clear and definitive closure leaves you and the other person on the same page of understanding and feeling like your time on the call was well spent. After you're done, say your goodbyes.

Leave Messages Worth Returning

Using voice mail is common in today's business world, so you may find yourself talking far more often to a person's voice mail than directly to that person in a live conversation. Nevertheless, having such an option may be better than leaving messages through another person.

The intent when you leave a message is to get the other person to call you back or to give specific information. When you leave phone messages, avoid rambling and stammering but don't leave breathless, choppy messages either. Likewise, avoid saying your name and phone number too fast, because if the other person doesn't understand you, your call probably won't be returned.

Keep your voice mail messages relatively short, briefly explaining your business or reason for calling, stating your name and telephone number slowly and clearly, and then requesting a callback if you want one. (Do make that request directly rather than assuming that the person you're calling knows you want him or her to call you back.) And even if you think the person knows your phone number, always leave it anyway so that you make it convenient for the individual to return your call. If you can be reached only at a few certain times, then leave information about when you can best be reached.

Chapter 19

Ten Tips to Enhance Teamwork

● ●

In This Chapter

▶ Increasing team productivity

▶ Enhancing team unity

● ●

*T*eamwork means working cooperatively and getting along well with others. When jobs required mostly independent thought and responsibility, teamwork was needed only in a general sense. Managers wanted employees to get along and help out when needed; otherwise, you did your job.

Today, in so many workplaces, people are organized to work in team situations for some or nearly all of their time on the job. At the core of effective teamwork is interpersonal communications. When you work primarily on your own, interpersonal skills are less critical. When your job requires you to coordinate efforts with others, which is what happens in teams, these skills increase tenfold in their importance.

To enhance effectiveness in teamwork for productivity and unity, this chapter gives you ten communication practices and tips to put into use.

Make Newcomers Feel Welcome

One of the challenges teams sometimes face is integrating new members. New members need to go through the learning curve and need to pay attention to the dynamic among all the members of the team. When little is done to help the new members fit in and feel a part of the team, the team tends to pull apart. New people feel like outcasts for awhile, and sometimes when more new members come in, two factions form — the old guard and the new guard.

When you're an established part of a team, always try to help the new person fit in as fast as possible. Use your active-listening skills to find out about the individual's work background. Ask what the person needs and help meet those needs. Ask others to help in showing the new person the ropes. Include the new person in social gatherings, such as going to lunch. When initiative is taken to welcome newcomers into a group, the integration happens far more quickly and smoothly than using *osmosis* (doing nothing and hoping everything will work out on its own), and everyone on the team gains from it.

Keep Information Flowing

In team situations, the need for members to keep each other informed is extremely important. Think of the flow of information as a *loop*. By opening and closing the loop, you keep the flow moving.

- **Closing the loop** means following through and getting back to others, informing them of what happened or what you found out about an issue.
- **Opening the loop** means taking the initiative to let others know something in advance, or passing on information that is immediately helpful for them to know — without being asked.

Closing and opening the loop involves thinking of others and keeping communication going at all times so that each person associated with the team feels well informed (in the loop).

Teach So that Others Can Learn

Part of what often is needed in teams involves cross-training or showing new team members how to do certain tasks, and most teaching involves communicating with others. To teach effectively, first remember that the person you're instructing doesn't know the task or job as well as you do. Explain the process step by step and translate any unfamiliar terms into common language.

In addition, allow for and be receptive to questions and then answer them clearly and directly. When people feel comfortable asking questions, they're engaged and learn well. In addition, check the understanding of your trainees by asking questions of your own. In particular, use open-ended questions so that trainees must provide feedback on what they're learning. Doing so lets you know what's sinking in and what's still confusing. Teach as a collaborative two-way process, not a one-way show and tell.

Offer Assistance

When your vocabulary includes comments like the following: "What can I do to help you?" or "Let me give you a hand on that," or "I can help you get that assignment done, if you'd like," you speak the language of a valuable team player. People want to know that they can count on you to help when they need it, and that you're willing to do so. When you're asked for assistance, always answer with a yes. If not now, then say when you can help and follow through. Someone who speaks and acts in the language of helpfulness and cooperation is a positive member that everybody wants as part of their team.

Ask for Help

Part of the benefit of working in a team is that you don't have to figure everything out yourself. You have other resources who can be of help to you when you need it. In fact, people often make preventable mistakes when they try to figure out for themselves what they don't know, instead of seeking assistance from others.

Asking questions is a sign of interest and assertiveness, not of stupidity. The only stupid thing you can do is not to ask when you don't know or you're uncertain about something. Don't apologize for asking — just speak up with confidence, stating your need simply and clearly. Then listen for the answer and probe deeper if you need more information or explanation. You may also want to paraphrase the answers you receive to make sure you understand. After that, you're on your way to putting what you found out into use. (See Chapter 5 for more on probing and paraphrasing.)

Speak Up in Meetings

The more you get involved in team situations, the more you're asked to attend team meetings. Teams need meetings to coordinate their activities and to collectively communicate to get everyone going in the same direction. For effective teamwork, teams need their members to do more than just show up to the meetings. (And indulging in the doughnuts and coffee is not enough either.)

Speak up assertively in every meeting. Offer your ideas and express opinions that help the team move forward in getting results. Even if you're the soft-spoken type, pump up your volume a bit and say what you have to offer to help the team — your thoughts and contributions are truly needed.

Actively listen, too, and show your interest in the meetings. Help turn your meetings into constructive two-way conversations.

Talk in Terms of Outcomes

A common pitfall for many teams is argument among the team members about how to get a job done. The outcomes needed are often lost in the debate over "your way versus my way."

Make outcomes the focus of these discussions, especially when you're problem solving and planning with your team members. Ask: "What goals are to be met?" "What results do we need to accomplish?" and "What customer needs do we need to meet?" Have questions like these enter your discussions and you'll generate a focus on achieving outcomes, not on methods.

Give Feedback Supportively

You can offer feedback to your team members about their performances. Doing so enhances teamwork, because it opens up honest communication. Just make sure that you *describe* your observations based on actions, instead of providing subjective commentary about other people's performances.

Give feedback to recognize good performance. When others help you or take other actions that help the team achieve results, express appreciation for it. Just be sure to give specific positive feedback, not general praise.

If something doesn't go well, providing observations about such issues in a straightforward and supportive manner helps team members reflect on their efforts and learn from their experiences. You're not giving feedback to judge others; you're doing so to reinforce performance and behaviors that make for effective teamwork. The fact that you regularly and constructively give this feedback to your team members elevates you to a leadership role among your peers — a valuable role to play for the team to be successful.

Take Problems to the Right Source

One inevitable effect of people working together in team situations is that problems happen. In fact, one way to determine whether a team will be effective is to look at how its members deal with problems and concerns that arise: Do they snipe at each other? Gossip behind each other's backs? Form factions? That doesn't encourage teamwork.

Team members need to work through their problems to grow and become effective as a team. When issues affect the team as a whole, put them on an agenda for a team meeting so that team members can deal with them collectively. When issues deal with an individual, go to that person to address the problem. In both cases, help facilitate the process by using the communication tools and problem-solving models of conflict resolution outlined in Part IV of this book.

Maintain a Sense of Humor

A sure sign that you have an effective team is people laughing with each other as a normal occurrence. They're not laughing at the expense of one another but are enjoying each other's company as they carry out the work of the day. They're not distracted by silliness, either. Their humor keeps a light touch that eases the stresses that come with the job.

Teams are made up of a collection of personalities. Trying to get them to work together effectively is no small task. If you can see the humorous side of this challenge and act upon it with your team members, you can transition from focusing on yourself in your own job to focusing on the group as a team.

Chapter 20

Ten Actions that Lend Credibility to Your Communications

In This Chapter
▶ Becoming reliable
▶ Earning a good reputation through your actions
▶ Building respect

You can't buy credibility; it can only be earned. Credibility means having others find you believable, trustworthy, and deserving of respect.

You earn credibility when you interact with others and take actions after those interactions. Credibility comes from actions that match your positive words and good intentions, because, after all, people can see only your actions. This chapter gives you ten actions to incorporate into your work practices that build credibility into your communications.

Following Through

One missing ingredient in today's workplace is follow-through. People want to count on you and know that you'll actually do what you say you'll do. If you say you'll take care of an issue, take care of it! If you say you'll check into the matter and get back to someone with an answer, do it!

More important, you must follow through in a timely manner. Say *when* you're going to do what you agreed to do, and get it done by that time. And when you need to get back to someone to tell that person that's it's been done, do so.

Forgetfulness and disorganization aren't acceptable reasons for lack of follow-through. Instead, they're signs of unreliability . . . that your word can't be counted on. So meeting every commitment you make to others is important. Consistency of actions supporting words breeds credibility.

Returning Phone Calls

Respond to your phone and e-mail messages too. When people call you at work and leave messages for you to return their calls, even if you don't know who they are, extend them the courtesy of doing so within a reasonable time. Waiting two weeks and three other attempts to contact you later do not constitute a reasonable amount of time.

Voice mail is useful technology and a handy way to receive messages. But if you treat it like a black hole, you hinder your credibility, and you may even be seen as someone who isn't on top of things. Even if your callback is to say no more than you're checking into the issue, at least your caller knows action is being taken. People can't read your mind, so no callback means the caller has been ignored. On the other hand, responsiveness builds credibility.

Being Passionate

You don't have to be a highly expressive individual to be passionate about your work and your communications. In your own style, permit your passion to come forth. Passion is about having interest and enthusiasm for what you do and what you say about it. It puts emotion into your message.

Communicating without emotion causes you to come across as bland and lifeless and that doesn't engage anyone's attention to listen to you. Out-of-control emotion, on the other hand, can turn people off.

A participant in one of my recent communication seminars said the following: "Allow yourself to be emotional enough to provide conviction, but not overly emotional to lose credibility." That's passion. (Thanks, Sara Nelson.)

Demonstrating Expertise

Be knowledgeable. Know your stuff and share it with others. If you don't communicate what you know and the subject expertise you've developed, you're not earning your keep at work. You're being paid to do a job. When others come to you for service or assistance, they want your expertise to come out in the interaction. No one wants to deal with incompetence.

Be sure to communicate your expertise with confidence but not with arrogance. And translate what you know in terms that others can understand. When you don't know something, that's fine. No one expects perfection, but do go find an answer. Don't rest on your laurels; keep building your expertise and sharing it with others.

Disagreeing without Being Disagreeable

You're entitled to your point of view and it can be different than someone else's. But when you say, "I disagree with you," you make the disagreement personal.

Instead, disagree with ideas and thoughts and make that the focus of what you have to say. Focus not on the fact that you disagree but also on the different points of view you have. That makes for a discussion of issues as opposed to a personal tug-of-war and debate.

Paraphrase the other person's point to make sure you truly understand it (see Chapter 11). You may find that you actually agree with some of the other person's stances on the issue. And when people know they've truly been heard, they're more likely to be open to hearing another point of view in return.

Avoid treating different opinions as right or wrong. They're just different ways people see something.

Staying Calm under Pressure

Stress is part of everyone's job: It should be the last item on your job description, something like, "Deal with stress without getting stressed out."

When you maintain relative calm under the stresses of the day, you improve your ability to listen effectively and communicate constructively. In the same way, when you show your stress, you sometimes inflame and distress others.

People want to know that you're approachable, especially in times of pressure. They want to know that you can listen to what's going on and help them work through the challenges. Do your venting privately; come ready to perform publicly. When you do, you command great respect.

Taking Positive Approaches to Problems

Problems are a part of all jobs. Much of what you're getting paid for has to do with fixing problems. Avoid dealing with them and they don't go away. Complain to others about problems and you become a drag on morale. Blame and verbally attack others for problems and you incite defensiveness in return — and often hesitancy to act in the future because no one wants to feel punished when a problem arises.

I've even met people who want to avoid saying the word problem and want to use euphemisms for it. "We don't have problems here. We just have challenging opportunities." Play with words all you want, but deal with the problem.

Involving others in constructive dialogue about how to fix a problem works best in first developing an understanding of what the problem is all about. Don't shy away; just fact find about the situation. Let people know that no one will be shot or tarred and feathered for the problem. Then lead the discussion to focus on solutions and don't stop until one is worked out. That's the tried-and-true, best, most positive approach to solving problems. And when you're a positive problem solver, you have credibility.

Listening First, Acting Second

Making snap judgments, jumping to conclusions, and reacting before you've gathered all the facts don't inspire confidence from others. They serve only as reinforcements that listening and thinking rationally aren't part of your modes of operation.

People want to be heard. They don't want you to cut them off and tell them what to do or what you're going to do. Exercising a little patience first usually goes a long way. When you understand first what someone else has to say, you have a better understanding of the best course of action to take. You can then act with reason and sound judgment, which is much better than flying off the handle and exacerbating the situation. And by achieving the understanding first, you may find there's nothing you need to do next.

Showing Sincerity

Nothing damages credibility faster than a lack of sincerity. Arrogance, manipulation, and dishonesty convince people to see the worst in your actions and not to trust your words.

Sincerity is the quality of coming across as genuine and honest. It is saying what you mean and meaning what you say, and doing so with respect for the other person. It is having your good intentions matched by your tone of voice when you speak, and it is showing when you listen that you care about what someone else has to say. Everyone can show sincerity, and when you show it as a consistent practice, you have credibility.

Being Straightforward

Many times, especially in problem situations, people purposefully decide *not* to be direct with others. They put all sorts of fluff into their messages trying to soften what they have to say. What they're doing, however, is diluting their points and creating anxiety in the listener, who often suspects that what they're talking about is far worse than what they're willing to say.

Being straightforward means being direct, candid, and clear. Being straightforward isn't the same as being blunt: Straightforward is to the point; blunt tends to smash the point and is personal and hurtful. Here's an example of the differences:

> ✔ **Direct:** "The numbers on page 4 of your report do not add up correctly."
>
> ✔ **Blunt:** "The numbers in this report are all screwed up and show you know nothing about using data."

Being straightforward means using language to make your points in the best way possible. Straightforwardness can be any degree from soft- to hard-edged, but you tailor the message based on how the individual best receives it. In either case, straightforward means you're being respectful, clear, and focused on the issue — no reading between the lines is necessary.

You'll find that being clear, respectful, and forthright in your communications are universally appreciated. When you do it consistently, you definitely have credibility.

Index

• A •

abusive language, avoiding in conflict
    situations, 157
acronyms, 124
action-focused communications. *See also*
    solution-focused communications
  can-do approach, 117–20
  in conflict situations, 160, 199–207, 216,
    222–223
  as customer relations tool, 262, 271–272
  importance of, 120–121
  as management tool, 332
  will-do approach, 120–121
action plans
  in conflict situations, 208, 216, 224
  preparing listeners for, 137–138
  in presentations, 245, 247
  recapping following conversations,
    139–140
  recapping in e-mail, 229
  writing down and disseminating, 208, 219
active listening, 10, 36–40
  in conflict situations, 160, 201, 205–206
  in customer relations, 261–262, 266,
    274–275
  definition of, 10, 27
  empathetic versus sympathetic listening,
    78–81
  examples of, 32–33, 38, 72–75
  importance of, 338
  during job interviews, 295, 304
  as a management tool, 310
  monitoring, 40
  during negotiations, 265–267
  during presentations, 255
  relationship to assertive speaking, 24
  during telephone conversations, 324–325
  tips for improving, 91–92
active listening tools
  checking the subject, 63–65
  door-opening devices, 58–60

echoing, 60–61
  paraphrasing message contents, 68–69
  probing, 61–63
  reflecting feelings, 67–68
  reflective paraphrasing, 69–70
  sharing relevant examples of, 70–72
  verifying understanding of messages,
    65–66
adversarial communications, 9
advice mode (nonempathic listening),
    avoiding, 39, 87, 310
agendas. *See also* communications plans;
    messages, clarifying
  during conflict resolution process,
    179–181
  outlining in presentations, 242
aggressive conflict-handling, 161–162,
    165–166
aggressive negotiating, 264
aggressive speaking approach, 10, 16–17
  examples of, 17, 23
  versus assertive speaking approach, 23
agreement, asking for
  at close of conversations, 140
  during conflict resolution process,
    207, 224
anecdotes. *See* stories
anger. *See also* conflict situations;
    disagreements
  customer, handling, 272–276
  nonverbal expressions of, 46
answering questions, 144–147
apologizing, 276
appeasement, using in conflict
    situations, 162
appreciation, expressing
  during conflict situations, 190
  during conversations, 144–145
  in intraoffice communications, 279,
    317–318
arguing, in conflict situations, 158
armchair quarterbacking, 20

arrogance, communicating, 12, 84
  browbeating, 162
  in conflict situations, 158
  during presentations, 238
  by tone of voice, 107
  when listening, 84–87
assertive conflict-handling, 164, 166, 167
  clarifying intentions, 176
  respect as component of, 169–173
  when to handle/not handle problems,
    168–169
assertive negotiating, 265–267
assertive speaking, 20–22, 97
  with angry customers, 275
  with bosses, supervisors, 314–315
  definition of, 10
  examples of, 22, 23
  with internal clients, 278
  learning/practicing, 24–25
  positive language and, 114–121
  speaking too softly, 106
  during team meetings, 331–332
assistance, when to offer, 331
assumptions, negative
  avoiding, 39, 70, 86–87, 126
  becoming aware of, 13
  in conflict situations, 157
  definition of, 10–11
  problems resulting from, 11–12
assumptions, positive, 11, 13, 160. *See also*
    positive (constructive) language
attention. *See also* audiences; listeners,
    engaging
  of audience, gaining, 242–244
  demonstrating during listening, 36, 93
attentive listening, 36
audiences
  addressing e-mail messages to, 233
  gaining attention of, 242–244
  handling questions from, 254–256
  participation in presentations, 243
  relating to during presentations, 239, 243,
    254–256
  target, identifying, 150, 152, 233
  using appropriate language for, 123
authoritarian expressions. *See* arrogance
avoidance, denial
  in conflict situations, 157
  in nonassertive speaking, 18

• B •

barriers to communication. *See also*
    negative language
  body language, 51–54
  nonempathic listening modes, 81–87
  physical barriers, 54
  tone of voice, 54–55
beating around the bush. *See* indirect
    language
behavior-focused language, for conflict-
    handling, 193. *See also* action-based
    communications
behavioral questions, during job
    interviews, 288
behaviors
  expected, communicating to
    employees, 309
  focusing on during conflict resolution
    process, 187
being-right mode (nonempathic listening),
    84–85
benefits, showcasing in presentations, 245
black-and-white thinking, 84
blame, 16
  in aggressive speaking, 16
  avoiding, 25
  in conflict situations, 157, 161, 194
blinking, excessive, 100
blunt language, versus direct language,
    189, 339
body language, 44
  during active listening, 48
  with assertive speaking approach, 21
  definition of, 100
  engaging listeners using, 101
  excessive movement, 53, 237
  with nonassertive speaking approach,
    17–18
  with passive-aggressive speaking
    approach, 20
  during passive listening, 34
  poor, examples of, 103–104
  during presentations, 247, 248-249
  during selective listening, 35
  unwelcoming, intimidating, 16, 52–53
body section, of presentations, 244–246
bold statements, in presentations, 243
bosses. *See* supervisors, bosses

brainstorming, 207, 216, 223
brevity, concise language
  during conflict situations, 205
  in e-mail messages, 232
  examples of, 122
  during job interviews, 290
  during sales interactions, 263
  on visual materials, 253–254
  when answering questions, 145–146
browbeating, verbal, 162

• C •

callers, putting on hold, 324–325
can-do attitude, 117–120. See also action-
    focused language
  can-do factors, in job interviews, 283–284
  in sales, 262
capitalized letters, limiting on visuals,
    253–254
challenging the speaker
  during listening, 85-86
  effect on communications, 9
changing the subject, 35
charts and graphs, how to use, 141
checking the subject tool (active listening),
    63–65
children, as passive listeners, 34–35
clarity, communicating with, 51,
    122–123, 125
  answering questions, 145
  approaching customers, 263
  in conflict situations, 183, 221–222
  in interviews, 302
  in presentations, 239
clients, working with. See also customer
    service
  communications plan for, 148
  listening to complaints, 88–89
close-ended questions, 61
  in job interviews, 287
closing communications, closure
  in conflict situations, 207–208, 211–212
  in customer interactions, 263–264
  importance of, 138–140
  in intraorganization interactions, 317–318
  in needs-based conflict resolution
    model, 216
  in negotiations, 267

in presentations, 238
in telephone conversations, 327
tools for achieving, 138–140
co-workers. See also intraoffice
    communications; team management
  handling conflicts with, 165–166
  viewing as internal clients, 276–277
coaching staff, 308–312. See also team
    management
collaborative communications, 9. See also
    mutual understanding
  diffusing anger, 164, 275
  establishing, 171
  importance of, 24
  improving performance, 173
  problem solving using, 126
commitments to action, asking for, 140
commonalities, listing in presentation
    introductions, 244
communications, 44
  basic types, 9–10
  components, 8–9
  goals, 9
  opening, 173
  two-way, 133
communications plans. See also
    preparation, planning
  for conflict resolution, 198–201
  examples of, 150–152
  for job interviews, 292
  outlining, 150, 200–201
  preliminary homework, 149
  for team meetings, 148
  when to prepare, 147–148
communications toolkit
  body language, 101–105
  checking the subject tool, 63–65
  describing tool, 186–191
  door opener tool, 58–60
  echoing tool, 60–61, 293
  eye contact, 98–100
  pace tool, 108–112
  paraphrasing tool, 68–69, 273
  probing tool, 61–63, 293
  reflecting feelings tool, 67–68, 70, 273
  reflective paraphrasing tool, 69, 273
  sharing relevant examples of, 70–72
  shift-and-show-understanding tool,
    182–186, 221, 274

communications toolkit *(continued)*
  stating-feelings tool, 193–195
  stating-thoughts tool, 192–193
  vocal tool, 105–108
complaints. *See also* conflict situations
  as avoidance technique, 158
  by clients, listening to, 88–89
  by employees, listening to, 89–91
compromise, 165
computer skills, evaluating during job
    interviews, 283
concentration. *See also* attention
  definition of, 49
  tips for improving, 50–51
concise language. *See* brevity; clarity,
    communicating with
conclusions, jumping to, 12
condescension, communicating, 116
confidence, expressing, 106
  in interactions with customers, 263
  in presentations, 239
conflict resolution process
  communicating positive intentions,
    176–179
  confirming outcomes, 183
  communications plan for, 198–199
  demonstrating understanding, 181–182
  handling challenging reactions, 220–222
  needs-based model for, 212–220
  resolving-concerns model for, 202–212
  setting an agenda, 179–181
  tips for facilitating, 224
  what not to do, 156–158
conflict situations, 155–156
  aggressive handling of, 161–162, 165
  assertive handling of, 164–167, 175–181
  discussing in conversations, 147
  discussing in e-mail messages, 231
  intraorganizational, 318–319
  nonassertive handling of, 162–163, 165, 167
  passive-aggressive handling of, 163–164,
    166, 167
  preparing to handle, 147
  team-related, 332–333
  tools for handling positively, 127,
    159–160, 337

  versus personality clashes, 155–156
  when to deal with/not deal with, 168–169
connecting statements, 71–72
consensus, 207, 216
consequences, considering, 223
constructive feedback, providing, 187. *See
    also* feedback
constructive language. *See* positive
    (constructive) language
context, of conversations, clarifying, 136
control
  maintaining, during conflict resolution
    process, 159
  maintaining when handling customer
    complaints, 274–275
  versus influence, 94
conversations
  closing, 138–140
  concentrating on the speaker, 49–51
  door openers, 58–60
  good, features of, 9–10
  laying out structure, 136–137
  opening, 134–138
  recapping in e-mail, 229
cooperation. *See also* relationships
  and good communications, 13
  intra-/inter-organizational, building,
    317–319
core messages, in presentations, 239,
    240, 255
creativity
  inspiring, 173
  of job candidates, evaluating, 285
critic mode (nonempathic listening), 81
critical language. *See also* negative
    language
  in conflict situations, 164
  in conversations, 145
crowding, 62
customer service. *See also* customers'
    needs/concerns
  communications and, 259–260
  customer anger, tips for handling,
    272–276
  in the public sector, 270
  quality, features of, 267–269

customers
  external, 7
  internal, 7, 276–279
customers' needs/concerns
  affirming understanding of, 262
  identifying, 269, 277–278
  listening to, 28, 266–267

● *D* ●

dark-cloud formula, handling liabilities
    using, 300–301
darting glances, eye movement, 100
data, presenting too much, 237
debating, during conflict situations, 221
defensive mode (nonempathic listening),
    82–83, 157
defensiveness
  how to handle, 138, 221
  during nonempathic listening, 82–83, 157
  during selective listening, 35
delegating, 309
demanding language
  in aggressive speaking, 16
  in conflict situations, 162
denying mode (nonempathic listening), 83
derogatory, demeaning language, 127,
  in conflict situations, 157–158
describing tool
  in conflict resolution process, 186–190
  examples of, 190–191
design, good, for visual aids, 254
destructive language, examples of, 115
details, limiting, 123. *See also* brevity
diagnostic mode (nonempathic listening),
    86–87
difficult customers. *See* customer service
direct language
  in conflict situations, 159, 164, 189
  examples of, 122
  importance of using, 114, 123, 339
  in presentations, 239
  in telephone conversations, 326–327
  versus blunt language, 339
  when answering questions, 145
disagreements. *See also* conflict situations
  during conversations, 145
  handling effectively, 126–127, 337

discomfort, allowing in conflict
    situations, 157
discussions. *See* conversations
disorganzied presentations, 238
distractions
  body language, 53, 104, 237
  eliminating, 92
  during listening, 39, 50–51
door-opener tool
  verbal door-openers, 59–60
  welcoming body language, 58–59
doubt, expressing, 18, 106, 130, 162, 237.
    See also qualifier words, phrases
dropping voice, 107

● *E* ●

e-mail communications
  flaming, 158, 159, 163
  limiting copies sent, 233
  message content, 232–234
  when to use/not use, 228–232
echoing
  definition of, 60
  during job interviews, 293
  when to use, 60–61
educational attainment, of job candidates,
    evaluating, 283
emotions. *See* feelings, emotions
empathetic listening, 78–79. *See also* active
    listening
  with customers, 268, 272–273
  examples of, 88–91
  versus sympathetic listening, 79–81
employees, working with. *See also* internal
    customers; team management
  asking versus telling, 309
  clarifying expectations, 308–309
  encouraging feedback, 311
  handling defensiveness, 138
  listening to complaints and concerns,
    89–91
  providing feedback, 310
  solutions-focused communications, 311
engaging the listener, 133
  body language, 101–104
  closing the conversation, 138–140

engaging the listener *(continued)*
  encouraging and answering questions, 144–147
  eye contact, 98–100
  opening the conversation, 134–138
  pace, 108–112
  preparing, doing homework, 137–138
  tone of voice, 104–108
  tools for, 141–144
enthusiasm, expressing, 93, 239, 250–251, 287, 336
enunciation, clear, 108–109
equipment, audio-visual, handling excessively, 237
example material, illustrations, using
  during active listening, 70–72
  to enhance messages, 141–142
  in presentations, 244
  when answering questions, 145
experience, demonstrating in job interviews, 283
expertise, demonstrating in job interviews, 283, 336
external customers, 7, 259
eye and head movements, 100. *See also* body language; nonverbal messages
eye contact, 34. *See also* body language; nonverbal messages
  during active listening, 48
  during attentive listening, 36
  engaging listeners using, 98–100, 248
  faces, looking at, 99, 248
  poor eye contact, examples of, 51–52, 98–100, 237
  during passive listening, 34
  during presentations, 237, 248
  during selective listening, 35

● *F* ●

faces, looking at, 99, 248
facial expressions. *See also* nonverbal messages
  during active listening, 48
  during attentive listening, 36
  effects on communication, 45
  engaging listeners using, 101–102
  during passive listening, 34
  poor, unwelcoming, examples of, 52
  during selective listening, 35
fact-finding, during job interviews, 304
facts
  focusing on exclusively, 36
  important or interesting, using in presentations, 243
  perceiving during active listening, 37–38
faking answers, 256
familiarity, advantages of, 92. *See also* relationships
fast, speaking, 110
feedback
  asking from employees, 311
  during active listening, 36–38, 67–68
  during attentive listening, 36
  during communications with bosses, 316
  during conflict resolution process, 182, 190, 205
  nonverbal messages in, 46
  in passive listening, 34
  providing to employees/team members, 310, 332
  requesting from listeners, 144
  using e-mail for, 229
feelings, emotions. *See also* communications toolkit
  communicating during conflict situations, 192–195, 205
  communicating during selective listening, 35
  handling during listening process, 36–38
  learning to control, 24
  in messages, perceiving, 45–46
  reflecting, 47, 67–68
  tone of voice as reflection of, 107–108
filler sounds, 111. *See also* nonwords
first impressions, importance of, 303–304
flaming, in e-mail messages, 158, 159, 163, 231
flexibility
  importance of, 24
  of job candidates, evaluating, 285
  when handling angry customers, 275
flow of presentations, 245–246

focus
  diverting, during selective listening, 35
  maintaining during conflict situations,
    159, 182, 188, 222
  maintaining during presentations, 257
  when speaking, 100
folding arms. *See* body language
follow-through. *See also* closing
    conversations
  clarifying agreed-on actions, 120–21
  as component of customer service,
    268, 274
  importance of, 92–93, 271, 335
follow-up
  e-mail, 230
  following conflict resolution process, 206,
    216, 224

• **G** •

gender-specific nouns, 128
generalizations, 13, 187
gestures, 102, 104, 248–249
get-even approaches, 9, 164
glaring, 99
glazing over, 100
goal-focused communication. *See also*
    action-focused communication;
    solution-focused communication
  communicating goals clearly, 136
  during conflict situations, 206
  during team meetings, 332
goodwill, promoting during job interviews,
    294–295
graphics, enhancing messages using, 141
greater good, emphasizing, 317–318
greetings, during telephone conversations,
    324. *See also* opening conversations
group meetings, creating communications
    plan for, 148

• **H** •

harshness, harsh language
  in aggressive speaking, 16
  in tone of voice, 107
headers, including on visuals, 253
hearing, versus listening, 27

help, asking for. *See also* conflict resolution
    process
  during team efforts, 331
  when dealing with angry customers, 275
  when dealing with internal clients,
    317–318
help, offering, during team meetings, 331
hemming and hawing negotiation
    phase, 266
homework
  before job interviews, 292, 303
  before presentations, 239
  before sales negotiations, 265
  as part of communications plan, 152
honesty, communicating, 114. *See also*
    sincerity
hopelessness, expressing, 18. *See also*
    qualifier words, phrases
hovering, 103
humor
  in e-mail messages, 233
  forced humor, avoiding, 143, 238
  sense of humor, value of, 333
  using to enhance messages, 143–144

• **I** •

I-/me-focused communications. 125
  in conflict situations, 178, 188, 192–194
  limitations of, 70
  versus You-focused communications, 75
identifier mode (nonempathic listening), 82
idioms, when to use, 123–124
imperatives. *See* trigger words and phrases
indirect communications, 158. *See also*
    passive-aggressive behaviors
  in conflict situations, 163
individuals, dealing with people as, 13. *See
    also* respect for others
industry knowledge, of job candidates,
    evaluating, 283
inflection, voice modulation, adding during
    speaking, 105
information sharing
  with customers, 269
  importance of, 315
  intraorganizational, 317
  with team members, 330

informational questions, asking during job interviews, 288–289

influence
   persuasion techiques, 148–152
   versus control, 94

inquiries. *See also* customer service
   handling on the telephone, 324
   responding to positively, 130–131
   responding to quickly, 317

insecurity, expressing, 106. *See also* qualifier words and phrases

insults, personal, avoiding during conflict situations, 157

intentions, of others, making assumptions about, 12

interest, expressing, 93, 239, 250–251, 287, 336. *See also* attention

interjecting, versus interrupting, 66

internal customers, 7, 259
   communicating with, 276–279

interpersonal skills, evaluating in job candidates, 285

interpreting, versus observing, 189, 204

interrogator mode (nonempathic listening), 84, 86

interrupting
   in conflict situations, 161
   handling interruptions positively, 54
   during selective listening, 35
   versus interjecting, 66

interviews, job (candidate's perspective)
   conducting positive interviews, 302–304
   handling potential liabilities, 298–301
   preparing for, 295–298
   questions to ask, 305
   what not to do, 301–302

interviews, job (interviewer's perspective), 279
   asking questions, 287–289
   can-do factors, evaluating, 283–284
   clarifying job requirements, 282–283
   common pitfalls, 289–291
   preparing for, 291–294
   promoting goodwill, 294–295
   will-do factors, evaluating, 284–286

intimidation. *See* arrogance

intraorganizational commmunications, 317–319. *See also* team management
   e-mail for, 228
   internal customers, 276–279

introductory section (presentations), 241, 242–244

introspective questions, asking during job interviews, 289

issue-focused language, using during conflict resolution process, 191, 193

• J •

jargon, avoiding, 123–124
   in communications with customers, 271
   during presentations, 237

job interviews (candidate's perspective)
   guidelines for positive interviews, 302–304
   handling potential liabilities, 298–301
   preparing for, 295–298
   things not to do, 301–302

job interviews (interviewer's perspective), 279
   asking questions, 287–289
   can-do factors, 283–284
   clarifying job requirements, 282–283
   common pitfalls, 289–291
   job requirements, communicating clearly, 282–283
   preparing for conversation, 291–294
   promoting goodwill, 294–295
   questions to ask, 305
   will-do factors, 284–286

jokes
   off-color, 143
   in presentations, 242–243

judgmental language, 183, 194

jumping to conclusions, 12. *See also* assumptions
   during selective listening, 35

• K •

key words/phrases, highlighting on visuals, 253

knowing-best. *See* arrogance

• L •

lack of confidence, expressing during speaking, 106
language, negative
  jargon and idioms, 123–124
  mixed messages, 130
  qualifier statements, 130
  rephrasing positively, 130–131
  trigger words and phrases, 128–129
  types of, 127–130
language, positive, 114
  clear messages, 122–123
  emphasizing action, 120–121
  emphasizing solutions, 124–127
  features of, 114–116
  handling disagreements using, 126–127
  importance of, 113–114
  positive spin, 116–120
lay terms, when to use, 123–124, 149
leading questions, 62
liabilities, personal, handling in job interviews, 298–301
listener talk, versus speaker talk, 75–76
listeners, engaging, 133
  body language, 101–104
  encouraging and answering questions, 144–147
  eye contact, 98–100
  pace, 108–112
  tone of voice, 104–108
  tools for, 141–144
  when opening/closing conversations, 134–140
listening, 8, 13
  attending, versus pretending, 47–49
  barriers to, 51
  definition of, 27
  focusing on the speaker, 49–51
  importance of, 13
  learning listening skills, 9
  poor listening, examples of, 30–31
  process of, 28–30, 32–33
  responding during, 30, 54–55
  during telephone conversations, 45
  types of, 10, 33–38

listening, active, 21, 32–33, 37–38, 338. *See also* active listening tools
  addressing customer concerns, 266
  checking the subject, 63–65
  in conflict situations, 160, 201, 205–206
  in customer communications, 261–262, 274–275
  empathetic listening, 78–81, 88–91
  examples of, 32–33, 72–75
  in job interviews, 295
  during negotiations, 265–267
  during presentations, 255
  in team meetings, 310
  during telephone conversations, 324–325
  tips for improving, 91–92
  tools for, 58–72, 78–81
listening, nonempathic, 83
  advice mode, 87
  being-right mode, 84–85
  critic mode, 81
  defensive mode, 82–83
  diagnostic mode, 86–87
  identifier mode, 82
  interrogator mode, 84, 86
  sparring mode, 85–86
listening, passive, 34–35
listening, selective, 35–36
loaded language, 127
looking away, 100. *See also* body language; eye contact
long-term relationships, value of, 13, 172, 265
loudly, speaking, 107

• M •

main ideas. *See also* messages, clarifying
  focusing on, 122
  identifying in messages, 91–92
  stating at opening of conversation, 135–136
management. *See* supervisors, bosses
management style, of job candidates, evaluating, 286
managing conflict-resolution process, 224

managing employees
asking, versus telling, 309
advising, 310
clarifying expectations, 308–309
encouraging feedback from, 311
providing feedback to, 310
using solution-focused
communications, 311
managing interorganizational
commmunications, 317–319
maps, using to enhance messages, 141
matrix management, 317–319
meetings, preparing for
conflict resolution meetings, 199–201, 224
presentations, 148–152, 240–241
messages, clarifying, 122–123
during conflict resolution process, 199,
221–222
in presentations, 240–241, 247
testing how message was received,
146–147
tools for, 60–65
messages, enhancing
at close of presentations, 247
providing examples of, 141–142
using positive language, 114–116
visual aids, 141
messages, mixed 130. See also qualifier
words, phrases; nonverbal messages
during conflict situations, 189–190
in response to questions, 145
messages, receiving, 10, 36, 78–81. See also
listeners, engaging; listening
capturing the whole message, 44, 48
clarifying unclear messages, 63–65
listening for emotions, 45–46
listening for main ideas, 91–92
paraphrasing, 68–69
verifying understanding, 65–66
visualizing the message, 50
messages, sensitive
in e-mail messages, 230
communication plan for, 147–152
in presentations, 240
messages, telephone, 327
messages, unspoken. See nonverbal
messages
mirroring, 109

mirrors, practicing in front of, 102
mixed messages. See messages, mixed
modulation, of voice, 237. See also tone
of voice
during presentations, 105
monotone voice, 237
motivation, of job candidates,
evaluating, 285
movement, excessive, inappropriate,
53, 104
during presentations, 237, 249
mumbling, 106
mutual understanding
demonstrating, in customer
communications, 261–262, 273
demonstrating, in conflict situations,
181–182, 221–222
as goal of communications, 9
testing in listeners, 146
tools for achieving, 9–10, 172

• N •

names, using
during job interviews, 294–295
when working with customers, 267
nasty grams, 231
needs
definition of, 214
of customers, identifying, 260–263
needs-based conflict resolution model
process, 212–217
using , example of, 217–220
needs-based job interviews, 304
negative language, 29. See also qualifier
words, phrases
in conflict situations, 162, 163–164
in e-mail messages, 232–233
loaded terms and phrases, 127
mixed messages, 130
rephrasing positively, 130–131
trigger words and phrases, 128–129
negative reactions, anticipating, 149–150
negotiating
aggressive approach, 264
assertive approach, 265–267
non-assertive approach, 264

nervousness, handling during
presentations, 256–257
newcomers, welcoming to teams, 330
no, when to say, 121
nodding, during attentive listening, 36
nonassertive behaviors
conflict-handling, 162–163, 165, 167, 221
during negotiations, 264
in speaking approaches, 10, 17–18, 23
nonempathic listening
advice mode, 87
being-right mode, 84–85
critic mode, 81
defensive mode, 82
denying mode, 83
diagnostic mode, 86–87
identifier mode, 82
interrogator mode, 84, 86
sparring mode, 85–86
nonjudgmental perspective
in conflict situations, 183
nonjudgmental question-asking, 63
nonverbal messages, 8, 44–45. *See also*
feelings, emotions; qualifier words,
phrases
emotions in, 36, 45–46
expressing positive intention using,
239, 255
importance of, 97–98
listening for, 48, 51–54, 275, 326
in passive-aggressive speaking, 20
nonwords
avoiding during presentations, 250–251
using during passive listening, 34
using excessively, 110–111
note-taking, 50
notes, using during presentations, 257

● *O* ●

objections
affirming understanding of, 262
overcoming, 38
observing, versus interpreting, 189, 204
offensive language, 143
office communications. *See*
intraorganizational communications

one-upmanship, avoiding, 71
open-ended questions, 61
clarifying message using, 62
in job interviews, 287
opening conversations, 134–138
telephone conversations, 324
organizational skills, evaluating in job
candidates, 285
organizing presentations, 239–241, 252
outcome-focused communications. *See*
goal-focused communications

● *P* ●

pace of delivery, 108–110. *See also*
modulation, of voice
pitfalls to avoid, 110–112
in telephone communications, 45
varying during presentations, 251
paraphrasing message content
during active listening, 68–69
during conflict situations, 182
in customer communications, 262, 273
when answering questions, 256
passion, expressing clearly, 336
passive-aggressive conflict-handling,
163–164, 166, 167
in e-mail messages, 231
passive-aggressive speaking approach, 10,
18–20
examples of, 19, 23
passive listening, 10, 34–35
patience
importance of, 45, 337
during listening, 39, 60, 93–94
during sales interactions, 266
during telephone conversations, 326
pauses
adding when speaking, 109
using during presentations, 251
perceived intentions. *See* assumptions;
positive intentions
performance expectations, communicating
clearly, 308–309
personal questions, comments, 128
during job interviews, 290–291
personal space, respecting, 103

personality clashes, versus conflicts, 155–156

persuasion, 148, 245

physical barriers, eliminating from conversations, 39, 92

physical skills, evaluating in job interviews, 283

placement of body, during listening, 54–55. *See also* body language

points of contact, 268

poor taste, 143

positive (constructive) language, 28, 114
  advantages of using, 115
  avoiding jargon and idioms, 123–124
  in communications with bosses, supervisors, 313–314
  in communications with customers, 269, 275–276
  in conflict situations, 126–127, 160, 164, 170, 178, 192, 195
  in e-mail messages, 232–233
  emphasizing solutions, 124–127
  examples of, 117–120
  features of, 113–116, 122–123
  importance of, 113–114
  in job interviews, 295, 303
  in presentations, 239, 255–256

positive intention
  assuming, 13, 188
  communicating clearly, 137, 176–179, 337–338
  displaying during conflict resolution process, 199, 222
  generating using positive self-talk, 276

posture. *See also* body language
  during presentations, 249
  welcoming versus unwelcoming, 101

preparing, preplanning
  for conflict resolution process, 198–201, 224
  for job interviews, candidate's perspective, 295–299
  for job interviews, interviewer's perspective, 282–286, 292–293
  for presentations, 148–152, 239, 240–241

presentation tools
  body language, 249
  eye contact, 248
  gestures, 248–249

presentations
  body section, 244–246
  conclusion section, 246–247
  creating communications plan for, 148
  features of good presentations, 239, 248–249
  handling the audience, 254–256
  handling stage fright, 256–257
  introductory section, 242–244
  pitfalls to avoid, 236–238
  preparing for, 148–152, 240–241
  visual aids, 252–254

probing. *See also* messages, clarifying
  during active listening, 61–63
  to identify customer needs, 261
  during job interviews, 293
  in response to questions, 146

problem-focused communications, 17–20, 124–125

problem solving, 172. *See also* conflict resolution; solution-focused communications
  active listening, 39
  during the conflict resolution process, 201
  flexibility and, 275
  focusing on solutions, 126
  positive approaches, 337–338

problem-solving ability, of job candidates, evaluating, 285

problem statements
  in need-based conflict resolution, 213–214, 218
  during presentations, 244–245
  in resolving-concerns conflict resolution, 203–205, 209–211

processes, service-provision, definition of, 279

processing messages (listening process), 30

productivity, listening and, 28

profanity, 128, 143

projecting voice, 105, 249–250. *See also* modulation, of voice
promises, 129, 271

• *Q* •

qualifier words, phrases, 130
  in conflict situations, 190, 192
  in e-mail messages,. 232
  in nonassertive speaking, 18
  in response to customer complaints, 269–271, 274
  in response to questions, 145
quality expectations, communicating to employees, 309
questions, 13
  answering with another question, 146
  asking during attentive listening, 36
  asking during communications with bosses, supervisors, 315
  asking during conflict situations, 183
  asking during job interviews, 287–289, 290, 304–305
  asking during selective listening, 35
  close-ended, 61
  encouraging during job interviews, 295
  encouraging from listeners, 144–147
  handling during presentations, 254–256
  importance of answering, 144–147
  leading, 62
  open-ended, 62
  tone of voice when asking, 63
  types of, 61–62
quick responses, avoiding, 39
quotes, using in presentations, 242

• *R* •

rambling speech, 145, 238
reactions, negative, anticipating, 149–150
reading, 8
  from slides/handouts during presentations, 237, 253
  of visual aids, by audience, type-size and, 252

recapping
  conversations, 138–140
  presentation messages, 247
receivers, 9
receiving messages, 29–30. *See also* listening
reflecting feelings, 67–68
  when handling angry customers, 273
reflective listening. *See* active listening
reflective paraphrasing, 69–70
  during conflict resolution process, 182
  when handling angry customers, 273
rehearsing presentations, 241, 256
relationship selling, 260–261
relationships, developing
  listening and, 28, 92
  value of, 13, 172, 265
relevancy of communications, in conflict situations, 178
reliability, importance of, 335–336
reports, communications plans for, 148
requests
  e-mail for, 228
  responding to positively, 114–21, 130–131
  responding to quickly, 317
  versus demands, 22
resolving-concerns conflict resolution model
  model process, 202–208
  using, example of, 208–212
respect for others
  communicating during job interviews, 294
  as component of customer service, 268
  demonstrating during listening, 28–30, 32–33, 40, 48, 93
  demonstrating during conflict resolution process, 206
  importance of, 25, 170–173
  positive language and, 127–129
  projecting during presentations, 250–251
  showing empathy, 78–81
responding to messages, 30. *See also* listening
responsibilities
  handling conflicts over, 166–167
  importance of accepting, 20

responsive listening. *See* active listening
results
  delivering to customers, 271
  improving using collaborative
    approaches, 173
returning phone calls, importance of, 336
rhetorical questions
  using in conclusion of presentations, 247
  using in introduction to presentations, 243
ridicule, 143
routine communications, e-mail for, 228
rumor-mongering, 158

• S •

sales interactions, 259–260. *See also*
  customer service
  identifying customer needs, 260–263
  negotiating during, 264–67
sarcasm, 143. *See also* tone of voice
  in conflict situations, 157, 163
say-it, prove-it chart (job interviews),
  296–297
second-guessing, and passive-aggressive
  speaking, 20
selective listening, 10, 35–37
self-control, practicing, 24
senders, 9
sense of humor, 333
sensitive issues
  avoiding in e-mail messages, 230
  avoiding or addressing in
    presentations, 240
  planning how to handle, 147-152
sequence, chronological, using
  presentations, 245
service. *See* customer service
service orientation, of job candidates,
  evaluating, 284
sexualized language, 128, 143
sharing knowledge
  in team efforts, 330–331
  when working with internal clients, 278
shift-and-show-understanding tool, 182–184
  using in conflict situations, 221
  using, examples of, 184–186
  using when handling complaints, 274–275

silence, learning to handle, 45
sincerity, communicating, 21
  during conflict resolution process,
    160, 178
  importance of, 338
  during interactions with customers, 263
  positive language and, 114
  during presentations, 239
  in tone of voice, 106
skills and accomplishments, emphasizing
  during job interviews, 303
snail mail, 228
slides, for presentations
  components of good slides, 252–254
  overloading, 237
slouching, 103, 249. *See also* body language
slowly, speaking, 110
soft-spoken voices, 106, 237
solution-makers, reluctant, 222–223
solution-focused communications, 21
  in communications with bosses,
    supervisors, 313
  in communicaitons with customers,
    272, 274
  in conflict situations, 160, 199–207, 216,
    219, 222
  examples of, 125–127, 210–211
  as management approach, 311–312
  in presentations, 244–246
  in team meetings, 332
sounding nervous. *See* uncertainty,
  communicating
source, going to, in conflict situations, 158,
  163–164, 332–334
space, personal, respecting, 103
sparring mode (nonempathic listening),
  85–86
speakers, concentrating on, 47–51
speaking approaches
  aggressive speaking, 16–17
  assertive speaking, 20–22, 97
  comparing, examples of, 23
  nonassertive speaking, 17–18
  passive-aggressive speaking, 18–20
  during team meetings, 331–332
  types of, 8–10
speaking effectively, toolkit for, 98–112

speaking positively. *See* positive (constructive) language

speaking too softly. *See* modulating voice

specifics, focusing on, 188. *See also* messages, clarifying; solution-focused communications

speculation, 126. *See also* assumptions

spin, 116

stage fright, 235, 256–257

stakeholders, identifying in needs-based conflict resolution model, 214–216, 218–219

staring, 99

stating-feelings tool, 193–195

stating-thoughts tool, 192–193

statistics, how to use, 124

stereotyping, 12, 13, 128

stories, anecdotes
  enhancing messages with, 142–143
  in job interviews, 304
  in presentations, 243, 246–247
  using when answering questions, 145

stress. *See also* conflict situations
  defusing tensions, 179
  handling effectively, 9, 337
  reducing through listening, 28

sugarcoated language, 115–116

supervisors, bosses
  communicating with, 312–316
  preparing proposals to, 147–152

supporting data, how to use, 124

sympathetic listening, versus empathetic listening, 78–81

• *T* •

talking at, versus talking with, 31

teaching, as management tool, 330

team management. *See also* employees, working with
  enhancing teamwork, 173
  evaluating job candidates, 284
  handling intrateam conflicts, 166–167
  information loops, 330
  teaching and assisting, 330–331
  viewing team as internal clients, 276–277
  welcoming newcomers, 329–330

technical knowledge, of job candidates, evaluating, 283, 292

technical language, when to use, 123–124, 271

telephone communications
  active listening, 45
  leaving messages, 327
  returning phone calls, 336
  tips for improving, 323–327
  voice mail, 234

tensions. *See also* conflict situations
  defusing, 179
  effect on communications, 9

thoughts, stating, in conflict situations, 192–193

threatening gestures, 104

time limits, clarifying during telephone conversations, 326–327

timing, in discussions of sensitive issues, 149

titles, including on visuals, 253

tone of conversation, establishing at onset, 137

tone of voice, 45
  adding emphasis and inflection, 105–106
  in aggressive speaking, 16
  communicating sincerity, 106
  as communications barrier, 55–56
  in communicaitons with customers, 270
  during conflict situations, 189–190, 194
  in e-mail messages, 230
  engaging listeners using, 102
  harshness in, 107
  during job interviews, 287
  listening for, 44
  nonjudgmental, 49, 63
  pitfalls to avoid, 106–108
  during presentations, 237, 249–250
  during telephone conversations, 325
  when asking questions, 63
  when giving advice, 87

toolkit, communications
  body language, 101–105
  checking the subject tool, 63–65
  describing tool, 186–191
  door opener tool, 58–60
  echoing tool, 60–61, 293

toolkit, communications *(continued)*
  eye contact, 98–100
  pace tool, 108–112
  paraphrasing, 68–69, 273
  probing tool, 61–63, 293
  reflecting feelings, 67–68, 70, 273
  reflective paraphrasing, 69, 273
  sharing relevant examples of, 70–72
  shift-and-show-understanding tool,
      182–186, 221, 274
  stating-feelings tool, 193–195
  stating-thoughts tool, 192–193
  vocal tool, 105–108
topic/theme of conversations, stating
    clearly, 135–136
transitions, in presentations, 246
trigger words and phrases, 128–129
tug-of-war metaphor, 8

• U •

ultimatums, avoiding in conflict situations,
    158, 162
ums, uhs. *See* nonwords; qualifier words,
    phrases
uncertainty, communicating. *See also*
    qualifier words, phrases
  during conflict situations, 162
  during conversations, 106
  during presentations, 237
understanding, mutual
  demonstrating in communications with
      customers, 261–262, 273
  demonstrating during conflict situations,
      181–182, 221
  as goal of communications, 9
  testing for, in listeners, 146–147
  tools for achieving, 9–10, 172
  verifying, 13, 65–66, 195, 222

• V •

vague messages, 60–61, 238
verbal barriers, 81–87
verbal browbeating, 16

verbal expression. *See* communications
verbal feedback
  during active listening, 36–38, 67–68
  asking for, 144, 311
  during attentive listening, 36
  capturing intangibles in, 46
  during communications with bosses,
      supervisors, 316
  during conflict resolution process, 182,
      190, 205
  during passive listening, 34
  providing to employees/team members,
      310, 332
verbose speech, 123
viewpoint, stating, 183–194
visual aids, 141
  how to use, 142
  in presentations, 239, 241, 252–253
voice mail, 234
vulgarity, 128, 143

• W •

walking away, 221,
weaknesses, personal, handling in job
    interviews, 301
welcoming newcomers, 329-330
will-do factors (job interviews),
    284–286, 300
wimpy words, 129
withholding, in conflict situations, 163
words, in messages, 44. *See also* language,
    negative; language, positive
working relationships. *See*
    intraorganizational communications
writing, 8
  of job candidates, evaluating, 283

• Y •

yelling, 156
You-focused communications, 75, 125

Notes

Notes

Notes

Notes